Georgia's Frontier Women

Georgia's Frontier Women

Female Fortunes in a

Southern Colony

BEN MARSH

The University of Georgia Press · Athens and London

Publication of this book was supported in part by the Kenneth Coleman Series in Georgia History and Culture, as well as by a grant from the Scouloudi Foundation in association with the Institute of Historical Research.

© 2007 by the University of Georgia Press
Athens, Georgia 30602
All rights reserved
Set in Minion by Bookcomp, Inc.
Printed and bound by Maple-Vail
The paper in this book meets the guidelines for permanence and durability of the Committee on Production Guidelines for Book Longevity of the Council on Library Resources.

Printed in the United States of America

10 09 08 07 06 C 5 4 3 2 1

Library of Congress Cataloging-in-Publication Data
Marsh, Ben 1976–
Georgia's frontier women : female fortunes in a Southern colony / Ben Marsh
       p. cm.
    Includes bibliographical references and index.
    ISBN-13: 978-0-8203-2882-9 (cloth: alk. paper)
    ISBN-10: 0-8203-2882-0 (cloth: alk. paper)
1. Women — Georgia History — 18th century.
2. Women — Georgia — Social conditions — 18th century. I. Title.
    HQ1438.G4M37 2007
    305.409758'09033—dc22 2006014975

British Library Cataloging-in-Publication Data available

ISBN for this digital edition: 978-0-8203-4397-6

Cartography by David Wasserboehr

CONTENTS

- *vii* List of Illustrations
- *ix* List of Abbreviations
- *xi* Acknowledgments
- *1* Introduction
- *7* *Prologue.* The Georgia Plan

PART ONE. THE TRUSTEESHIP

- *21* *Chapter One.* Population
- *36* *Chapter Two.* Economy
- *67* *Chapter Three.* Family and Community

PART TWO. THE ROYAL ERA

- *95* *Chapter Four.* Immigration and Settlement
- *124* *Chapter Five.* Expansion and Contraction
- *142* *Chapter Six.* Consolidating Gender
- *179* *Epilogue.* Revolution?
- *187* Conclusion
- *193* Appendix
- *197* Notes
- *231* Bibliography
- *245* Index

ILLUSTRATIONS

PHOTOGRAPHS

14   William Hogarth's *Gin Lane*

17   Selina Hastings, Countess of Huntingdon

54   *Caroline of Ansbach*, by Jacopo Amigoni

58   Seal of the Trustees for the Establishment of the Colony of Georgia

64   Mary Musgrove Matthews Bosomworth, with Creek warriors

103 1757 Map of Carolina and Georgia

133 Elizabeth Lichtenstein, in early life

157 Elizabeth Lichtenstein Johnston, in later life

173 Runaway slave notice in the *Georgia Gazette*

184 Letter from Abigail Minis to (probably) Mordecai Sheftall

FIGURES

23   1. Estimated Population of Trusteeship Georgia

122 2. Black Population of Georgia

MAP

xiv Colonial Georgia

TABLES

24   1. Georgia Immigrants by Gender

96   2. Royal Governors' Estimates of Georgia Population

110 3. Slaveholding among Applicants for Land

ABBREVIATIONS

Col.Rec.	*The Colonial Records of the State of Georgia,* vols. 1–32
Col.Rec.	Colonial Records of the State of Georgia, vols. 33–38
Col.Wills.	*Abstracts of Colonial Wills of the State of Georgia*
Collections	*Collections of the Georgia Historical Society,* vols. 1–22
Det.Rep.	G. Jones, *Detailed Reports on the Salzburger Emigrants*
Egmont	Percival, *Diary of Viscount Percival, afterwards First Earl of Egmont*
Gaz.S.Ga.	*Gazette of the State of Georgia*
GG.	*Georgia Gazette*
List	Coulter and Saye, *A List of the Early Settlers of Georgia*
Rev.Rec.	*The Revolutionary Records of the State of Georgia*
Roy.GG.	*Royal Georgia Gazette*

ACKNOWLEDGMENTS

During the seven years that I researched and wrote this book, I accrued many debts, most of them happily of a nonfinancial variety. I would like to thank staff members at the following institutions for their professional help and use of resources: the Georgia Historical Society in Savannah (whose archivists not only recommended manuscripts and sources but were kind enough to introduce me to minor league baseball); the National Archives at Kew (formerly the Public Record Office); the University Library at Cambridge and the Bodleian Library at Oxford; the British Library and British Museum; the National Library of Scotland in Edinburgh; various University of Georgia libraries (especially the Hargrett); the University of Warwick library; local archives in Norwich, England; and the State of Georgia Department of Archives and History in Atlanta.

I have a tremendous intellectual debt to colleagues and friends across the modern Atlantic world who have offered insight, criticism, support, and many enjoyable nights out along the way. I would like to thank participants at a host of conference sessions in recent years, at the Southern Association of Women Historians, Organization of American Historians, British Group in Early American History, Southern Historical Association, and various research seminars at British universities. At conferences in the United States, Catherine Clinton, Carol Berkin, and Kathryn Braund have offered penetrating and positive feedback as chairs and commentators; copanelists Tim Lockley, Jules Sweet, and Steven Hahn have offered great camaraderie, good humor, and priceless bibliographic recommendations; and Ed Cashin, Cynthia Kierner, Michael Morris, Connie Schultz, and many others have been kind enough to share their time and their expert thoughts. I had only a vague inkling of the notion of "southern hospitality" when I made my first research trip to Georgia, and, having handed over my wallet at 4:00 a.m. to muggers who frequented Atlanta's Greyhound Bus terminal (evidently lying in wait for unsuspecting hungry English graduate students), I must confess I was skeptical. But since then my faith has long been restored, and I have been repeatedly overwhelmed by the generosity and enthusiasm of Lee Ann Caldwell, Michelle Gillespie, John Inscoe, Annette Laing, and the people of Georgia more generally.

In Britain the study of early American history has never felt like a frontier, largely thanks to the comradeship of a community of scholars who have kept me on the straight and narrow yet brought depth and breadth to my understanding of the Atlantic world. I have benefited immeasurably from conversations, workshops, car journeys, pub lunches, seminars, walks, dinners, and arguments with Tony Badger, Emma Hart, Peter Marshall, Mike McDonnell, Simon Middleton, Colin Nicolson, Sarah Pearsall, Don Ratcliffe, Steve Sarson, Matthew Ward, and Natalie Zacek and the fleeting visits of Sylvia Frey, Carol Karlsen, Mary Beth Norton, Linda Kerber, the late Lance Banning, Laurel Thatcher Ulrich, Jack Greene, and others.

I owe a sizable debt of moral and intellectual support to a host of students, graduates, and former and current colleagues at institutions where I have learned and taught. Particular mention must go to Trevor Burnard for innumerable words of wisdom, rugged enthusiasm, and dry wit at Brunel University and to Inge Dornan, with whom I shared many enjoyable lowcountry coffees. At Oxford University I had the pleasure of the company and acumen of the teaching staff at Brasenose College and a host of Americanists, including Rick Beeman, Richard Carwardine, Gareth Davies, Clive Holmes, Michael Heale, Jack Pole, Stephen Tuck, and Peter Thompson, whose passion for ideas was infectious. More recently, like many of my historical subjects, I have experienced a move to another country, and my new colleagues in the history department at Stirling University in Scotland have naively welcomed me with good humor and kindness.

In researching and writing this book, I have been dependent upon funding from various bodies, and I owe special thanks to the Economic and Social Research Council, which funded a doctoral studentship some time ago; Downing College and the History Faculty at Cambridge University for various postgraduate travel grants and awards; and the assistance of the Modern History Faculty at Oxford and the Faculty of Arts at Stirling in getting me to various libraries and conferences. The editors at the *Georgia Historical Quarterly* worked with me to refine my understanding and articulation of the history of women and the American Revolution in Georgia. Nora Jaffary has also helped me to clarify and develop elements of my thesis, by carefully editing my essay in her forthcoming book, *Gender, Race, and Religion in the Colonization of the Americas*. The expert recommendations of two anonymous readers at the University of Georgia Press lent direction and focus to the ongoing process of revision.

I would also like to convey my appreciation to staffers at the University of Georgia Press not only for their patience but also for their support and guidance. Particular tribute must go to Andrew Berzanskis, Jon Davies, and Polly Kummel, who offered a thoroughly welcome combination of sharp copyediting, good humor, and enthusiasm and vastly improved the manuscript.

Conceiving of and embarking on this project would not have been possible without the inspiration and encouragement of two supervisors at Cambridge. To Richard Smith, who calmly guided me from the medieval towns of East Anglia through to a personal new world of eighteenth-century philanthropy and demography, and for his richness of interests, depth of knowledge, and Cole Porter karaoke, I am deeply grateful. I would always have been indebted to Betty Wood anyway, simply for introducing me to the history of colonial America with which I have been, and continue to be, spellbound. But her unfailing enthusiasm for rediscovering the worlds of the overlooked, for finding humanity in historical context, and, when necessary, for a pint of ale and plate of fish and chips at the Granta Inn, she has been an enduring and most welcome influence. A practitioner of the Annales school of graduate supervision, she continues to be a mentor, critic, counselor, and warm friend.

Completing this project, or, more accurately, stopping it at a satisfactory point, has required a high degree of perseverance. This would have been impossible without the support of friends and family—some of whom have looked through the manuscript in its various drafts, and others of whom have done a fine job of distracting me from it as necessary. I especially would like to express to my wife, Lils, my love and deep appreciation for her patience, time, and careful proofreading and for her continued interest and irrational encouragement. My greatest thanks this time around are reserved for my parents, to whom this book is dedicated in a pitiful attempt to acknowledge their unfailing support in everything I do.

Note: Settlers of English and later African and South Carolinian origin were dispersed throughout the province.

Georgia's Frontier Women

INTRODUCTION

Colonial American women of the eighteenth century do not seem to share the historical exuberance of their seventeenth-century predecessors. After all, women of the eighteenth century inhabited a more settled, stable world. Huts had become houses and villages had become towns; wealth was becoming class, and color was becoming race. Gone were the days when Thomas(ine) Hall could masquerade in the Chesapeake of the 1620s in either male or female guise. Gone was the time in New England when conditions had allowed Anne Hutchinson to usurp male authority and challenge the social and religious precepts of her day. Fewer women now experienced at first hand the shock of Indian captivity, as Mary Rowlandson or Hannah Dustan had during the last decades of the seventeenth century. And never again would the female association with witchcraft be allowed by the pressures of a pubescent society to explode into a bloodletting on the scale of the Salem trials of 1692. Only the events of the American Revolution saved women from what might otherwise have been a disturbingly quiet century and dragged them insistently back to the forefront of scholarship.

The history of the colonization of Georgia reminds us that eighteenth-century America still had frontiers. Despite the budding urbanization, growth of institutions, and consolidation of social hierarchies in older territories, there remained many new worlds ripe for exploitation. The most perceivable frontier was geographic. During the century Europe and West Africa hemorrhaged enough migrants to fill up settled seaboard areas of North America, as well as the banks of navigable waterways and fertile eastern plains, and flow westward into the Appalachian backcountry. Sandwiched between the three great European colonial powers and two major southeastern Indian peoples, Georgia constituted a clear geographic frontier of British settlement between 1732 and 1776.

The significance of the geographic frontier, though not the engine of American identity that Frederick Jackson Turner once described, is that it was a prerequisite of other frontiers: it provided a site for the exploration of other boundaries in society, the laboratory in which practical and theoretical experiments were conducted. By the time of Georgia's founding, many other regions had already played their part. Each new colony had shipwrecked its settlers' expectations upon the rocks of reality. The debris was gradually reconstructed as it drifted ashore, a product of both European origins and American environments. As fledgling settlements became functional societies, perceptions of gender, rank, and race had hardened and stuck fast like old barnacles.

In *Georgia's Frontier Women* my goal is to construct a comprehensive account of women's contributions to the demographic, economic, and social processes of settling the youngest of the British American colonies that declared their independence in 1776. Here, on the margins of settlement, perceptions were initially pliant, social systems were supple, and the population was colorful. Eighteenth-century Georgia women were more diverse in origin than the vast majority of formative colonial populations. Georgia's women drew not only on a pluralistic Old World heritage but also on New World migration and experience.

In a sense, writing a history of eighteenth-century frontier females is subject to the same hazards that they faced: navigating a practical route through the dense theoretical fog of gendered oppression. Some alarming gaps in source material compound the dangers of a patriarchal bias within the historical record. Perhaps it is asking for trouble to focus upon women, limit oneself to the colonial lower South, and seek to encompass race and ethnicity. But as with early settlers, instead of casting envious glances at the more fertile northern regions (and their excellent recent scholarship), I found my energies were best channeled into a redoubled determination to persevere in the hope that this book at least serves as a foundation for future refinement. The records may not be as comprehensive as the diaries and letters of New England or the demographic data of the Chesapeake. But sufficient sources have survived the ravages of time—and Sherman—to shed varying amounts of light upon female roles in early Georgia.

Naturally, the elite educated white woman is prone to basking in the spotlight, while her counterparts among the lower classes and non-European populations remain shadowy reflections. She reminds us that there was no single generalizable female experience; gender was only one vector in a larger social matrix that encompassed age, nationality, occupation, race, and class. Equally, the public documentation of her activity in newspapers, wills, church records, and obituaries far outstrips information about more private locations—about her home, her relationships, and her thoughts. Just as one cannot sit in on a stranger's memorial service and be remotely confident that one has a firm grasp of her actual character in life, the unevenness in the data available tends to transform certainties into probables, probables into possibles, and possibles into unfathomables. In places the unknowables bestow a (somewhat) tentative tone upon my analysis. It is important to be aware at the outset that any interpretation of the historical record, my own included, is profoundly shaped by such omissions.

In 1995 Phinizy Spalding and Pamela B. Wilson lamented that in an era of admirable historical reappraisal and integration of women's life and work experiences in early America and eighteenth-century England, "colonial Georgia . . . has been largely ignored . . . or bypassed entirely in virtually all studies dealing with the role of women," particularly in comparison with the better-documented colonies of New England and the Chesapeake.[1] One consequence of such widespread disregard is that historians who do engage with the field can be tempted to overemphasize elements of their study, showing no reluctance to highlight how women triumphed, scored on issues, or struck a blow for women's rights to counter the supposed inconsequentiality of their subjects. Such justifications are unnecessary. The identification of the colonial era as a golden age for (white) women, as first expounded in Elizabeth Dexter's *Colonial Women of Affairs* in the 1920s, has long collapsed under the pressure of more recent research. The model has been rejected as oversimplistic and unsophisticated, caricaturing colonial female behavior with an anachronistic brush that overstates public economic opportunities in the earlier period (often overlooking sociocultural constraints), and contrasts them too favorably and abruptly with a paradigm of female domesticity in the nineteenth century.[2] But abandoning the search does not mean rejecting that at certain times, or in certain places, some women secured a higher economic or social status than the cultural norms of their society theoretically permitted. The converse is equally self-evident, as localized conditions could also bring a downturn in female fortunes.

The acceleration of research into the women of eighteenth-century Georgia in recent years, spearheaded by Betty Wood, Lee Ann Caldwell, and Michelle Gillespie (among others), has only begun to move historical focus away from that dinosaur of historiography, the elite white male. This is a reflection not only of the truism that colonial Georgia has historically stood in the shadow of its more populous and patriotic neighbors. Within the historiography of the colony and state itself, women's actions and lives have too often been left in the shadows of men's, and nonelites' in the shade of the wealthy and prominent. This seems particularly strange, given that contemporaries were so quick to acknowledge that, as Robert Parker put it in January 1735, "Women in a New Colony are the Very Sinews of it."[3] This exploration seeks, as far as the sources allow, to demonstrate that the presence of females on the frontier was critical to the evolution of the province. In turn, the impact of the frontier on females was instrumental in structuring their lives. The theoretical regulation and practical operation of gender together lay at the heart of Georgia's formative identity. Despite their early freakishness, by the end of the eighteenth century the regulation and operation of gender would be ideologically and mechanistically bound together with race and class in a durable web that confirmed Georgia's status as a southern society.

THE COLONIZATION OF Georgia during the eighteenth century was an erratic process, one that had few constants and many variables. Georgia's evolution would incorporate sporadic outbreaks of violent warfare, sweeping shifts in government, opposing attitudes and responses to racial slavery, and the coexistence of broad religious toleration with localized antipathies. A province whose economic growth was stagnant and whose population relied on imported foodstuffs to survive would become one in which productivity and exportation were prolific, and commercial ties sprang up across the Atlantic world. Right up to the Revolution, Georgia's colonization was largely characterized by the arrival of distinct communities and their interaction with each other across linguistic, cultural, and ethnic boundaries. The colony's own societal progress was constantly indexed against changes in the world outside and diplomatic relations with the Spanish, Native Americans, French, Carolinians, and ultimately the British Crown.

It is fair to say, then, that finding change in the history of early Georgia is easier than finding continuity. Diversity, not similarity, is far more apparent in the words and actions of those who experienced these years, all seeking to explain and define themselves against the shifting world outside. External disruptions and alienations encouraged the vast majority of settlers to seek stability *within* the family and the local community. From this angle, which spotlights the centrality of marriage and the family to the settlement of Georgia, it is possible to find a continuity worthy of study and one with which contemporaries identified. Because families are based on axioms of human nature, studying the formation and function of families offers insight into a subject that interested and shaped the behavior of almost every settler.

Marital partnerships were the building blocks of the population of early Georgia and came in many shapes and sizes. Although all were distinct blends of personality and function, most operated on the premise that the union was beneficial, a positive investment that combined sexual, social, emotional, and economic factors. In the colonial domain, particularly on the frontier of settlement, the stability offered by marriage and kinship links assumed even greater import. Precisely because settlers were far from their home countries, they drew on those influences that were most embedded and that they could most easily re-create in their efforts to adapt to the circumstances of the New World. Many hopes and dreams about family prosperity proved impossible to realize. Natural and man-made obstacles seemed to conspire to damage colonists' prospects: the hostile climate induced high levels of infant mortality, while the initial banning of female inheritance of property discouraged some from settling. In response, individuals and communities swallowed their pride and shook off their aversions. They married people of different religions, colors, and national origin; they married extremely soon after the death of a spouse and adopted new children; and they married young. But this was not so much changing the rules of the game as moving the goalposts. Few would go so far as to discard the valuable assets offered by the institution of marriage itself.

Though this book focuses on Georgia, and offers a skewed narrative of the evolution of the colony, it does not do so in isolation. Insofar as this is a history of adult women, it is also, indirectly, a history of men and of children. I have tried, where appropriate, to locate the history of Georgia within a larger "Atlantic" context—to think about how experiences in Georgia contrasted with experiences in other colonies, in metropolitan Britain, or in continental Europe. Elsewhere the "Middle Ground" of the American interior has been a more suitable backdrop. This reflects that the colony in its infant years had links to a motley collection of influences: the trading customs of Creek Indians; the utopian machinations of aristocratic English peers; the enslaving patterns of West African chieftains and their trading clients. My intention herein is to highlight rather than expound on such linkages, and where practicable I have introduced a comparative dimension—for instance, in exploring demographic patterns, changing economic roles, or the codification of race and gender.

The resulting book is divided, largely chronologically, into a prologue, six chapters, and an epilogue, with a brief conclusion. The prologue, "The Georgia Plan," explores the preconceptions, motives, and expectations that drove a set of trustees to sponsor the new colony and what roles the trustees expected women to play in it. Part 1, comprising chapters 1 to 3, addresses the trusteeship that ruled Georgia between 1732 and 1752. In this section I outline the distinctive characteristics of the early population before exploring the ways in which migration, mortality, and fertility influenced women's life cycles and economic functions within their communities. People had to swiftly adapt their courtship and parenting patterns, domestic and extradomestic labor, intercultural relations, and social behavior to cope with the realities of life on the frontier of settlement, often belying the trustees' original hopes and expectations.

Part 2 addresses the period following the collapse of the trusteeship, when for more than twenty years Georgia came under the direct jurisdiction of the British Crown, until the American Revolution tortuously terminated that jurisdiction. During the royal era the province experienced a radical transformation, set in motion by a range of factors: the arrival of new migrants, new government, slavery, economic investment, and Indian land cessions. Chapters 4 to 6 explore the ways in which these changes depended upon and influenced the roles of women in the colony, returning to the themes of familial behavior, economic activity, and interracial relations. By exploiting such mechanisms as land granting, legislation, and fashion, a self-defining white elite consciously and publicly distanced itself from subaltern groups, although the theory never equated fully with private practices in Georgia. As each subsection of the population (including females and slaves) sought to advance its own interests, it helped construct a patriarchal cultural web that mirrored other southern colonies in its endurance and elasticity (see chapter 6). The epilogue engages with the ways in which the

Revolution and Revolutionary War intersected with women's behavior. For all the constitutional and physical upheaval in Georgia, and despite the individual actions of many women of different races and different loyalties, the Revolutionary frontier proved transitory; the gendered and racial ordering of society survived unscathed. As several historians have posited (though not without dissension), in the aftermath of the Revolution patriarchy would return undeterred with a new gender ideal, "Republican Motherhood." How far the weary women of independent Georgia subscribed to this northern, educated ideal is a matter for future scrutiny.

PROLOGUE

The Georgia Plan

Beliefs about gender have always shaped the character of colonization. From their first fumbling attempts in the sixteenth century to graft English populations onto lands in Ireland, and later onto lands three thousand miles across the Atlantic Ocean, British colonizers had relied on assumptions about the interaction between males and females and how such interaction would, could, and should affect society. Some of these beliefs were of long standing: cultures and institutions throughout Britain had evolved to uphold the dominant position of men, from the monarch down to the father of the lowliest family. Beliefs about gender and sexuality, particularly in the sixteenth and seventeenth centuries, were accorded greater credence because they were attached to a world order designed by a higher being. The Creek and Cherokee peoples, no less than the British who would encroach upon their lands, believed that a higher being had shaped human nature, had endowed men and women with certain inalienable characteristics—in the same way that we might acknowledge today that our genes affect our characteristics, that we are somehow predestined.[1]

By 1731, when a British writer was drafting a justification for the founding of yet another new colony, some beliefs about gender were in transition.[2] Attitudes toward sex, for instance, were shifting because of a growing body of medical literature, a weakening of religious orthodoxy, and a newfound familiarity with other races and their gender systems. The sexual voraciousness that had once been associated with all women (interpreted as innate sin) was now disassociated from white women. The regulation of female sexuality was viewed less as a moral matter to be dealt with by church courts and more as a matter of public order or a medical concern. Newspapers and magazines designed specifically for middle- and upper-class women were beginning to appear, and these periodicals were identifying subject matter and role models that would come to characterize a distinctly feminine world. A growing number of writers emphasized women's capacity to inculcate the population with virtue—and even satirists, like the playwright Henry Fielding (whose production of *Tom Thumb* opened in 1730), could not "seem to move beyond imagining separate domains of masculine and feminine power."[3] Essayists and novelists increasingly advocated responsible motherhood, and although they may not have represented the sentiments of the population at large, their appeal for moral improvement followed three decades (1690–1720) in which English parents alone had abandoned about one thousand infants each year.[4] James Edward Oglethorpe, the author setting out his plans for a new colony in 1731, sought consciously to put into practice the most up-to-date, cutting-edge theories about empire, commerce, philanthropy, and gender. Like many political commentators, moral philosophers, and colonial apologists before him, he realized that to create an orderly society, he would have to establish a stable system of relations between men and women.[5]

King George II conferred a charter for settling Georgia upon a group of trustees, or proprietors, in 1732. These men, originally numbering twenty-one, would direct the colony's affairs independent of direct royal control and had more in common than simply their gender. They were all prominent in English society—they included ten members of the House of Commons, two members of the House of Lords, and five ministers of the Church of England. They had all been linked at some point with the Associates of Dr. Bray, a colonial missionary organization, and were intimately connected with the philanthropic projects of their day. The two most influential members, John Viscount Percival (later Earl of Egmont) and James Edward Oglethorpe, lavished considerable amounts of time, energy, and money upon the Georgia plan, to relocate thousands of disadvantaged people to a new productive utopia across the Atlantic. It is important to understand that this undertaking was purely paternalistic and altruistic. The trustees' reward was not to be found in patronage or power or profit, the motives for earlier proprietary schemes such as the colonization of Pennsylvania or Carolina, but in the emphasizing of their good deeds and the gratitude of the recipients. The founding of Georgia, as one historian has put it, was "a unique experiment in the history of English colonization."[6]

As revealed in a number of publications and sermons intended to boost support for the venture, the Georgia plan was carefully constructed and unambiguous. Three practical motives underlay the philanthropic sponsorship. First was the desire to relieve the worthy poor in Great Britain (particularly London) and place them in an environment where they could be productive and therefore happy. Second, the province was thought to be rich in resources that would benefit British trade policy. The climate was believed ideal for the production of silk and wine, commodities that Britain was forced to import at great expense. Finally, a key motive for establishing Georgia, one that guaranteed large amounts of parliamentary support, was military. The province would act as a buffer for South Carolina, which had no southern line of defense and was threatened by attacks from the Spanish in Florida and the French in the Mississippi Valley. In terms of the actual functioning of the settlement, the trustees intended Georgia to be a colony of and for small farmers. Every man (excepting indentured servants) was to have fifty acres, with no one receiving more than five hundred. The institution of slavery was also prohibited, another means of preventing the emergence of a plantation society, as had happened in the colonies to the north of the territory.

These motives and measures structured the formation of Georgia as a colony, but through their policies and regulations the trustees maintained extremely close supervision of the evolution of their experiment. They searched, selected, and sometimes interviewed charity colonists whose passage to America and provisioning for one year the trustees would underwrite. They handpicked experts to supervise the cultivation of targeted commodities, insisting that each farm grow a set number of mulberry trees for the silk industry. The trustees marked out townships in neat geometrical shapes. They dictated that the prescribed fifty acres be laid out so that a dwelling was within the town, a five-acre garden plot was set near the edge of town, and a forty-five-acre farm was in the countryside.

The trustees ruled indirectly through their appointed officials, whose control of the focal points of the larger settlements—the storehouse, the courthouse, the jailhouse—gave them power if not popularity. But the trustees' hands-on approach to the government of Georgia from across the Atlantic provoked serious problems, as did their resolve on restrictions concerning landownership, slaveholding, and the consumption of hard liquor. Although the trustees brought a great deal of experience in charitable and missionary work to the venture, their economic credentials were considerably more spurious. In fact, many settlers believed that the trustees' meddling in the colony's economy was to the detriment of its development. Opposition grew in the province, particularly from "adventurers," people who brought with them some capital and traveled across the Atlantic by their own means but who found their investments negated by conditions and regulations in the colony. This group, labeled the Malcontents, campaigned for changes in policy from Georgia, Charlestown (later Charleston, South Carolina), and eventually through representatives in London.[7]

This opposition put greater pressure on the trustees to reveal the extent to which their Georgia plan had succeeded. Despite some early political victories and Oglethorpe's successful repulsion of a Spanish invasion during the War of Jenkins' Ear, the trustees had little to show for such a considerable investment. Many lost heart, their morale sapped by criticism and by each colonist who fled the struggling province. Attendance at the trustees' Common Council waned as they turned to other philanthropic projects in the 1740s. The project had become hampered above all by a lack of funding, as well as flagging public interest and enthusiasm, and continual complaints from the Malcontents. The Earl of

Egmont despondently remarked that it was "a melancholy thing to see how zeal for a good thing abates when the novelty is over."[8] In 1751 the experiment was officially terminated when the trustees surrendered their charter to the Crown.

By the time the first royal governor of Georgia, John Reynolds, arrived in 1754, Georgia was already moving rapidly in a new direction. Planters and adventurers were flooding into the colony to take advantage of the legal relaxation of slaveholding and landholding regulations. Colonial historians have closely investigated the failure of the trusteeship and characterize it as anything from a humanitarian tragedy to a bumbling farce. But however faulty were the economic precepts behind the Georgia plan, its propaganda and promotional literature lent unusual prominence to the importance of women in the trustees' grand, idealistic scheme.

The founders of Georgia communicated their philanthropic aims so effectively throughout the British Isles and the American colonies—and the trustees' connections and credentials were so well respected—that a generous flow of private gifts and parliamentary grants poured in during the first years of the venture. The promotional literature reveals the founders' aspirations for female roles within the colony, though these would bear a limited resemblance to actual experiences.[9] These preconceptions were dictated partly by cultural norms and partly by more prominent factors that dominated the promotional literature: the wealth of the British Empire as measured by population size, poverty, and production. Propaganda writers such as Benjamin Martyn (secretary to the board of trustees) and Oglethorpe himself distributed numerous pamphlets explaining the rationale behind the Georgia venture, often expressed in political arithmetic learned from the likes of William Petty, Sir Josiah Child, and Charles Davenant.[10] From these pamphlets and published annual sermons presented by prominent Anglican ministers before the trustees and the Associates of Dr. Bray, we learn that women were far from peripheral to the Georgia plan, an assumption that some historians have made explicitly and others implicitly by simply ignoring the presence of women.[11] Indeed, the centrality of women to the venture, as confirmed in the sex ratios of immigrants, comes across strongly in the literature of 1731–33, when the trustees made their greatest effort to secure benefactions.

James Oglethorpe's *Some Account of the Designs of the Trustees for Establishing Colonys in America* was never actually published at the time, but it was read to Dr. Bray's Associates and served as a blueprint for the design of the colony. It was quoted at length and paraphrased in later published pamphlets attributed to Benjamin Martyn.[12] The primary role of women in the Georgia plan, we learn, is to encourage the continued dedication of the male workforce, to save what would be wasted male labor on menial tasks, and to preserve the health of the colonists:

A Wife and Children are security for a Mans not abandoning the Settlement; and the presence of those dear pledges who will reap the advantage of it will the more strongly incite him to labour. Even in the beginning Women and children will not be useless Mouths since there will always be some business which they may do and save so much labour to the Men, such as preparing their Food, cleaning and mending their Cloaths, gathering Wild Fruits, Roots, or Shell fish etc. The being kept clean and having wholesome food prepared at regular hours would tend greatly to the preserving the health of the people; and in Sicknes the having their Wives to nurse them may recover many who would inevitably perish were they to have no succour but from careless or unskilful Comrades.[13]

Women were not expected to labor in the fields but rather to tend to the domestic sphere as loving wives and dedicated housekeepers under the complete rule of the head of the household. Oglethorpe stresses this, stating that the husband should be answerable for the behavior of his wife and children and that he should have "proper authority" over them to enable him to keep them in order.[14] However, Oglethorpe maintains an emphasis on the need for hard work—even away from the fields, which were to be the exclusive domain of men. Women were to be inspired with the same "spirit of labour" as were the men. In particular, those who were most proficient at making clothes, spinning linen, and performing other household services were to be encouraged to make others emulate them and to instruct the ignorant. The trustees even envisaged that "little prizes for those who are most expert may be perhaps a good way of incouraging industry both in Men and Women."[15]

Preconceptions of women's domestic roles in the colonization of Georgia were thus heavily based on traditional norms and the existence, or, rather, creation, in the New World of separate spheres. Females were necessary because of their particular skills in the familial arena; their home-keeping virtues were to be encouraged and imparted. These expressions of conventional and conservative beliefs in the value of the family served an important function for the trustees. They underlined the trustees' intention that Georgia was not to be a military outpost, colony of convicts, religious haven for dissenters, or money-grabbing scheme in the mold of early Virginia. Georgia was for unfortunately poor but otherwise perfectly normal men with wives and children. Like swarming bees— a simile used frequently in the promotional propaganda—they would simply re-create their proscribed gender and familial roles in a new locale.[16]

In addition to their customary domestic responsibilities, women in Georgia were expected to perform vital labor in the cultivation of silk—an industry that the trustees expected to thrive in the supposedly ideal climate. Indeed, they partly justified the prohibition of slavery by the notion that they could mobilize women and children as an alternative, lightweight labor force in the production of raw silk. In a pamphlet published in 1732, *A New & Accurate Account of the Provinces of South Carolina & Georgia,* Oglethorpe offers a second justification for women's presence, which appears to be slightly at odds with the idea that they would be based within the home.[17] But this inconsistency reflects a very specific intention. The trustees aimed to attract a large number of benefactors from among those who were dissatisfied with the way local charity was organized in England. Those who footed the bill perceived poor relief, distributed in parishes by local officials, as corrupt, ineffective, and above all expensive. Oglethorpe now offered an alternative that would place the most paupers, women and children, in remunerative employment: "The Easiness of the Labour in winding off the Silk and tending the Silk Worm would agree with the most of those who throughout the Kingdom are chargeable to the Parishes . . . the Number of Poor, last mention'd [i.e., women and children], being thus dispos'd of, would send us Goods, at least to the Value of Five Hundred Thousand Pounds annually, to pay for their English Necessaries; and that would be somewhat better than our being oblig'd to maintain them at the Rate of Two Hundred thousand Pounds a Year here at Home."[18] The notion of female colonists' generating half a million pounds' worth of silk each year exposes not only the oft-noted naïveté of the trustees' economic precepts but also the remarkable centrality of women to their plan. Martyn was confident that the silk industry would provide employment for twenty thousand people on each side of the Atlantic; Oglethorpe believed that, when transported to productive Georgia, a man's "Wife and eldest Child may easily between them earn as much as the Man."[19]

The trustees therefore envisaged a colony in which women played a crucial role in both the economy and society. Economically, women were construed not only as domestic processors of primary goods cultivated by the men—although this arguably remained their most important responsibility—but also as producers of raw silk at enormous profit to themselves and their nation. Their economic contribution in Georgia was expected to compare favorably with their husbands', and to save a sizable amount on the annual bill for parish relief. In contrast, their familial role was designed to imitate rather than deviate from British norms; they were expected to remain firmly rooted in attending to the needs of their husbands and children, a task recognized as vital to safeguarding stability, health, and happiness in the New World.

Finally, women were necessary to increase the wealth of the colony, and by extension the nation, in another sense: population size.[20] The trustees aimed to "encourage Marriage and make Children a profit instead of a burthen to their Parents" in order to guarantee the rapid population growth that would provide another potential benchmark of success.[21] The trustees particularly wanted to avoid demographic problems that had plagued other colonial efforts in which men "cast away their Bodys upon rich old women" or made other kinds of unequal and unhealthy matches solely for the purpose of gain. The trustees wanted infertile wives to be construed not as a blessing but as a curse.[22] In these aspirations, as in so many others, the trustees would be disappointed. But to stimulate public subscription it was important to emphasize the links between philanthropy, female roles, and population growth. Georgia's patrons, like their peers in metropolitan Britain, believed that the engine of imperial prosperity was human expansion. To make Britain more powerful one had only to tap its unfulfilled potential—to rescue the thousands of wasted bodies crowding into urban slums and mobilize them. The Georgia plan was only one of a number of charitable projects intended to address the issue.

Patterns of English benevolence reflect a change in attitudes in the early eighteenth century. The great "age of philanthropy" was spurred on by moralists who highlighted the shortcomings of contemporary society using every medium possible. Hogarth's satirical etchings rammed home the urban decadence that pervaded London. Daniel Defoe and John Gay (among others) captured the criminality and vice in print. Religious societies railed from the pulpit and prayer meeting against immorality. Politicians, though by profession corrupt, occasionally addressed related issues of policing, military recruitment, and debtors' prisons. The creation of several major charitable ventures between the 1730s and 1760s, in response to the apparent moral crisis of the era, shared not only a spirit of humanitarianism but also clear objectives. The recipients of their benevolence had to make a valid contribution to the machine of empire.

Women's capacity to reproduce and to invest new generations with proper moral fiber—and thus women's welfare—was of central concern to social policy makers, political economists, and moralists. Contemporary writings relied heavily on both the metaphor of the family and the notion that charity must be so directed that it would raise the "deserving" poor from indigence and fit them into a national engine of economic productivity. The heightened responsibility placed on the shoulders of the donor for avoiding indiscriminate benevolence represented a significant step away from the almsgiving by bequest so characteristic of previous centuries. With the Poor Laws under heavy criticism from the likes of T. N. Alcock (in his famous 1752 *Observations on the Defects of the Poor Laws*), and as more and more philanthropists disposed of their wealth during their lifetimes, so new forms of charitable associations emerged.

The philanthropic foundations between 1730 and 1750 display not only the specific targeting of poor women but also a significant number of links within the wide web of wealthy individuals and corporations that contributed to charitable endeavors and encouraged others to make donations. At least 25 percent of the 138 philanthropists whom the historian Donna Andrew categorizes as

William Hogarth's *Gin Lane* (1751). In this engraving, the British satirist and artist depicts some of the worst excesses apparent among the poor of mid-eighteenth-century London. The various scenes of mayhem in the background are framed around the figure of a drunken woman whose unattended baby falls to its death in front of the Gin Royal Tavern. Hogarth's concerns about alcoholism, debt, and criminality were shared by many of Georgia's trustees, with whom he was intimately acquainted.
© Copyright the Trustees of The British Museum.

"major donors" to metropolitan causes between 1740 and 1769 also contributed—directly or indirectly—to the trustees for the colonization of Georgia.[23] The renowned Capt. Thomas Coram, for example, was a member of the Common Council of Trustees and therefore heavily involved in donating and collecting funds for the expedition. In an earlier project he had supported a program of conversion and education for Native American girls in the colonies, but his tour de force was the establishment of the Foundling Hospital in 1739 to nurture abandoned or orphaned London children. Lord Carpenter, another member of the trustees, found himself solicited by a representative of the Lock Hospital (for the treatment and cure of venereal disease) to be a vice president in 1746. These two London charities were more controversial than others. They raised questions about what might happen if help were made available to illegitimate children and the sexually promiscuous. Critics argued that such charities would only abet sexual misconduct, prostitution, and infant abandonment, undoubtedly discouraging a number of potential subscribers. Women in particular are surprisingly absent from the subscription lists.

However, a number of other ventures—including the trustees' plan for colonizing Georgia—were more attractive to those looking to assist "deserving" women without getting their hands dirty. The opening of the Lying-In Hospital in 1749 for poor married women was shortly followed by the opening of the London Lying-In Hospital. As one historian has remarked, "The theme of the pregnant woman in danger of death was seen to be ripe with possibilities for eliciting charitable donations."[24] Of the listed subscribers to these two charities, women constituted 33 percent and 14 percent, respectively. This compares with an average of 21 percent of donors to the Georgia trustees between 1732 and 1738 (excluding those who gave to parish and corporate collections, whose number and gender cannot be measured). If we take the absence or presence of female subscribers as an indication of the reputability of the charity—that is, its supposed tendency to increase or decrease vice while relieving affliction—it becomes clear that the colonization of Georgia was an openly laudable charity for assistance given both *to* women and *by* women.[25]

The trustees' female benefactors often appear to have specified the area to which they desired their donations to be channeled. This may reflect a considerate nature and genuine concern on some occasions but equally a shrewd approach on the part of collectors who sought the best means of soliciting contributions. Lady Saunderson, for instance, paid five pounds and five shillings in 1732 "for the use and Relief of the Necessitous Women and Children on board the Ship in their Passage to Georgia."[26] Apart from targeting these specific female circumstances requiring support, women were overwhelmingly prominent in advancing the cause of Christianity in Georgia. Although women contributed less than a tenth of the total benefactions to the trustees between 1732 and 1734, women donated more than 70 percent of the money collected "for the Religious Uses of the Colony."[27]

Women might have been so generous in this sphere and not in others for several reasons. First, giving for religious uses was evidently the highest form of charitable benevolence both in terms of its affiliated spiritual rewards and, more important, its untouchable reputability. Women with disposable wealth may have been reluctant to give to charities for the relief of prostitutes, support of fatherless children, or treatment of venereal disease, which were not only socially distasteful but also potentially detrimental to the nation. But wealthy women viewed the provision of spiritual direction for both Georgia's colonists and its natives—in the form of building churches, maintaining ministers and missionaries, and providing religious exegetical materials—as a purer, socially acceptable way of disposing of their charity. Indeed, although some benefactors, such as Mrs. Katherine Southwell, were content to donate large sums of money "to be applied in cultivating Lands for the Religious Uses of the Colony towards the Maintenance of a Catechist in Savannah," many women went as far as sending religious volumes themselves. A "Lady Who desires to be Unknown" donated fifty books, whereas other anonymous females gave five hundred copies of an "Explanation of the Church Catechism" and, later, four hundred books.[28] Their anonymity was in keeping with the selfless modesty and/or assurance of spiritual rewards that went hand in hand with such actions.

The assurances of spiritual rewards, given by prominent clergy, indicate another reason for women's disproportionate interest in underwriting spiritual direction: they were targeted by reverends and learned men. Famous and well-connected preachers associated with the venture, such as the reverends Hales, Whitefield, and Wesley, personally handled a large proportion of women's contributions and evidently encouraged the practice through sermons. "Lady Cox and several other ladies at Bath" petitioned the trustees in 1737 to allow Whitefield to preach a sermon for a collection intended for missionaries in Georgia.[29] Dozens of benefactions and bank receipts from female donors give details such as the fifty pounds "paid in by the hands of the Rev. Mr. Whitefield to be Applied for the Religious Uses of the Colony" or the typical case: "Receiv'd by the hands of Dr Hales One hundred Pounds the Benefaction of a Gentlewoman Who desires to be Unknown to be applied towards the Support of the Missionaries and Schools for instructing and converting to Christianity the Native Indians in Georgia. Resolved that Dr Hales be desired to return the thanks of the Trustees for the said Benefaction."[30]

The system in operation was highly personalized, largely anonymous, and evidently extremely efficient. However, these women were more than wealthy

Selina Hastings, Countess of Huntingdon (1707–91), portrayed by an anonymous artist in 1770. Hastings was one of many female philanthropists in the 1730s and 1740s who donated resources to the Georgia project. After forming a close relationship with Rev. George Whitefield, later her personal chaplain, Hastings founded a sect of Calvinistic Methodists in Britain and maintained an active interest in the welfare of Whitefield's Bethesda orphanage in Georgia. National Portrait Gallery, London.

victims of well-directed exploitation. They were targeted successfully because they were willing to give to a cause they considered proper and productive, like those men who chose to sponsor "the Advancement of Botany." The female assumption of religious authority and the notion that women were responsible for families' spiritual well-being also was becoming more pronounced in the eighteenth century, at least among the wealthier classes. Aniti Guerrini has argued that changing medical understandings of female physiology helped underwrite this redefinition and notes that several prominent women who were patients of the Bath physician George Cheyne exemplified the new model of elite womanhood. Several of his patients also played a prominent role in sponsoring projects in Georgia. Lady Betty Hastings, the daughter of the seventh Earl of Huntingdon, became something of a celebrity renowned for her beauty, piety, and munificence in the early eighteenth century. Her various charitable activities, made possible by a large Yorkshire estate that she had inherited from her maternal grandfather in 1704, included benefactions to schools and colleges and to the Society for the Promotion of Christian Knowledge (she also held stock in the Royal Africa Company and the South Sea Company). The heiress took an active interest in the welfare of Georgia colonists, writing a letter of recommendation for a dyer and his wife from Barnard Castle whom the trustees promptly dispatched across the Atlantic.[31]

Lady Betty's sister-in-law, Selina Hastings (Countess of Huntingdon from 1728), similarly pioneered both the interconnections between elite Englishwomen and religion, and the welfare of Georgia colonists. Convinced by the charismatic revivalism of George Whitefield in particular—Selina Hastings made him her domestic chaplain a decade after her own evangelical conversion in 1739—the activist countess was almost certainly one of the secret book donators mentioned earlier, and after her husband died in 1747 she harbored designs for Georgia land. She later extended her investment in Atlantic world revivalism, funding numerous chapels and ministers as part of her English connection and taking over the administration of the Bethesda orphanage in Georgia in 1770, an undertaking that would cost her thousands of pounds for very little return. Such elite female donors could no doubt consider themselves as quasi matriarchs over both indigent Europeans and indigenous Indians.[32]

In summary, promotional literature for the Georgia plan held clearly identifiable objectives and expectations for female roles within the colony. Most drew heavily upon contemporary conservative European ideals, although it is worth noting that they were tailored to some extent to suit the purposes of the propaganda: to heighten public interest and attract donations to the venture. Locating the Georgia project within the context of eighteenth-century English philanthropy reveals that women, though a minority, were unusually prominent as subscribers. This reflects a public approval of the merit of sending "deserving" paupers to America, relative to other less sanitary charities at home. The part played by elite Englishwomen in sponsoring the Georgia plan may have been covert, but their response to the trustees' direct appeals demonstrates that the venture was considered bona fide. In delineating the expected relative positions of men, women, and families in their colonial society, the trustees offered only limited concessions to the New World environment—mainly an optimistic anticipation of female silk production and the theoretical prohibition of female landholding in the colony.[33] They embarked upon their project secure in the knowledge that a significant female presence on the frontier would generate piety and permanence. Above all, it would increase the population of the colony and, by extension, the prosperity of the nation.

PART ONE

The Trusteeship

CHAPTER ONE

Population

The trustees seriously underestimated the gulf between New World and Old World environments and seemed to have learned little from past colonial mistakes. This, in part, reflected their desire to embark on an entirely new and humanitarian experiment that demanded that they spurn the imitation of patterns that already had emerged in North America (and particularly the lower South). Georgia was not to be an offshoot of the Carolina lowcountry but rather was to establish a new type of colony. Yet a study of the population of Georgia highlights the contribution of the trustees' ignorance of colonial conditions, as well as their selection of settlers, to the failure of the venture in demographic, economic, and societal senses. In particular, the trustees' preconceptions of women's roles were falsely premised on the notion that the familial cycles of Georgia colonists would imitate those of Europeans. Instead, circumstances in the colony dictated that marriage and familial formation would be very different, and settlers quickly adjusted their life-cycle patterns to fit their new environment.

Studies of the demography of British America have multiplied in recent years, as colonial historians have rallied around family reconstitution and the possibilities it holds for untangling population history and related economic processes. Unfortunately, most of these studies have focused disproportionately on the population history of New England and the Chesapeake, leaving a chasm between our understanding of the demography of the northern and southern colonies, and leading John J. McCusker and Russell Menard to state, "The Lower South still awaits its demographic historians."[1] This chapter constitutes an attempt to build no more than a thin rope bridge across the chasm, highlighting the similarities and differences between the population makeup of the Georgia colonists and their counterparts elsewhere and exploring the implications.

For the purposes of most of the comparative analysis, I have used the first decades of colonization as my benchmark. Establishing a new settlement in the supposed wilderness—for whatever reason—was the fundamental experience shared by the earliest European populations of North America, and it makes better sense to compare the demography of colonization across these common lines than across the years 1732–52, by which time other colonies were far advanced in the evolution of economy, settlement, and capacity for natural increase. That the depressing population history of trusteeship Georgia "contrasts sharply with that of other [contemporary] American colonies"—which, especially in New England, were approaching the Malthusian formula of doubling every twenty-five years—is unsurprising.[2] Georgia's demographic failures undoubtedly accentuated the disappointment in the venture and galvanized emigration from Georgia (especially to the flourishing South Carolina), but to approach it in isolation is to overlook important common demographic traits.

The first statistic required for the study of historical demography is population size. In most broad estimates Georgia's diminutive contribution to the European and African peopling of British America in 1732–52 is subsumed into its larger sibling of South Carolina, which already numbered an estimated thirty-five thousand when the *Anne* anchored at Yamacraw Bluff in 1733. This is partly due to the insignificance of the colony and partly to the lack of reliable data. True, an impressive number of extant letters and official reports contain estimates of militia or settlement populations, as well as the listings of early settlers recorded by the Earl of Egmont and trustee officials. But these are compounded by the high levels of unrecorded migration, particularly to and from South Carolina, the West Indies, New York, Pennsylvania, and England. As a result of migration, the high incidence of disease, and the continual state of war with the Spanish and the French, as well as their Indian allies, the population size of trusteeship Georgia fluctuated considerably—clearly too heavily to be calculated as a residual (as attempted by H. A. Gemery for net migration to several colonial regions in the seventeenth century).[3]

A significant proportion of early Georgia settlers, for example, consisted of Sephardic Jews and Moravians. Only a handful of Jewish colonists remained in 1740, although about eighty had arrived before 1735. Most, sponsored by the London Sephardic community, had come from England, but others had arrived from Portugal and the West Indies, as well as other colonies. They had been frightened into fleeing Georgia by the very real threat of Spanish invasion and the religious Inquisition that would no doubt have accompanied it. Forty-three Moravians, consisting of twenty-one men, fifteen women, and seven children, arrived at Savannah between April 1735 and February 1736. They departed for Pennsylvania after an unhappy sojourn, having produced only two children and having generated much hostility from other settlers who were unsympathetic to their refusal to serve in militia units or to perform public duties on religious grounds. Despite the problems of unrecorded migration, however, enough evidence (both quantitative and qualitative) exists to throw some light on the demographics of early Georgia.[4]

Figure 1 Estimated Population of Trusteeship Georgia

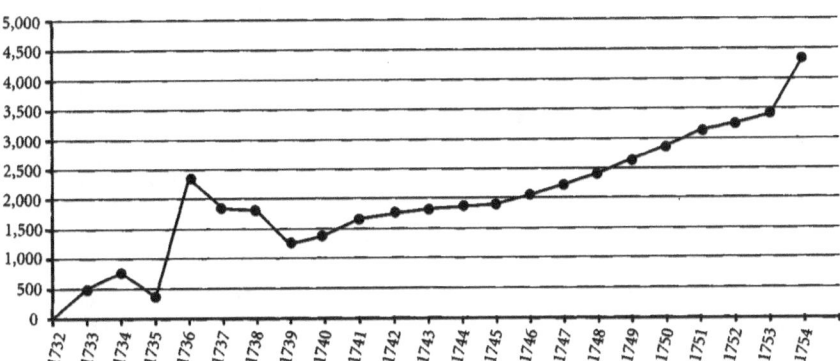

Note: The graph does not take account of the Native American presence in the province.

Sources: Ready, *Castle Builders*, 41–47; E. B. Greene and Harrington, *American Population*, 180–86; *List*; B. Wood, *Slavery in Colonial Georgia*, 89; and Cates, "'The Seasoning,'" 146–58.

Figure 1 represents an attempt to reconstruct the population of trusteeship Georgia by drawing from a number of primary sources as well as more recent estimates. The chart highlights several patterns that tie in well with accounts of contemporary military, epidemiological, and migration events. For a long time Georgia relied on immigration simply to sustain, let alone increase, the population. The flight of the Jews and Moravians, for example, along with the abandonment of settlements and the dispersal of a significant number of Malcontents between 1737 and 1741, brought about a reduction of nearly 50 percent in the population. This is even more notable, given the arrival in September 1738 of a regiment of seven hundred soldiers under James Oglethorpe.[5] The process of "seasoning," the period during which colonizing communities suffered from new diseases in a new climate, is also in evidence between 1733 and 1741. By the mid-1740s the colony was at last capable of limited growth. These were the major trends in the early population of Georgia, which was characterized paradoxically by high immigration *and* high emigration, as whole communities— Lowland Scots, Moravians, Sephardic Jews, and Salzburgers—made decisions to relocate elsewhere in Georgia or to abandon the colony altogether.

Better evidence exists for estimating the sex ratio of a large proportion of Georgia immigrants than for estimating the population size as a whole. Trustee officials such as John Vat, Hugh Mackay, and George Dunbar, who were responsible for the collection and transportation of settlers, were impressively diligent in documenting the immigrants under their care. Officials in Georgia were forced to maintain fairly close supervision of at least the consumption of

Table 1. Georgia Immigrants by Gender, 1733–41

Year	Men	Women	Children*	Total	Percentage Female
1733	77	44	48	169	40%
1734	292	129	179	600	36
1735	190	47	33	270	24
1736	315	96	99	510	29
1737	21	9	8	38	34
1738	158	69	88	315	36
1739	44	37	64	145	48
1740	4	5		9	56
1741	89	80	116	285	48
Unspecified	283	64	36	383	21
Total	1,473	580	671	2,724	34%

*Available evidence supports an assumption that half the children were female.

storehouse goods by the new arrivals. The first boatload of immigrants on the *Anne* consisted of 114 people of whom 44 were female (39 percent), a percentage that seems to have persisted in the arrivals of the next decade. If half the children brought to Georgia were female—an assumption supported by the evidence that specifies the genders of the children—the proportion of immigrants who were female would have been about 34 percent of the 2,724 immigrants recorded between 1733 and 1741 (see table 1). Furthermore, the evidence from the *Anne* shows that 87 percent of the females aboard traveled in family groups: they were overwhelmingly wives, mothers, and daughters. Their presence is testament to the trustees' selection policy of industrious but disadvantaged *families* (as emphasized in their promotional literature) and confirms the importance in the trustees' view of the paragon of woman as guardian of the family and its virtue. It is clear from the composition of immigrants that the trustees had not, as one historian has suggested, "attempted to develop . . . a womanless society."[6]

These figures display close parallels to the makeup of a group of 1,960 immigrants to New England before 1650, 35 percent of whom were female and more than 70 percent of whom traveled in family groups. These data show that, purely in terms of the ratio of male to female, the women of Georgia had far more in common with their Puritan Goodwife counterparts than with the women of the early Chesapeake. The seventeenth-century South had suffered an emphatic shortfall of females, who numbered one to every five or six men—accounting for the high rate of bachelorhood in Virginia (25 percent) and considerable imbalance in Maryland, where "comely or homely, strong or weak, any young woman was too valuable to be overlooked, and most could find a man with prospects."[7] Given the similarities in the sex ratios and family groupings of the immigrants who initiated the colonization of New England and Georgia, the difference in their early demographic evolution becomes all the more striking. If, as David Galenson suggests, "these sex ratios clearly indicate why rapid natural increase could begin so early in New England," they fail to explain Georgia's endurance of no natural increase until well into the 1740s.[8]

The qualitative evidence from the first two decades of Georgia's existence appears to contradict the relatively healthy sex ratios of new arrivals. Much of the problem in Georgia, in short, was a scarcity of marriageable women: too many of its female settlers either were already married or were young children. Like the early Chesapeake and New France—and unlike New England—Georgia had a conscious awareness of the need for marriageable women as a positive and necessary inducement for the recruitment and reproduction of settlers.[9] James Oglethorpe wrote to the trustees on several occasions, asking that they send over "industrious wives" for the men in his regiment, since for "single men there are very great Inconveniences."[10] By February 1743 the subject was taking over his entire correspondence:

> Gentlemen,
> The first Measures for us as Trustees to take is after supporting Religion to encourage Marriage and the rearing up of Children. Here [in Frederica] are a great number of married people and yet there is now in this place only above 700 men more than there are Women most of these would marry if they could get wives. The sending over single Women without Familys that could protect them might be attended with Indecencys but the giving passage to the Wives, Sisters and Daughters of Recruits and a small maintenance till they go on board would be a remedy to this and much the cheapest way of peopling the Country since after their arrival they are no further expense for their Husbands can maintain them.[11]

Oglethorpe's embarrassed request for mail-order brides for the southern frontier was echoed on the northern boundary of the colony. Here, Rev. Samuel Urlsperger conveyed the message that the Salzburgers in Ebenezer required a new transport of a hundred migrants "especially to the End that they might have more single women to Marry."[12] Because of the advantages that the trustees perceived from an increase of such "Useful Inhabitants," they agreed to pay extra to defray the cost of passage for a number of women who were inclined to hazard the trip to Georgia.[13] The greater presence of females among the immigrants of 1738–41, as shown in table 1, may well reflect this concern. As early as 1736 Archibald MacBean, a Highlander who was acting as a recruiting agent in Inverness, had offered to provide "twenty Young Women None of them Whores nor Transporters But to be Indented servants."[14] His implication was that the women would at least be useful as laborers before they became useful as wives. Like the officials of the Virginia Company, who decided to send over a boatload of one hundred maidens in 1620, the authorities in Georgia were obviously acutely aware of a scarcity of marriageable women, without whom the population could never achieve natural replacement rates, let alone growth. By 1735 more than a thousand people had immigrated to the colony, yet Elizabeth Stanley, the official midwife, had delivered just fifty-nine babies, a number of whom were likely to have perished (although she was proud that none of the women had died). Only after ten years had elapsed, in February 1745, did William Stephens, who served as the trustees' secretary in Georgia and was designated president of the colony between 1741 and 1751, find that "the Increase of Children among us of late years is (I think) worth remarking."[15]

Another reason why Georgia struggled to reach the impressive reproductive rates of New England is to be found in the high mortality of the early "seasoning" years, which meant that fewer marriages completed their normal fertility cycles. Of the colonists who came to Georgia, Milton Ready and Gerald Cates have estimated that 30 percent to 39 percent were dead by 1752.[16] Such was the disease toll in the first summer that the trustees had to open an orphan house for those who had lost both parents. Outbreaks of disease were worsened by an Atlantic crossing that assured inferior standards of nutrition for a period of several weeks and sometimes inflicted scurvy and dysentery. This was particularly dangerous for the 1,809 charity settlers, people from the lower social classes whose health was likely to have been compromised even before the journey. Oglethorpe reported that the two children who died during the voyage were already weak when he came on board and that they had been half-starved before they even left London.[17] Upon arrival in Georgia the settlers discovered that malaria and typhoid thrived there, especially around the swamps and river deltas of the lowcountry, claiming a considerable number of lives in the summer of 1733. The popular contemporary explanation for these "feavers" lay in the excessive consumption of rum by idle colonists. Others attributed the illnesses to drinking the unhealthy river water. Neither beverage would have helped, but the colonists' susceptibility to fever is most probably associated with their exposure to a new epidemiological climate, more deadly than the environment of New England. The early demographic regime is best summed up in the report of the minister in Savannah, Rev. Samuel Quincy. By July 1735 he had conducted 38 marriages, 34 christenings, and 156 burials, figures that seem to confirm the healthy gender ratio, the low birthrate, and the high mortality that afflicted the colony in its early years.[18]

A further reason for the unimpressive fertility becomes apparent when this mobile population is broken down not only by gender but also by age. A cursory glance at the migrant lists shows that many married women who traveled to Georgia were well advanced in their childbearing years. The average age of married women on the *Anne*'s voyages, for example, was as high as thirty-five, and the women brought with them on average fewer than two children. Only 27 percent of the women in the first shipload were aged twelve to thirty. The first group of Salzburgers who arrived was similarly made up of older family units, as was a large proportion of the indentured servant-settlers (both English and foreign). The most likely explanation for the failure of fertility in the colony is this aging, family-grouped population and, more important, its interaction with the high mortality of the early years. The concerns of the trustees' officials about the scarcity of *marriageable* women reflected the difficulty, above all, of finding women of marriageable *age*.

Studies of eighteenth-century English families suggest that average parents produced children at roughly thirty-month intervals, beginning at the time of marriage and extending to about the wife's fortieth or forty-fifth birthday.[19] As the female aged, the birth interval increased and children were born less often. But even the limited remaining potential for childbearing of most of the married women who arrived in Georgia was wiped out by the likelihood that she or her spouse would die in the first few years, given that they were at even greater risk from disease because of their age. Many widows remarried, some more than once and often in an extremely short space of time. However, few of these second or subsequent marriages produced children—often the marriage was simply a convenient way both to protect and provide for the widow and her existing children and to furnish the new husband with a housekeeper and perhaps a house to keep. The relatively advanced age of many immigrants is likely to have placed added pressure on the women at the younger end of the spectrum to marry young and therefore have children early. The combination of the distorted age structure and the disease-conducive environment was to prove disastrous for a large number of births among first-parity females in early Georgia.

The colonists were evidently aware of the cumulative effect of age, gender composition, and climate on their fertility. John Vat remarked of the Salzburger community that until June 1735, all the childbearing Salzburger women had delivered early and most had died. "Such of our Women as are now pregnant," he added, "are in deadly apprehensions that ye present Soil is pernicious both to the Growth of Children & Seeds."[20] Of the forty-two Salzburgers who were dead by Christmas 1738, thirty-one were women. Concurrently, infant mortality in this community approached 53 percent by 1740. Of fifty-six Salzburger children born in America or who were younger than three when they emigrated, about thirty were dead by January 1739. These deaths, although probably occurring at a higher rate in Ebenezer than elsewhere (because of its unhealthy lowland location), played a significant part in extending the regime of low fertility across colonial Georgia. First, in purely mathematical terms, these deaths removed from the equation an important number of young women and with them their potential future children. Second, the high mortality rate created a dearth of women of marriageable age, which forced men to migrate and look elsewhere for brides—as many Salzburgers did in Purysburg, South Carolina. Finally, the mortality rate may have actively discouraged women from having children at all, as is suggested in Vat's comment that I quoted earlier. The soil, interestingly, was believed to be responsible for both the failure of agriculture and the dangers of childbirth in Ebenezer. The travel diary of the two German pastors who accompanied the Salzburgers, Johann Martin Bolzius and Israel Christian Gronau, notes that many Salzburger wives were "in a miserable physical condition" and getting worse because they were nursing. During the first months of 1735 the ministers requested from the stores a few oxen for a fresh supply of meat, remarking that "this is particularly important for the lying-in women and for those who are pregnant."[21] By late April, though, eight young women in the Salzburger community and their infants had died in little more than three months, clearly from complications arising from their pregnancies—described as anything from feebleness to "internal gangrene"—and a new midwife had taken over.[22]

Midwifery problems persisted for a considerable time in Ebenezer. The new midwife (Schweighofer) suffered a stroke, the next (Holtzer) died in 1737, and for a number of years any pregnant woman found that "nobody knew in what way to help her." A French woman from Carolina was called in to help, but her long journey was problematic so a German widow from Savannah (Bischoff) was lured to the community in 1739. She remarried and moved away eight months later, so an inexperienced rookie (Rheinlander) filled in temporarily, although she soon decided to give up the task. An older woman (Bacher) next brought a strong spiritual element to the practice of midwifery but frequently fell short in regard to the practicalities. Such was the crisis of midwifery and the lack of knowledge and confidence among the women of the congregation that the community wrote to the city of Augsburg in Austria. A midwife there wrote a long and detailed response—answering questions and explaining "various very necessary means . . . to proceed in certain delicate circumstances, for which we have lacked advice up to now." A chest arrived a month later containing hot water bottles, a few remedies from the Augsburg midwife, sponges, herbs and roots, and also porridge pans and drinking cups for eventually weaning children off breast milk.[23]

In Savannah the plight of pregnant women and infants was similarly identified but differently diagnosed. In separate incidents during the early 1740s, autumnal fevers afflicting women and children were blamed on eating too much fruit and on taking the wrong medicine or "dose of Physick" while pregnant.[24] The illnesses of pregnant women were often remarked upon, and the colonists of Georgia became progressively more aware of the need to attend to them. Several women expected children during the journey to Georgia, a problem that the trustees had evidently not anticipated. Three unfortunate passengers were accidentally abandoned on shore at Portsmouth, having been sent "to engage a Midwife to go to Georgia for the sake of Women Passengers near their time on board the said Ship [the *London Merchant*]."[25] The settlers demonstrated an awareness of the special dietary requirements of pregnant women. The fresh meat that the Salzburger pastors requested coincided with the planting of celery, turnips, "or anything else that is green," while Samuel Eveleigh (a Charlestown merchant heavily involved with the Georgia project) recorded that he had delivered a great bundle of asparagus. As soon as Oglethorpe received it, he magnanimously ordered that the spears be given to "the woman with Child without reserving any for himself."[26]

In January 1735 Elizabeth Stanley, whom James Oglethorpe informally commissioned as public midwife at the start of the venture, wrote to complain of a number of problems affecting the completion of her duties. She entreated him to prevent nonspecialists from performing midwifery duties, sensing that if the current trend continued, more lives would be jeopardized. "One gentel woman has atamted itt," she remarked, "and ye 2d woman She Delivered She Died and Lifte her infant behind har." Stanley suggested that new arrivals should immediately be given her name as a way of preventing future miscarriages. This recommendation was not entirely selfless, of course, for Stanley relied upon her services' being remunerated—and she hinted at the close of her letter that she was owed some money.[27]

Nonetheless, as Stanley intimated, the existence of a number of practicing, unqualified, and inexperienced midwives—even if only from among the "gentlewomen" of Savannah—may certainly have damaged the chances of a successful birth. One might speculate that these women were called in to attend to their social peers, who may well have refused to accept the help of a lower-class specialist (Stanley's rough writing style reveals her origins). Oglethorpe asked Stanley in February 1736 to "examine a pretended midwife."[28] Lack of professional assistance, whether from choice or because frontier life meant that an expert midwife might rarely be close at hand, only compounded the dangers of childbirth. Rev. John Wesley grouchily complained about the nursing methods used during the birth of Mary Welch, who was born in February 1736; he bemoaned the lack of solemnity displayed by the midwives, who seemed to prefer "laughing and jesting" with their patient to prayers and "exhortations to each other to fear Him who is able to inflict sharper pains than these."[29] The more telling decision of the professional midwife Elizabeth Stanley, to leave her husband and return to England to have her own baby in 1736, speaks volumes about contemporary confidence in the practice as performed in Georgia.[30]

By 1739 the posts of public midwife at Savannah and Frederica were recognized as important enough to merit a full salary of five pounds per annum "besides five shillings per laying; and to be obliged to go on all Occasions when required." In 1741 the task of officiating at Frederica fell to one Elizabeth Harrison, who accordingly sent her bills to the trustees. A further sum was put aside to reimburse "Midwife Nurses" for their attendance.[31] The extent to which these measures contributed to the gradual improvement in infant survivorship in the 1740s is impossible to gauge, but the regulation of professional help for pregnant women must have improved success rates. While the perils of childbirth would continue to afflict Georgia's mothers and infants throughout the colonial era, and particularly among the enslaved population, victims in the early years tended to be unseasoned young white women, who were often experiencing their first pregnancy with an already weakened constitution and poor levels of hygiene and nutrition. These factors combined with the high mortality, imbalance in age structure, and constant migration in and out of the young province to at least delay the possibility of natural increase in the population and, at most, to fundamentally damage it.

The peculiar demographic conditions in trusteeship Georgia heavily influenced processes of marriage and family formation. Although the trustees were increasingly aware of the importance of achieving a balance in the ages and genders of settlers to counter the mortality of the seasoning years, patterns in the province obstinately refused to adhere to European norms. Early ages at first marriage, particularly for females, and extremely rapid remarriage after a spouse's death both were prevalent in the colony.

One of the few defining characteristics of the South as a discrete area before the antebellum period was that marriage, widowhood, and remarriage were all extraordinarily commonplace occurrences.[32] Marital turnover was disproportionately high among the early settlers of Georgia, as both younger female immigrants and widows with property were snapped up by predatory males looking to start a family, earn a larger land grant, or pick up acreage that had already been cleared or cultivated. For their part the women were more than passive victims. They looked to find a source of economic support, to move a few rungs up the ladder of society, or simply to ensure their own safety and protection in what was a dangerous and turbulent new world. As Jacques Dupâquier observes, remarriage was most frequently a defensive measure intended to safeguard the continued existence of surviving family members.[33]

The demographic regime of trusteeship Georgia, with its stable sex ratios but unbalanced age and fertility levels, induced the high rates of remarriage that are conspicuous within the primary sources. Although the average age at first marriage was undoubtedly much lower than in England and probably many other colonies, the likelihood of remarriage was substantially higher. Robert V. Wells has calculated that 88.1 percent of Quaker marriages in the Middle Colonies were first marriages for both bride and groom and that these marriages had an average duration of 30.8 years in the late seventeenth and early eighteenth centuries. Although the quantitative evidence for the trusteeship period is too sparse to generate a statistical average age at first marriage or a figure for average duration, marriage patterns in Georgia were clearly at the opposite end of the spectrum.[34]

The colonial records of Georgia highlight the young age of many first-time brides and the celerity with which they became wives after their arrival in the province. Some women married even before they left home, in anticipation of the need for domestic stability in the New World. Rev. Samuel Urlsperger records that nine young Salzburger "newly engaged" couples were married by November 1734, more than half of them before they had left Europe.[35] The trustees' principal on-site official, William Stephens, emphasized the speed with which young brides were snapped up. On 4 April 1745 he reported in his journal "that another of our Magistrates, was Smitten with Love, and making what speed he could, to enter into the Conjugal State with a young Damesel."[36] Such marriages were clearly to the advantage of both parties, because young women could achieve considerable upward social mobility and relative security by procuring a well-to-do husband. In 1744 the trustees gave extra encouragement to young men, such as three Dutch servants who had completed their terms of indenture, to seek wives as quickly as possible by the offering those who had families a larger land grant (up to five hundred acres).[37] Anticipating such beneficence, Sir Francis Bathurst, who was in Georgia, even sent his daughter and her new husband back to see the trustees in England to boost their chances of securing a profitable land grant in 1735.[38]

As I explore in greater depth in chapter 2, for many other European immigrants, the need for a wife represented little more than a need for domestic supervision, a housekeeper, without whom many men could not maximize their economic potential. The household economy, by definition, depended upon having a processor of the primary resources produced in the field, the garden, or elsewhere. A man without a wife would have to pay someone to perform such domestic duties; male colonists preferred the purchasing of a wife, capable of fulfilling other needs without arousing suspicion, to the hiring of a maidservant. On occasion the two could be combined, as demonstrated by James Moore (or

Muir), who married in December 1734 by buying the indenture of servant Mary Woodman before she had been in the colony for three weeks.[39] The average age at first marriage for women in trusteeship Georgia is therefore extremely likely to have been lower than it was in the early years of more northern colonies, as intimated in the work of Russell Menard and David Galenson. The marriage age in Georgia was certainly younger than was customary in England, a phenomenon documented in the eighteenth-century demographic writings of Thomas Malthus, and Benjamin Franklin, who observed that "marriages in America are more general, and more generally early, than in Europe."[40]

A similar contrast with the northern colonies and Britain is found with respect to *remarriage*. Wells noticed that his "eighteenth-century Quakers did not rush into a second or third marriage. . . . Those few who did marry more than once did so after a surprisingly long delay," an average wait of 6.2 years for the woman. This compares with an average interval of 47.6 months (about four years) for Englishwomen in the period 1700–49.[41] Twenty-five traceable and datable remarriages during the trusteeship give an average wait of just 8.4 months for the Georgia widows, nearly half of whom had found new husbands in three months or sooner.[42] This speed of remarriage was a feature of trusteeship Georgia that is remarkable even when compared with other colonies—let alone twenty-first-century norms. It was remarked on by contemporaries such as Thomas Causton, whose language in a letter to the trustees dated 16 January 1735 is testament to the ability of both male and female settlers to put the past behind them: "Mr Antrobus having buried his wife has married the Widow of Joseph Taylor."[43] The intervening period in this case was seven months. The sources also confirm that this pattern did not apply to women of one age group, class, or nationality but outlined a general tendency throughout the province.[44]

No one example describes the centrality of economic motives to the high incidence of the remarriage of widows better than Ann Harris's courtship by John Slack, as outlined in the journal of William Stephens. Slack, a mason by profession but more recently a disciple of George Whitefield's, was struck by the profitable household run by Harris—who had cleared and planted her five-acre plot, regularly raised plentiful crops, and had noticeably increased her livestock. Slack, according to Stephens, thus became "carnally minded, and was such a successful Woer, that the Widow in a little Time yielded to be his wife." However, Slack rescinded his offer when he learned that much of this prosperity would have to pay off her late husband's debts—and that Slack would become liable to satisfy these creditors upon marriage: "His Interest outweighing his Love, [Slack] thought it too great a Price to pay for a Wife."[45] This episode is unlikely to have been typical of most potential remarriages. The widow Harris was clearly an exceptional woman, and the gold and pewter mentioned in Stephens's account suggest that John Slack was not without some substance himself. However, it plainly reveals many of the prevalent characteristics of remarriage and the mechanisms of courtship in colonial Georgia—including the yielding of the female "in a little time."[46]

The justification of rapid remarriage was perhaps best captured by Robert Parker Jr. in a letter dated 30 January 1735, to the brother of his new wife, the former Elizabeth Sale. He stated: "As Women in a New Colony are the Very Sinews of it Your Sister being left a Widow & Designing to leave this place, I thought I cou'd Not do my Self or the Setlement a greater Service than by laying an Embargoe Upon her by Way of Marriage, which I in few Months put in practice."[47] Parker's less lofty motives were revealed in a letter written by Noble Jones, who, in his capacity as surveyor, was approached by the prospective groom, who wanted to know where the Sales' land was going to be and attempted to bribe Jones to change the plot.[48] A man who married a trusteeship Georgia widow knew he was apt to reap some benefit from her first husband's labors, as well as from the special treatment afforded her by the colonial authorities in the early years.

The driving force behind so many men's desire to marry widows was evidently the men's capacity to increase their material means without too long a wait or too much hard labor. It is more difficult to explain female motives, but in the widespread absence of local support networks of family and friends, and the conventional societal expectations that accompanied women in Europe, we find a clue that once again self-interest outweighed love. The distribution of age and sex ratios left a great number of widowed women (whose deceased husbands had been relatively old) who were not old enough to be sexually inactive but unlikely to have many more children—and for whom it made sense to settle down with another partner (often also well beyond his sexual peak). Death, indentured service, or simply distance often separated younger women from any paternal influence or protection in their marital decisions. Conditions on the southern frontier thus weakened parental authority and, with the exception of one or two pious congregations, limited institutional control. The frontier milieu removed psychological obstacles to marriage, even as it provided practical incentives. A marriage theoretically provided not only personal protection against manifold dangers but gave widows and pregnant women the potential to safeguard property and goods for their children—even after their mother's death if the widow drew up a marriage agreement.

Other features of Georgia families during the trusteeship were also functions of the demographic regime of high mortality and migration. Adoption and family separation were uncharacteristically common. The dearth of marriageable women necessitated interethnic and even interracial marriages. Landholding regulations that prohibited female ownership were circumnavigated, if not openly flouted, by direct appeal to the paternalistic trustees—until the trustees dropped these strictures altogether in 1750.[49] These socioeconomic conditions were direct consequences of the demographics of the colony, and I investigate them in greater depth in subsequent chapters.

Just as population evolution failed to meet the trustees' expectations, so women's roles in the colony differed from their utopian European preconceptions. Despite considerable encouragement, mothers and their children never happily staffed the mulberry groves, plucking leaves for the silkworms. Circumstances on the frontier and the exploitation of indentured servants left many women vulnerable to abuses that would have appalled the paternalistic trustees. Equally, the trustees expressed concern when women made the most of their opportunity to marry favorably or illegally and bettered their situation by taking advantage of such factors as the diversity of employment permitted on the margins of settlement. The trustees' plans for the colony did not embrace the levels of prostitution, extramarital cohabitation, and criminal activity that a number of female colonists engaged in.

However, the experience of colonizing Georgia proved the trustees correct on one score: their acknowledgment of the centrality of women and the family to the process of settlement. The trustees' selection of colonists reflected this centrality but failed to take into account the devastating effect of the "seasoning" period upon European immigrants to the malarial lower South, the relatively advanced age of many settlers, and the constant need for more women of marriageable age to remedy demographic deficiencies. Encouraging marriage, a prime objective identified by Oglethorpe, was a necessary policy to guarantee an upsurge in fertility in the colony. But the presence of wives and mothers held other attractions for European immigrants. On the frontier of settlement (as I discuss in chapter 2) it was quickly realized that female labor—and particularly labor in the domestic environment—was a prerequisite of making a living in Georgia. The trustees' dismissive assertion that there would always be "some business" that women could do was borne out in ways the founders had not anticipated.

The experience of marriage and widowhood, endured or enjoyed by the majority of colonial women, sets the stage for any analysis of female roles in Georgia or, for that matter, in England, Europe, or the northern colonies. But the universality of the state of marriage or widowhood is prone to insinuate a homogeneity of character that simply did not exist. Even within the province the patterns of marriage differ from settlement to settlement. For most of trusteeship Georgia, however, marriage and widowhood were extremely frequent and highly unstable. The motives that compelled men and women to marry or simply to cohabit were more material than religious, more practical than conventional. Women used the social and economic protection offered by the traditional sacrament of marriage to safeguard their interests against the dangers of the New World, yet the complete legal absorption of a wife into the husband was less absolute in Georgia than elsewhere. In many instances women retained direct control of the resources and finances at their disposal. The proliferation of marriages of expedience and the high mortality and migration rates are best perceived as mutually reinforcing phenomena. But the complex and often broken family structures that resulted were not the kind of families that the trustees had hoped to cultivate. Immoral reproduction was no laughing matter for the Earl of Egmont, who vetoed the involvement of a Scottish minister in 1735, on account of his having published *An Essay upon Improving and Adding to the Strength of Great Britain and Ireland by Fornication,* or as Egmont succinctly put it, "a pamphlet to justify that whoring is no sin."[50] Instead of establishing the family homestead unit as the basis of the colonial economy, the reality was that patterns of marriage and widowhood in trusteeship Georgia were symptomatic of the failure of the venture.

CHAPTER TWO

Economy

The economic fortunes of the women of early Georgia, as the trustees expected, more often than not were closely intertwined with those of their husbands and fathers. As in England, Europe, and colonial America, for the most part women's conventional responsibilities as workers within the household dictated their everyday employment. But although domesticity was the nucleus of their work, the unfamiliar circumstances gave rise to new permutations of women's work within and outside the household. The frontier required a range of tasks and occupations that made the activities of early Georgia women literally groundbreaking. In addition to bringing unforeseen encumbrances, the scarcity of labor and the absence of a functional market economy offered favorable opportunities to women. This was a miniature golden age, when institutions were in their infancy and women could expect greater power in the public sphere and more direct control of economic resources than was usual in Britain or America. An English farmer's wife could become "Conqueror Over the whole place"; a half-breed Creek woman could claim that "she could command every Man" and become the largest landholder in the colony; and an Italian mother—despite many children—could "domineer over all."[1]

At the same time, the colony's institutional infancy created conditions liable to constrain female economic agency and restrict activities and opportunities that were uncontested in the Old World. For many Georgia resembled something more akin to a dark age—a step back into a bygone, barbarous era. Elizabeth Bland declared in an abjectly miserable letter to Oglethorpe in June 1735 that "I have lost my liberty," describing the colony as a veritable hell on Earth and conjecturing (rather prophetically) that King George could never get away with treating his people in a like manner in Britain.[2] In the absence of a caste of slaves, female indentured servants were particularly vulnerable to exploitation of their labor and of their bodies—as one woman learned in the summer of 1739 when she broke into a property to find that her indentured granddaughter had scars across her body "from her Neck down to her Heels."[3] Similar atrocities were reported across the province. Women were theoretically prohibited from landholding and inheritance, denied an economic identity within marriage, and exploited outside it as vulnerable orphans and needy widows. They were commodified and on at least one occasion actually bought and sold, which would be more startling were it not that the institution of slavery was only just around the corner.

In short, the complexities associated with the settlement of a colony extended both ends of the spectrum of female economic experiences—offering both greater latitude and greater menace than were to be expected elsewhere. Of course, the economic behavior and labor patterns of early Georgia women were not metaphorically groundbreaking—the continent's colonial past was littered with antecedents in the Chesapeake, New England, the Carolinas, and the Middle Colonies. These were echoes of older patterns of colonial female employment that were now softened by the onset of normalization, maturity, and, in some places, gentility. In her study of the colonial courtrooms of Connecticut, for instance, Cornelia Dayton Hughes found that women became less and less conspicuous as the organizing principles of society changed and the economy commercialized.[4]

As had occurred fitfully in other colonies, the economic lifestyles of Georgia's frontierswomen would change significantly as the province aged, a process that I describe more fully in chapter 5. But the initial conditions of their existence remind us that the evolution of colonial female experience—even among white women—evinced no national trends. Simply put, to view colonial female experiences through a national chronology is to overlook the crucial importance of regional age (that is, the length of time that a colonial population occupied an area). Focusing on regional age allows a more sensitive accommodation of the local influences that affected colonial evolution. It also mitigates the historiographical dominance of colonies established in the early seventeenth century—when Filmerian political theory and formative race relations were more resonant influences than they were one hundred years later. Though these influences ultimately seemed to collect like migrating birds, it is vital to appreciate that the evolution of gender relations in each colony started from a different point and at a different time.

Georgia provided a distinctive human environment. The scarcity of labor, demographic imbalance, and absence of a functional market economy were fairly unusual for their time, although parts of the backcountry, the Ohio Valley, and New Hampshire were similarly configured. But Georgia was made more distinctive by its location in a South increasingly dominated by slavery. The labor scarcity and economic disability were made more noticeable, felt more acutely, because of the colony's proximity to lowcountry South Carolina, the most lucrative location in mainland America at the time.

The prosperity of Georgia's nearest neighbors in the British Atlantic world, both on the mainland (the Carolinas and Virginia) and offshore (the Caribbean islands of Jamaica, Leeward Islands, and Barbados) was overwhelmingly based upon their exploitation of slave labor. By the early eighteenth century British traders and New World planters had established a highly profitable symbiosis in which Africans were transported across the Atlantic and forced to work, typically in appalling conditions, on plantations that generated staple crops (such as tobacco, sugar, and rice) for sale in Europe. Economic forces had intertwined with cultural practices over time. The voracious New World demand for field laborers, who were needed to satisfy the expanding tastes of Europeans, meshed with a growing British capacity to supply European planters with West Africans. Typically taken captive by other Africans in the course of internecine warfare, they were shipped across the Atlantic initially through the Royal African Company and subsequently through separate traders. Long-standing suppositions and beliefs about the inferiority of Africans were revitalized and creatively expanded upon in order to justify the treatment meted out to them: they were variously held to be a people bearing a divine curse, morally and culturally perverse, physiologically suited to tropical soil and toil. Such cultural stigmatizing helped to allay any lingering guilt about the exploitation of slaves, and before the close of the eighteenth century white expressions of opposition to slavery tended to be few and far between. The Georgia trustees had not prohibited slavery as a matter of principle but because it was inconsistent with their social and economic intentions for the colony.

The Georgia records illuminate a wide variety of economic roles fulfilled by women during the trusteeship, but the overwhelming majority of these roles can be described in two ways. First, "domestic employment" preoccupied the vast majority of females for the vast majority of their working lives. In "domestic employment" I include all specialist housekeeping skills that pertained to the household domain. These skills were remarkably diverse and wide ranging and have been comprehensively expounded and explicated by historians, from the classic "pots and pans" of Julia Cherry Spruill to the excellent recent scholarship of Laurel Thatcher Ulrich, Carol Berkin, and Cynthia Kierner.

The second category of "extradomestic employment" that I would like to apply incorporates female activity that fell appreciably outside the boundaries of typical household maintenance. In fact, for the most part it incorporated activities that were specialized or hybrid extensions of unpaid domestic or familial responsibilities, including making millinery, providing lodging, engaging in midwifery, dressmaking, and retailing foodstuffs and dry goods. Nursing the sick for a fee or teaching children for money were no great distance from family health-care duties or the imparting of critical skills to sons and daughters. Running a large tavern demanded the focused application of cooking, occasional cleaning, and—most important—shrewd accounting techniques. Full-time agricultural labor was literally a few steps down the road from garden upkeep and cultivation. Even prostitution can be viewed as a debased extension of more conventional domestic pursuits. In short, female economic behavior outside the official homestead was overwhelmingly based on tasks within it.

In fact, inconsiderate Georgia settlers (presumably occupied with other, more pressing concerns) defined no such thing as an "official" homestead—and would have looked confusedly and disdainfully upon the artificial categories that I have just mentioned. Individuals frequently undertook both kinds of labor or switched between one and the other, configuring their economic activity to best meet their personal and family needs. Besides, it rarely mattered where a daughter or female servant worked, for their labor was directed by a higher authority: a mother or father, a master or mistress. Equally, in the eyes of the law it did not matter where a wife worked, for all the proceeds of her labor notionally devolved to her husband. The ends not only justified the means but made quibbling about their exact nature rather pointless. Given these limitations, the historical value of differentiating between female domestic and extradomestic economic activity relates not to the purpose of the work but rather its nature. Where the first category of "domestic employment" entailed tasks that were short, varied, numerous, and unpaid, the second tended to be more specialized, more time consuming, and much more likely to be remunerated.

As I have noted, the trustees' promotional literature heavily emphasized the importance of women's work in the domestic environment. In Georgia as well as in London the idealized woman was rooted in familial domesticity. Lady Frances Bathurst, arguably the most highborn female settler in the colony, was remembered in 1736 as "a loving Wife, an affectionate Mother, and a true Housekeeper"—not quite as verbose, perhaps, as Anne Bradstreet's famous fifteen-line eulogy for her mother in 1643 Massachusetts but embracing similar principles. Such acclamations were more remarkable when recorded about the living rather than the dead, who were prone to be shrouded in respectful mumblings. John Wesley was sufficiently impressed by the hospitality shown him by two ministers' wives that he made a note in his journal, wondering that "it appeared to be their delight as well as their custom to be the servants" of all visitors. It was one thing to do one's duty but quite another to enjoy it. Given the nature of much of the work—an interminable sequence of arduous, unsociable, and fatiguing chores, punctuated only by less mundane tasks—it is fair to say that the ratio of enjoyment to fulfillment for domestic employment was quite low, and the arrival of special visitors might well provide welcome diversions. It is also worth noting that John Wesley's track record in Georgia—as Carol Ebel has demonstrated—does not suggest he was a particularly shrewd judge of female appearances.[5]

Nonetheless, the centrality of females in the context of the household was axiomatic to the eighteenth-century colonists of Georgia. Thomas Causton took great pains to describe the houses of the fledgling colony in a letter to his wife in England, on the implicit understanding that this area, along with the garden (whose dimensions he recorded), would fall within her domain; this was the information that pertained to her interests. Causton concluded, "We shall have a fine prospect," and urged his wife to bring furniture, thread, and linen. Even before their arrival in the colony, wives were fulfilling expectations in caring for their families. Francis Moore reported the activities of those awaiting departure from the English Channel as they prepared for life in the New World. He records that while the men practiced using small arms, "there were also thread, worsted, and knitting needles given to the women, who employed their leisure time in making stockings and caps for their family, or in mending their clothes and linen." Upon arrival on the coastline of Georgia, the women washed their linen and dressed their meat on shore with fires made of cedar and bay trees, an extraordinary luxury for Englishwomen used to scrounging or gleaning for furzewood and unused to the teeming oyster banks that were accessible at low tide.[6]

Moore's casual observation reminds us that settling the New World required a reconfiguration of domestic tasks as well as better-documented adjustments in husbandry practices and commercial enterprises. The first dwellings of Georgia—and indeed the vast majority of houses during the trusteeship—probably were crude log cabins consisting of one multifunctional room that served as kitchen, dining room, and bedroom. The fireplace was the most important feature with a variety of cooking utensils hung around it. Archaeological excavation of the lot of a family that lived in Frederica between 1736 and 1748 recovered several items relating to the construction and maintenance of clothing, including brass thimbles, sewing pins, and buttons. The actual tasks of cleaning, mending, and cooking probably differed little from what might be expected in England—or, for that matter, in other colonies. But the sparseness of materials meant that women were more often obliged to produce the ingredients they needed for preparing foodstuffs, medication, and other household products. Admittedly, Georgia settlers had some advantages over some of their forebears—not least the accessible goods and services in nearby Charlestown, and the trustees' stores, which initially provided basic supplies and equipment. But the majority of wives—and especially the inhabitants of more remote settlements—remained heavily dependent upon their own labor and ingenuity for securing subsistence provisions.[7]

At first glance such domestic responsibilities do not appear to have held much worth in the eyes of colonial women's contemporaries. Their activities are submerged, even in the relatively barren historical record of female economic activity, beneath a pool of other, more exceptional and notable occupations that only a minority of women were willing or able to follow. Anne Ewing has rightly identified early Georgia women's domestic activity as a salient contribution to settlement, stating that their importance "can best be seen through their accomplishments within household boundaries." But although the women's importance in this sphere is undeniable, their visibility is more questionable. As Anne Frazer Rogers has remarked of the Fort Frederica settlement, female cooking, cleaning, and nursing tasks tended to leave little archaeological evidence. Equally, contemporary writers rarely felt the need to describe any kind of domestic activity in a direct or complete manner. William Stephens described the buildings at the Bethesda orphanage as including a workhouse for women and children, an infirmary, and two large kitchens facing one another "for Washing, Brewing, &c." This "&c" is a reflection of the quotidian character of the feminine tasks that Stephens did not even bother to describe to his readers. It may even be suggestive of a contemporary undervaluing of the female labor patterns associated with domesticity.[8]

In fact, regardless of what they chose to record in official and personal accounts, contemporaries were keenly aware of the fundamental contribution made by female domestic labor to the maintenance and advancement of colonial society. Women's work, paradoxically, was at its most obvious when it was absent. In a sense, a refreshing feature of writing in the twenty-first century is to have to emphasize that most male contemporaries were confounded by and many incapable of undertaking domestic responsibilities in the absence of an adult female—regardless of whether they held women in disdain or not. Settlers reported in 1738 that bachelors lacked the necessary domestic skills; that they "endured much disorder in their dwellings"; that they needed women in order to "establish an orderly household." Bolzius expressed considerable admiration for two sons who were notable because they managed to operate their household during their mother's illness. The struggle of neighbors who had lost spouses or could not find one were obvious for all to see, atomically unstable. Widowers consciously and subconsciously reminded their married brethren of the usefulness of a wife—how many "could not keep house without her." Without women's performance of their functions within the homestead, men could not perform theirs outside or achieve self-sufficiency, let alone increase their assets. The recurring obsession with attracting large numbers of young women to become wives in the colony, then, was to satisfy an economic thirst as much as a demographic one.[9]

If available, female relatives were expected to fill in domestic duties in place of wives, though less reliance could be placed on adult daughters who swiftly married and moved off. In the absence of wives or relatives, female servants—indentured to the trust or individuals, or paid independently—fulfilled many vital domestic needs of the young colony. Women in service, although occasionally employed in the fields and gardens (see discussion later in this chapter), were most often used as housekeepers and maids. It was reported in October 1743, following the expiration of a number of indentures, that the colony was suffering desperately from a shortage of servants—both male and female, either for agricultural labor or "the most necessary Domestick Uses." Samuel Hill requested information about maidservants before even crossing the Atlantic, realizing that he was "too unskill'd in the making a Bed or boiling the Pot."[10] The eagerness with which female servants were sought in the absence of wives, mothers, and other relations demonstrates first and foremost that this kind of labor was fundamental to the welfare of every inhabitant of the colony. Second, it demonstrates that this kind of labor was intensely gender specific.

Europeans made thousands of adjustments in the process of acclimating to the New World environment. But the inability of the vast majority of men, when faced with a crisis, to improvise domestic duties that they were physically capable of (though admittedly unfamiliar with) underlined the depth of psychological commitment to gendered place. Female inheritance patterns and testamentary activity could bend and flex over time, relations with other races and ethnicities could fade in and out of fashion, religious piety and slanderous tongue wagging could be interpreted in manifold ways, but female domestic work patterns were one gender parameter that was not to be tampered with. In Georgia, away from the stability of kinship and communal links in the Old World, these traditional patterns took on added import. The value accorded women's work—though invisible to economists, concealed from archaeologists, and neglected in the historical record—was still determined by its demographic and geographic context, by supply and demand. Given the later involvement of bondswomen within Georgia households, the trusteeship period established the high-water mark of white female domestic labor for centuries to come. In July 1750, just six months before slavery was officially legalized in the colony, a Salzburger announced that because he could not find a white servant-girl to help run his household and deal with his three children during his wife's prolonged illness, "necessity had forced him to buy a black female servant." Nine years later significant numbers of Salzburgers regularly trekked to Savannah to inspect the newly arrived cargoes of slaves.[11]

The second category of "extradomestic employment" is considerably more noticeable in the colonial records, which document women who were active across a wide range of vocational pursuits, from agricultural labor and sericulture to tavern keeping, manufacturing, interpreting for Indians, and retail. In particular, the trustees' obsession with careful land layout and distribution, and their insistence on nearby gardens for town lots, extended the compass of the household to incorporate agricultural work and work with livestock.

Female household work had never been restricted to four walls in the way it would be in later centuries, but the frontier insisted upon an even larger sphere of activity. At one time or another in trusteeship Georgia, women cultivated Indian corn, asparagus, vines, European wheat, peas, beans, potatoes, barley, turnips, rice, rye, oats, peaches, nectarines, limes, oranges and apples, and fish and shellfish—a good deal more than the gathering of wild fruits and roots that Oglethorpe hypothesized. The independent reports of two officers recently returned from Georgia—Lt. Col. Alexander Heron and Capt. George Dunbar—both commented on the remarkable plantations of a number of widows on St. Simons Island, with Heron stating not only that they raised enough for their own support but that "he has often bought of them Pease, Sallading, Fowls & Other Things." The plantations of these widows and their families were evidently exemplary to the lackluster soldiers and idle settlers of Frederica.[12]

Of course, capabilities varied enormously depending upon the origin of settlers. It is no coincidence that the majority of women found to be active in agriculture or animal husbandry were not from London but from the peasant societies of Germany and the Low Countries. Milton Ready noted that many Londoners, and particularly the "unfortunate city-folk . . . lacked the special skills of the farmer and backwoodsman"; equally, their wives and daughters often lacked the skills required to cultivate and process garden produce, to thresh or winnow grain, to tend to livestock, "&c." The notion of preadaptation, that some ethnic communities were more successful in the New World because of an ecological or at least occupational similarity to the culture of their homelands, appears particularly applicable to the advances made by the Salzburgers, who were mainly farmers and craftspeople. Indeed, the records show a heterogeneity of agricultural responsibilities falling to women, which dispels the illusion of the trustees' expectations. Conditions on the frontier of colonization—land rich and labor scarce—were such that wives were often forced or allowed to fill a wide variety of occupational loopholes.[13]

Most of those extradomestic responsibilities taken on by women (and children under their direction) did not require a strong labor force. Still, the clearing of land—the first step before farming could be attempted—was by no means an exclusively male preserve. John Vat commented that several female Salzburgers resolved to clear some ground, in the process motivating a number of single men to do likewise. Bolzius similarly noticed in 1736 that "some people have very good assistance by their strong Wives" in clearing land and laboring, and later he stated with pride that in the Salzburger congregation, neither the men nor the women were "afraid of work."[14] Although women rarely worked on their husbands' allocated forty-five-acre plantation, many examples demonstrate that the five-acre gardens laid out on the fringes of towns and settlements were exclusively managed by wives and widows. One woman was so pleased with her experimentation with rye in the summer of 1741 that she resolved to send some of the product back to a benefactor in Europe—a gesture not only of gratitude but also of triumph.[15]

English immigrants were generally less successful than their continental European counterparts in the pursuit of agricultural self-sufficiency (let alone profit), a disparity that many historians have attributed to the makeup of the colonists. Of 827 listed settlers who were sent over "on the charity" before 1742, only 97 had occupations related to husbandry. Despite a lack of husbandry experience (particularly among the urban settlers), many tried their hand at farming, only to drift into shopkeeping, coastal trade, day laboring, or simply abandoning the colony. In the early years even the highest social classes within the colony were not exempt from engaging in agricultural labor, however distasteful. Samuel Eveleigh visited the plantation of Sir Francis Bathurst in May 1735 and remarked that the baronet needed two more servants because his wife and son were working in the fields themselves. There were few exceptions to the general deficiency in English husbandry, and most colonists found themselves relying heavily on the trustees' stores in Savannah, Frederica, and Darien, where they could purchase provisions on credit if need be. The widow Ann Harris's clearing and planting of her own five-acre plot, and her supplying of milk to several families, earned her an award as "one of the most valuable Inhabitants amongst us, remarkable for Industry."[16]

Small-scale animal husbandry was a responsibility that often fell to wives and was less exclusively the domain of continental European settlers than arable farming. The feeding and killing of chickens, geese, goats, sheep, and hogs, and the tending of both trust and private cattle herds demonstrate that women played an active role in generating as well as processing the products of livestock. Women even practiced beekeeping at both the northern and southern boundaries of trusteeship Georgia—at Ebenezer by the Salzburgers, whose hives were allegedly damaged in May 1734 by "malicious Negroes," and at Frederica.[17]

Some aspects of work with livestock, most notably milking, held traditional associations with female labor; pragmatic philanthropists in South Carolina sent the Georgians a gift of one hundred cattle, which Oglethorpe distributed among the settlers so that every family that included a woman received a milk cow. However, where in England the work of the dairymaid was becoming increasingly professionalized during the eighteenth century, in trusteeship Georgia few women brought sufficient experience to make more advanced products such as butter and cheese. In late December 1734 Robert Parker complained that the only dairy wife capable of making decent butter had been punished excessively for a minor offense, made to sit in the stocks for three hours during a rainstorm, carried aboard a sloop, and ducked so forcefully that she was lame for months.[18]

In addition to free wives who turned their hand to small-scale husbandry and those involved in sericulture, many indentured female colonists were given agricultural responsibilities by the trustees, another indication of the scantiness of laborers. The trustees employed seventeen German male servants and twenty-three females "at the Crane and in the Garden," perhaps because the trustees were aware of the Germans' superior proficiency at agriculture. A number of indentured Swiss families were similarly instructed to tend to the cow pastures on Hutchinsons Island. The women servants were to be employed as directed by overseers or petty officials at each location and paid the sum of six pence per day (compared with eight pence for men) to maintain themselves in food and clothing. However, the pay was conditional upon completion of allocated tasks, and if they failed to perform their work as directed, they were to be paid in proportion only to the work they did. Though a superficially reasonable stipulation, it was one that left them dangerously dependent upon the character of the overseers, and economic muscle frequently buttressed other forms of exploitation. Even wives in the service of freeholders often found themselves laboring in the fields rather than in a domestic environment. When a tree fell on a boy in 1743, breaking both his legs, his indentured parents received relief of ten shillings a week. This was to pay for someone to help support and exercise him because neither his father nor his mother could afford to give up the "plantation work" they were doing.[19]

Other common extradomestic female occupations, particularly for older women, were teaching and nursing (including midwifery, discussed in chapter 1). Teaching took place for the most part in the home, although early schools were founded in Ebenezer, Savannah, and Bethesda, and some evidence of peripatetic instruction survives. The education of young children was a mother's responsibility, and, although mothers were not yet endowed with the higher status afforded maternity by the discourses following the American Revolution, their informal instruction of their children in early Georgia was crucial to the survival and prosperity of their sons and daughters. Reading and writing on the frontier were implicitly acknowledged as less important for girls than learning to sew, cook, spin, knit, and keep house—practical skills that they would apply and perfect before they reached adulthood.

Women's responsibility for the upbringing and informal education of their own offspring often expanded to the teaching of larger groups of children—particularly in community-based settlements such as Ebenezer. Salzburger teachers imparted not only practical but religious wisdom using a pamphlet entitled "The Little Order of Salvation," which was thought to be of great benefit to children. Religious virtue was a key area of instruction that women were expected to instill in their children, but other subjects held similar significance. The trustees hired Henry Hamilton and his wife, Beguina Charlotta, a couple who had indentured themselves for four years, to teach English to German speakers in 1741. Paid teaching in proprietorship Georgia was unusual for either gender, though the trustees later sponsored the exclusively male post of schoolmaster in Savannah (providing for any children who were sent), as the trustees did teachers in Ebenezer like the Ortmanns.[20]

Women were employed to teach the forty children enrolled at the Bethesda orphan house (established in Georgia by Rev. George Whitefield), though women were never afforded the same status as their male counterparts. A visitor described the arrangements in 1745–46: "After Dinner they retir'd, the Boys to School, and the Girls to their Spinning & Knitting."[21] The girls were to learn the arts of managing a household—including washing, cleaning, and sewing— and their female instructors assumed that practice made perfect, serving the dual role of teaching the children and attending to the domestic needs of the orphanage. Only a handful of girls received an education in a particular trade, since one specialized skill was not as useful as a variety of abilities in the absence of a well-developed market economy, though the daughter of William Kilbury was put out by the trustees as "Apprentice to a Mantua Maker" as a reward for her dead father's services.[22]

The trustees remarked in their promotional literature that the presence of women was necessary to provide succor to the afflicted. Nursing, particularly in such a death trap as the disease-ridden lowcountry of colonial Georgia, was an extremely common pastime. In an oft-quoted letter written by Oglethorpe upon his return to Georgia in August 1733, in which he bemoans the mutinous and idle environment in the colony and the sickness raging among the population, he states that "some of the Women (most handy about the Sick) dyed; so that we had neither Doctor, Surgeon nor Nurse." Clearly, the position demanded experience, time, and exposure to a variety of transmittable diseases and perhaps for these reasons was more often remunerated than was teaching.[23]

Some women undoubtedly maintained themselves entirely by attending to the sick, for example, Ann Bliss, who was sent across on the *James* specifically to "act as Nurse in Georgia," but generally nursing and the practice of medicine, unlike professional midwifery, were only sidelines by which the poor supplemented their meager earnings. Evidence of such part-time employment is found in the expenses of Thomas Hawkins, a doctor and apothecary who died in Georgia; the expenses included reimbursements for nurses who had assisted him. Margaret Fitz, herself an indentured servant, was employed by the trustees to nurse sick servants in Frederica—but she and others like her could expect to collect a limited income for time, travel, and expenses spent caring for the sick. Mrs. Creon and her husband were bequeathed the entire estate of William Harvey in 1745 for having taken care of him during his sickness, although their efforts evidently fell somewhat short of his survival. The potential profitability of nursing is also evident in the capital accumulated by a Dutch nurse who was appointed to keep a house in Savannah where she took care of the infirm. When she was the victim of a theft in 1739, it was found "to the Admiration of every Body when known" that she had saved a sum of seventeen guineas (roughly $3,500 today).[24]

The reality of female extradomestic labor patterns belied the status of married women at law. Formal responsibility for most economic activities was prohibited to married women, as all their unprotected property and goods—and anything they earned—became subsumed into their husbands' estates. But the principle of tacit consent appears to have been widely applicable, aided and abetted by the confused state of legislative affairs during the trusteeship. Given the high level of widowhood, the prolonged absences of many husbands, and the sparse pattern of settlement, it appears that women frequently operated with comparative independence from men.

This was not necessarily a question of acting outside the law, despite the assertion by some historians that there existed "laws forbidding women to work."[25] For one thing, since the trustees held the absolute right to legislate for the colony in its first two decades, they were able to make exceptions to normal practices. Arguably, as a bunch of paternalistic philanthropic males, they were liable to be peculiarly receptive to female petitions—as evidenced in their willingness to grant women land despite the trustees' own strictures. For example, when Penelope Fitzwalter's husband died in 1742, she successfully applied to be appointed to the traditionally male office of wharfinger, a position that attended to the maintenance and organization of the rudimentary shipping facilities at Savannah, though it paid only small rates.[26] Second, even English common law made some provisions for unusual commercial circumstances. When a couple ran a business together, the law did allow the female to act as her husband's "agent." His approval of all her transactions was assumed, and she became a "feme sole trader." Such a condition existed in most American colonies in the eighteenth century, although interestingly Marylynn Salmon has documented a more liberal and comprehensive protection of women's legal rights in the southernmost colonies and in particular in South Carolina (sadly, Georgia was not part of her study).[27] Women's capacity to act with a degree of economic independence was therefore informally legal, established by precedent and custom rather than by statute. Given the lack of competition, and the critical shortage of labor and facilities, few people cared that women (and often married women at that) played a more active role in the trades than might be expected elsewhere. In this period in England women tended to find their economic activities restricted as the locus of trade and manufacture moved away from the household.[28]

During the trusteeship, then, wives were allowed extensive control of finances across the whole spectrum of exchange—from marketing and bartering for home produce to large-scale transactions. Indeed, given that the variation in property laws from colony to colony stemmed from the diversity of English boroughs, counties, and towns, it may well be that in proprietorship Georgia the high incidence of women's owning—or expecting to own—the monetary proceeds from their personal transactions was born of early eighteenth-century London idiosyncrasies. Such ethnic origins certainly explain the frequency of female control of proceeds in German American households in other colonies, and the Salzburger women appear often to have spent their own cash and profited from their own endeavors. Mrs. Ortmann was personally awarded £7 and 5s, after presenting to the trustees a "Bill of Charges" for an orphan who was lodging with her and her husband. Reverend Bolzius recorded in his will that his wife was to keep a small hundred-acre plantation that "she had bought with her own money by raising cattle."[29]

One might speculate that the independence of their German counterparts motivated female English immigrants' desire to control the proceeds of their own labors. Martha Causton bought tablecloths and pewter for nearly three pounds, a purchase that may well have been made out of her own profits. She evidently considered her own earnings to be distinct from her husband's work, for in April 1739 she delivered an impressive torrent of abuse and foul language when she was denied cash payment for mulberry leaves that she had cultivated and that she apparently thought "a Perquisite of her own."[30] Mary Hodges Townsend, wife of a trader frequently away from the province, wrote to the trustees in March 1740 complaining that *her* prices (probably for provisions) were being unfairly undercut by their official. Ann Emery, whose husband piloted ships into the mouth of the Savannah River, successfully petitioned the trustees "that She may have a license to sell Beer" on Tybee Island in 1739. Her enterprise had paid off by 1741 when she kept a chandler's shop, sold a "good store of retail ware," and allegedly flogged rum under the counter.[31]

One incident in particular illustrates how conditions on the colonial frontier—away from close-knit communities and institutionalized proprieties—allowed disadvantaged minorities the latitude to command significant degrees of economic and social authority, given the opportunity. On 29 May 1739 an English tradesman named Pope, new to the colony, considered it well within his rights to administer a slap to a slave woman who had had the tenacity to argue with him about prices. But his actions that afternoon generated an uproar in

Savannah. The trustees' secretary recorded the incident in his journal, remarking that this girl was more than just a slave, as she was the mistress of Capt. Caleb Davis, a colonial trader of some reputation. The captain, he wrote, "suffered almost every Thing to pass through her Hands, having such confidence in her, that she had the Custody of all his Cash, as well as Books.... It may easily be supposed the Life of such Slavery was not a heavy Burden upon her, and that she had Art enough to shew, all Persons who had any Business with Captain Davis, were expected not to treat her with Contempt."[32] Pope, familiar only with European attitudes toward both women and slaves, misunderstood the ability of the colonial frontier occasionally to distort such norms. His imprudent blow was delivered in ignorance of the special status that Captain Davis's slave, nurse, mistress, and accountant had forged for herself, belying her appearance. The records do not reveal whether Pope faced any consequences for his actions.

Wives traveling to fulfill specialized extradomestic labor activities were a common sight in trusteeship Georgia. The silk industry was a popular outlet for supplementing family income, but other options were also available. Magdalena Sanftleben traveled to Ebenezer to help with the hog slaughtering at the orphanage. Maria Gruber similarly worked at the orphanage threshing flour. In July 1741 Juliana Ortmann spent a great deal of time picking fruit, which she sold or "like others, tries to put to good use by making dried fruit and spirits." Margaretha Kalcher installed herself in the public house near the mill, where she baked bread and brewed beer from syrup from the West Indies and Indian corn. Wives often traveled long distances to engage solely in trading activities: on several occasions Maria Magdalena Rauner traveled from Ebenezer to Savannah, where she boasted of earning much money from the produce of her fieldwork, knitting, spinning, and apparently selling the labor of her three children.[33] Many wives, especially when sick and/or unable to assist in fieldwork, would compensate with their needlework, by which they could earn a significant amount, as local people might "bring them all sorts of tailoring and women's work."[34]

The women who gained access to the most de facto economic agency more often than not engaged in manufacturing, retail, and tavern keeping. Women involved in manufacturing contributed to the production of their families to varying degrees but might be expected to spend any free time—that is, after fulfilling their domestic duties—by helping to ply the trade in question. This could range from the minimal verbal efforts of Mary Duchee to persuade her obstinate husband to "stick to his Trade of Pottery" to more substantive contributions.[35] By 1750 such was the level of female involvement in home-based crafts that one commentator observed that while "there is still a shortage of carpenters, turners, brickmakers, carriage builders and potters in Georgia . . .

weavers, hosiers, knitters, needlemakers, bakers, millers and so on are not necessary here."[36]

The level of contribution a wife made to a given trade can be measured to some extent by her capacity to continue production in the absence of her husband. When her husband returned to England in 1743 to obtain servants, a Mrs. Smith of Frederica continued to profitably operate the baking business initiated by her spouse. Catherine Perkins was responsible for running the same settlement's most prosperous store during her husband's frequent absences—and her successful management impressed clerk John Brownfield sufficiently to warrant his noting it in his copybook.[37] The widowed Anne Dorothy Helvingstine petitioned to resettle with her children in Abercorn, to pursue their trade as leather dressers, a request that the trustees granted to avoid losing "so promising a family."[38]

However, for every case that displays a salient female economic contribution to extradomestic pursuits, another reminds us of the considerably worsened status of a family without a father. Many women who lost husbands had no alternative but to seek relief. Elizabeth Anderson, who continued to run a bakery after the death of her husband, did so because she found "Business failing and Times growing hard with her for Want of Employment" in 1746—and the trust extended to a number of widows small cash payments, provisions, and occasionally servants. Other widows, such as Lucy Mouse, sought work as mantua makers; she wrote a letter dated May 1747 in which she requested the lot of a deceased family, insisting that she "must follow her Business in Savannah."[39]

Extradomestic work in manufacturing, retail, and education, as Helen Bartlett, the first historian of early Georgia women, noted in 1939, could be a worthwhile pursuit only in settled towns and older communities. Tavern keeping and lodging, however, were businesses that could find customers even in the most remote outposts of trusteeship Georgia. The tavern hostess, found equally in the backwoods and backcountry districts as well as in the larger seaboard settlements and towns, appears to have shared largely in the business; the enterprise, after all, was predominantly based on domestic skills and demanded little outlay. Moreover, as Sarah B. Gober Temple and Kenneth Coleman have remarked, though there was precious little currency around in the colony, some money could be made from the tavern business, a point reinforced by the complaint of the Earl of Egmont himself about the sizable sums wasted in Georgia taverns.[40]

Many activities that occurred behind the doors of taverns were frowned upon by the trustees, whose moral concerns led to the prohibition of hard liquor and the severe punishment of gambling and prostitution. But this could not detract from the taverns' usefulness as communal focal points, sources of information, and places where guests could be accommodated: dined and especially wined. Public houses were often used to entertain visiting Indian or European dignitaries; here, William Stephens reports, several strangers "pass'd their time of waiting merrily and by Invitation" and found plentiful entertainment.[41] Where Puritans congregated inside churches, Virginians convened outside courthouses, and Quakers massed in meetinghouses, early Georgians went down the local pub.

The trustees attempted to maintain stringent control of the activities that took place in taverns. They insisted, for instance, that tavern keepers have an official license, give accommodation to travelers, and sell neither dry goods nor any other articles usually kept in shops, a regulation that, as I shall describe shortly, was enforced in regard to Mary Hodges in the summer of 1733. Rum and gin, in particular, were commodities dangerous enough to have a moral value attached, a not-inconsiderable achievement in the heyday of the slave trade. Such spirits were construed as evil: the scourge of metropolitan London society and a disease poised to infect the colonial experiment. The trustees encouraged their officials to name, shame, and prosecute miscreants to the letter of the law, like John and Henrietta Scott in Savannah, who were twice convicted of selling rum, by the testimony of two sailors between 1736 and 1738.[42]

However, a large number of tippling houses existed without licenses; these catered to the tastes of laborers, soldiers, sailors, and travelers in the colony. The most popular and successful unlicensed tavern was that of the Penroses, and it even hosted a public banquet in 1735. John Penrose spent little time in Georgia, leaving the running of their inn and their shop to his wife while he traded in New York. Elizabeth Penrose, already forty-six when she left England in 1732, would become known in the colony as "Mother" Penrose. This nickname, like "Godfather" or "Daddy," beautifully highlights the importance of popular notions of hierarchical familial authority. Penrose was an extremely influential woman whose reputation and connections allowed her considerable ascendancy in Savannah. She illegally employed a servant contracted to work for Joseph Hetherington in March 1735, but Hetherington wistfully observed in a letter to Oglethorpe that "troubling my head with her, is what I did not Care for, She still remaining Conqueror Over the whole place."[43]

Mother Penrose's dominion apparently extended beyond retail, tavern keeping, and rum selling, for she was convicted in May 1736 of "keeping a bawdy-house."[44] As in the 1930s, prohibition had a tendency to amalgamate all insalubrious activities under one roof, under one sovereign. This provoked rather hypocritical complaints from other tavern keepers, such as Mary Hodges and the Mercers, who wrote to the trustees informing them that "your honours good intentions were intirely frustrated by Mrs Penrose being encouraged not only to keep public House without license, but also to Sell rum, and punch publickly, and in great quantities, by which means all Strangers and many of the Towns people frequent there . . . notwithstanding that Said Penrose has been twice fin'd in Court, for Said practice."[45] The rival tavern keepers even went as far as to allege that the trustees' storekeeper, Thomas Causton, had supplied Penrose with large quantities of rum and held public events at her tavern. It is impossible to gauge the accuracy of such allegations, but in Causton's defense the task of enforcing the law was problematic, to say the least.[46] For one thing, members of any jury empaneled to hear a case against a tavern keeper were more than likely to be regular customers. It was only "by an absolute Charge upon the Consciences of the Grand jury" that both Elizabeth Penrose and Mary Hodges were convicted of retailing liquor without a license, and since reliable testimony and proof could realistically come only from a colonial official, most retailers escaped prosecution.[47]

Again, taking women's capacity to continue to work after a husband's death as an indicator of the importance of her contribution to a given trade, one finds that the tavern hostess played a key role in the working relationship—perhaps an unsurprising conclusion given the pseudodomestic nature of the business. Mary Hodges continued to operate after her husband's death and the revocation of her license; she was paid £7 7s. 9d. for the "Diet and Lodging" of an official translator, and in March 1735 the trustees owed her as much as one hundred pounds for provisions. In 1735 her activities were again legalized when at forty-five she married Edward Townsend, who held a license to keep a victualing house. Their pooled resources and shared discontentment with the administration of the colony led to her tavern's becoming the first gathering station for Malcontents. She therefore became infamous in Savannah not for being a woman fulfilling a maverick economic role but for being a deliberately disruptive social influence. The Earl of Egmont noted in his *List of Early Settlers* that she was a "vile foul mouthed Malecontent," an assessment based on a number of unsavory incidents in which she had damaged the reputation of the trustees—circulating letters, for instance, that claimed the king had rescinded their charter. William Stephens's response to her departure from Georgia was to "Thank God."[48]

The cases of Mother Elizabeth Penrose and the "Venom-Scatterer" Mary Hodges Townsend offer instructive instances of women who were operating as economically independent and socially powerful agents in early Georgia—and were mirrored elsewhere in the colony. But it is critical to note that these female tavern keepers, though they played the major role in the business and challenged local authority in myriad ways, remained psychologically attached to preconceptions of gendered place. None remained unmarried for long. Penelope Wright's second husband apparently took great delight in her experience and expertise in tavern keeping. Ann Bennet married Samuel Lee shortly after the death of her first husband, and within a year her prosperous tavern in Frederica had been ruined. Widowed tavern hostesses were evidently attractive propositions for single men, but the women's command of income and influence was rarely sufficient to discourage them from seeking the solace of someone whose masculinity underwrote the validity of their daily transactions. Just as these women's work after widowhood discloses their key economic role, their marital choices disclose a paramount need to reconstruct familial attachments.[49]

As I have noted, in most of their domestic and extradomestic activities, Georgia women emulated female patterns of employment in other colonial settings. But in one trade, in one occupational respect, the labor of Georgia women was quite distinctive. For about forty years the silk industry offered female colonists considerable employment opportunities that were impossible in northern Europe and most other colonies on account of the climate. The mulberry trees from which silkworms were fed could flourish only in warm conditions, which meant that Britain was forced to import—at great expense—silks from elsewhere (especially from the Mediterranean and India) to fulfill its consumer needs. The trustees, aware that the Georgia experiment had to appeal to Parliament and the British public for funding and support, showed in their promotional literature that they were keen to advance the cultivation of silk and wine (another commodity imported for climatic reasons) while emphasizing that domestic goods produced in Britain would not be threatened by competition from the colony. Indeed, the Salzburgers were specifically prevented from bringing people skilled in glassware or pottery from the continent in order to assuage such concerns. Achieving immediate results in the production of silk was a prime objective that occupied a great deal of the trustees' time, energy, and funding. In 1736 Queen Caroline arrived at the birthday celebration of her husband, George II, in a resplendent gown of raw silk from Georgia that had met the approval of a host of British experts, been processed in Sir Thomas Lombe's revolutionary mill in Derby, and tailored by one of London's most eminent silk weavers. At a dinner event a year later she leaned over and commented to Catherine Parker Percival (wife of the Earl of Egmont) that "Georgia was a good thing, and particularly for the silk."[50] An official presentation was later made to the king's customs commissioners of the first full chest of silk to arrive from Georgia on 23 February 1742.[51]

Such publicity stunts, and the wider machinations of the British politicians and economists who directed trade policy, depended enormously on the willingness of a sufficient number of women who had no previous training to take up the cultivation of silk—while striving to establish their families and homes

Caroline of Ansbach, by Jacopo Amigoni, 1735. An influential figure in the Hanoverian dynasty (queen consort of Britain and Ireland between 1727 and her death in 1737), the fashion-conscious Caroline would pose a year after this portrait was painted in a court dress made of silk from Georgia, thereby promoting the colony named after her husband, King George II. The trustees named Georgia settlements after her son (Frederica) and daughter-in-law (Augusta). National Portrait Gallery, London.

in the New World. Although they could make supply and cultivation of mulberry trees compulsory in colonial statutes, they recognized that these measures would be futile if the labor force was disinclined to work. The trustees needed to appeal directly to every age group of women, from young girls to old widows, as well as to foster a proclivity in husbands and fathers who might encourage the women's interest and dedication. The trustees achieved this by offering a great deal of financial, technological, and educational support that ensured swift returns on labor. The trustees offered salaries, bounties, and bonuses; procured equipment and specialist literature; and institutionalized apprenticeships. The comparative success of the trustees' endeavors in silk production—which stood in sharp contrast to many of their other economic policies—can largely be ascribed to the nature of the labor required.

In terms of actual time and exertion, the appeal of silk production to female colonists is easy to understand. The work with which women were associated included first the cultivation of mulberry trees and leaves; then the feeding and care of worms until a sufficient number had cocooned themselves; and, finally, the drawing off, winding, and refining of the silk itself. Employment was therefore seasonal, typically comprising a six-week feeding blitz of the silkworms between early March and late April, followed by a refining and reeling-off period that lasted into late May and often beyond. The exertion required was demanding but not particularly physical, except for picking the leaves. Wives needed to manage their time effectively and ensure that they paid sufficient attention to the delicate tasks of feeding and drawing off, but aside from these times of increased application, it was more than possible to perform other necessary familial functions, though space for the operation might be at a premium. Moreover, women handled most of the work inside the household, where they could call upon supplementary child labor and where they could closely watch the worms, an important facet because the quality of the worms' winding would ultimately determine the price returned for the silk cocoons. In this way the labor can broadly be categorized as seasonal, domestic, nonphysical, and of course remunerative—again offering women some degree of control over their own finances. They were paid in proportion to the weight and quality of *coquons*, or the silk balls, that they delivered to the appointed officials.

One lively incident taken from the journal of William Stephens highlights the prominence of women in sericulture. In April 1739 Marie Camuse, a Piedmontese silk winder employed by the trust, persuaded official Thomas Jones to purchase a number of prime mulberry tree leaves at a plantation at Ockstead at the rate of three pence per tree. Three German indentured servant-girls were dispatched to gather the leaves, which they did somewhat carelessly, in the process damaging the branches. When Martha Causton, wife of the owner of Ockstead, discovered what had happened, she was understandably enraged. Not only had her mulberry trees been spoiled, but the money she had expected to receive herself had been credited to her husband's (overdrawn) account at the trustees' stores. Suspecting herself "defeated in such Payment as she looked for," she embarked on a tirade of abuse on such a scale that Jones warned Causton's husband to keep his wife's tongue in order. Though ultimately limited, significant extradomestic employment opportunities were clearly available to women through the silk industry.[52]

Many women in proprietorship Georgia were willing and able to take up the challenge of a new occupation that offered then so many advantages, and many exciting predictions were made for the future of the silk industry in light of their pioneering production—although none reached the level of £500,000 posited in the trustees' pamphlets. The trustees paid out top salaries of twenty to sixty-five pounds per annum to highly skilled women who were willing to train others. The trustees paid bonuses of up to five pounds to those apprentices who successfully learned the art of winding from scratch. And they offered bounties of up to two shillings per pound of cocoons that were brought to their filatures (silk factories), as well as cash payments for mulberry leaves. As a result it wasn't uncommon to see young girls on their way to town in late April, carrying boxes on their heads with their own silk yields. It also wasn't uncommon to hear of husbands' relocating their households and families to areas with more pine barren, to allow their wives better access to mulberry trees.[53] James Habersham estimated that if five hundred women in Georgia could be put to work at the silk business, their product would be worth over £28,125.[54]

The trustees' enthusiasm was to prove misplaced. By the 1780s the silk industry was dead, the equipment buried in cellars and the women forced to other alternatives. The white mulberry, with leaves suited to a silkworm's diet, obstinately refused to grow in the wild, unlike its cousin the black mulberry, whose leaves were too sharp for the silkworms' taste. Hundreds of thousands of trees of the white variety, *morus alba*, were successfully imported and planted, reminders that, as Mart Stewart has best articulated, "the natural environment was not merely a scene in which action took place; environment was entangled with action."[55] But the white mulberries tended to survive only in richer soils, which, after the legalization of slavery in 1751, brought mulberries into direct competition with the rapidly expanding cultivation of agricultural crops in the lowcountry. As early as 1741 one influential South Carolinian, Hector Beringer de Beaufain, had warned the trustees that the mulberry trees required the "Best Corn land."[56] But it was the tried-and-tested formula of lowcountry rice cultivation that stifled, in Georgia's planters, the kind of experimental spirit that motivated more cosmopolitan contemporaries.[57] Rice needed a complex and grueling sequence of hoeings and floodings between late March and May, which coincided precisely with silk's highest labor demand period.[58] It would be one ancient Chinese commodity or the other.

Sericulture dominated the metropolitan depiction of Georgia in its first years. In a pamphlet entitled *Reasons for Establishing the Colony of Georgia*, Benjamin Martyn painted an idyllic picture of a utopia across the Atlantic that promised to provide rewarding work for both genders. He described the women and children's feeding and nursing silkworms and winding off the silk while their menfolk plowed and planted their lands. The trust adopted the mulberry leaf as part of its official seal. Even in contemporary poetry the silk workers were portrayed as idyllically at work:

> Here tend the Silkworm in the verdant Shade
> The frugal Matron, and the blooming Maid.
> Th'expiring Insect's curious Work resume,
> And wind Materials for the *British* [sic.] Loom.[59]

To be fair, the trustees matched their imaginary flights of fancy with substantial backing. In addition to sending the white mulberry trees, silkworm eggs, instructional pamphlets such as Thomas Boreman's *Compendious Account of the Whole Art of Breeding, Nursing, and the Right Ordering of the Silk-Worm*, and, later, copper basins and winding looms, they recognized the need to invest in expertise in the form of a number of European specialists.[60] These specialists were located and approached for their talent and/or experience in the field. They were often consulted on the progress of the industry and given special employment, either in Georgia or back in England, to monitor the results. The "scientific" aspects of the industry—botanical literature and market economics—were predominantly male-oriented spheres. This was demonstrated in the exclusively male authorship of tracts pertaining to the silk business and the exclusively male patronage of botanical development. As a result a number of male consultants and specialists were employed to supervise the planting and nursing of mulberry trees. But the "artistic" aspects of sericulture also rendered a handful of women particularly conspicuous as experts in the care of worms, drawing off and winding, and refining the silk itself.

On 18 November 1732, while on board the *Anne*, which carried the first batch of colonists ready to populate the new settlement, James Oglethorpe wrote to the trustees concerning the arrangements made with two Italian silk weavers from Piedmont. The Amatis brothers were contracted to bring two men and four women "who understand the whole of the Silk Business." The agreement is remarkable not only because the women were required in an equal ratio to men as specialists but also because they were afforded the same wages, a pattern

Seal of the Trustees for the Establishment of the Colony of Georgia. This original seal placed heavy emphasis on silk cultivation in early Georgia, detailing a mulberry leaf and silkworm egg. The hope was that women would take up raw silk production by the thousands and that the project would prove its worth, as the Latin inscription reads, "not for [the trustees] themselves, but for others." Courtesy of the Georgia Historical Society, Administrative Files #1361.

that was not repeated in other areas (such as indentured service, where women received half to two-thirds of men's allowances). It was a woman, the mother of three young sons, who became the most prominent specialist in the early years of the colony after she and her husband offered their services to the trustees and embarked in April 1733.[61]

A series of deaths and desertions left Marie Camuse with a virtual monopoly on silk knowledge in early Georgia that she manipulated regularly and effectively to her advantage, leading one contemporary to complain that "this Wicked Woman domineer[ed] over all." In July 1740 Major Horton warned the Earl of Egmont that "if that woman should die, the art would be lost," and she certainly knew it. Camuse fiercely guarded her technique, or art, from potential competitors. Trustee officials described her as secretive and unwilling to instruct others. She was prone to angry outbursts if she felt her finger movements were being studied, and she refused to permit her reeling wheel to be copied. Camuse also misused the trustees' apprentice system by artificially restricting the number of apprentices and habitually employing her apprentices in domestic tasks (in which they were already proficient). Bolzius bemoaned in 1745 that she was "unwilling to tell us the least Article concerning this Art," and two years later his wife undertook to make absolutely certain that no woman in Ebenezer could likewise "pretend a Monopolium" in the art of winding.[62]

For a long time the trustees and their officials had no choice but to acquiesce to the machinations of Marie Camuse, whose work was attested to in the first chest of silk to arrive from Georgia (in February 1742), which she had wound from 220 pounds of cocoons. She was offered a gratuity for every person "certified to be properly instructed by her in the Art of winding Silk," although a visitor in 1735 rightly judged the training of apprentices to be a burden to her. The profits were not inconsiderable, for Camuse was a shrewd businesswoman. In early May 1741 William Stephens had noted that she "knew what use she was of," and he found himself compelled to supply her with what she asked for (including ten pounds in cash and various provisions), simply because she "must not be disobliged." That September he was forced to show her the colony's account books to silence her suspicions, while he was forced to grant her claim for twenty-nine pounds two months later "for the Sake of keeping her Quiet." Camuse even spread rumors that she would return to England if she were not better accommodated. When the Board of President and Assistants, the administrative body of officials appointed by the trustees, tentatively asked in November 1743 whether she would accept a salary of sixty pounds per annum and the assurance of a pension offered by the trustees, Camuse rejected the offer—haughtily stating that Oglethorpe had allowed her one hundred pounds, and "she would accept of nothing less." Needless to say, the board complied, its minutes wearily recording that its members had given way "to her perverse Temper Rather than hazard the loss of a Manufacture always designed by their Honours as a Staple of the Country."[63]

Ultimately, Marie Camuse's monopoly collapsed in the face of prolonged pressure, as her demands exceeded her worth. Her salary was suspended at the end of August 1747, as her worst fear—that of one of her own students' actually becoming educated—was realized in the person of Elizabeth Anderson. Anderson had been under Camuse's instruction for three seasons and was soon installed as the new silk diva in Savannah—complete with a larger rent-free house and a cash sum of twenty pounds. She proved a far more amenable teacher than her predecessor, regularly providing the board with an account of the industry's progress and content to share her trade knowledge. All were impressed when she showed the Salzburgers how to operate new winding machinery that she had assembled according to instructions sent from England.[64]

Winding apprenticeships like Anderson's were actually paid for by the trustees, and they gave rewards of five pounds each to three young Salzburg women to encourage their further interest. But little technical proficiency was required to attend to the earlier step of feeding and nursing the worms, which also brought cash remuneration. Payment for the cocoons was to be immediate (literally "upon the Spot") and carefully measured according to the quality of the product and the role of the worker. Cocoon production increased after a number of "careful Housewives, had taken Thoughts about it, and were persuaded it might be time well bestowed." When they were delivered to Savannah, an expert like Camuse or Anderson was on hand to value them. Many women took up these labor and training opportunities, and some tried to squeeze even more out of the trustees. Rev. Johann Martin Bolzius increased the profitability of female silk labor in the Salzburger community by gently threatening the trustees. After he explained that their regulations might discourage Salzburgers from engaging in sericulture, the trustees doubled the bounties, from one to two shillings per pound of the finest cocoons, and from four pence to eight pence for the poorest quality.[65]

As more boxes arrived in England, the trustees responded by providing equipment, such as the two dozen copper basins exported in June 1750, and the machine for reeling in August of the same year, and by approving a recommendation to construct filatures in Savannah and Ebenezer. By 1750 fourteen young women in Ebenezer were proficient at winding, while in Savannah James Habersham was assured that even more women—both married and single—intended to learn it in the coming season. Husbands were looking to buy copper basins and machines for their wives and daughters, though some expressed concern at the "neglect of their private House Business."[66]

The legalization of slavery in Georgia signaled the long-term erosion of mulberry tree (and therefore silk) cultivation. But for a short period the high-water mark of investment in sericulture coincided with the introduction of slavery—an intersection that threw up novel situations. At a grassroots level one shoemaker earned so much money through his wife's spinning of silk that he was able to buy a female slave in Carolina in 1750.[67] At a constitutional level the trustees did not insist that those elected as deputies in the new assembly hold a certain amount of land or wealth. Rather, the candidate had to conform to the limitation of the number black slaves in proportion to white servants in his household and have at least one female in his family who had been instructed in the art of reeling silk. The two main contemporary concerns, in other words, were minimizing the negative consequences of slavery while maximizing the positive advances in sericulture. Racial language gradually permeated measures relating to the silk industry: the trustees now specifically offered "To each White Woman" an allowance of forty shillings to those who learned the art of reeling.[68]

Yet in the formative years of slavery in the province, sericulture was peculiarly biracial. At public filatures it was recorded that "young People, both white and black, are employed in a work," while James Habersham, Pickering Robinson, and James Harris all made reference to planters' sending "their Daughters and Negroe Women" or "their Daughters as well as Young Negroe Slaves" to acquire the art of reeling. Sadly, nothing is known about conditions inside the filatures. Patterns of socialization, treatment, and task distribution may well have been racially demarcated. But for a short time white and black women were engaged in an identical pursuit, offered the same training, and labored in the same extradomestic factory. Such shared conditions did not last long—and by the 1760s the silk industry had become the dwindling preserve of poor white women, for, as Gov. James Wright noted, "People of Property can make more by Employing their Negroes about other things."[69]

The withdrawal of planter interest in sericulture in this defining moment of Georgia's growth would prove to be a crippling blow, although metropolitan agencies continued to pour in capital, and women in provincial strongholds—particularly around Ebenezer—continued to use their newly learned skills each spring, producing more than fifteen thousand pounds of cocoons annually in the early 1760s.[70] In 1772 James Habersham wrote something of an epitaph for sericulture in Georgia, difficult for a man whose own plantation was named "Silk Hope." He too associated silk's failure with slavery, concluding that silk would never become "a considerable Branch of Commerce" in Georgia until the province had "a number of white people of middling circumstances."[71] Silk failed in Georgia not purely for climatic reasons but because of a lack of expertise and a failure to divulge it before the 1750s, because of an understandable reluctance among planters to dissent from the orthodoxy of rice and indigo cultivation after the 1750s, and because of occasional disasters such as late frosts or fires in buildings housing the silkworms—which crippled supplies for subsequent years.[72] But for a short time silk production altered the landscapes of a host of Georgia settlements and the livelihoods of a host of female laborers.

CONDITIONS ON THE COLONIAL frontier dictated that its female inhabitants engage in a wide variety of economic pursuits—both domestic and extradomestic. This need for occupational flexibility was as true for the poor and low-status as it was for the comfortable and high-status women (for few could be described as wealthy). At the upper end of the status spectrum, flexibility allowed women to coordinate their activities to maximize unique advantages—whether they had a monopoly on trade knowledge, a unique skill like Indian interpreting, or controlled access to rum, retail goods, or information. Such advantages differentiated the prominent and successful women from the bulk of frontier females, who lacked access to either economic or social capital. At the lower end of the spectrum, adaptability was not so much about profit or power as a strategy critical to survival.

Many wives, like Lucy Mouse, found that the rapidly changing conditions on the frontier demanded occupational diversity and tried their hands at various vocations and in different locations. Thomas Mouse, a clog maker, arrived with his wife and five daughters to take up a land grant on Skidaway Island in January 1734. The Mouses kept a small-scale public house, but having failed to establish a workable farm after seven years, they moved to Savannah, where Lucy found occasional employment as a midwife and also took on work in textiles.

She lost her husband to a fever in the summer of 1742, by which time her house on Skidoway had been destroyed—the boards stolen and the frame burned by Indians—prompting her to sell her share of the cattle for £8 10s. and search for permanent accommodation in Savannah. Like Lucy Mouse, many women found that their survival required constant adjustments of their working regime to adapt to novel circumstances.[73]

The exceptional and well-documented career of Mary Musgrove Matthews Bosomworth most clearly outlines the remarkable scope of wives' potential employment on the frontier of settlement. A mixed-race niece of one of the kings of the Creeks, she was born around 1708 in Coweta Town on the Ockmulgee River with the tribal name of Cousaponakeesa. She married the prosperous Indian trader John Musgrove around 1725, but her greatest opportunities arrived with the *Anne* on Yamacraw Bluff seven years later—opportunities that she seized with open and dexterous arms. Her success in translating for Oglethorpe and dealing with the Indians gave her great influence over the young colony as well as more material rewards. She was the largest landholder in the first years and operated a trading post and storehouse with which she supplied both the Europeans and Indians with meat, bread, and liquor.[74]

Her first husband died in 1737, but E. M. Coulter suspected that "all along he had appeared the lesser half of the household, overshadowed as he was by his influential wife."[75] Her activities, if anything, became even more vigorous. She set up a communications point, Mount Venture, on the southern bank of the Altamaha River from where the Spaniards' activities could be surveyed and reported, and in 1740, when open warfare had broken out, she rallied the Creeks to Oglethorpe's side. By now she had married again, this time to her own servant, Jacob Matthews. Her crucial role in providing intelligence (if not full-fledged espionage) was often called upon to deal with tense situations, and Col. Alexander Heron referred to her as "a Woman of such consequence."[76] The historian Michelle Gillespie has more recently concluded that Mary Musgrove Matthews Bosomworth "wielded substantial power as a cultural broker."[77] Her marriage to a third husband, Rev. Thomas Bosomworth, in 1744 prompted her to try to make further gains from her exulted position, culminating in claims that she was both "Empress and Queen of the Upper and Lower Creeks."[78]

In a remarkable showdown weekend in August 1749, Mary Musgrove Matthews Bosomworth, once a lowly interpreter, asserted that she was no subject but rather the equal of King George II. She claimed that she could command every man in the Creek nations to follow her, and she threatened the colony with extinction. Nor were these entirely idle threats—for at her behest, hundreds of Creek warriors had descended upon Savannah, and the townsfolk were understandably paranoid. Faces and tempers were strained, words carefully chosen, doors barred, and the militia stood armed. As Savannah officials looked on aghast, she stomped her foot on the ground and screamed that "that very Ground was hers." Only by arresting the Bosomworths, procuring an independent interpreter, dividing the Creek leaders, and distributing plenty of gifts were Savannah officials able to turn the diplomatic tide in their favor. The Indian leaders were assured they had been deceived, and though several remained unconvinced, the Creek headman Malatchee professed that he had not understood that he had been "Ranked with an Old Woman." The supposed empress was contrite after the event—though not as contrite as her husband, who openly wept while promising that he would use his utmost endeavor to prevent his wife from creating any more disturbances. Escaping with little more than an embarrassing caution, she retained what Governor Ellis described as "questionless great ascendancy over some of the Indian tribes" in the 1750s and was finally granted sixty-two hundred acres in St. John's Parish in recognition of her services on 13 June 1760.[79]

The situation in which Mary Musgrove found herself was partly fortuitous, but she certainly took full advantage of her prospects. She was active, mobile, diplomatic, and remarkably forceful. In 1735 the Indians had complained of the behavior of the trader Joseph Watson, desiring that either "another man might trade with us," or that Musgrove could trade by herself. These objections were raised after Watson endeavored to shoot Mary Musgrove and would have done so had she not overpowered him in her own defense, in the process apparently wrestling the gun from him and breaking it. As the historian E. Merton Coulter concluded, "A woman with far better opportunities than Mary ever had might have done much worse."[80] Yet, on the colonial frontier it is hard to envisage what these better opportunities might have been. Mary's work as a translator, diplomat, trader, herdswoman, negotiator, and landholder of course depended partly upon her strength of character and ambition but mainly upon her social capital. Her subsequent marriages (albeit to lower-status men) served to emphasize her quasi-European status, while her strong Creek connections and the reliance of the European colonists upon her cooperation lent her more material advantages. Her unusual employment opportunities were a product of the frontier's capacity to allow a greater diversity of roles for free white, red, or black people than did older, more established societies.[81]

The labor patterns and flexible occupational experiences of Georgia women during the trusteeship challenge any suggestion that the eighteenth century witnessed a universal narrowing of women's economic roles and a decline in their public economic activities. But while these experiences show that the late colonial frontier remained capable of extending females considerable economic latitude, they also convey a number of important qualifications.

MARY BOSOMWORTH INCITING THE INDIANS TO VIOLENCE.

A nineteenth-century depiction of the upheaval caused by Mary Musgrove Matthews Bosomworth, an influential woman of Creek descent, who angrily (and allegedly while drunk) led a contingent of Creek warriors to harass colonial officials in August 1749. Though not the Amerindian "Empress and Queen" that she claimed to be, she was remarkably influential and opportunistic as a cultural broker. From Hezekiah Butterworth, *Zigzag Journeys in the Occident* (1885), 79, courtesy of the Hargrett Rare Book and Manuscript Library, University of Georgia Libraries.

First, though many women benefited from the disrupted market and labor conditions, these self-same conditions proved intensely detrimental to a significant proportion of female settlers. Elasticity in the range of opportunity could rebound in either direction. Second, though several women were able to exercise an unusual degree of economic and social power, their behavior was never fully disassociated from their gender. This qualification was captured most clearly in the frames of reference that male commentators used to describe influential women. Mary Musgrove Matthews Bosomworth may have been "Mary" to the Indians, but colonial officials insisted upon using her formal European identity ("Mrs. Bosomworth" or "the wife of Mr. Matthews") despite her obvious independence and even though this frequently required some clarification. Elizabeth Penrose's nickname, "Mother," served as an ironic reminder of her womanliness. Marie Camuse was explicitly likened to the stereotype of the recalcitrant *male* English artisan. Writers also freely assumed mitigating circumstances to account for the unseemly behavior of such women—most commonly drunkenness or simply madness. In short, the activities of these women were never conceived in isolation, or on their own terms, but squeezed into preexisting gender categories. There would be no new episteme that might have facilitated the persistence of such phenomena in early Georgia.

Third, because women's economic gains were underwritten by the demographic instability outlined in chapter 1, any financial success on the frontier came at a high price and was temporary. How far Georgia women could enjoy their comparative freedom, given their extra time spent grieving for lost relatives and partners, migrating around the province, and struggling without assistance, is questionable. Equally, the duration of this liberality would be limited by the speed with which the demography of the province normalized in the second half of the century, as I discuss in part 2. Finally, despite the myriad ways in which frontier females assumed greater latitude than their counterparts in more settled societies, it remained absolutely clear that nothing was more important to wives' economic experiences than their relationship with husbands.

Families functioned most productively when their most basic components, husband and wife, operated as a unit. Failure of wives to streamline the economics of the domestic environment could become a serious problem for families. Anna Riedelsperger apparently failed to take part in farm work, failed to economize in her housekeeping or cooking, and squandered money on unnecessary luxuries. As a consequence her family found it impossible to prosper. Some husbands went so far as to implore local authorities to intervene, and Reverend Bolzius agreed with one man who dragged him into his hut, confirming that the wife paid "too little attention to her household and its economy, and this causes much loss and places a double burden on the husband." At the opposite end of the spectrum were those women capable of shrewdly balancing the demands of the colonial world upon their time and energy, and another husband in the same community proudly displayed a new tile oven that his wife had set up with her own hands, almost as tidily as a mason.[82]

Husbands and wives had to function as an efficient team in order to maximize their household income. This did not necessarily mean working together, nor did it mean getting on with one another, although a number of families—particularly in the fields of artisanry, manufacturing, teaching, tavern keeping, and retail—operated best this way. John Teasdale and his wife ran a tavern that was profitable and popular because they acted "in a double Capacity." The Hernbergers were the only tailors in Ebenezer, and Bolzius remarked that "he and she are always busy and receive cash." Even in an employment as male oriented as soldiering, husband and wife could operate in tandem: Maria Magdalena Rauner followed her husband (who had enlisted) to the War of Jenkins' Ear, "because she could earn money there as well as he." More usual cooperative practices were part time and agricultural—including the grinding of corn, weeding, making hay, and mowing grass.[83]

In the same way that wider female economic agency remained formally unacknowledged, the high level of practical cooperation necessitated by the frontier never effectively challenged the contemporary gendered labor paradigm. In other words, though women might work side by side with menfolk and were obviously vital to the colonial economy, though a few might occupy critical socioeconomic positions and in practice commanded significant commercial power, this never afforded them a higher status in theory or at law. In part, this reflected how deeply the paradigm was psychologically entrenched within every settler, whose understanding that a wife was absolutely subordinate to her husband was as unquestioned as the settlers' understanding of her importance to household economy. In part, it reflected the peculiar executive and legislative powers held by the trustees, which were uncommonly supple—and thereby accommodated a wide range of female economic activities. But the persistence of the paradigm unscathed through the upheaval of the trusteeship would make it far easier in later decades for male authorities to "legitimately" deny women (and especially wives) the practical latitude that the frontier had demanded.

CHAPTER THREE

Family and Community

On 23 November 1744 the Board of President and Assistants met in Savannah, and all the members trudged off to the house of Margaret Avery. This was the second time they had seen her in two weeks, and the atmosphere was tense. She had in her possession a detailed map of the province, compiled by her husband, Joseph, that would be extremely dangerous if it fell into Spanish hands, and it was imperative that she relinquish it to the proper authorities. They appreciated her state of distress—for she had been widowed just four weeks earlier—but in the face of her continuing intransigence, their tone darkened. They threatened to prevent her from collecting on debts owed to her late husband unless she allowed them to place the map in safe custody. Margaret Avery's behavior reflected many facets of early Georgia life that I outlined in chapter 2: she was shrewdly opportunistic in trying to make the greatest financial gain from the map in her possession, a contingency brought about by the need to survey uncharted lands, yet she was consciously vulnerable to the pressures placed on her by the death of her husband and the growing chorus of disapproving male officials. Avery grudgingly yielded the map six weeks later, when she was given (at her insistence) a signed certificate from the board, twelve pounds, and passage to Charlestown.[1]

Seen through another's eyes, the same incident is equally revealing about another aspect of early Georgia life, the process of family formation and reformation. One of the Savannah officials, William Spencer, had arrived at Margaret Avery's house with this different agenda at heart. While the debate about the right course of cartographic action raged on, Spencer's concern was not with matters of colonial security so much as personal affairs, for he sought to marry the widow's stepdaughter. The experiences of the Spencer and Avery families, though they can only be partially reconstructed from surviving details, typified the social complexities that were rife among the households of early Georgia.[2]

William Spencer, an English vintner, had arrived in Savannah two years earlier, in May 1742, to undertake official responsibilities as an assistant and bailiff for the trust. He brought with him a wife and four children, but his wife and two of his children died during their first Georgia summer. With two young daughters to look after, Spencer desperately sought a surrogate mother—or, as he put it, a proper person "to learn them how to live in this World." After several months he became captivated by the stepdaughter of Margaret Avery, who apparently was less than half his age. His colleagues recorded that he had a great deal more to say to her than to her stepmother, with whom he should have been conducting official business about the map. The pair were married on 6 January 1745 by a minister (named Chisette) who was from Purysburg and happened to be in Savannah, and the speed of proceedings took even Spencer's contemporaries by surprise. According to one commentator, the sudden wedding was the talk of the town for several days.[3]

In September 1746 Spencer elaborated on his motives in a letter to the trustees' accountant, Harman Verelst, explaining that "for the Sake of my two Daughters, having met with a Woman Suitable to my mind, I thought it was best for me a Second time to enter into a Marriage State."[4] Yet though his motives appear to have been simple—driven by the need to protect the welfare of his two daughters—his improvised reconstruction of a family had a number of more complex implications. The ramifications of the young age of his new bride, for instance, could be substantial. How would his daughters respond to a stepmother only a fraction older than they? What would happen to their inheritance when he died, as he presumably would, years before his new wife? How would the arrival of half-siblings affect the dynamics of the household and the distribution of assets in coming years? Many settlers asked such questions, which often held more importance and immediacy than the grander issues that occupied colonial authorities. This was evident even before any settlers had disembarked in America. When the passengers about to board the first ship for Georgia were consulted about colonial regulations, they expressed four concerns. Two related to female inheritance laws, indicating that they already recognized that such matters were a high priority. The other two related to what would happen to their luggage at either end of the trip, a pragmatic concern well familiar to travelers today.[5]

Rapid courtship and swift remarriage were natural responses to the demographic upheaval of the frontier, but they also brought cumbersome baggage involving stepchildren, widowhood, and inheritance. Both William Spencer and Joseph Avery took second wives to take care of their households and their original children. In doing so, both threatened the otherwise simple processes of inheritance and the stability of their children's future. Spencer's young bride received nothing from her dead father's estate while her stepmother, Margaret Avery, was alive. After Margaret Avery died, her stepdaughter received the figurative bequest of only the clothes on her back. The reason was not poverty, for Margaret Avery had received a handsome gratuity from the trustees for eventually delivering up the map. Rather, her stepdaughter received nothing because her own half-brother had acted extremely quickly to seize the family's assets, ensuring that his siblings and half-sibling received little. The staggered deaths of the senior members of the Avery family had left only a legacy of disruption.[6]

Nothing happened slowly in the evolution of families in early colonial Georgia, and it seems both logical and inescapable to assume that in the whirlwind of marriages, births, and deaths, people were less emotionally attached to one another—their feelings numbed by constant exposure to familial changes. But such an assumption receives no explicit support from the primary sources and for this reason must be treated skeptically. What the evidence does suggest is that most unions formed after a parent died were formed with a view to the welfare (both material and emotional) of the children of the deceased. In many cases, as with the Averys and Spencers, this paradoxically led to disruptions and discontent as new births complicated the process of inheritance. In fact, the Avery and Spencer examples are comparatively simple—for the women the men chose did not bring to their marriage any of their *own* children from previous marriages to further complicate the equation. Irrespective of the role in courtship of emotional or sexual attraction, parents generally considered foremost the best options for their children's future.

In 1750 William Spencer remarked that his young wife had made an excellent stepmother despite her age, teaching his daughters to be "Good House Wifes and also expert at their Needles." In other words, the benefits to his children justified his remarriage. As it transpired, Joseph Avery had been equally concerned about his daughter's welfare after his death. He had secretly given her a deed to properties in Pall Mall (London) that she revealed to her husband several years into the marriage. Perhaps the concealment of valuable written documents was a trick she had learned from her stepmother. Either way, the second Spencer marriage was reproductive as well as productive. By July 1750 the partnership had added three healthy boys to the family, with another baby forthcoming—and a year later they were happily described as "a numerous and encreasing young family." By the time William Spencer, now a "gentleman" of Christ Church Parish, died in August 1776 (having presumably outlived his second wife), his nine legatees were all sons and daughters.[7]

PROCESSES OF FAMILY formation naturally proved extremely sensitive to the disrupted demographics and economic elasticity of the trusteeship. By the 1730s in Europe, across most of the northern colonies, and among the Indians of southeastern America, the selection of a female sexual companion (in most cases, a wife) could be made from a substantial pool of suitable partners. This was far from the case in frontier Georgia, which had many fewer young British single women than men desirous of marriage. Colonial officials themselves were swift to capitalize on their greater socioeconomic status to secure wives. The domino effect left a significant number of male colonists with no alternative but to seek brides outside what might be termed their preferred catchment area. And these unions, limited though they were, necessitated to some extent a reappraisal of both ethnic and racial preconceptions. In the process of loving the one they were with, both male and female settlers consciously and subconsciously bridged cultural gulfs of varying dimensions.

Lutheran Salzburgers reluctantly married Rhineland Germans, while Dutch servants and French Swiss proved equally willing to hurdle linguistic and cultural obstacles in the quest for legitimate sexual union and, more important, household economy. Englishmen consorted with Highland and Lowland Scots, Irish, and South Carolinians, and, according to one source, a number of Sephardic Jews managed to accept Christian wives. Processes of courtship and ceremonial practice varied according to class and community, but certain responses were nevertheless common to local conditions. In the early years of the colony courtship periods were briefer and target nets cast wider because of the dearth of potential spouses. Several factors became less important on the frontier—for instance, females were married at ages considered young even by contemporaries. Equally, geographic or linguistic obstacles that were prohibitive in other environments became far less important. The timing of courtship also responded to immediate conditions: short (sometimes extremely short) periods between time of first encounter and date of engagement were common. Systems that had appeared fixed by tradition and custom proved to be malleable—to the benefit of many participants and to the disgust of a few righteous observers.[8]

If conditions on the frontier sanctioned the existence of what might be called transethnic unions, the same conditions also sanctioned a more limited degree of interracial unions—on rare occasions between white and black or brown inhabitants but more commonly between white male newcomers and female natives. Slavery, as Betty Wood has comprehensively documented, was theoretically prohibited in Georgia until 1751. But the presence of limited numbers of bondspeople and free blacks was well known. Although the records allocate these inhabitants a typically low profile, a number of references are tantalizingly suggestive of the kind of "sawbuck equality," or frontier liberality, that has been identified within other early colonial settings. By the middle of the eighteenth century slavery was comprehensively institutionalized across British America and the West Indies, embedded in the legal tissue of every colony. But like a spreading plague, it was also somewhat misunderstood and less virulent away from the epicenters of infection.

On 24 September 1742, a courageous slave girl, just twelve years old, sought to escape her master in Charlestown by joining a shipload of settlers that was en route to Georgia. Her fellow passenger, the German pastor Henry Melchior Mühlenberg, recounted in his notebook that she seated herself slyly among the Salzburg children. The Salzburgers, no doubt excited and bewildered at the imminent prospect of arriving at their new home after such a protracted journey, assumed that she belonged to the boat's skipper. The skipper, in turn, assumed that she was one of the new settlers, for the summer transatlantic crossing had left the Salzburg children "burned almost black by the sun." Mühlenberg, fearful of arrest for harboring a fugitive, raised the alarm. In a short while the twelve-year-old had been given a "sound thrashing" and returned to her master in South Carolina, which had established rigid slave codes and practices against such behavior.[9] The forlorn girl had tried to take advantage of the new settlers' lack of familiarity with slavery or blackness and their lack of knowledge of one another. And at least for a short time before Georgia became contagious, before slavery was firmly entrenched in the lowcountry, circumstances in the colony threw up the kinds of racial unorthodoxy that were typical of marginal zones in the Atlantic world.

Augusta, for instance, was a unique place beyond the effective reach of European prescriptive authority. Indian traders used the town as a point of departure on journeys into the Creek territory, and Augusta's mobile population was made up of an assortment of traders, settlers, visitors, half-breeds, and refugees. Here, when Ann Magdalena Heinrich, a teenage Swabian servant, complained to her white master of an attempted rape by one of her two black overseers, the master first beat her with his cane, then ordered her stripped stark naked, attached by her arms and hauled up to a beam, and then terribly whipped—all specifically "in Presence of these two Negroes."[10] Her race was no guarantor of preferential consideration and in this case evidently less of a factor than her gender, class, age, and national origin. In a less disturbing manner the absence of institutional support was evident in Augusta a few years later when an elderly free black man, who apparently had been baptized in Virginia, was found to be cohabiting with a German woman who had immigrated to Georgia. Their relationship was recorded not so much for being exceptional or unacceptable but because the pair had requested to be married; perhaps they hoped his Christianity would render their union less illicit.[11]

But before the mass influx of slaves heralded by the collapse of the trusteeship in the 1750s, by far the most common interracial unions in Georgia involved Native American females and European males. Thomas Christie noted that so many "bastard orphans belonging to the Indian traders" lived in Augusta in 1741 that it would be worth apprenticing them in sericulture.[12] Sufficient features of southeastern Indian marriage patterns were compatible with European customs that a number of immigrants intermarried with Creeks, Chickasaws, and members of other tribes. As Kathryn Braund notes in her painstaking survey of contemporary references to Creek women in the eighteenth century, "the nuclear family, having a husband, wife, and offspring, was the basic economic unit in Creek life," as it was among Europeans.[13] First-generation settlers sought to secure advantageous unions, maximizing on the positive relations with the Creeks during the two wars with Spain and France in the 1740s and 1750s, as recently highlighted by Julie Anne Sweet in her account of British-Creek dealings in the trustee era.[14] Many English and Scottish traders took Native American brides, thus assuring them of influential allies and support in the dangerous Indian Territory. These unions were beneficial also to the villages, which gained not only a secure route to European goods, and advantage over neighboring tribes, but also a degree of influence over the so-called Beloved Men who determined Georgia's Indian policy. Joseph Fitzwalter was married to the daughter of the Creek headman Tuscanee in April 1735 in an elaborate ceremony whose guests included the local Yamacraw leader Tomochichi and his queen, Senauki, and a number of colonial officials and their spouses. Fitzwalter reported to the trustees four months later that this union had greatly satisfied chiefs of both the Upper and Lower Creeks. As a secondary consideration he hoped that time would wean his bride "Molly" off what he described as her "Savage way of living." His optimism proved unfounded, for she ran away from him some time afterward.[15]

Many of these red-white relationships, then, were no more than temporary unions of expedience. George Galphin, for instance, apparently had wives in Ireland, the Indian country, and at his plantation at Silver Bluff on the Savannah River. For traders like Galphin or Joseph Fitzwalter, who quickly remarried an English tavern keeper, having ceremonial ties to Indian villages was simply, in a sense, a perk of the job. Other marriages adhered more closely to Native American norms, as British traders moved into the homes and clans of their new wives—but some degree of negotiation between white and red perceptions of family structures was always required. Lachlan McGillivray, for instance, took only one wife and insisted on a compromise between the two cultures' customs with respect to inheritance and the upbringing of children. Lachlan, unusually, demanded that his son, Alexander, be educated in Savannah but was apparently content for his daughters to remain in the Wind Clan.[16] That Creek systems of child rearing and inheritance tended to be dominant reflected the demographic preponderance of Amerindian communities, the indifference of many traders, and the remarkable cultural conservatism of Creek women, whom Kathryn Braund has labeled "guardians of tradition."

Mary Musgrove Matthews Bosomworth, though not a full-blood Creek, similarly found ways of balancing Indian and European customs.[17] Her second marriage, to her own servant—a loud, excitable, and lusty young Englishman—raised a number of eyebrows when it occurred. One contemporary described Jacob Matthews's wedding as no less than a "Promotion from Obeying to Commanding." However, it was evident that this marriage was unconventional. While the married Jacob Matthews may have dressed more resplendently and acted with airs and graces, no one doubted that his new bride retained the balance of power in their relationship. In his last will and testament, written in January 1740, more than two years before his death, he formally bequeathed her all her belongings—a way to enforce Creek inheritance customs over English legal practice.[18]

Certain features of family and community organization were common throughout the province, despite the extraordinary national, ethnic, and racial diversity of the early population. For though inhabitants tended to conglomerate around what was familiar—the Highland Scots in Darien, the Lutheran Salzburgers in Ebenezer, assorted Indians at Augusta and Musgrove's Cowpen, the urban English in Savannah—each shared in the upheaval of the frontier.[19] Customary controls over processes of family formation had eroded everywhere. At best, this was manifested in women's working and wooing outside the parental household and marrying at younger ages; it involved a gentle tinkering with traditional marriage practices. At worst, the erosion of traditional values spilled over into cohabitation and sexual intercourse outside wedlock. Participation in these phenomena was widespread, even if described differently by the various settler groups—from the godly Salzburgers to the worldly Londoners.

Perhaps the most constant feature of family formation, as one might expect, was the alluring influence of high social status. Naturally, the heyday of elite flamboyance would come with the arrival of wealthy, slave-owning families in the 1750s through 1770s. In fact, many would scoff at the idea that any recognizable elite existed during the trusteeship, as one Robert Parker discovered after he absolutely refused to serve on juries or drill with the militia, insisting that he was a gentleman and it would be beneath him.[20] Nonetheless, status is a relative measure. There existed hierarchies in early Georgia borne both of Old World rank and New World function. That officials such as William Spencer, James Habersham, and Johann Martin Bolzius were able to procure brides where others had failed suggests that positions of authority (including those without substantial wealth) held their own attraction to available women and their parents. Age was rarely a barrier, and all three proffered excuses in their letters for taking brides substantially younger than they.[21] When Habersham married one of his pupils, the sixteen-year-old Mary Bolton, he felt compelled to point out that she was a true Christian maiden whose "pious prudent behaviour exceeded those of twice her years."[22]

President William Stephens looked upon the actions of his younger colleagues among the magistrates with the vigilant eye of an elderly widower. He observed that they found marriage (and indeed remarriage) a relatively easy process to complete—an indication of the importance of social capital and rank in attracting a mate. In his journal Stephens recorded on 4 April 1745 that Charles Watson, "who from the time of his arrival last from Augusta on the 12th March (it seems) commenced Wooer; and I am informed has so far Succeeded, with the approbation of her Mother and Brother, that tis talked of as a sure thing; but whether or not we may expect such a Suddain Consumation, as we Saw in Mr. Spencers Case or that they'll abstain till Lent is over, we must wait to know." Salzburger men occupying positions of responsibility and authority, generally better off than their counterparts, were also more likely to be able to procure a bride even when the numbers of available women were limited. In these cases age differences were again often significant. Johann Lodowich Meyer, a forty-year-old judge, remained a widower for fourteen months (an impressive period by trusteeship Georgia standards) before taking Barbara Zorn, an eighteen-year-old orphan, as his second wife in 1750. The pastors in Ebenezer, Johann Martin Bolzius and Israel Christian Gronau, noted in their diary that he had apparently been experiencing "the usual sorrow and practical drawbacks" of lacking a helpmeet—by which one may assume they are talking about domestic assistance, not sexual gratification.[23]

Across trusteeship Georgia engagement was not marked by a ring or by any great length of time but rather an oath or a pledge. This promise of marriage could normally be made only with the consent of parents or guardians—although young men were given more latitude in this regard than women. Once made, the promise was deemed to be final and in the overwhelming majority of cases not retractable. But parental involvement often was not possible because many young people had been orphaned by the high mortality across the province. Unfortunately, few records or entries leave any information about the relative roles of male and female paramours and their interaction with authoritative parental figures in the course of courting. One incident, however, does offer some insight. Matthias Zettler, a young shoemaker, proposed in April 1741 to Elisabetha Catharina Kieffer. Initially, in the absence of their parents and at her brother's plantation, she accepted, and the pair promised themselves to each other. Only retrospectively did they receive full parental consent. A few weeks later the eighteen-year-old changed her mind, deciding against the marriage and obviously upsetting Zettler. The matter was brought to the church authorities to mediate: Zettler wanted her word to be her bond, while Kieffer claimed not to be bound by it.

Legally, of course, young Elisabetha was not bound by her promise—which she was entitled to withdraw. But her father was disgruntled and vexed. His daughter's behavior reflected poorly upon his own paternal authority, and it is rather ominously recorded in the pastors' diaries that he performed his "fatherly functions" on her and proceeded with "*ratione Disciplinae* as she has deserved it." In the next weeks both Kieffer and his wife spent a great deal of effort convincing their daughter to marry Zettler. Eventually, Elisabetha Kieffer claimed that her heart was "now inclined towards him quite otherwise than before." On 19 May the couple were finally married, and her parents were described as "very glad."[24]

The first matter this incident touches on is the abnormality of promising engagement before obtaining parental consent. Parental consent was customary across most cultures, communities, and classes in Georgia. Engagement was an agreement reached not only by the potential bride and groom but also upon the advice and approval of their immediate kin. To skip this advice and consent was to endanger the process of marriage by leaving it at the mercy of impulsive decisions or, as one commentator discreetly, put it, "overhaste." Furthermore, the prior consultation with another party made rescinding an engagement promise considerably more difficult. Elisabetha Kieffer was brave and willful in going back on her word, but she had the comparative advantage of having initially accepted without her parents' awareness. Her father certainly threatened and punished her, but undoubtedly a combination of carrot and stick was what led her eventually to accept the advances of Zettler. Embarrassment and rage gave way to cajoling and persuasion—and it is probably not coincidental that Elisabetha's mother, Anna Margaretha, is mentioned only in association with the latter. Unsurprisingly, the marriage was punctuated by disagreements and disputes—and at one stage a homesick Elisabeth actually moved back to her parents' home.[25]

Conditions during the trusteeship—particularly for those living outside defined communities—allowed some young women a greater degree of jurisdiction over their own courtship and marriage patterns than their contemporaries were accustomed to. A young German girl in Savannah, in contrast to Salzburger Elisabetha Kieffer, defied the wishes of her father—who was firmly set against her betrothal to a young man living in the nearby settlement of Abercorn. The daughter ignored her father's insistence and went to Abercorn. The records do not reveal what happened to her and her intended. The difficulties that this episode brought to light were probably occasioned by the age of the girl in question. According to their pastors, an important custom brought over by settlers from the Rhineland was the acceptance that children who had attained "a certain age" could marry against their parents' wishes, a practice that apparently caused much vexation. The lack of institutional control across the colony during the trusteeship was such that religious authorities bemoaned as late as 1750 that "if permission to marry is denied, nothing but considerable trouble results." Even when the concept of parental advice was taken to its absolute limit and a marriage was arranged without consulting the bride, conditions on the frontier allowed too much agency for such unions to be widely practicable. One unnamed woman, who had been forced to marry an older man against her will, was troubled by her adulterous conception of a child.[26]

Despite the high incidence of marriage of younger women and remarriage of a sizable proportion of older women in trusteeship Georgia, cohabitation outside wedlock was a frequent occurrence. This naturally attracted the attention of moralists such as Rev. George Whitefield, who vilified several people in the town of Savannah who, as he put it with typical mildness, "lived most scandalous Lives with their Whores." For some widows cohabitation with a new partner may have been preferable to remarriage. About a quarter of the husbands who wrote wills between 1733 and 1775 specified that certain bequests would fall to their widows only while they remained single. Just such a situation might explain the relationship between John Lyndall and Elizabeth Gilbert, the widow of William Mears. Contemporaries were confused that this pair had never been married, yet everyone looked upon both her children by her first marriage and those she had borne since as Lyndall's. The rules, it appeared, could easily be bent. A minister reprimanded the merchant Thomas Christie for living in open adultery with his "housekeeper," Sarah Turner, the wife of an indebted sawyer who had run off to the West Indies. Edward Jenkins was concerned about the fate of two orphans placed with Nicholas Amatis, who had taken "a scandilous wench to himself instead of a wife." For a person who had little capital, wasn't overly God-fearing, and could bear the occasional haughty comment or disdainful glance from the well-to-do, being married or not made little difference. Besides, someone could always claim, like Elizabeth Hughes West Kellaway did, that she had been married privately by the good old French minister at Purysburg.[27]

The prevalence of cohabitation confirms the importance of the element of mutual need in the spectrum of relationships between the men and women of proprietorship Georgia. The rite of matrimony was not always considered necessary to the requirements of colonists whose desires revolved around the axes of domestic economy, emotional stability, and sexual appetite. The difficulty of finding a suitable and/or a nearby minister was sometimes simply not worth the effort. In fact, most clergymen who were dedicated (or unfortunate) enough to find themselves operating in Georgia found that that stable religious attendance was a problem. Many, including future evangelist greats like George Whitefield and John Wesley, undoubtedly learned lessons that would come in handy.[28]

The Salzburger pastors were more successful than their counterparts in reducing the number of unorthodox courtships and defective marriages among their congregation. Unlike Whitefield, Wesley, and company, the Salzburger pastors had the advantage of living among and intermarrying with members of their congregation. The pastors were also working with more impressionable and devout parishioners, although their edited diaries somewhat glorified their activities. Their relative success at Ebenezer was predicated upon a twofold approach. This involved scrutinizing and monitoring the behavior of local inhabitants very closely. And it required that outsiders be kept at a polite distance—the ministers erected a psychological barrier to differentiate the Salzburgers from other colonists. It was a little late for a city upon a hill, for the North American continent was no longer the barren wilderness that ethnocentric Puritans had described a century earlier. But the Society for the Promotion of Christian Knowledge would have been delighted with the alternative allegorical simile provided by George Whitefield in his letter dated 20 June 1740. He described the stark difference between the community at Ebenezer and the rest of the colony as equivalent to the time "when there was darkness among the Egyptians, but light in the land of Goshen."[29]

From 1742, and on all subsequent occasions when the opportunity arose, the Lutheran pastors encouraged prospective married couples among their parishioners to get engaged in their presence—along with parents and guardians. The pastors were also keen to assemble the entire congregation to attend such important ceremonies as the publishing of banns, though this was rarely possible in practice. Considerably less consideration was extended to those outside the congregation. The ministers treated even German colinguists from other parts of the province suspiciously and required them to provide the oral or written consent not only of their parents but also of the master in whose service they were employed. The Lutheran pastors proved extremely wary of dirtying their hands by marrying or baptizing strangers, and they apologetically turned away a number of aspirants to make long journeys homeward.[30]

The earliest such occasion occurred on the afternoon of 1 July 1734, when a "very insistent" Englishman asked Reverend Bolzius to marry him to a widow in Savannah because the visitor could not get an English pastor to perform the ceremony. Bolzius's armory of diplomatic skills allowed him subtly to evade the matter. Sorry, he mumbled, but his vocation covered only those of Lutheran religion. He explained that he had written to London for clarification but had not yet been answered. In order to perform such a ceremony, he imagined he would need at least an order and permission from the vice governor. Also, of course, he would need a different marriage book because the ceremony would have to be conducted in English. The Englishman was apparently satisfied with this and, having dined with the pastor, happily set off home, considerably further from his objective of snapping up a Savannah widow.[31]

By 11 November 1734 the pastors had made it clear to a number of people that they would not embroil themselves in complicated ceremonial difficulties, complaining that "in this country such matters are frequently handled in quite disorderly fashion."[32] The most surprising request came from an Englishman involved in the Indian trade, who brought with him his Native American wife and their child to have it baptized. The pastors refused on the ground that they had no assurances that the child had not already been baptized, noting privately that they were suspicious of any man who openly declared his child to be illegitimate and who did not wish to go to the clergymen in Savannah. Beneath their ceremonial objections the pastors were clearly concerned that English influence would contaminate the relative purity of the Salzburger settlement. The pastors warned Mr. Ortmann not to permit his wife to lodge English travelers, because they were liable to cause scandal—though in fact he had little influence over his wife's actions. The pastors were similarly displeased when a widower agreed to indenture his daughter for seven years to a woman in Savannah to act as a nanny. Deeply mistrustful of English settlements, the ministers warned that the girl would be harshly treated, forget all she had learned, and be led astray by the bad examples around her. A number of incidents involving German female servants seemed to validate the pastors' opinions. Courts inconclusively investigated the alleged rapes of women in Frederica. Several other references were made to episodes involving premarital sex and prostitution, and the abuse of underage girls.[33]

German girls outside the Ebenezer settlements were obviously more vulnerable and likely to yield to the advances of English soldiers, despite the pastors' admonitions. One such woman was labeled a "whore" but probably in the sense of the eighteenth-century German equivalent *Hure* by which one meant a woman who had premarital sexual relationships. The woman in question eventually married her seducer, Capt. William Francis (a ranger), and the pair were killed along with their child during a raid upon Fort Venture on the Altamaha River, by Indians allied with Spain, that the pastors thought to be "an especial judgment of God."[34] Another German woman, Ann Magdalena Heinrich, had been sold into service in Augusta by Captain Thomson, the owner of her transport ship. Following her abuse there at the hands of an Indian trader, she served out her time in Savannah, where she was reportedly "in great peril . . . of seduction and also had opportunity to marry ill-bred people." She resisted the temptations, however, and married Carl Sigismund Ott in February 1743.[35] When John Terry, recorder at Frederica, complained of rapes committed by military officers there, some of them suborned a Palatine woman (Elizabeth Yootire) to accuse him of the same crime.³⁶ Finally, the experiences of Mary Simeon—a young French indentured servant who was transferred for money from Arthur Edgcomb to James Moore and sold to James Wilson, who later "found means to hire her to" Paul Cheeswright—are strongly suggestive of prostitution. Bailiffs found her one night with a wanted felon and three other men on several beds in one room of a "debauched house" in Savannah. The bailiffs removed Simeon from these squalid acquaintances, by which time the midwife Elizabeth Stanley believed Simeon to be pregnant and placed her as a maidservant with a married couple, but this account of "the Girls misusage" is unlikely to have been unique and may not have been wholly compelled. Although Mary Simeon was obviously exploited by the men involved in the ring, some observers assumed that her involvement was partly out of choice—as indicated by the comment of Edward Jenkins while referring to her new employers, Mr. and Mrs. Fallowfield: "If any in ye Town can Breck her from her ill habbit they will."³⁷ Such incidents led the bailiff Thomas Causton to declare in December 1736 that he had "found many Inhabitants of this place guilty of . . . Petty Larceny, Whoredom, [and] Adultery."³⁸

Over time, relations between the communities of early Georgia improved. In large part this was a reflection of the spread of interethnic associations (both formal and informal) precipitated by the frontier environment. For instance, Anglo-German links were more amiable in the aftermath of the frightening episode of the War of Jenkins' Ear, when settlers of all creeds were united in their opposition to a Spanish invasion. A number of refugees, mostly women and children from Savannah and Frederica, fled northward, where they were lodged in Salzburger homes. After General Oglethorpe's victory at Bloody Marsh repulsed the Spaniards on 12 July 1742, the former refugees sent letters to Salzburg families thanking them for their kindness—and included coffee and silk ribbons as tokens of their gratitude.³⁹

The increase in the number of interethnic families during the 1730s and 1740s facilitated such expressions of colonial solidarity. The dearth of women of childbearing age among European settlers prompted unmarried males in all parts of the province to forge transcommunity links. Even in the Ebenezer settlement, unmarried males looked to Purysburg (in South Carolina) as well as the rest of the Georgia colony to furnish them with available women. Abraham Grimmiger, for example, found a wife as far south as Frederica; she was a young Scottish woman of handsome appearance and "in great danger of seduction." Perhaps for this reason Grimmiger wanted to bring her to Ebenezer, at the opposite end of Georgia, though it apparently cost him much to tear her away from her father and other people. Her first few months must have been harrowing, for she knew only her husband and spoke only English and Gaelic, her mother tongue. Other Salzburger men married German-speaking immigrants who worked as indentured servants in and around Savannah and Frederica. The linguistic transition may have been easy, but they still had religious differences to overcome. Prospective husbands from the Ebenezer settlement made it a condition of marriage that their prospective Palatine wives convert to evangelical Lutheranism rather than their native Reformed Protestantism—and many parents refused to yield on this important spiritual point. Ultimately, the Salzburger pastors became less rigid about the English, Scottish, and Irish settlers whose marriage ceremonies they were willing to perform, and by the early 1750s—bereft of Oglethorpe and the trustees' support—they reluctantly complied with an increasing number of marriage requests.[40]

Families and communities could not help but be affected by the increasing intermarriage rates between English, Germans, Scots, Irish, Carolinians, and Indians. The structures that emerged in Georgia would replicate neither Old World patterns nor the equally unsuitable expectations of the trustees. Institutional authority was too weak and kinship networks too diffuse. Relationships in Georgia were less static and stable than in most of Europe and the northern colonies: adultery, infidelity, and cohabitation were common, marriage and remarriage were frequent, and circumstances often facilitated the opportunity to flee an unhappy union. Joseph Fitzwalter's Creek bride, "Molly," ran away from him, as did Daniel Derizous's wife, Olive, to whom he bequeathed "one shilling sterling for poisoning me."[41] Plenty of settlers had left Britain with the specific intention to sever their familial attachments and relished the anonymity of a new life and a forgotten past. "No Body would Leave his native Country," observed the surgeon Samuel Pensyre to James Oglethorpe, "if they had not some Crosses or Misfortune to venture their lives in Crossing ye ocean." Pensyre's cross was a London wife whose alcoholism had become unbearable; his solution was to travel to Georgia in 1733 and cohabit with another woman and her two sons. Indeed, so rare were well-matched and successful unions that the marriage of a young clerk in February 1745 to a "young Damesel of Modest Behaviour and a good Character . . . is looked upon among us as a good Fortune here."[42]

Some of the earliest so-called marriages were sufficiently fraudulent to warrant public censure. Londoner Elizabeth Malpas was convicted of pretending to be the wife of one William Bully while "lyeing between two fellows naked & leading a dissolute life," which brought a punishment of sixty lashes at the tail of a cart that was then dragged up and down Savannah's Bull street.[43] Other marriages disguised rings of sexual exploitation through which one female was actually bought and sold by different men. In 1738 two soldiers were almost indicted—one for offering his wife for sale, and the other for offering to buy her—but, for lack of evidence, the case was eventually treated as a "Misdemeanor only." More verifiable was the episode involving Hannah Willoughby Watkins Mellichamp. When her original husband, the wig maker James Willoughby, died in October 1734, she privately married the forty-six-year-old surgeon William Watkins through an obscure minister. In the late spring of 1735, by which time Hannah was pregnant, a letter revealed to their distress that Watkins's previous wife was alive and well in England. Fearful of a conviction for bigamy, William Watkins persuaded Hannah to marry another man—warning her that if news of his previous marriage came to light, her pregnancy would make it seem that she had "played the Whore." In August Hannah Willoughby (Watkins) married Richard Mellichamp, with William Watkins looking on—his fake congratulatory smile no doubt bolstered by a sense of relief. But when Mellichamp realized he had been taken for a chump, discovering that his new wife was not only defiant but also pregnant, he auctioned her for a fee of five pounds. She, of her own volition, publicly bedded the buyer. In October a grand jury convicted Hannah Willoughby (Watkins) of bigamy, which brought a mandatory whipping. Ironically, her marriage to Mellichamp, which had been intended to deflect accusations of "playing the whore," had resulted in her public prostitution. Equally ironic was that the pregnancy that would have convicted her now commuted her punishment, from a whipping to a period of confinement in Savannah's jail. For his involvement Watkins received a hundred lashes and imprisonment. The wife buyer escaped with a suspended sentence, thanks to his honest testimony, despite his having a prior conviction for keeping a bawdy house. Mellichamp, construed as the victim, was acquitted of blame.[44]

Such incidents confirm that many relationships and marriages in trusteeship Georgia were occasioned by mutual interest or convenience rather than being based on romantic love, built on practical notions of lasting interpersonal bonds, or even matched according to social status or common networks. Although some of the first Georgia marriages, such as William Spencer's, undoubtedly functioned successfully and productively, a number faltered on their weak foundations in the absence of a strong and operative societal protocol.

Though mutual interest or convenience were the traits that tended to characterize family formation across the province, there remained plenty of scope for distinctive practices. Among such an extraordinarily diverse population, idiosyncrasies remained for years among settler groups. Fringe populations—like the highly mobile Jewish settlers and equally itinerant Indian inhabitants—managed to retain the most independent structures at family and community levels. Even among those other groups more prone to integration, a number of features betrayed their diverse origins. Georgia was no melting pot that homogenized its components but rather a simmering stew whose ingredients shared some of their flavor while retaining much of their original distinctiveness.

The early Jewish population was far from insignificant, numbering about eighty people in 1735, most of whom were Sephardic (of Spanish origin), although there was a small group of Ashkenazi (German) Jews. This aroused consternation among the majority of colonists, who were at best wary of non-Protestants and at worst anti-Semitic, though the feelings were to some extent mutual. One Jew (probably Benjamin Sheftall) described the town of Savannah in April 1741 as being riddled with abominable horrors, including adultery and fornication, that were practiced with impunity—and at Frederica he suspected it was even worse. This did not preclude Jews from fostering positive relations with gentiles, as Holly Snyder has demonstrated in her absorbing account of Jewish dialogues with Christian pietists in the British and German Atlantic worlds. Indeed, while a few Jewish settlers apparently took Christian wives, like Isaac Compass, who married the daughter of the English wheelwright Thomas Young, most would go to considerable lengths to ensure that they were married to a Jew, often scouring the Atlantic seaboard for appropriate matches for their children. Coreligionist networking was nothing new to colonial America—it had previously smoothed the progress of both Puritan settlement in New England and Quaker settlement in the Middle Colonies, and by the eighteenth century it had already helped to establish small but significant Jewish communities in a number of port cities around the Atlantic basin (including the Caribbean). Jewish marriages during the colonial era in Georgia saw unions formed with families in Rhode Island; Jamaica; St. Croix; New York; Philadelphia; and Port Royal and Charlestown, South Carolina.[45]

Nonetheless, for all their remarkable resilience Jewish marital and communal practices in Georgia undoubtedly reflected the demographic stresses and strains of living in an Atlantic outpost. Benjamin Sheftall waited two years after the death of his wife, Perla, in November 1736 before marrying the Dutch Ashkenazi Hannah Solomons. In the context of the colony this period of mourning was exceptionally long. But it reflected the dearth of partners available to those, like Sheftall, who held to unwavering principles of selection, for at the date of their marriage Hannah Solomons, newly arrived from Holland, had been in Savannah for just seven weeks. Frontier circumstances would predictably complicate religious and ritual practices, not least because the opportunities in Georgia had attracted such a diverse and often discordant Jewish community, the members of which disagreed about eating customs, festivals, dogma, and the construction of a synagogue. Even the flight of most of the Sephardic population did not resolve the difficulties, for after 1741 the devout Sheftall found himself (and his two young sons) in a community bereft of sufficient men to form a minyan, and he therefore decided to temporarily relocate his family to Charlestown to ensure that his sons' commitment to Judaism would match his own.[46]

Initially, Native American inhabitants of the "empty" lands that they had cheerfully granted to the trustees had little need to adjust the organization of their families and communities in the face of European settlement. By the 1730s the Creeks and Cherokees of the interior had proved successful adaptors to the new world in which they found themselves. Sheltered from the tidal waves of disease and warfare that had crippled so many seaboard tribes, both confederations established a powerful role for themselves in the geopolitical balance of the region through a combination of shrewd diplomacy and fortuitous location. Their large numerical size (with the Cherokees numbering about 12,000 people, the Creeks 20,000, and the Chickasaw 2,000) also ensured that Indian-European marriages would involve far more white adjustment than red acculturation, though as Michelle Gillespie has remarked, these unions often dramatically affected the lives of individual women and children who occupied "contested terrain between distinctly different cultures."[47]

Native American marriages were structured around an oral contract between husband and wife, ceremonially sealed on a designated wedding day. As with European marriages, each partner swore to uphold certain gendered duties: the husband promised to hunt and supply his wife with meat; she pledged to provide him with corn and to prepare food. This agreement was the formal centerpiece of a larger customary ceremony that was carefully choreographed. Indian suitors followed a protocol that Edward Cashin has aptly described as "as intricate as that practiced by the gentry of Virginia or Carolina." The most obvious difference between the Euro-American population and both the Creek and Cherokee communities was in defining and *understanding* the family through male rather than female relatives. Kinship links, a primary mark of identity, ran through Indian female bloodlines and were more important to the Indian population than to most European settlers. For Native Americans the selection of a partner was a more careful and deliberate decision than for most early white colonists, who neither valued kinship so highly nor had the luxury of much choice. Because both the Creek and Cherokee societies were dominantly matrilineal, female relatives played a central part in courtship and matrimonial affairs.[48]

Mothers and sisters, working alongside clan elders, were crucial to the obtaining of consent for marriage. The women determined whether a male suitor, who was necessarily from another clan, was suitable for incorporation. They judged his character and paid particular attention to his martial and diplomatic reputation, as well as the gifts he was able to provide such as furs, food, and blankets. Following the ceremony, a trial period of varying length offered the last opportunity for either partner to dissolve the marriage without incurring blame, though this rarely occurred. In contrast to European traditions, marriage gave husbands no rights over their wife's property or their children (present and future). Households consequently often incorporated extended family, consisting typically of a woman, her husband, their unmarried sons, daughters, and those daughters' children. Indian marital practices in the Southeast, despite their matrilineal orientation, shared a number of features with European customs— from courtship to the provision of a dowry to the giving away of the bride to the necessity of consummation. This facilitated the high number of interracial marriages with traders. After all, Indian traders not only brought ready-made dowries to the bargaining table but were also often of Scottish or Scots-Irish origin and therefore culturally familiar with at least patrilineal notions of clan identity. In some ways German settlers also perceived themselves to be culturally closer to the local Amerindians than to many neighboring Europeans, for instance, in sharing a more modest dress sense than English ladies'. One diarist noted: "The [Indian] women are fully clothed, almost like the peasant women in Germany. Those who have no clothes cover themselves completely with a woollen blanket, and in this respect they show more modesty than the English ladies."[49]

But there remained key differences, which were frequently a source of confusion in Indian-European relations. Among Indians, divorce was easily obtained—being simply a matter of mutual consent—and as a result marriages (described in Cherokee as "uniting the blankets") could last for only a short time. White onlookers tended to view this serial monogamy as another manifestation of native savagery or debauchery. As the historian Michael Morris has noted, such an attitude operated to the benefit of white traders (and was largely propagated by them), allowing them to abandon Creek wives in the Indian country without facing censure from other whites. Indians' partners seemed inconstant and adulterous, though few whites could have cast stones from Georgia, because many evidently subscribed to just such a pattern in practice. Native opinions of Christian marriages could be equally impudent: "Not one in a hundred of them had anything to do either with happiness or common sense," observed an Indian, famously quoted by Thomas Paine.[50] But though it was comparatively easy to divorce in native society, this by no means resulted in a devaluing of formal marital relations.

Unlike Europeans, Creek and Cherokee women suffered no stigma for indulging in casual sexual encounters before they were married. But Georgia observers noted that local tribes had no such relaxed attitude toward sexual promiscuity within wedlock.[51] Native American punishments for adultery by married women were severe (often effectively prostitution as far as sexual relations with white traders were concerned) and were intended to mark out and scar the guilty party for the rest of her life. Philip Von Reck explained in his

Short Report on Georgia and the Indians that those whose ears had been cut and whose hair had been shorn had been punished for whoring, whereas adultery was punished by "cutting off nose and ears."[52] Native Americans punished all activities that transgressed established sexual boundaries by removing the very symbol of female status, the hair. Indeed, a glance at a Creek female was all that was required to gauge her marital status: adulterers and whores bore facial deformities, married women braided their hair, and widows wore theirs naturally, leaving it uncombed for a period. All Indian women went bareheaded, thereby giving a clear and open indication of their status.[53] Indeed, marital status was so revered that it was protected after death. According to one observer, Indians instituted a custom of burning or burying all the household effects, provisions, and other things owned by an Indian brave in order to prevent a wife from being tempted to murder her husband to obtain his goods. Male ownership of material possessions was undoubtedly on the increase among southeastern Indians during the late seventeenth and eighteenth centuries, as trade with Europans and reliance upon European goods became increasingly dominant within native society. The destruction of goods during death ceremonies in part sought to ensure that the new conditions did not overly influence deeply rooted gender conventions among Amerindian families and communities.[54]

Nonetheless, though cultural persistence generally characterized the social relations of southeastern Indians during Georgia's formative decades, there was also some clear evidence of change. Creeks and Cherokees had survived and profited by proving adaptable in the first part of the eighteenth century, and their interaction with European settlers naturally influenced certain facets of their culture. Politically, the period witnessed a gradual move toward centralized tribal leadership and the partial recognition of patrilineal dynasties—largely because French, Spanish, and English diplomats preferred to deal with European-style leadership hierarchies rather than more complex configurations. The proliferation of European trading lent disproportionate weight to the importance of deer hunting—and, by extension, male roles within society.[55] Finally, the high levels of interracial marriage produced a growing number of mestizos. In colonial society these individuals were liable to face discrimination. But among Amerindians being a mestizo often proved to be an asset. Thanks to their mixed-race connections, many were able to exercise considerable power, assuming important diplomatic, commercial, and political roles, as evidenced by Mary Musgrove Matthews Bosomworth, or Alexander McGillivray, future leader of the Creeks who would broker the Treaty of New York with George Washington in 1790 that supposedly would guarantee federal protection of Creek territory.[56]

Given the fuss made over the unusual willingness of William Johnson, the

Irishman who became the British Crown's first superintendent of Indian affairs in 1755, to accept Indian customs, adopt their dress, learn the Mohawk language, and intermarry in mid-eighteenth-century New York, it is clear that the boundary between Georgia settlers and southeastern Indian communities was initially far more porous than boundaries elsewhere. British traders, more than fifteen of whom were reported in the lists of early settlers without mention of wives, were known to be keen "to associate even more closely with these heathen people by marrying an Indian woman." Even the priggish Salzburgers expressed admiration for Indian families, believing, wrongly, that polygamy was unknown to Indians, and that their communal welfare system provided effectively for widows and children. Polygamy, and especially sororal polygamy (whereby a man married two or more sisters at once), was a traditional practice among the Cherokees and Creeks but one that they appear to have used less and less because a husband's ability to sustain more than one wife was increasingly limited by war, land cessions, and game depletion.[57] Because the white presence was too small to be threatening, and the sexual interaction overwhelmingly involved munificent white males and (surplus) Indian females, expediency was able to get the better of prejudice. Marriages between Native Americans and Europeans in Georgia were generally restricted to those members of either group who were willing to risk cultural stigma for material benefit. It is no coincidence that with the removal of the French threat in the 1760s—effectively presenting the British with a monopoly in the Indian trade of the Southeast—examples of interracial marriage seem to dry up. A key motivation for the uniting of British and Indian blankets had disappeared: French competition fell away after their defeat in the Seven Years' War, while trade relations became more centralized and coordinated. Although by the late eighteenth century the proximity of increasing numbers of Cherokee, Carolinian, Creek, and Georgian inhabitants invited extensive interaction with respect to European modes of dress, building construction, animal husbandry, slavery, and agriculture, marriage was no longer as significant a factor. As relations deteriorated in the backcountry, Creek and especially Cherokee clans discovered a growing inclination to spill rather than share blood with the white settlers.

In the processes of courtship, celebration of marriage, and naming of children, the various communities of early Georgia reflected their various racial, ethnic, and religious origins. Marriage-day antics ranged from the minimalist Salzburger solemn congratulations to the grander celebrations of young Creek couples married at the annual green corn festival. Somewhere in between, the bulk of continental European immigrants of the Reformed religion and provincial British folk brought customs of great vivacity in their celebrations of marriage—getting together to eat, drink, and dance after the ceremony.

The coexistence of these various approaches allowed for some degree of cross-influence. Bridal couples from German communities turned to English preachers to perform baptisms and marriages—as they were then permitted to drink and dance to celebrate. "If everybody who danced and enjoyed a good time were to be damned," muttered one German servant woman, who was fed up with her sanctimonious counterparts, "only a very few would find salvation." Nonetheless, communities also retained signifying hallmarks of their own homelands. Among the Salzburgers, for instance, children continued to receive the names of their godparents (rather than the biblical names that the pastors preferred); women in childbed received customary gifts of food; and mothers and children were ceremonially "churched," or blessed, together.[58]

Married women's familial responsibilities, like their economic chores, were rendered more difficult by their new environment. Given the complex living arrangements that were prevalent, the role of the mother-wife was critical to the management of relationships and the establishment of family harmony. As children acquired half-sisters and -brothers—often of a significantly different age—it was important that maternal authority was well respected. For young brides this was far more problematic than for remarrying widows, who frequently brought their own assets into the new marriage (occasionally protected by a formal contract). But there were no surefire ways to safeguard either personal livelihood or children's futures in such a disrupted social environment. As soon as thirty-two-year-old Elizabeth Little West died, her two-year-old son by her first marriage was promptly evicted and dispossessed of his Savannah lot by his hard-hearted stepfather.[59]

The welfare of orphaned or half-orphaned children in early Georgia was dangerously dependent upon the attitudes of their guardians, whose incentives varied from the opportunity to abuse control of extra labor to the need to replace lost children and/or a genuine concern to provide an appropriate domestic environment. Upheaval was commonplace, as orphans were often required to relocate according to changing circumstances. Both parents of the Huber family had died of dysentery by May 1734 in the village of Abercorn, leaving behind four daughters. On her deathbed Maria Magdalena Huber, the mother, tearfully forced her minister to swear to look after her children so that she could "die gladly now and would not worry any more." The oldest girl died in September, apparently of epilepsy, and by October the three remaining girls were lodged in the common shelter, essentially a spare hut in Ebenezer. Two of her sisters followed the oldest to the grave in the first months of 1735, leaving the seven-year-old Margaretha the only survivor in a family of six. Margaretha, bereft of parents, siblings, and any kind of stability, was adopted by a well-respected couple, who apparently cared for her "as if they were her real father and mother," but her tortuous journey was interrupted again. Sickness descended upon her adoptive parents, and she was moved in August 1735 to the Bachers' house, where she remained for some time before moving to the Grubers' house, where she lived in January 1738 (at the age of ten). There she was reunited with her adoptive mother, who had married Peter Gruber in February 1736. Margaretha battled through the difficulties of her childhood, though, and by 1759 she was married to an Englishman, Samuel Graves, in Bethany. The pair got on well, despite her frequent illnesses, and now it was she who stepped into a quasi-maternal role, becoming a diligent stepmother to his two infant children.[60]

Margaretha Huber, incredibly, was more fortunate than many. Though riddled with their own afflictions, at least her various adoptive and foster parents appear to have been conscientious. Other couples were less avid about caring for new recruits within the family. Edward Jenkins, appointed by Oglethorpe as one of the first trustees of orphans in Georgia, remarked that many Savannah women into whose care orphaned children were committed (for a fee) did not always adopt and raise them as they would their own children. "I am sorry I cant help but say the wimen Turn out but very Badly," he observed, "which makes the orphans' live miserable." The labor of orphaned children was particularly vulnerable to being abused by self-interested guardians or custodians. Children without one or both parents often were sent away to be an apprentice or servant, which usually made them the victim of the universal need for cheap and menial labor. Equally, unrelated children in the household were likely to face more extreme punishments, as no bond of kinship restrained adults' actions. One little English girl was treated so violently by her German mistress-mother that neighbors complained. In May 1737 another foster father insisted that an orphaned girl living in his household be removed because his wife abused her frequently and vehemently. Bolzius accepted a third girl into the Ebenezer community when he heard of her treatment at the hands of her current master and mistress in Savannah; they beat her so severely that she would run away and hide for days under clapboard houses. When hunger and thirst drove her out, she was reportedly hung up and whipped—with her wounds washed in saltwater.[61]

This mistreatment of orphans and apprenticed children was by no means out of place in the barbarous climate of the early modern Atlantic world, but it was symptomatic of the struggles of European women to deal with the unfamiliar family arrangements on the frontier. First, their time was greatly constrained by their labor obligations. More noticeably, they had considerably less recourse to mechanisms of support. In Georgia they could rarely rely upon the support of extended family. Nor could they expect much welfare assistance from institutions like the established church or community devices like poor relief. Unlike Native American villages, European settlements lacked flexible models of welfare provision—principally because their inhabitants subscribed to a more narrowly defined conception of the family. Naturally, mothers ardently defended the interests of their own children. One mother incited her son to break into his master's house in Savannah, steal his indenture of apprenticeship from a chest, bring it to her to burn, and then hide in her cornfield. But rarely were stepchildren or adopted children extended equal regard.[62]

Those families that, as a result of remarriage, included either stepfathers or stepmothers often experienced strenuous difficulties in accommodating new relationships. One man wept when he recounted how badly he was faring in his child raising, because his wife's oldest son could not "be brought to order by any discipline on his or his wife's part." Another couple habitually locked their six-year-old daughter up like a prisoner and were eventually persuaded to relinquish her, to be brought up by another family. Other manifestations of dysfunctional households saw stepfathers refusing to pay school fees for their wives' children by previous marriages. Such incidents led Bolzius to remark that "in this country children are not well provided for . . . it is as if they were to be sacrificed to Moloch."[63]

Families and communities may have arrived in Georgia arranged according to traditional European models. But each witnessed a rapid declension upon exposure to the disruptive conditions on the frontier. Marriages became irregular, distorted, and unconventional. Families became diffuse, ethnically mixed, and fragmentary. Communities became porous, mobile, and disorganized. Women's roles were necessarily reconfigured by such circumstances, a shift made more noticeable by the traditionally more static position that females occupied within society. There was no question that conditions made family life extremely uncomfortable and unstable. The new environment weakened the boundaries of acceptable marital practice—readily encouraging young ages of female marriage, extremely swift remarriage, and often cohabitation. Behavior was driven by expediency more than any other influence.

Whether this was a liberating or a constraining change for European female settlers is open to debate. Pioneers in the field of women's history, spurred on by the feminist movement of the late twentieth century, have explored this question, or variants of it, across an impressive range of colonial backdrops.[64] Were Chesapeake planters' wives more powerful in the community because of their marital value? Was the status of New England's goodwives enhanced by their longer lifespan or greater literacy? Were Dutch women compromised in New York by the arrival of restrictive English legal controls? Did Quaker matriarchs in Pennsylvania or Delaware gain from their family stability and independent meetings? It seems strange that the pioneers themselves made remarkably little reference to any change in status, especially since contemporaries were not slow

90 · CHAPTER THREE

to pass judgment upon other new juxtapositions in their new worlds: forms of servitude, slavery, or Indian neighbors. Naturally, the omission is partly explained by the overwhelmingly male authorship of the records that remain. Equally, it is perfectly clear that most of the females who settled the frontier were heavily preoccupied with more pressing questions.

Yet all Europeans who traveled across to Georgia, in their quieter moments of reflection, must have compared their new lifestyles with what they had known before. Some were pushed, driven to America by persecution, debt, or some other "Cross or Misfortune." Others were pulled, allured by the promise of profitable commerce or fertile land. All would remember the moment when, at a crossroad in their lives, they had chosen this transatlantic path rather than another. After all, the decision to embark upon a brand new colonial venture—even in the 1730s—was a decision momentous enough to require consultation in all but the most fiercely patriarchal and proscriptive families. Attempting to amalgamate this range of motives and experiences into one collective gendered expression produces only a baffling cacophony.

In short, the Georgia example reaffirms that the New World proved to be liberating for some European women and constraining for others. There were clearly opportunities for many low-status females to marry above their Old World rank—whether first-time brides or more experienced wives. By marrying up, they might gain access to a more comfortable lifestyle, larger landholdings, and exert more influence than would have been conceivable elsewhere. The personal nature of justice and the limited extent of institutional control could also, on occasion, operate to the benefit of a gender whose formal authority was minimal. But the self-same conditions proved enormously detrimental to another set of women. Though a twice-remarried widow might have been well off economically, she (unlike some historians) would not have disregarded the negative emotional impact of losing three husbands—quite apart from the implications of those losses for her family and their future. Equally, for every young woman who manifested significant freedom in her social behavior, another found herself ostracized and neglected by her community and its slack policing. The opportunities appeared to pale into insignificance relative to the dangers. For many widows remarriage was not so much an empowering as a survival device. Anne Laurence has argued that a broad shift toward a culture of individualism in England between 1500 and 1760 "deprived women of the support of the community while not substantially increasing their opportunities for personal choice and action," and the same can certainly be said for a high proportion of females on the Georgia frontier.[65]

Since it is manifestly impossible to take a statistical average of female experiences, index them against precolonial expectations, and compare them with other societies, the most salient question then becomes what differentiated those women who benefited from those who suffered in the colonial environment. In general, those women who were best able to negotiate their way around the perils of the frontier environment drew heavily upon three criteria: control of information, connections, and character.

As demonstrated by those monopolizing businesswomen introduced in the previous chapter, a particular expertise or proficiency could offer females a relatively exalted position among their peers—and this was far more likely to occur on the frontier than in more established societies. Control of information in a locale plagued by uncertainty also lent added import to those with access to reliable news or communication, which became powerful social weapons. Tavern keepers most frequently fit this category, but there were plenty of other instances: two women discredited Charles Wesley as a minister in Frederica, while the Creek Indians almost came to blows with the Savannah militia following false complaints by Mary Musgrove Matthews Bosomworth. Social connections were also critical in determining the relative standing of immigrants. Those able to draw on kinship networks, for instance, or construct new associations, found themselves better able to cope with the changes demanded by the frontier by sharing the burden with others. This might range from using young children to scare birds from the seedbeds to conducting diplomatic negotiation with highborn Indian warriors. But personal situations were undoubtedly reinforced by an ability to rely upon others—whether at church, down at the pub, or in the fields. The most vulnerable inhabitants among the diffuse settlements of early Georgia were those who had no social capital to compensate for their predicament: isolated indentured servants, orphans, and secluded housewives. Finally, it is plain that some personalities proved better suited to the coarseness of the frontier, better able to display adaptability in the face of changing circumstances. Those willing to improvise solutions to unfamiliar obstacles, to anticipate expedient solutions rather than respond to outside forces, were at an advantage when it came to using information or cultivating social connections.[66]

Naturally, none of these criteria was as important as luck, wealth, status, race, or nationality. Nor could these factors ever fully offset the degree of gender domination facilitated by hundreds of years of patriarchal programming. But among the chaotic families and communities of trusteeship Georgia, such factors helped determine whether the colonial condition would prove liberating or constraining to a diverse and distinctive female population. In 1753, for the first time on record, an unmarried girl reported that she would prefer to stay single in the face of a marriage proposal. For twenty years women in Georgia had either jumped at the opportunity to marry or, in the words of this girl, had been "forced to accept." By the 1750s such opportunities and obligations were already becoming somewhat less intense, as Georgia society began to experience a quite remarkable transformation. As institutional authority dramatically increased with royal control and population explosion, the economic and social latitude previously extended to (or forced upon) women would become a faded memory. Increasingly like their counterparts in other colonies, they would operate inside of, rather than in spite of, an established patriarchal society.[67]

PART TWO

The Royal Era

CHAPTER FOUR

Immigration and Settlement

In 1752 the dwindling number of trustees surrendered their charter of government for the colony of Georgia to the king after twenty years of failing to stimulate substantial demographic or economic growth in the province. Once again utopianism had proved to be an inept midwife for the birth of a British American colony. Prohibitions on landholding and slavery had undermined the kinds of economic incentives that stimulated migration to the Chesapeake in its early years. The social, gender, and age composition of the Georgia settlers had hampered the kind of rapid population growth that the colonies of New England attained in their early evolution. In particular, the lack of young marriageable women or young married couples seriously damaged Georgia's demographic potential—explaining to some extent the inclination to abandon settlements such as Frederica or leave the province altogether. Just as military threat, economic prohibitions, imbalances in the age structure, high mortality levels, and land and community abandonment served as disincentives to colonization in the 1730s and 1740s, so the reversal of many of these factors in the decades that followed prompted a considerable change in the colony's fortunes.

The removal of the trustees and their sanctions changed the pattern of settlement of Georgia permanently, although many of their measures (such as forbidding the use of imported slaves) had already begun crumbling into disregard.[1] The sudden influx of thousands of planters, their families, and their bound labor force heralded an era of tremendous growth, the population reaching about thirty thousand by 1775.[2] No longer a struggling European experiment in these years under direct royal government, Georgia would adopt the outlook of South Carolina and the West Indies, and would rapidly integrate into the larger southern economy.

Naturally, the transition from trusteeship administration to royal government was a little messy. It was influenced by the opportunism of settlers, the personalities of newly arrived governors, and the mandates of the Board of Trade (formally, the Council of Trade and Foreign Plantations), a body appointed by the commission of the Crown since 1696 to oversee the direction of colonial business and that now issued directives directly to Georgia in place of the trustees.[3] Within twenty years or so the province became intricately connected to

Table 2. Royal Governors' Estimates of Georgia Population

	1756	1760	1761	1762	1766	1773
Whites	4,500	6,000	6,100	6,800	9,900	18,000
Blacks	1,855	3,578	3,600	4,500	7,800	15,000
Total	6,355	9,578	9,700	11,300	17,700	33,000

Sources: *Col.Rec.*, 26:415 (President Graham); 27:104 (Governor Reynolds); 28:pt. 1, 44, 178 (Governor Ellis); 28:pt. 1, 309 (Governor Wright); 28:pt. 2, 185 (Governor Wright); *Col.Rec.*, 37:141 (Governor Wright). Only Gov. James Wright's 1773 figure is likely to have been particularly inaccurate.

larger movements in the Atlantic world: great wars for empire, mass migration, the slave trade, formation of a distinctive if somewhat indistinguishable backcountry, and ultimately the erosion of British authority in the colonies. As the trustees' blueprint faded, Georgia's development drew upon both the hard-nosed practical experiences of its new immigrants and the equally hard-nosed realism of veteran colonial administrators. Concerns about settling indigent paupers or Protestant refugees disappeared. Imperial administrators were preoccupied instead with securing Indian trade, establishing a constitution and economy that best fitted the needs of empire, and protecting the southern frontier. Georgia mattered not because it was a worthy pursuit in its own right but because it was a vital piece in a much larger puzzle.

The Georgia governors and their advisers on the Board of Trade, which had been reinvigorated in 1748 when the dynamic Earl of Halifax was appointed as its president, faced something of a dilemma in resolving the most visible problem with the colony—it didn't have enough people. On the one hand, the territory needed populating as quickly and as comprehensively as possible. The province would prosper economically (through the cultivation of rice, silk, indigo, or livestock herds) only if provided with a large labor base, while it could be defended effectively and inexpensively only if it were guaranteed a large enough militia. But it was equally critical that the new migrants be governable: occupying surveyed and registered land, divided into administrative parishes or counties, not encroaching upon Creek territory, and ideally paying taxes through a lower-house assembly whose powers would be limited. Governors wanted to avoid the creation of either a bastard offshoot of plantation-dominated South Carolina, which would be indefensible, or a disorganized haven for refugees, which would be unprofitable and ungovernable. They sought to secure what James Wright, the last royal governor, called "the Middling Sort of People, such as have Families and a few Negroes," who would "most effectually People, enrich and strengthen the Province."[4] The key mechanism that the administrators used to resolve this dilemma was the land-granting system, which was designed to encourage the right migrants to flow legally into the province.

When Georgia's first royal governor, John Reynolds, arrived in 1754, he devised an attractive package to offer abundant tracts of free land to potential settlers. The system of granting these tracts, which was based on headright schemes that had already proved effective in other colonies, ensured that the authorities retained some influence over the selection of recipients—and could therefore keep tabs on both the quantity and quality of new arrivals. The land grant applications offer considerable insight into the process of settlement in the years between the trusteeship and the Revolution. Though a problematic and inconsistent data set, they sketch at least an outline of Georgia's evolution in the late colonial era and allow us to make cautious inferences about the character of the population—where people were from and where they ended up. Ratios of white to black, and adult to child, ram home the different demographic characteristics of the royal era relative to the troublesome trusteeship. Ultimately, the statistics are testament to a continued contemporary recognition of the importance of female roles in the consolidation of a stable and profitable society.

The governor and his council met at the start of each month to consider petitions for land that they could reject, make conditional, or accept. Grants were based on the principle that each applicant was entitled to a hundred acres for himself or herself and a further fifty acres "in family right" for every member of the applicant's family—which included spouses, children, indentured servants, and slaves. These allowances were then added together to create a single grant of acreage that was eventually made out to the head of household after the land had been warranted, surveyed, laid out in diagrammatic form (known as a plat), and finally signed by the governor. In September 1765 Joseph Turner submitted a prototypical petition setting forth "that he had been in the Province about six Months from Roonoke North Carolina had had no Land granted him and was desirous to obtain Land for Cultivation having a Wife and two children Therefore praying for two hundred Acres upon great Ogechee near the north Creek and about five Miles on this side a Place called old Town."[5] Petitioners could further increase their holdings in a given area by purchasing extra land from the royal government.[6] If successful, grantees were expected to clear a certain proportion of their land in a given time and to begin paying quitrents for their holdings a year after occupation (although there is little evidence that such rents were ever collected), and after a year the occupants were free to sell, bequeath, or distribute the land.[7]

In the seventeen years between 1755 and 1772, the colonial government considered 5,387 land grant applications and made 3,685 grants. If the sheer volume was a burden for the governors and their council members, they could take some comfort from the personal benefits that accrued from sitting on the land-granting committee, which gave them an opportunity to exercise a significant degree of patronage. Whether applicants were needy, well connected, reputable, married, possessed slaves and/or children, and so on ultimately determined the success of their application. While the historian Robert Lipscomb is right to emphasize that the rapid settlement of land was the committee's main concern, it was by no means the "sole purpose of policy," for it also sought to control the *type* of migrants.[8] Over time the policy formulated by the thousands of individual decisions made by the land-granting committee prompted changes in patterns of application. Frustratingly, many applications were incomplete, hundreds were postponed, and petitioners often mistook their entitlement (under- or overestimating their family right) or tried to change the location of their grant. Setting aside these problematic petitions and those concerning town lots (which did not require petitioners to outline the composition of their family group) leaves a data set of 3,689 petitions made by about 2,369 applicants.

In theory, all applications should have provided the name of the petitioner, an account of the petitioner's lands and length of residence in Georgia (or, failing that, her or his place of origin), a breakdown of the members of the family group (which determined the size of the acreage), and of course the actual location of the grant. Yet even if all applicants had provided these details, the records are silent about the age of most petitioners and their families, which bars many avenues of demographic analysis. Moreover, applicants frequently applied more than once, which seriously complicates the data set. Norman McDonald, a Highland Scot with little capital, decided to settle on the Sapelo River, where many of his countrymen lived, but the committee rejected his application in 1755, without explanation. His second application, bolstered by the inclusion of a wife and two children, was successful, and the addition of a third child in 1759 prompted him to claim a further fifty acres in Turkey Camp Swamp. The flexibility of the distribution system allowed the committee to modify or extend grants, and many names (like Norman's) recur over the years, reflecting patterns of life-cycle development: birth, marriage, widowhood, and inheritance.[9]

The evidence aggregated from these land grants registers the presence of 18,837 people in nonurban districts between 1755 and 1772. Reassuringly, this fits reasonably well with several guesstimates that dutiful royal governors sent to the Board of Trade (see table 2). Though several thousand Georgia residents, and, more important, the urban dwellers, are missing from the land grant data set, and though we might expect that at least a few hundred families never took up their lands, the data offer some useful indicators of the nature of settlement. Petitioners claimed that they held in bondage 11,143 African slaves, whose gender and age were unspecified. White adults numbered 3,370 and brought with them or raised 4,130 children. They had embarked for Georgia from across the Atlantic world—from Newfoundland, Jamaica, Maryland, Scotland, Bermuda, Ireland, New York, Barbados, Pennsylvania, England, Honduras, New Jersey, St.

Kitts, and elsewhere. Of the 291 applicants who specified their place of origin, about two-thirds had arrived from the Carolinas, a fifth from other Atlantic colonies, and the remainder from the British Isles (including Ireland). Those from South Carolina, the Caribbean, and the Chesapeake brought about five bondspeople per applicant, accounting for almost 90 percent of the slaves. Arrivals from elsewhere averaged one slave per petitioner.

The timing of immigration, as about two-fifths of the petitions indicate, reflected a variety of stimuli that pushed or pulled Euro-Americans to settle in Georgia. In contrast to the years of the trusteeship, when Old World issues frequently dictated migration patterns, most of the new arrivals in royal Georgia were responding to economic pull-me factors. Without doubt, the availability of large and fertile tracts of free land with few strings attached was the lure—not only for those with experience in plantation agriculture and large numbers of slaves but also for smaller families or those looking to start one. Immigration occurred in a series of waves that corresponded to the shifting tides of land availability.

The first wave saw the original seaboard area claimed by settlers hailing from South Carolina and the West Indies during the 1750s. James Habersham, a wealthy merchant and respected member of the Governor's Council, which acted as the Upper House of the legislature (as it was also called), as well as a court of appeals, reported that from 1750 to 1754 people came regularly to Georgia, culminating in the settlement of a Congregational township at Midway, but that immigration later declined and did not really revive until about 1760.[10] The historian David Chesnutt confirms from a purely South Carolinian perspective that interest in migrating to Georgia "subsided" between 1753 and 1756.[11]

South Carolinian tidewater planters were organically attracted to their neighboring province because of its identical natural environment. Having helped Malcontents to undermine Georgia's prohibition on slavery in the 1740s, and to overturn it on 1 January 1751, they literally capitalized on their chance to increase their landholdings and productivity—whether they were starting a new plantation from scratch or expanding an already established enterprise. For them the prime rice lands to the south of the Savannah River represented quite simply the least expensive and most profitable investment in the American colonies. Carolina had been heavily influenced in its early years by the experiences of Barbados planters, and the colony was founded in the late seventeenth century on the understanding that slavery would feature in Carolina—even before any exportable crop had been secured. By the middle of the eighteenth century, merchant-planters had established markets for rice and indigo and had institutionalized a captive African labor force in the lowcountry. Many were attracted to the ideal tidewater swamplands around Georgia's major river systems (the

Savannah, Ogeechee, Midway, Satilla, Altamaha, and later St. Marys) because of a scarcity of such lands in South Carolina. Others may have been prompted to diversify their holdings because of a depression in rice prices during the 1740s. Moreover, affluent migrants from South Carolina knew that they could benefit not only from establishing new plantations but also from controlling the growing markets in Charlestown and Savannah.[12]

Historians of the late colonial Southeast have debated the extent to which political opportunity was a further factor in influencing white male immigration. David Chesnutt argues that those men "just below the planting aristocracy of Carolina," although well above the middling rank, were unlikely to hold any major political offices and says this was an important reason for their departure to Georgia.[13] Alan Gallay has since questioned the value of attaining high political office in Georgia—noting that the vast majority of Carolinians preferred to "pursue their opportunities in Carolina."[14] If political influence was not an aspiration in itself, it was certainly imperative to migrating planters that their economic interests be effectively protected at law. Perhaps the earliest and most obvious example of the link between socioeconomic needs and legislation was the drawing up of royal Georgia's first slave code in 1755. Unsurprisingly, this was closely modeled after that of South Carolina, marking the abandonment of trustee humanitarianism: the slave code contained more restrictions and more severe punishments for blacks than previously while allowing whites larger slaveholdings.[15] Sixteen years later the Georgia Commons House of Assembly (which consisted of two representatives from each county and acted as the lower house of the legislature) continued to look to its northern neighbor for inspiration, augmenting the fees of public officials "so far as to make them Equal to those taken by Officers of the like respective denomination in South Carolina."[16] Whether the result was intended or inadvertent, the South Carolinian migrants' need to nurture their economic interests guaranteed that they would eventually dominate Georgia's government and structure a plantation economy parallel to that of South Carolina. This was as much a function of timing as of migrant numbers. By the time that Georgia's greatest population growth began about 1760, many of the influential planters (like Jonathan Bryan) had already arrived. The dusty pioneers migrating to Georgia in the 1760s and 1770s found that mechanisms of credit, labor, commerce, government, law, and even land granting were already rather monopolized by a Carolinian clique.

The second wave of migration bringing a host of new settlers to the colony was delayed several years by the declaration of war with France in 1756. While Georgia's population continued to increase at a constant baseline rate, its moments of noticeable change were dictated by major events such as war or the opening up of new lands. The dip in migration vexed Governor Reynolds, who remarked in May 1755 that "there are but very few Settlers arrive here" because of the fear of war.[17] Only eleven families arrived in 1756, according to their land applications, compared with thirty-five the previous year. The Seven Years' War, which was known as the French and Indian War in North America, where the struggle first broke out in 1754, spread across oceans and continents between 1756 and 1763, culminating in a genuinely global conflict between the great European powers. It not only tended to discourage communities and individuals from risking a dangerous Atlantic journey but also made the prospect of setting up in Georgia far less appealing. The lack of military protection in the fledgling province was a source of great consternation for all three governors before the war ended.[18] Georgia's frontier position rendered it particularly vulnerable because of the proximity and size of Indian tribes that were open to French influence in the Alabama country and Spanish influence in the Floridas. Little wonder that the few hundred Acadian refugees (of French Catholic origin) who rudely disembarked at Savannah in late 1755 were treated with such suspicion and contempt by the government and that the vast majority were elbowed out by the time the war had ended.[19] But as the arrival of the Acadians presaged, and as progress of the French and Indian War made clear, the principal theaters of conflict would remain in the North. More important, the British were gaining the upper hand, culminating in the conquest of Canada. As it became increasingly apparent that enemy forces or Indian allies in the Southeast were unlikely to make any serious incursions, Georgia was once again open for business.

The migrants who arrived in this second wave still tended to move from nearby colonies, but their origins and ambitions were more varied than those of the plantation-orientated first wave. David Chesnutt observed from his nonquantitative data that even South Carolinian settlement after 1757 was "composed primarily of small planters and non-slaveholding farmers who settled mostly in the backcountry on the Great Ogechee and the Savannah rivers."[20] More than sixty petitioners claimed to have arrived in 1759, and in that year the colonial authorities distributed a record 72,530 acres. In the subsequent three years both applications and acreage grants dropped off, reflecting that the best parcels of land had been snapped up and that fewer migrants were competing for the marginal plots.

On 10 November 1763 Governor Wright secured the Treaty of Augusta, sparking the highest rate of immigration and consequent population growth in the history of the colony. Under the treaty the Creek Indians agreed to cede about 2.4 million acres to British Georgia, a parcel more than an eighth the size of Scotland. This land cession had as much effect as the official termination of war with France in encouraging settlers (besides, the British victory had made the French and Spanish colonial presence all but inconsequential). The new land, extending south beyond the Altamaha to St. Marys River and northwesterly past Augusta to tributary branches of the Savannah, was rich, fertile, and virtually empty of whites.[21] In buying this chunk of land from the Creeks in return for minor concessions (such as the waiving of trading debts), Governor Wright was picking his way through the conflicting desires of British politicians, frontier settlers, planters, and Indian traders. But he succeeded—with Indian acquiescence, British blessing, and an American appetite—in securing an inflow of migrants that was either prohibited or improbable elsewhere.

As all eyes focused greedily upon the enormous potential of the American continent, now that the war was over, migrants to the lowcountry were inspired by the opening up of prime rice territory in the tidewater lands south of the Altamaha River, which had been made safer by the Spanish cession of Florida. To this newly ceded southern corner immigrants brought many more slaves than had their counterparts in the earlier migration; the greater number of slaves allowed the migrants to take full advantage of the sudden availability of ideal plantation lands, and competition for jurisdiction between Georgia and South Carolina prompted a bitter struggle.[22] But far more significant were the farmers and small landholders who now flooded into the backcountry, which, as the historian Kenneth Coleman has noted, constituted the best land available in the southern piedmont.[23]

Analysis of the applications for land in the royal era helps explain this parallel occupation of rich lands for slave plantations (in wetland areas) and yeoman farms (in nonwetland territory), by yielding information about the characteristics of migrants and the behavior of the land-granting committee. When the land sought is categorized as lowcountry or backcountry according to topographical precepts, the 1,833 petitions between 1755 and 1769 split almost evenly: 882 correspond to the lowcountry and 886 applications are for nonwetland territory.[24] Broadly speaking, "wetland" or "forested wetland" areas pertained to the parishes along the seaboard that many historians have used as a definition of the lowcountry: Christ Church, St. John, St. Andrew, St. James, St. David, St. Patrick, St. Thomas, and St. Mary. In modern-day Georgia this corresponds roughly to the area east of Interstate 95. However, a topographical categorization allows greater precision in the identification of land grants. Parts of these parishes were neither low nor suitable for plantation cultivation. Equally, areas in the northwest of the province were well suited to labor-intensive crops or pursuits. In fact, though migrants to the lowcountry may have applied in equal numbers to those in the northwest, those to the lowcountry tended to bring more wealth and certainly more bondspeople into Georgia—averaging 9.35 slaves per petitioner compared with a backcountry average of 2.49 slaves. But backcountry migrants dominated the postwar flood of settlement as they

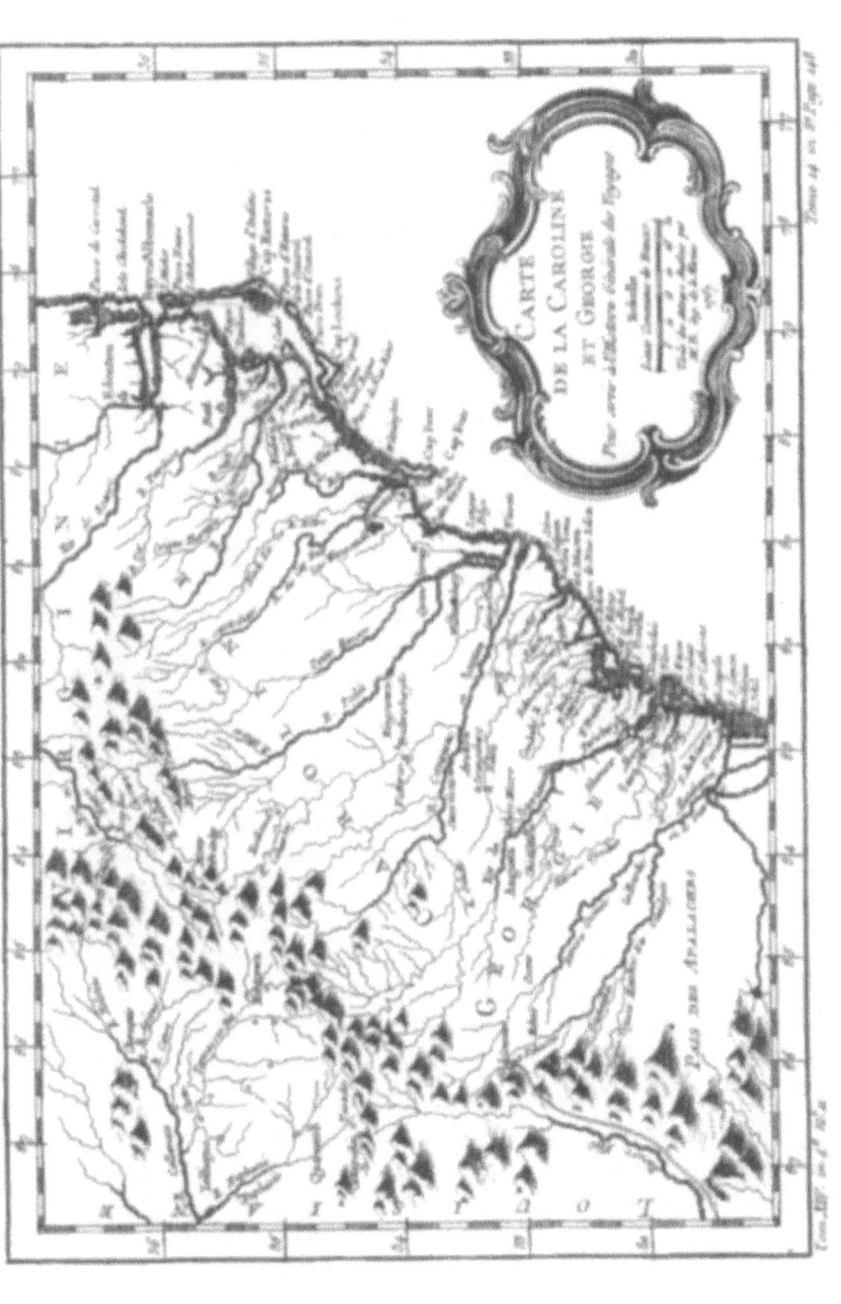

Map of Carolina and Georgia drawn by a French naval officer in 1757. This map offered information on numerous place names, topographical features (for example, mountains, river systems, and islands), and estimates of longitude and latitude (around the periphery). As it was being drawn, Georgia settlement was beginning to expand from the coastline lowcountry up the veins toward the backcountry. Courtesy of the Hargrett Rare Book and Manuscript Library, University of Georgia Libraries.

poured into the province—outnumbering their eastern counterparts in every year but one between 1763 and 1769. They settled far up beyond Augusta and filled out the sparse areas of St. George's Parish, typically reapplying for adjoining acreage to facilitate the pursuit of small-scale husbandry and especially livestock farming. Loveless Savage was one such farmer who, perhaps belying his name, registered for land next door to the plot that he, his wife, three children, and one slave "had some time improved and settled with a stock of cattle and hogs" in St. Paul's Parish in 1768.[25]

These contrasting types of settlers—lowcountry planters and backcountry farmers—were both associated with stereotypes that the royal government was desperate to avoid. According to the worst-case scenario, the lowcountry could become an insurgent society of single white male overseers running rice and indigo plantations for employers elsewhere. To circumnavigate this problem the two governors during the lowcountry migration waves made it clear that men who wanted land in Georgia would have to live in Georgia. John Reynolds's administration (1754–56) tightened up the whole process of land regulation, and the council required that men must first move their families to Georgia or put up a large bond.[26] Gov. Henry Ellis (1757–60) sought to curtail the acquisitions of even large landholders. His concern for the military and defensive implications of a slave majority led him to suggest that petitioners receive only twenty acres (instead of fifty) for each additional slave above the sixtieth.[27]

The worst-case scenario in the backcountry involved its occupation by lawless young crackers, lazy men whose sole ambition was to drink heavily, steal, and stir up trouble with the Indians. Though all three colonial governors reported banditry on the frontier, such backcountry problems would become a perennial headache for James Wright, who was in office during the third wave of migration (1761–76). He urged his General Assembly at the start of its session in October 1765 to give every possible assistance to inviting "good" settlers to cultivate and improve the ceded lands.[28] Naturally, this involved weeding out the unworthy—like Samuel Fry, who was refused a grant in August 1766 "on Account of his Bearing a Bad Character."[29] The land-granting committee believed that such people were undesirable and would contribute little to the colony's prosperity.[30] The unworthy were typecast as miscreants—wenchers, debtors, and petty criminals who were frequently blamed (especially in and around Augusta) for causing trouble with the Creeks. Like all stereotypes, these contained elements of truth—and during a short period the behavior of unruly inhabitants on the western frontier *would* help erode Anglo-Creek relations.[31]

For all their differences, the fears about both lowcountry and backcountry settlement had one thing in common: they were highly gendered. Each emphasized the negative consequences of large numbers of poor single white males.

The presence of these men, as lowcountry overseers, would result in imbalanced demographics and landownership, nonresident planters, slave disturbances, and puppet government from abroad. In the backcountry the presence of such men would result in increased criminality, uncontrollable Indian relations, and economic waste. In seeking to circumvent both eventualities, the governors and their land-granting committee recognized the need to nurture and support an extensive female presence across the white immigrant population. James Wright spoke in particular of "the many and great Advantages that will result to the Province by having a Settlement of a Number of sober, regular, and industrious, Families."[32] In 1773 he instructed Edward Barnard, captain of the Rangers (a military unit commissioned by Wright to patrol the backcountry), to compel vagrants to leave ceded lands in the northwest of the colony, but the governor qualified this by emphasizing that "if you should find any familys there . . . you may suffer them to continue."[33] Vagrancy was perceived as being at the evil end of a moral polarity that elevated "the family," and therefore women-as-mothers, to a righteous and transcendent instrument of settlement.

The behavior of the land-granting committee, through its power to sanction legal habitation, provides a quantitative manifestation of the government's intentions. About two-thirds of the applications (65.86 percent) were from men with wives. Of these applicants, more than three-quarters (77.28 percent) had five slaves or fewer. The new arrivals in Georgia were responding to the well-tailored demands of the royal colonial authorities. Wives were naturally as central to the royal Georgia plan as they had been to the original trustees' formation, but unlike the trustees, whose remarks on the subject were overt in their propaganda publications of the 1730s, the royal authorities offered only indirect and implicit acknowledgment of wives' importance. The royal officials did not publish their intentions with the clarity or zeal of their predecessors, but the actions of the land-granting committee spoke louder than words and were evidently heard by its target audience.

Put simply, a petitioner's marital status played a statistically significant part in determining whether he was successful in obtaining a land grant. Though the committee turned down only 4 percent of applicants, being married appears to have dramatically increased one's chances of success, alongside other considerations.[34] A petitioner's bid obviously improved if a committee member could verify the petitioner's claims or vouch for the petitioner's character. Rejection was more likely to occur when applicants were strangers—such as William Evans, whose presence in Georgia for six months was insufficient to warrant his being allowed a grant near Augusta until he "brings his family into the province and a Certificate of his character." In October 1770 two absentee applicants were denied, Ezekiel Williams of South Carolina, "till he comes to reside in the province," and Thomas Wilson, "till he attends and produces a certificate of his character."[35] The authorities were increasingly on the lookout not only for petitioners of debatable character but also for men lying about the amount of land for which they qualified—for instance, by pretending to be married.[36] Land grant applications by single men were rejected more than twice as often as those submitted by their married counterparts. In attaching marital status to landownership in this way, royal authorities transcribed their urgent need for women into an ideal of masculinity that placed added emphasis upon the importance of being a husband—of existing as the nucleus of a familial molecule, not just as an independent atom. The evolution of a distinctive form of paternalism would become more defined in the next decades, as I explore in chapter 6. If the trusteeship had borne witness to the impact of gender upon settlement, with its communities dependent upon a female presence to perform supposedly "female" tasks, the royal era testified to the reverse, insisting that settlement could equally affect social constructions of relations between the genders, by describing and defining ideals among society's men and women.

The governors' measures provoked something of a response from their target audience, for the proportion of married applicants rose noticeably from an average of about 58 percent in the first three years of the records to 66 percent throughout the period 1759–72. And while the land grants indicate that the proportion of white adult women remained constant, about 34 percent during the royal era, the new arrivals—unlike their trusteeship counterparts—were producing children at rates comparable to those of other late colonial populations' (for instance, the population of Bristol, Rhode Island, as estimated by John Demos).[37] This reflected, above all, that most of them had come directly from other late colonial populations. The stabilizing of sex and age ratios during the 1750s and 1760s, concurrent with the arrival of a majority of colonists unfamiliar and uninfluenced by earlier Georgia courtship patterns, meant that many earlier sociodemographic traits faded as Georgia's communities began to merge into a heterogeneous whole. For the majority of white settlers courtship was less likely to involve girls aged thirteen to sixteen, less likely to be brief, and less likely to span long distances—whether geographic, linguistic, or religious.

One unlikely source provides a useful indication of perceptions of adulthood and progression through the familial life cycle. Wills written by parents (and other relatives) often left conditional bequests to children, requiring that they would receive them only when they had reached a certain age or "come of age." Little variance is displayed in those conditional bequests to young men, who could almost always expect to inherit control of their assets at twenty or older, usually twenty-one. Twenty-seven wills that outline such clauses for female children specify acquisition ages ranging more widely, from sixteen to twenty-one.

On average they stipulate an age of 19.1 years at which young women were deemed to have "come of age," and parents were confident that these young women could assume control of (sometimes substantial) bequests. Furthermore, 41 percent of these conditional clauses stipulated that the bequest would immediately fall to the female upon marriage as a kind of postmortem dowry. In other words, a substantial proportion of parents expected that their female children would be married before they had reached the age of full adulthood. The ages specified in these testamentary stipulations show little disparity between wealthy and poor testators. Planters in St. John's Parish such as Matthew Smallwood, who specified that his only daughter, Mary, should receive his entire estate upon marriage or at the age of sixteen, held the same conceptions of their children's adulthood as Savannah saddlers like Palser Miller. Successful Indian traders like Isaac Barksdale made the same provisions as hard-up carpenters such as Barak Norman, whose daughter's inheritance at age eighteen was largely dependent upon the amount snapped up by his many creditors.[38]

As a result of these stipulations, as well as information from other sources and records, a picture can be sketched of expected patterns of personal development among whites in late colonial Georgia. The majority of settlers regarded females as marriageable at about fifteen and considered that young women had reached full adulthood—by which they meant psychological maturity rather than physical development—at about nineteen. In fact, the vast majority were married (for the first time) before the age of twenty-two. Georgia women, then, probably married at younger ages than their counterparts elsewhere: Galenson estimates a mean age at first marriage of 20 to 23 for New England women and gives figures of 25 to 27 for the brides of Old England, although more recent analysis of English population history has this figure two years younger, at 23 to 25.[39] Georgia males rarely married during their teenage years, which gave them time to inherit and/or establish their own fortune before entering into courtship and marriage during their early to midtwenties—and sometimes later. Girls usually became receptive to (and engaged in) courtship between the ages of fourteen and eighteen, and the evolution of courtship for both male and female was heavily dependent upon parental attitudes as well as local community protocols (see chapter 6). However, these general trends conceal significant variance in courtship patterns and customs among the various communities that made up late colonial Georgia.

Attempting to measure the average number of children per family from the land grant data in any given year is rather awkward, not least because we can assume that most people chose to reapply only when they had already produced another mouth to feed—another mouth for which they could claim fifty acres. In other words, it is not reasonable to simply compare the overall petitions for, say, 1762 with those of 1772 because at least 543 applicants applied for additional acreage several years after their first land grant. However, assuming that those people who did *not* reapply had *not* had more children (for otherwise they would likely have claimed land), and that their family size was therefore static, it is possible to factor in the yearly arrival of new children to estimate that the overall average number per family was gently rising, worth an extra fifth of a child in the decade between 1762 and 1772. On average, married land applicants registered 2.92 children in their last known petitions. This figure may seem unimpressive as far as completed family size goes, but it shows that many migrants brought families that were relatively young. Families with one to three children predominated among all applicants, for few unions had yet reached their full capacity—though by the second half of the period in question (1764–72) a far greater proportion of applicants registered more than three children than had done so earlier. Those who reapplied for land were likely to average another 1.5 children, and at least 809 children were born into families that had already claimed land.

Other sources provide some support for my tentative conjecture of a comparatively young population, provoked to migrate by land shortage, lower social status, and/or opportunism. Chesnutt identified a number of South Carolinians who were living in Georgia in 1759, noting that several factors "suggest that they were probably young men who were just beginning their careers," while Betty Wood emphasized that for younger sons, "Georgia held out the tantalizing promise of an upward social mobility apparently denied them in South Carolina."[40] In marked contrast to those who had traveled across the Atlantic during the trusteeship, many "next-generation" immigrants to Georgia from other colonies in British America were able to retain kinship, social, and therefore economic links with their place of origin. Indeed, a common feature of Georgia immigration—whether in the lowcountry or the backcountry—was the importance of kinship networks to settlement patterns. In many cases the arrival of families was staggered over several years. Only when a given area of land was in high demand was it likely that relatives would be split up across any significant distance. To avoid such difficulties John Graves of South Carolina attempted to submit his own petition and one for his brother at the same time. Other prospective immigrants took fewer risks, and large groups encompassing several families often arranged their settlement months or years in advance—such as the Bermuda families who moved to St. Marys River in 1766, or the Dunn families who moved from South Carolina to Buck Head in 1764.

Of course, blood relations were not the only groups that settled together in Georgia. Neighbors and even whole communities often relocated in entirety or partially. Indeed, a high proportion of new arrivals migrated as whole communities, including the Puritans, who had moved inexorably south from Massachusetts by way of Dorchester, South Carolina, to form the congregation at Midway in the early 1750s. Several Quaker families from North Carolina arrived to establish Wrightsborough in February 1768 under the leadership of Joseph Maddock, and many others were to follow in subsequent years.[41] Other groupings were occupational: in 1764 a number of shipmates in the Royal Navy decided to settle on the Great Ogeechee, acquiring neighboring tracts; they included the captain, first lieutenant, surgeon, and a number of "indentured servants" who were most probably crew members. Typically green offshoots of older societies, these small communities were driven to move by the prospect of localized religious homogeneity and economic prosperity, as well as the comfort and familiarity of old acquaintances—often, but not always, across kinship networks. Better supported and connected than their trusteeship counterparts, they were well placed to take advantage of the high-water mark of the first British empire. Their societal models and expectations, though far from homogeneous, were simply more workable than those of their European precursors'. The pattern of settlement for these communities heralded changes in gender and in women's roles in the colony that facilitated Georgia's swift absorption into a southern way.

As table 3 shows, more than half of all married women registered on land granted in Georgia between 1755 and 1772 lived in households that did not own African slaves. These women, together with their husbands and children, probably performed duties that were typical of most eighteenth-century subsistence-based farming families. About 70 percent settled in nonwetland territory where livestock and crop farming were easiest, and away from the eastern tidewater and swamplands, which were best suited to plantation agriculture. Arrivals from northern colonies (North Carolina, Virginia, Maryland, and Pennsylvania were the largest contributors) were accustomed to oak and hickory land, or pine barrens for lumber and livestock pasturage. Many no doubt migrated down to the foot of the piedmont as a result of Indian disturbances or to evade the kinds of grievances that found expression in the Regulator movements—including contests about landownership and high taxation.[42] The proliferation of creeks and streams that fed into the larger Atlantic river systems, particularly the Savannah's, provided an environment fertile enough for their needs (and by the early nineteenth century it would prove viable for cotton growing). Their small family-operated farms yielded little commercial output but provided livestock and grains for home consumption, along with small quantities of tobacco, flax and hemp, and forest products. These households, which often eked out a miserly existence, shared much in common with the antebellum Carolinian yeomanry described by Stephanie McCurry, with women playing a

Table 3. Slaveholding among Applicants for Land

Slaves in Household	Number of Applicants	Percentage of Applicants	Total Slaves	Percentage of Slaves	Average No. of Children per Married Applicant
None	1,104	54.49%	0	0.00%	2.97
1–5	483	23.84	1,164	10.45	2.79
6–10	171	8.44	1,340	12.03	2.97
11–20	135	6.66	2,002	17.97	2.61
21–40	78	3.85	2,474	22.20	3.25
More than 40	55	2.71	4,163	37.36	3.41
Total	2,026	100.00%	11,143	100.00%	2.91

"critical role" in securing self-sufficiency and in transforming some items of household production into market exchange.[43]

The 190 wives identified as living in households with more than ten slaves are, for obvious reasons, likely to have led lives extremely different from their backcountry counterparts'. These women often arrived in Georgia only after the preliminary clearing and often building had been accomplished; they brought with them fashionable habits and accoutrements from Charlestown, where they retained important social contacts. By the early 1760s the colony contained, according to Gray and Wood, "a pyramid-shaped distribution of landholders with a handful of large, slave-owning rice planters at the apex and small family farms with one or no slaves at the bottom; precisely the class structure which the Trustees [had been] determined to avoid."[44] Two hundred sixty-eight land applicants claimed among them a total of eight-five hundred slaves, a group that represented more than three-quarters of all blacks who were declared in the land applications as being held in bondage. Land grant applicants with the highest numbers of slaves tended also to have a higher average number of children in their families, suggesting that these applicants were further advanced in their familial evolution upon arrival. Although family wealth usually meant a more varied diet for children, constant nursing, and more opportunity to escape outbreaks of disease such as smallpox, it is unlikely that the higher average number of children is solely a reflection of infant survivorship.[45] If many backcountry migrants moved into the colony because they had nothing to lose, slaveholding whites on the eastern seaboard had much to gain.

Joseph Gibbons, a member of a wealthy South Carolinian family, arrived in Georgia with his wife, Hannah, three children, and thirty-one slaves in 1755.[46] Hannah gave birth four more times at intervals of no more than eleven months, two and a half years, two years, and four years. The Gibbonses acquired slaves rapidly, building a captive labor force of 106 blacks by March 1766 to work on plantations on the Newport and Altamaha rivers. At his death in July 1769 Joseph left 8,834 acres in Georgia to be divided among his eight children and his widow. Other members of the Gibbons family, including John Martin (father-in-law), John (brother), and William (brother), settled nearby. William, like his older brother, steadily increased his household size from two children and eighteen slaves in 1756 to six children and seventy-one slaves twelve years later. From secondary sources it is apparent that William was often concerned about the welfare of his labor force. In 1765 he paid more than twelve pounds sterling to doctors for thirty-nine medicinal items—a variety that included febrifuges, tonics, anodynes, and worm powders. Between May and June of the same year he also paid Henry Bourquin more than two pounds for treating his slave Peter and for "sundry dressings . . . of a negro fellows finger."[47] According to the land grant data, at this stage he claimed to own forty-two slaves, which makes it possible to estimate that Gibbons spent, on average, more than seven shillings per slave on medicine. This expenditure was more likely to have been made on the ground of protecting his investment than any altruistic bent: at least two blacks took the risk of running away from the Gibbons plantation—"a short well set black Ebo fellow named Nero" in 1768 and "a Negro Wench named Darque or Darchus," who had run away in 1769 with her eight- or nine-month-old child. Gibbons believed that Darque might "be harboured in or near Savannah, as she has many acquaintances in and about that town." He advertised, seeking the whereabouts of both fugitives, in the *Georgia Gazette*.[48]

Between the small group of wealthy slaveholders and the far more numerous less-affluent backcountry yeomanry lay a wide spectrum of inhabitants, many of whom owned small numbers of slaves and who accounted for about a third of land applicants. Some were failed planters who had fled creditors with whatever they could take with them. Others were freshly arrived from outside South Carolina or the Caribbean and sought to enmesh themselves in the network of power that had been so swiftly constructed. Still more would gradually invest in what labor they could afford to, in order to supplement their own household income and ultimately guarantee financial solvency for their future generations. The tidal wave of slavery largely drowned the use of indentured servants by those of middling stature, and although servants did continue to arrive in small numbers from provincial parts of the British Isles, they were rarely a cost-effective alternative to enslaved Africans. In January 1771 the *Hopewell* arrived with a number of Scots-Irish servants from Belfast and dozens of families that settled in the vicinity of Queensborough. They were joined in March 1772 by 217 colonists from Ireland, brought aboard the *Brittania*. Both Thomas Brown (who brought 108 people from the Orkney Islands in September 1774) and William Manson (who brought 100 from Newcastle upon Tyne a year later) organized boatloads of indentured servants to settle Friendsborough Township.[49]

Females constituted a minority, only about 4 percent, of land applicants. Two-thirds of these women were widows, running households that ranged from Elizabeth Anderson's small plot in St. George's Parish with her remaining child to Elizabeth Elliott Butler's ten thousand acres in St. Phillip's Parish, where she had amassed more than 131 slaves by 1771. In general, female applicants could expect munificent treatment from the land-granting authorities, partly because of their concerns about balancing the demographics of the province. The illustrious Elizabeth Butler, for instance, was turned down only once, in August 1768, because the governor wanted the same land. Widows' applications increased over time, as more male landowners died and left land and/or slaves to their relicts. Many of these widows sought to collect on grants for which their husbands had applied but had not yet formally occupied at the time of their demise. Other widows simply required more acreage than that which had been left to them in wills or as dowers. Ann Moodie had been renting property in Savannah for a year when her husband died, leaving her with six children and no land until her petition was granted. After her husband died, Mary Venning requested that she be allowed to "take out his Majesty's Grant for the said Lot in her own Name the better to enable her to educate and bring [up] her Family" of five children.[50] Most widows (75.44 percent) still had children to provide for in the household, and widows were more likely than other applicants to have large numbers of slaves.[51]

Even widows who had immigrated from other colonies were freely given land grants. Among them was Jean Graham, who arrived from Pennsylvania with sons aged eleven and seventeen; she was "desirous of finding an Asylum and Protection in this Province" in 1759. The affluent Heriot Crooke from St. Kitts brought dozens of slaves and repeatedly harassed the committee to protect the interests of her children and grandchildren. Ann Wilkins was organized enough to purchase four hundred acres in Georgia before she even left South Carolina with her three children and twenty-six slaves to claim her headright on Satilla River in 1766.[52]

Widows' petitions could be expected to pull on the heartstrings of the paternalistic land granters. The governors and committee members were, after all, in the rather attractive position of being able to bestow large chunks of property at no personal loss—and could look to enhance their reputation among the elite by favoring prosperous but single female arrivals. The petitioners milked this advantage: widows' applications were wordier than others and carefully tailored to appeal to the land granters. The women frequently included justifications that belied many widows' relative prosperity. Thus two years after

Jane Barnard's husband died in 1757, she found herself "greatly in want" of land on which to graze her cattle; ten years after his death she possessed more than one thousand acres and twenty slaves. Mary Shortner requested a tract "for the better support of herself and her family." Sarah Fryer begged to be allowed to take up her husband's grant "the better to enable her to bring up and educate her said [eight] children." Beseechingly phrased and eloquently expressed, some applications from women received abnormal latitude from the authorities. Ann Fitch, owner of thirty slaves, went so far as to obtain a caveat and win a ruling against two men; their grants were revoked because their lands would "deprive her of the Front of her Land whereon She is Settled and made large Improvements."[53] Hannah Vincent was more premeditative, obtaining a further grant in addition to her one thousand acres on the ground that "if granted to any other person [it] would be very inconvenient for her," since this tract led from her property down to the Great Ogeechee River.[54]

Even when female petitioners' claims to land were dubious, the authorities were likely to be beneficent. Sarah Breed sought one hundred acres on Tybee Island on the ground that her father-in-law, Edward Townsend, who had died intestate of yellow fever, had "always in his Life-Time expressed his Desire that the Petitioner should enjoy the said Land and would have given her a legal Assurance thereof had he not been suddenly taken."[55] Winiwood Mackintosh nonchalantly claimed that her brother Roderic had signed over to her five hundred acres near Darien but that the documentation for the transfer was "lost or mislaid." (Her petition was rejected not because her claim was spurious but because the area had already been reserved for settlers from Williamsburgh, South Carolina.)[56] The authorities' generous attitude toward female petitioners, like their favoring of married males, underlines again the committee's concern with the population makeup of the province. Its measures coaxed many widows into remaining in Georgia, rather than returning to their place of origin, even though most had lived in the province for only a few years when their husband died.

The character of widowhood, as evidenced in the land grants, had changed dramatically since the trusteeship. Whereas few early women had been large landowners (with the notable exception of the "Empress" Mary Musgrove Matthews Bosomworth), widows in the royal era owned significant amounts of acreage, cattle, and bondspeople. Given a generous dower or simply a good source of credit, widows no longer felt quite so constrained to remarry. Within three months of the death of her husband, Robert, in November 1766, Mary Bevill was embarking upon a joint venture with three men to erect a saw mill upon Brier Creek, where she presumably employed the nine slaves she had inherited, but she took none of her partners as her husband.[57] The likes of Elizabeth Butler, Abigail Minis, and Jane Barnard slipped effortlessly into the role of widow-matriarch, comfortable enough at the head of a large family to eschew suitors. Remarriage remained more commonplace among those with less wealth and especially among widowed mothers looking to protect the interests of their children.

Just as it was common for widows to claim in their own names land for which their late husband had petitioned, so it was common for the spouses of those who remarried to seek to maximize upon their union. Of course, the vast majority of remarriage petitions were made by the new husband and encompassed not only the acreage for which their new wife was eligible but also any allowances for new stepchildren, each of whom qualified for fifty acres. John Niess, for instance, as a result of his marriage to Luke Greger's widow, was awarded a grant in the name of Christian Greger, his stepson, and it was Niess's to manage until the seven-year-old came of age.[58] John Wilson wanted his new wife, Mary, to have redress in the form of a parcel of land for the "considerable sum of [his] money" she had spent on the maintenance and education of her children by her first husband, Christian Riedelsperger. Mary took up the case in January 1768 after John Wilson's petition had been postponed. She explained that her first husband, Riedelsperger, had been born illegitimate and had died indebted and intestate, meaning that their land had been escheated (i.e., had reverted to the Crown) upon his death, and neither she nor her children had therefore received their headrights; the governor rejected her claim because he could not grant escheated lands without express permission. Although these claims were opportunistic, the stewardship of stepchildren's lands was a temporary post, and a woman who became a single parent upon the death of her husband and then married again stood to gain from ensuring that her new husband duly claimed her headright and her children's headrights (i.e., their combined acreage allowances), so long as they had not yet been granted. It was, after all, theoretically outside a guardian's power to dispose of property in another's name—as William Norton discovered to his disappointment when in September 1768 he tried to sell land that his late mother-in-law, Lucy Mouse, had bequeathed to his son.[59]

Other ways of capitalizing on a new marriage included building up small land empires around a widow's existing holdings: Francis Arthur purchased two hundred acres of pineland adjacent to property that his wife, Mary, owned on Bermuda Island in September 1765.[60] Such actions not only facilitated the efficient harvesting of crops and resources but also solidified the merger of two families; in this way a new husband could establish a family base without threatening the existing property of the widow and by displaying a commitment to their joint marital enterprise.

The remaining third of female applications were lodged because a spinster or minor had inherited slaves, which entitled the survivor to fifty acres for each slave now in her "family." Again, unsurprisingly, most applications were brought by male relatives of the spinster in question "on her behalf." Fathers, guardians, uncles, in-laws, male neighbors, and trustees all took measures—whether selfless or selfish—to ensure that these (often young) women received their due, which was not insubstantial, averaging seven slaves. These slaves were generally incorporated into the household in which the spinster lived—though a number may have been hired out or simply employed by the guardian until the girl's marriage or coming of age. Other spinster petitions involved the direct inheritance of property—usually when a patriarch died without male heirs.[61]

The colonial administration, then, did much more than hand out vast amounts of free land to the waves of immigrants between 1755 and 1772. No matter what the immigrants' religion or their origin (French Catholics excepted), the administrators welcomed with open arms the requests of married men and families that came to live in Georgia, and of women widowed there; the officials were careful and considerate in protecting the interests of the widows' children. In contrast, administrators confronted lone males and absentee requests with pursed lips and suspicion. Still, the settlers poured in, unevenly and eclectically dispersed around the major transportation waterways and dependent upon networks of kinship and religion as well as agronomy and land suitability. By the early 1770s Henry Yonge, the surveyor general of lands, reported with certainty that the decent land was again running out. Estimating that only three thousand "plantable" acres remained—and noting that these were dispersed in small parcels in far-off locations—he concluded that the "Pine Lands remote from Navigable rivers are unprofitable, and even Useless for the Timber, and the Salt Water Marshes being Boggy sunken Lands are only Improveable at a heavy Expense, and Labour."[62] The amount of acreage granted in the colony had been in sharp decline since 1769.[63]

Yet Governor Wright announced in December 1773 that the population exceeded 18,000 whites and 15,000 blacks—nearly twice that of his 1766 estimate.[64] This apparent discrepancy is probably not as dramatic as it seems—Wright probably overstated the population in 1773 by as many as 4,000 (or 12 percent).[65] But two other factors figured prominently. The average number of children per family was rising throughout the 1750s and 1760s, and by the 1770s the province probably was reaping the demographic rewards of the comparatively high proportion of young families (both black and white) who had migrated there. Despite the momentous interruptions of the Revolutionary War, the general upsurge in fertility evidently continued, for by 1800 Georgia's white women aged sixteen to forty-four had the highest number of children younger than ten per thousand in all the United States.[66] At the same time the mortality rate was dropping—at least among white settlers—as more of the population than ever lived in upland areas away from the malarial swamps and more people were seasoned to the sultry climate.

It was also evident by 1773 that more and more inhabitants of the backcountry were not living on properly registered and surveyed lands but were squatting, or "straggling," and as Capt. Edward Barnard lamented on 8 January, they "paid little or no regard" to authority.[67] A second reason, then, for the discrepancy between diminishing land grants and population growth in the early 1770s was that migration had continued beyond the confines of officially grantable plots—echoing what had occurred during the early 1760s. The solution was obvious: it was time to acquire more land from the Indians.

The so-called New Purchase of 1773, like previous cessions, was the direct product of pressure for land. Tracts of frontier territory in northwestern (and to some extent southern) Georgia were released like a safety valve whenever Euro-Americans' desire for settlement exceeded the bounds of land availability and Native American reluctance. On this occasion the valve released more than 1.5 million acres known as the Ceded Lands (modern-day Wilkes County), and they attracted hundreds of families from American colonies and other locations in the British Empire. The Ceded Lands were effectively sold by the Cherokees to the royal government, in order to redeem debts they owed to Indian traders.[68] Though a number of Creeks disputed the sale, laying claim to the lands between the Ogeechee and Oconee rivers, Governor Wright brushed aside their appeals, using trading embargoes as sanctions until the Creeks made a disgruntled compromise.

Wright planned to recoup the money spent on the New Purchase by selling acreage in the Ceded Lands rather than giving it away.[69] This was more than just an easy way of raising revenue—at a time when British officials were finding that increasingly difficult to do in the American colonies. The great advantage of selling land rather than distributing it for free, as Wright explained in a letter to Lord Hillsborough, secretary of state for the colonies, was that people of substance would settle in the area: "They will, of course, be something better than the common sort of back country people," he observed.[70] He was averse to the continued presence of infiltrators, people who had settled, unauthorized, in crude huts and whose hunting and plundering was also angering the Creeks. Habersham, in his capacity as acting governor while Wright was in London, issued a proclamation banishing the trespassers, who were apparently "by no means the sort of people that should settle those lands."[71] Battling doggedly to secure a moral society, Wright looked again to families and communities—not rogue males. Between 1773 and 1775 he orchestrated the arrival of about three hundred families, and, according to records compiled by R. S. Davis (a cross section of 183 arrivals), 45 percent were female, more than 90 percent of the adults were married, and the average number of children per family was more than four.[72] These were large young families hailing principally from North Carolina (47 percent), South Carolina (27 percent), Virginia (13 percent), and Maryland (7 percent).

Ironically, only on the eve of tumultuous revolution did the consolidation of settlement in Georgia find expression—in normalized gender ratios, improved birthrates, a flourishing plantation economy, and a growing administrative structure.[73] Between May and October 1772, no fewer than seven new justices of the peace were appointed to handle the needs of the growing populations of St. George's Parish, Sunbury, Queensborough, and (unusually) the Creek country.[74] With its two overlapping worlds of lowcountry and backcountry, slave majority on the tidewater, and deteriorating relations with western Indians, Georgia had graduated in thirty years to the status of a southern province in more than a purely geographical sense. The death penalty for horse stealing in the colony, for instance, was commuted in 1773 in recognition that English legal practice was inappropriate "in these Southern Provinces."[75] The Caribbean was becoming equally alien: a year later Lachlan McIntosh warned his traveling son Jack about the different "fashions" and the dangers of "vicious and immoral company" in *Jamaica*.[76]

What lay at the heart of Georgia's newfound southern identity was not the institution of slavery per se. Slavery was legal, after all, in every one of Britain's Atlantic colonies in the mid-eighteenth century—slaves were owned and recognized from Quebec to Florida and from the Ohio Valley to the Caribbean. Heavy concentrations of enslaved Africans and their enslaved descendants could be found in the towns of the late colonial North—Boston, New York, Newport, and Philadelphia—as well as on the tobacco and wheat plantations of the Chesapeake and along the tidewater of South Carolina. Slavery alone could not render Georgia southern. But the converging attitudes toward race, sexuality, and gender carried in by migrants between 1750 and 1775 underwrote the development of an identifiably southern society (see chapter 6).

By the middle of the eighteenth century, European settlers had long established firm parameters for the institutions of slavery in the Americas. So while, as Ira Berlin has most adeptly demonstrated with reference to North America, the structure and format of slaveries varied significantly over time and space, slavery (in whatever form) had become an entrenched part of life in the Americas—indeed, one of its most distinguishing features.[77] Capturing Africans, shipping them across the Atlantic Ocean, selling them off, and forcing them to live, labor, and frequently die in a new locale had become so feasible that throughout the eighteenth century alone, about six million people were transported to the Americas—more than one person every ten minutes for a hundred years. Although the purpose of slavery was quite simple—a socially determined condition that allowed one person to exploit the labor of someone else—British colonists in the seventeenth and early eighteenth centuries had sluggishly refined and aligned their racial, sexual, legal, and social definitions to manufacture an enduring engine of exploitation. The condition of slavery transformed humans into property, forced laborers for the duration of their life who would pass on their subaltern status to their children through the female line. The condition was stringently demarcated: limited racially to nonwhite peoples (and increasingly black ones), enforced legally and physically, and transferable from one owner to another, though some slaves were harder to transfer than others. A Georgia doctor, Noble W. Jones, complained about one of his more recalcitrant bondswomen in a letter to his wife: "I have no expectations of selling Dye, and believe must do the best we can to try to conquer her."[78]

Georgia administrators debated whether to legalize slavery in the province before 1751, and Georgia settlers brought thousands of slaves in the subsequent decades. They therefore had a pretty clear idea of what American slavery was—in a way that their antecedents had not in the early decades of settlement of Virginia or Barbados (or, for that matter Hispaniola, New Amsterdam, or Saint Domingue). Georgia slavery, first fully articulated in a slave code of 1755, was a variant of British American slavery that was modeled along lines already drawn in South Carolina. As chattel property, slaves had no legal rights to private lives and had no protection under the law. They were prohibited—among other things—from taking any physical action against whites, learning how to read and write, assembling in large numbers, traveling, visiting, working or bearing firearms without a permit, testifying in court, wearing ostentatious clothing, and beating drums and blowing horns in slave quarters. Recommended punishments included execution by hanging or by fire for major crimes (such as violent resistance or plotting insurrection), and whipping with horsewhips or sticks, shackling, jailing, or a spell in the workhouse for other misdemeanors. Perhaps the cruelties associated with slavery are best evidenced, however, in the measures that the Georgia General Assembly would *not* countenance. The code rather vaguely prohibited owners from working their slaves for more than sixteen hours a day or on the sabbath; from murdering, starving, or burning them (which brought a fine); or from "Barbarity," such as castration, cutting out tongues or eyes, or scalding.[79]

As table 3 shows, most bondspeople in Georgia were owned by a small number of planters who laid claim to twenty-one slaves or more in their application for land. According to late colonial land applications, about 60 percent of slaves were owned in a large unit of twenty-one or more, about 30 percent were owned as part of a moderate unit of six to twenty bondspeople, and about 10 percent were part of a smaller unit of one to five slaves. We might generally expect that the slaves' work patterns were correlated to the size of their owners' slaveholdings, but larger holdings could be divided across a number of plantations and town dwellings, while individuals and small groups of slaves often found their labor hired out by their owners, depending on their own skills and their owners' circumstances.

Although little evidence exists regarding the growing enslaved population of late colonial Georgia, blacks' demography clearly displayed properties that were distinct from those identifiable among the Euro-American populace. Because each application simply recorded the number of slaves owned (or the number added since the applicant's previous grant), the land grant data sadly leave no information pertaining to black sex ratios or ages; in subsequent chapters I will make use of alternative sources, such as runaway advertisements, to embellish on enslaved experiences in the colony. But people of African origin clearly constituted the largest block of new arrivals in royal Georgia, bought firsthand in chains from the kingdoms of western and central Africa, or secondhand from the islands of the Caribbean, where they had been creolized, and the mainland American colonies. Relegated to a legal status that did not recognize them as people, the slaves of necessity erected physical and psychological walls that have left few historical windows on their brutally exploited lives. However, despite their damning skin color(s), Georgia's earliest bondspeople were actually extraordinarily diverse in their *recent* origins, before the direct shipment of slaves from Africa was regularized in the final third of the century. Those who had already suffered slavery in Jamaica, Virginia, Mobile, St. Kitts, or the Carolinas brought customs, practices, and assumptions about economics, religion, race, and gender, no less than their white owners did.

From an analysis of 202 inventories and lists between 1755 and 1777, Betty Wood established that in Georgia the "ratio of slave men to women on all estates was in the region of 146 to 100," or 59.3 percent men and 40.6 percent women.[80] Slave-owning migrants appreciated that slave reproduction was an easy route to increasing owners' capital—and a route that differentiated mainland North America from the Caribbean islands, where the punishing nature of sugar production undermined black fertility.[81] As Jennifer Morgan has argued, South Carolina slaveholders often articulated the social and economic value of slave women, mainly through purchasing and bequeathing patterns.[82] Drawing on more than a century of inherited familiarity with the Atlantic slave trade, the Georgia settlers appear to have actually brought fractionally *more* females than the 35.8 percent calculated by Peter Wood in neighboring South Carolina. The overall sex ratio among arriving slaves in North America, about two males per female, varied by ethnic group. Some ethnic groups, such as Mandingo and Ibo, were near the African coast; slaves from these groups included about 50 percent women. Other groups, such as Bambara and Hausa, lived as much as eight hundred miles inland; slaves from these groups were almost all male.[83]

Information about thirty-three ships that disembarked slaves in Georgia between 1766 and 1774, available from the *Trans-Atlantic Slave Trade* database, indicates that about 41 percent of Africans were embarked from Senegambia, 22 percent from Sierra Leone and the Windward Coast, 8 percent from Angola, and 7 percent from the Gold Coast—a fairly low proportion of Angolans, considering the significance of the region as a source of human captives in the wider transatlantic slave trade.[84] In all, these voyages brought 5,617 Africans to Georgia in ships built in Britain (57 percent), the Chesapeake (29 percent), and New England and the Middle Colonies (14 percent). The ships varied in size, with the smallest carrying 56 slaves and the largest 392, but on average they bore a human cargo of 196 people. Only two ships left details of the length of their voyage from Senegambia and the Windward Coast to Savannah; both took about sixty-seven days to make the crossing. In all, 839 Africans died in the time it took to cross the Atlantic, a Middle Passage mortality rate of about 7.7 percent.

Lutheran pastors remarked as early as 1750 that the two principal uses of blacks in Georgia were work and reproduction. They identified a direct causal link between reproduction and the fact that often "a Negro man is permitted to have as many women and a Negro woman as many men as they like," a practice that the ministers described as a "loathsome horror."[85] Many West Africans would have been familiar and comfortable with the "horror" of polygamy, and it is not an infeasible assertion that on occasion polygamy was transplanted across the Atlantic to exist as a basis for sexual reproduction on larger plantations. But how representative this observation was is impossible to determine, and on another occasion pastor Bolzius stated categorically that slaves had no choice but were forced to take as wives or husbands whomever the master gave them.[86]

The age structure of the Georgia slave population was similarly a reflection first of the patterns predominant in South Carolina and second of the demands of those involved in direct Atlantic trading in the 1760s and 1770s. Plantation owners, hence merchants, expressed a preference for young labor—usually people younger than twenty-five. Skilled and seasoned slaves in this age range constituted the most expensive investment a planter could make, and imports concentrated unerringly upon this age group. In 1773 the merchants Telfair, Cowper, and Telfair expressed that in their opinion the most "advantageous," or profitable, slaves in the Georgia market were "prime Men & Women, with a few Boys & Girls, the Men & Women not exceeding twenty five years of age."[87]

Despite the relatively even sex ratio and an age distribution unusually weighted toward young adults, Georgia's early slaves initially failed to achieve a high birthrate. According to Betty Wood, between 1755 and 1777 the number of children per slave woman in Georgia averaged less than one.[88] A few qualitative sources indicate that owners bemoaned this slow rate of natural increase, which was particularly galling to those for whom children represented long-term financial capital. James Habersham, for instance, stated in 1772 that "until a year or two past, the Births in my Family fell considerably short of the Number I bought and dyed."[89]

A primary determinant of the low birthrate was undoubtedly the intensification of staple agriculture. Plantation conditions, suggests Peter Wood, served more to frustrate desires for enduring intimacy and "reduce the likelihood of procreation" than to give license to a promiscuity imagined by white masters to be innate.[90] Betty Wood points also to the damaging social and psychological context in which black partnerships were formed.[91] Other factors pertained more exclusively to the African origins of bondswomen, who usually maintained a spacing pattern of three years between children because they had long lactation periods. The horrific trials of the Middle Passage contributed physically and psychologically, while those mothers torn from infants or young children in Africa could expect longer intervals between their later children than had been true of their earlier births.[92]

A simple solution was found to the problems associated with the low birthrate and high mortality among the slave population: the continuation and acceleration of the slave trade in the lower South. In addition to fairly high numbers of adult females, merchants indicated a preference for slave shipments that contained a significant proportion of adolescent boys and girls, a measure that compensated demographically for the dearth of plantation-born children. Children in their early teens were not only more likely to survive the seasoning period but also had considerable labor potential, as they could be apprenticed to a profession or become generally acclimated to plantation conditions with greater ease than a person ten or more years younger or older. The presence of a comparatively high proportion of unrelated adolescents among the slave population injected new momentum into the birthrate. Rather than waiting for the emergence of an underrepresented generation of slaves born in America, slaveholders had only to wait only a short while before a number of their bondsmen and bondswomen were in a position to bear their own children.

According to a variety of contemporary estimates, the black population of Georgia spiraled from a few hundred people up to roughly 13,000 during the third quarter of the eighteenth century (figure 2). The land grant data record the presence of 11,143 slaves registered in or before 1773. The shortfall in this

Figure 2 Black Population of Georgia

figure compared to the governors' estimates may be accounted for partly by slaves owned by masters who had not yet claimed land according to their headright, partly by those slaves laboring within the urban environment, and finally by the presence of a few hundred free blacks. As early as 19 July 1750, a letter to the trustees from the president and assistants recorded that numbers of blacks in the province were on the increase. According to an "exact list," there were 202 men and 147 women, "besides children too young for labour."[93] The earliest black Georgians, then, constituted a community that at least held the potential for a positive natural growth rate—the population was comprised of 42.12 percent women and a number of children—but was soon engulfed by the influx of unacclimated African slaves.

Georgia's slave population before 1766 was overwhelmingly a result of forced immigration from nearby provinces rather than actual African importation. As a result many early fugitives did not run away in a straightforward bid for freedom but because, as one observer put it, they did "not like to be separated from their friends and relatives and frequently run off from Georgia to Carolina."[94] The relatives of Carolina's slaves were as certain as the younger sons and relatives of Carolina's white planters about their prospects in Georgia. Others sought to return to family elsewhere on the mainland: a man of mixed heritage named John fled back to the "Indian nation"; Cassandra was thought to have headed for Mobile, where her parents and other relations lived.[95] Slaves, such as seventeen-year-old Hannah, who ran away soon after her importation from Jamaica, also made up a majority of arrivals from the West Indies. From the perspective of familial stability it was far more advantageous to be brought into Georgia by/with a settler than to be transported there and sold at auction.[96] At an auction of slaves from St. Kitts on 18 April 1753, an observer remarked that "most of the children had to leave their mothers behind, which must have been just as painful for them as it was for an old Negress at the auction who had to see her children sold to different masters." It was unusual for children younger than about eight to be sold without their mothers, but it happened on occasion.[97]

About five thousand creolized slaves were brought into the province from South Carolina and the West Indies, though Georgia planters purchased an increasing number of Africans at slave auctions in Charlestown.[98] When the institution germinated in the lowcountry, Savannah merchants instigated direct importation, ensuring more rapid growth; the slave population doubled during the late 1760s and early 1770s. By this time it is likely that the proportion of Georgia-born slaves constituted the majority of black children in the province though a minority overall. The importation of high proportions of female and adolescent Africans gradually raised the birthrate so that by the Revolution, the black populace was probably at last capable of limited but noticeable natural growth.

During the royal era colonial authorities had made public decisions to endorse the arrival of free women of European origin. These were increasingly matched at the private level by slaveholders looking to expand and consolidate their personal domains through the importation of enslaved women of African origin. The first group of women held the key to legitimacy—to societal and moral value, to a balanced and worthy future for the colony. The second group assured material prosperity as a source of present and future labor. Their continued separation, thanks to the transposition of a gendered slave-owning ideology, would assure Georgia of its southern status. To keep whites and blacks distinctive, through the use of rigid racial laws and narrow gendered behavioral guidelines, was to mark out common ground for both groups and sow the seeds for the collective identities that had been lacking.

CHAPTER FIVE

Expansion and Contraction

The new waves of settlers that rolled into Georgia's lowcountry swept aside much of the occupational flexibility that had characterized women's extradomestic work during the trusteeship. Diversity of opportunity began to ebb away from the settled seaboard, as normalization contracted the scope of individual women's activities. The rapid growth in the population sated the hunger for white women's labor. The proliferation of slavery now meant that the most menial, marginal, and emergency work was foisted upon bondspeople—on the plantations and, gradually, in the cattle pens, stables, and larger kitchens too. In part, this was simply a case of black women's replacing white women in the labor market. Yet the employment of female slaves in the royal era tended to limit bondswomen to one discrete occupation with a distinct set of responsibilities—as a field hand, cook, or maid. With the entrenchment of slavery and the consolidation of settlement, the variety of women's work as *individuals* contracted as the frontier moved.

The energy saved by narrowing white women's occupational breadth allowed for the specialization of female behavior in the lowcountry. Georgia could now afford a genuine elite, whose obsession with gentility and fashion was virtually a full-time job in itself; for these women the concept of laboring in the fields was utterly alien. Among the middle classes, and particularly in the growing towns of Savannah, Darien, and Sunbury, female occupations became increasingly specialized to cater to a market whose consumer needs were becoming more predictable, reliable, and profitable. Only for those hardy pioneers who continued to settle the western backcountry and the southern frontier did the abiding principles of self-preservation mean that women's work would continue to approximate strategies revealed in the trusteeship period.

While the changing contours of the labor pool and the market were, in all likelihood, the most immediate influences on women's employment history, other factors played important supporting roles. Two related to the outgoing colonial regime and the removal of the trustees. The proportion of personal decisions made by paternalistic aristocrats and their appointees now shrank as colonial authority shifted away from on-the-spot arbiters and became attached to more formal processes. The abundance of historical records, a reflection of the trustees' thirst for information, also evaporated in the early 1750s. As a result both the possibility and the visibility of female activity outside the conventional declined. Moreover, society's conventions were also now in a phase of transition, as new forces within Georgia—lowcountry and backcountry, urban and plantation, Carolinian and West Indian—competed for ascendancy in politics and commerce. As I suggested in chapter 4, the incoming British colonial regime was concerned with order and regulation, enlightened empire and standardization. Women's work was far from peripheral to these shifting sands: one of the first bills to which the newly constituted Georgia Assembly turned its attention in January 1755 related to the legal status of female extradomestic labor.

On several different occasions in the 1750s and 1760s, legislators addressed women's economic status and legal capacities during and after marriage. This reflected both that ownership of land in the lowcountry was becoming steadily more profitable and that families were becoming more stable and cohesive. This stability was evidenced in the declining proportion of husbands who, in their will, nominated their wife as the sole executor of their estate. Whereas in the first decade of the colony's existence, about half of all the wills specifying a wife as an executor listed her as the sole executor, by the final decade of the colony's existence this proportion had dropped to less than a quarter of wills. In a comparison of 411 colonial wills, 37 were made by women, and 249 of the remainder made reference to a wife; wives were named executors in 154 cases and sole executors in 43 cases. The proportion of wills that named the wife as sole executor declined as follows: 1733–42, 50 percent (4/8); 1743–52, 33 percent (1/3); 1753–62, 30 percent (10/33); 1763–72, 26 percent (20/76); 1773–82, 24 percent (8/34). This pattern of wives' finding their testamentary access to property dwindling over time was extremely common across North American colonies as they matured.[1] Georgia legislators' efforts were manifested, above all, in repeated attempts to ensure procedural consistency in the transmission of wills, conveyances, and mortgages. Contemporaries were acutely aware of the problems of inheritance that had emerged at the end of the trusteeship, and the legislators debated and passed bills on the subject in 1760, 1762, and 1764. In so doing, they brought Georgia into line with a wider southern paternalistic legal trend. To protect white women's interests, members of the Assembly invoked regulations that confined and typecast women.

On 24 April 1760 Gov. Henry Ellis assented to a bill whose final title was "An Act to enable Feme Coverts to convey their Estates and for confirming and making valid all Conveyances and Acknowledgements heretofore made by Feme Coverts." Dissent over the bill had required calling a special conference to resolve disagreements between the upper and lower houses of the Georgia legislature, but eventually most of the all-male members of the Commons House of Assembly (the lower house) and the Governor's Council (the upper house) established a framework that that they could agree on.[2]

The act was intended, specifically, "to prevent husbands disposing without the consent of the wife, what of right did or would belong to them."[3] In order to achieve this, the law instructed judges and justices to read a declaration of consent that wives were to repeat before them whenever a deed was recorded. The officials were paid two shillings and sixpence to ensure that the wife lent her assent of her own free will, without any compulsion or force used by her husband to oblige her to do so. According to the wording of the act, this protection of the interests of married women from their husband's coercion was "customary in His Majesty's American colonies." But the historian Marylynn Salmon, in her study of women and the law of property in early America (she excluded Georgia), documented a more "overprotective, patriarchal fashion" in the southern colonies than in the northern ones.[4]

The instigation of this act in Georgia, constructed in emulation of similar statutes in Virginia and South Carolina, gave legal title to the notion of female helplessness and underlined the growing sense that the southern ruling elite shared a certain mentality. The legislation helped protect property, such as the house adjacent to the market square in Savannah that was given to Anne Bard by her father in trust, irrespective of her marriage to Peter Bard. Thus, regardless of her husband's death, Anne was able to dispose of the lot independently, choosing to sell it to the baker John Smith for three hundred pounds in 1786, having previously leased it to him.[5]

The first act of 1760 was amended in subsequent years as Georgia judges and legislators repeatedly voiced concerns for the rights of married women. Grey Elliott presented another bill on the subject of married women's conveyances to the Governor's Council in December 1762.[6] This second bill sought to prevent fraudulent transfers of capital and to uphold transactions and agreements that predated the bill of 1760 and therefore did not conform to its more rigorous standards. By the eighteenth century most colonial courts required some kind of examination procedure; when a married woman wanted to execute a conveyance of property, she went into a separate room with an officer of the court, and he read the contents of the deed and ensured she understood the details. This was one of the methods used, although it was hardly foolproof, to protect married women from coercion by their husband or other parties. Since her acknowledgment, if forthcoming, barred her forever from establishing claims to the property, it was recognized as hugely important to at least attempt to guarantee that the woman in question was happy with the disposition. The wording of the act was careful to emphasize that nothing in it should "be construed ... to bar any widow ... from her dower and right ... who did not legally join with her husband in such mortgage."⁷ Grey Elliott's bill, like drafts of previous legislative proposals, was heavily debated in both houses. Alterations and amendments were agreed upon in another conference on 8 March 1763, and Governor Wright gave his assent a month later. Further legislation was drawn up to amend the "Act for preventing fraudulent mortgages and conveyances" in November 1764.

If the proportion of conveyances of property in Georgia signed by both husband and wife is an indication of the effectiveness of the acts, they appear to have proved useful. Of 317 conveyances made before Governor Ellis assented to the new legislation, not a single one was made in which a wife signed a document that disposed of her husband's present property and her future property forever.⁸ In the books of colonial conveyances that follow until June 1771, more than a third of all recorded transfers (36.94 percent) named both husband and wife as grantors.⁹ Of course, in reality this meant only that husbands now had to go to the added trouble of asking and, if necessary, coercing their wives to assent to property transactions, and there is no evidence of wives' putting up resistance or being any less inclined to dispose of land. But the necessity of wives' giving their supposedly free consent represented at least a formal step toward the protection of certain female legal and economic prerogatives. Evidently, concern for proper procedure, the protection of married women from their husbands' acquisitive tendencies, and, above all, the smooth transmission of property were important and endemic stimuli of legislative action in early royal Georgia. In a positive light, the tightening up of legal controls protected women from domineering husbands and ensured consistency in women's treatment at law. In a negative light, it limited their economic agency and portrayed them as weak and submissive.

In fact, the standardization of procedures for married women's conveyances in the 1760s was not the first matter relating to women's economic roles that the royal legislature considered. The issue of regulating female traders prompted a substantial debate in the fledgling Georgia Assembly during the previous decade, as legislators attempted to smooth the transition from the anarchy of the trusteeship to a stable southern society. In early 1755 evidently enough women were acting economically and independent of their husbands—because of absence, separation, or mutual agreement—to warrant the introduction of a bill allowing the status of feme sole trader to be applicable in Georgia. In practice this meant that certain married women were extended financial rights usually denied them: the right to sue for and recover debts, and, conversely, the right to be arrested and sued for any debts contracted by them as sole traders.¹⁰

What remains tantalizingly obscure is the driving force behind the arrival of this measure regulating female traders on 31 January 1755. Invited to prepare the bill were James Habersham, Alexander Kellet, and Noble Jones, all men with dual interests as both merchants and loyal and upright servants of the colony, all of whom were made council members under Governor Reynolds. On the one hand, they might have benefited personally from the ability to recover debts from recalcitrant wives who were pleading coverture (marriage) to evade the bailiff. On the other, their history of concern with disadvantaged people's welfare and their own experiences of marital absenteeism may have inclined them to draft the bill with a view to its progressive or liberal aspects: facilitating a greater degree of financial cooperation within marriage and extending to women the ability to act as economic agents in their own right.

The Georgia debates about the introduction of feme sole trader legislation were almost certainly inspired by the example of South Carolina. As Marylynn Salmon has observed, South Carolina enacted two statutes on the subject in 1712 and 1744 and consistently "demonstrated a strong commitment in the colonial and early national periods to the right of married women to act as feme sole traders."[11] In fact, South Carolina was the only British American colony to offer formal recognition of married women's right to act in such a capacity. Providing the husband gave his approval—a provision that could be assumed if he had abandoned his wife—his partner was allowed to own and operate businesses in her own name as if she were single. Such women were no longer able to plead coverture to avoid creditors' demands. But the law did help women in recovering debts from their customers, as the doctrine provided a way for women to sue without the presence or explicit consent of their husband. The higher the number of married women working in businesses and, especially, retail, the greater the pressure and demand for sole trader legislation to smooth the progress of economic transactions in the absence of a husband. South Carolina's thriving commercial metropolis of Charlestown—with its myriad Atlantic mercantile connections—offered a fertile rationale for legal permissiveness, and the idea would spread south.

During the trusteeship in Georgia married women had had no real need of formal recognition of their economic status. The trustees were entitled to enact their own regulations, which often offered great latitude according to individual circumstances—as the supposedly barred female landholders of the 1730s and 1740s discovered. Moreover, in the frontier conditions of a struggling colony whose settlers often relied upon the trustees' storehouses, the ability to legally sue and be sued for debts was generally unnecessary. Informal transactions were the norm, and an abundance of evidence (see chapter 2) suggests that married women were willing and able to partake in economic activity in the absence of husbands—and, in a not inconsiderable number of cases, even when he was present. Wives' activities in tavern keeping, sericulture, cattle raising, land purchasing, retailing, and so forth were not protected by feme sole trader legislation but by more direct, informal appeals to the trustees. With the arrival of direct royal control many previously informal processes peculiar to the colony, such as land granting, needed to be set on a firmer basis. The planned introduction of a bill in Georgia to legalize married women's independent economic activity may therefore best be seen in the light of these administrative and legislative changes, as well as the influence of South Carolinian practices.

The bill, first drafted on 3 February 1755, was entitled "An Act to empower and enable a Feme Coverte, who is a sole Trader," language strongly suggestive of a genuine concern for extending the economic capabilities of married women engaged in business. However, disagreements about the intricacies of the bill were rife, especially between the Governor's Council and the Commons House of Assembly, whose concurrence was required in order to submit the bill for the governor's (and, later, the Privy Council's) approval. Amendments were hotly debated, refused, and refashioned, but ultimately the Assembly reached an impasse in late February. No other bills to date had caused such consternation in the province's formative legislative processes, yet the issue of married women's trading rights disappeared from the record books after a resolution to adjourn further consideration of the bill's amendments until 18 March. Apparently, it was neither assented to by the governor nor accepted as law by the Privy Council in Britain since the records reveal no mention of the "Act to Empower and enable a Feme Coverte."

The bill may have been abandoned for one of several reasons. An insufficient number of married women in Savannah may have been deemed economically active for the bill to be worthwhile—although this seems unlikely since some popular demand must have instigated its introduction in the first place. Other business may have taken priority in the legislature, or Governor John Reynolds may have expressed a reluctance to assent to the bill in advance. Perhaps most plausible is the suggestion that the feme sole trader bill became a casualty of the growing factionalism that permeated Reynolds's short occupancy of the governorship. The governor took little time in alienating members of the Governor's Council from the lowcountry (among whom were the three drafters of the bill); Alexander Kellet would later travel to London to give evidence of Reynolds's alleged malfeasance.[12] In the absence of any corroborating evidence, all we can surmise with any certainty is that an acute and contentious debate occurred in regard to married women's formal financial independence in early 1755 and that this debate highlighted the high number of commercially active wives in Georgia, the sense of transition and redirection from the trusteeship to a new order, and the growing influence of South Carolina in that new order.

The new economic order was built around slavery's staples: rice, indigo, naval stores, provisions, and lumber. Exports doubled between 1761 and 1766 and had reached a value of one hundred thousand pounds by 1773.[13] White women's extradomestic labor would have comparatively little to do with any of these mainstream raw products directly. But even as the changing contours of the market bypassed earlier female functions, urban and plantation prosperity brought its own economic opportunities. At the top of the social hierarchy a prosperous plantation elite ensured a market for fashion and high-status commodities, for quality schooling and well-fitted clothes and hats, and for libraries, newspapers, and leisure venues. At the other end of the social spectrum slaves too needed equipping and managing, mass-produced linens and equipment, and dried goods and pharmaceutical products. Specialization, previously a handicap for all except the most knowledgeable silk winders, now became a viable strategy, particularly in urban environments such as Savannah.

In the historical record widows tend to be more visible than wives, because widows acted almost exclusively in their own names. With no husband to provide for them, although often with his commercial capital still intact, trading widows emerge prominently—as demonstrated in the family papers of William Gibbons Jr. (1728–1803).[14] The widow Mary Bateman, for instance, was one of the first victualers for the Gibbons family and its slaves when the family moved from the Bahamas to Savannah. In the spring of 1753 Bateman sold the senior William Gibbons two loaves of bread, four pounds of cheese, and more than twelve gallons of rum.[15] The tavern of the widow Abigail Minis became a favorite haunt of William Gibbons's when he visited Savannah: between 1757 and 1758 Gibbons ate there sixteen times, paying on average one shilling and sixpence for his dinner and in later years enjoying punch, wine, beer, and vinegar with his meals (presumably having had enough rum).[16] The Gibbons family papers also show that widows could be dragged into the economic record not through experience or desire but simply in their capacity as executor of their husband's estate. Such was the case with Martha Lines, who sought to tidy up some financial clutter from the estate of her late husband, Isaac, by getting the money owed him by Thomas Carr (for thirteen hogs, five steers, and a cow) repaid to one William Dunham.[17]

However, the participation of white women—whether single, married, or widowed—in the economic sphere during the royal era has left its deepest impression in the historical record in the form of several advertisements in the Savannah newspaper called the *Georgia Gazette*, published from 1763. These announcements can broadly be categorized as two types: advertisements posted by women for goods available or services offered, and notices published by husbands who wished to bar an estranged wife from purchasing goods on their credit. Overall, dozens of examples highlight the dynamism and frequency of female commercial labor.[18] The occupations advertised by these women were narrow and similar to those extradomestic pursuits offered by their trusteeship precursors: tavern keeping, millinery and mantua making, retail, boarding, and teaching. But the marital economic partnerships of the 1750s through 1790s were more specialized, thanks to the establishment of a fixed urban market and its expanding consumer base.

In retail the contribution of wives might vary from no practical assistance at all to full-time complete commercial autonomy. David Cunningham owned a wharf and naval stores in January 1764, while his wife, Ann—in a separate advertisement in the same *Gazette*—announced that she was selling spirituous liquors, sugar, molasses, and other goods.[19] Henrietta Bourquin, widow of the widely used doctor Henry Lewis Bourquin, who had died in 1774, continued to distribute pharmaceutical products in his absence, including "Turlington's Balsam, Godfrey's Cordial, Stoughton's Bitters, British Oil, Liquorice, Manna, Rhubarb Preserved Ginger, and Tamarinds" in August 1775. (The English merchant Robert Turlington was granted a patent for his miraculous all-curing "balsam of life" only in 1744, suggesting that the products offered by Henrietta Bourquin were fairly current. Turlington's Balsam was used to treat a variety of ailments, from bronchitis to hemorrhoids. Godfrey's Cordial was a soothing syrup of opium tincture, a dependable way to keep children content and docile. Richard Stoughton's "bitters," mixed from an elixir patented in 1712, promised relief to those with a weak stomach or a lack of appetite. British Oil was a liniment to relieve pain or stiffness.)[20] Florence Mahoney's description as a "vintner" by her daughter Winiford in the *Gazette* a couple of months later similarly indicates that wives and widows among the middle class were active not only in selling goods produced by their husbands but also in the manufacturing and refining processes.[21] Hannah Vincent gained considerable experience in retailing in Georgia before she returned to England after her husband, Thomas, died in 1767.[22] From her new base in London she continued to milk the contacts and clients she had established in America—such as the prominent and prosperous family of Noble Jones, one of the very members of the Governor's Council who had sponsored the feme sole trader bill a dozen years earlier. Vincent acted as the Joneses' agent in Britain, both making goods herself and contracting out other requests to upholsterers and fabric dealers, offering with cheerfulness to "execute future Commands and Gratefully remember all the kind Favours conferred on me when in Savannah." Vincent thanked Sarah Jones for the pots of preserved plums that came with each package from Savannah, but she was also careful to enclose invoices, bills of lading, and a tally of the Joneses' current account in her replies.[23] Like the majority of wives whose husbands ran mercantile operations, Vincent had played an active part in administering her family's business, as her ability to prosper in that vocation during widowhood suggests. The William Gibbons Jr. Papers show that retailing wives frequently received payments on behalf of their husband: the women calculated sums owed and signed receipts to confirm that balances had been paid off and debts satisfied.[24]

Tavern keeping continued to be a pursuit that allowed and often demanded a high degree of marital economic cooperation. John and Sarah Lyon ran a popular tavern in the 1750s and 1760s, and until her "greatly and justly regretted" death in November 1765, it was always Sarah's name that was listed on advertisements for balls or meetings of the Union Society and Freemasons.[25] As with many of the trusteeship taverns, the mistress of the house often attained a higher profile than her spouse. Margaret Pages, who had the protection of a marriage contract when she married again, to a goods retailer, in September 1763, gradually widened the scope of her husband's business on the Bluff in Savannah. She expanded his business to offer boarding facilities as well as a baking business and, ultimately, a tavern, which was licensed in her name after he died, sometime before 1765. Margaret outlived him by just four years and specified that her estate was to go to her son by her first marriage, Michael Lucas, and that her mulatto slave Peter was to be clothed, maintained, and educated in a "beneficial trade" until he attained the age of twenty-one, when he was to be manumitted.[26]

Marital occupational partnerships came no more naturally than in the field of education, whose scope had outgrown the rudimentary instruction offered during the trusteeship.[27] By working in tandem, husbands and wives could now upgrade the facilities offered from itinerant tutoring to boarding schools and class teaching: the home became the school, where they could most efficiently invest all their skills and resources. Husband-and-wife occupational partnerships in teaching could also attract a wider cross section of pupils, both male and female—and many advertisements emphasized this advantage to good effect. The archetypal advertisement listed the husband's myriad abilities and experience and outlined the subjects he would be teaching, before giving his name and contact details. The advertisement often then named the wife in a postscript as a collaborator who would undertake to teach particularly "feminine" skills such as sewing and cooking, and she would sometimes offer boarding facilities.[28] Instruction tended to include a basic menu of reading, writing, and sewing, but several tutors offered more advanced and specialized tuition in grammar, arithmetic, foreign languages, embroidery, dancing, and music.[29] As today, students preferred some subjects to others: ten-year-old Elizabeth Lichtenstein used to hide a book beneath her sewing. She recalled that her education at schools in Savannah was supplemented in the evenings by the attentions of her aunt, who "endeavored to make me a notable needlewoman . . . [but] declared at last that I should never be anything but a botcher at it."[30]

Elizabeth Lichtenstein "in early life." An only child, Elizabeth was born on a small farm beside the Little Ogeechee River on 28 May 1764, to a father and mother who reflected the diverse roots of Georgia's earliest immigrants (of Russian and French Huguenot stock respectively). Her tranquil country life was brought to an abrupt halt by the death of her mother in 1774, and she was sent, reluctantly, to be schooled in embroidery by an elderly aunt in Savannah. Courtesy of the Hargrett Rare Book and Manuscript Library, University of Georgia Libraries.

The Jacobses, a Jewish couple, were running an academy in Savannah by 1786. They had lived together since Jacob Jacobs, a merchant, had moved into the then-widow Sarzedas's lodging house a week after it opened in May 1775—and they had married in November that year.[31] In June 1786 Mrs. Jacobs (the records do not reveal her first name) advertised that a dancing teacher would be gracing her academy, and in 1793 the couple offered to accommodate three or four more boarders at low rates.[32] By 1796 she was running the academy alone, presumably because Jacob had died.[33] Although in this case the extent to which either partner actually taught is unclear, both husband and wife had turned over new occupational leaves in launching their educational venture. Occasionally, such a marital partnership straddled related occupations. Elizabeth Bedon opened a boarding school for young ladies in Savannah in 1769, while her husband, George, offered his services in the same *Gazette* as a clerk and bookkeeper. He evidently believed that he could earn a better income from his education in this capacity than as a teacher, although he probably contributed to parts of the curriculum.[34]

Of course, only a tiny proportion of white girls received such specialized tutoring. Whether the remainder of the free nonelite population received even a rudimentary education was heavily dependent on their parents' outlook and occupations—becoming more likely, for instance, if they were devout, urban, or commercial. Most girls were at best semiliterate, taught what they needed to know about domestic maintenance and child care by example, and they worked out for themselves how to dance. Planters' fears about the education of slaves generated a widespread belief that "Were the Negroes universally taught to read . . . there would be little doubt that the next ships informed us of a general insurrection."[35] Nonetheless, on extremely rare occasions enslaved women and men might have access to a limited education, and there is evidence that some owners, including Jonathan Bryan and James Habersham, encouraged this on religious grounds. One bondswoman, owned by the Kieffer family, had been promised in 1745 that her child would not change hands and would be raised and educated as a Christian. When her daughter died at about the age of fifteen, the mother thanked her mistress, Maria Kieffer, for "making it a Christian child."[36] Another, more defiant slave mother was so distressed at the death of her daughter (who had been baptized Sulamith in 1751, separated from her mother within a year, and died at the age of two) that the woman undertook to accept an education "because she wished to get the child again and would [only] have hope of doing so through the Christian religion."[37] This mother and daughter were initially owned by Matthias and Elisabetha Zettler (whose problematic courtship I described in chapter 3) but sold to different owners in 1752.[38]

While many of Savannah's merchant houses, academies, ballrooms, and coffeehouses catered to the fashionable tastes and trends of the self-conscious elite, the provisioning of the slaves also brought specialized vocational opportunities to a smaller number of middle-class white women. Lucretia Triboudet supplied slaveholders with sturdy oznabrig linens for their workforce—either in whole pieces or already fashioned into thick shirts and trousers. After someone looted her shop in February 1765, she offered a reward of five pounds to any white and fifty shillings to any black informants.[39] Slaveholders also sometimes relied upon nonelite white women to assist in the management of a plantation and to handle the day-to-day running of estates.

Although historically the slave overseer has been characterized as a single white male from the lower class, a significant minority of plantation owners actually specified that they wanted a married overseer. About a third (35 percent) of advertisements in the *Georgia Gazette* seeking an overseer stated that preference would be given to men with families—and often small families at that. Such specifications were probably perceived as a way to insure landowners against the dangers associated with single overseers: laziness, disloyalty, corruption and exploitation, drunkenness, and, ultimately, lack of productivity. On a smaller scale such concerns closely mirrored the fears of gender imbalance in the colony as a whole, as expressed by the land granters. A married overseer, after all, had a vested interest in performing his functions to the best of his abilities: his occupation was closely tied to the prosperity of his family.

Some advertisers particularly wanted men with wives "on account of raising poultry," suggesting that plantations with married overseers were more likely to operate virtually independently of the owners and to engage in a variety of pursuits such as the production of lumber and livestock as well as staple crops such as rice and indigo. Single men were more frequently required to bring "vouchers" or "written recommendations" of fidelity, industry, and especially sobriety. A majority of advertisers still preferred single overseers because they were relatively less expensive and their term of contract more flexible.[40]

In addition to the advertisements placed by married women, notices from sixteen husbands between 1763 and 1775 offer further evidence of wives' activity in the marketplace—examples of what happens to marital economics when the marriage fails. These were all husbands whose wives had taken the drastic step of running away, which was the only way to effect a separation without resorting to a criminal act. In itself, running away (which often meant returning to live with her family) was a reactive measure when marital living conditions had become intolerable. It is likely that men absented themselves as frequently as women, but the humiliating notices published in the *Georgia Gazette* are testament to the imbalance of the marital economy. If a wife withdrew her domestic and sexual contribution to the marriage, a husband could take the ultimate sanction of withdrawing his spouse's access to his credit.

The sixteen men all made public their reasons for refusing to pay any debts contracted by their wives. In part, this reflected the embarrassment of having to admit to a personal and social failure, and the gradual development of a formulaic notice structure (as occurred with advertisements for fugitive slaves) may have served to distance the individual from a heightened sense of culpability. Sadly, the other side of the story—and arguably the more interesting side—is missing in the overwhelming majority of cases, sometimes, we may assume, because the wife actually left the colony altogether. Husbands were always careful to explain that their wife was the guilty party, using language such as "eloped," "absented herself," and "left without leave"—and including justifications such as "notwithstanding she had every necessary provision made for her," "carried off with her a gold sleeve button and several other things," "contracted debts . . . to a considerable amount," or "refuseth to return on any reasonable terms." The notices as a whole—however similar in format—orchestrate a medley of emotional tones, ranging from those offering rewards for information about their wife's whereabouts to those threatening to prosecute anyone who harbored her, entertained her, or carried her out of the province.[41]

In just three of the sixteen incidents do the records reveal anything significant about the nature of the marital discord, and two of these explanations come from husbands again seeking to justify their withdrawal of financial support. Elizabeth Oates, for instance, was barred from her husband's credit for taking it upon herself to move to Savannah, rent a house, and run up other "unnecessary" expenses, contrary to the express order of her husband, John.[42] Robert Hamilton of Augusta went the furthest in insisting to the public that he was blameless and that (even so) he had taken all the measures he possibly could to resolve his marital predicament. His lengthy advertisement in the *Georgia Gazette* of 20 April 1774 describes his efforts to organize a meeting with his wife, Ann (née Rasberry), who had taken residence with her mother and sister. Hamilton suggested that they might meet at a place of her choosing, each accompanied by friends or family, so that he "might hear what reason the said Ann had for so absenting herself, and likewise every complaint that she, her said mother, or sister, could make known or allege against him." His proposition having been repeatedly refused, Robert's advertisement stated that he thought "himself now sufficiently justifiable" to forbid the public from contracting debts with her on his account. The notion of being "sufficiently" wronged by a wife to warrant financial sanctions suggests that a line existed that could be crossed, a finite limit implicitly understood and accepted, if not recorded, by contemporaries. Although we cannot know exactly why the Hamiltons separated, or who (if anyone) was the more responsible, we can glean from this incident, first, that a popular social conception existed of what merited the withdrawal of financial support and, second, that the ferocity of the mother-in-law is a constant of human nature.

The third incident ties in with the notion of a "just" disenfranchisement insofar as a third party testified that the behavior of the wife in question, Lydia McCarty, had not merited the sanctions taken against her by her husband, Cornelius; the punishment did not match the crime. The writer was a tailor named Jonathan Remington, who had lodged with the McCartys for eighteen months spanning 1765–66. Remington felt the need to respond to reports that were "greatly prejudicial to the character and conduct" of Lydia and had presumably culminated in her husband's refusal to support her in May 1766. Remington declared on oath before two justices of the peace, and not without a sense of irony, "that he has never had, directly or indirectly, any indecent freedom or criminal conversation with the said Lydia McCarty, or she with him: And this deponent also declares, That he now is, and will at all times hereafter be ready and willing to give any further or other satisfaction that the said Cornelius McCarty may require for the justification of his wife's character."[43] Extramarital sexual relations obviously met the criteria of sufficiency, except when the husband's suspicions were misplaced and publicly challenged, as on this occasion.

The notices placed by disgruntled husbands, more than any other, reveal that in most relationships married women were granted daily access to their husband's credit and fulfilled many commercial responsibilities, which merchants (both male and female) were all too happy to accommodate. Husbands who denied their wife commercial autonomy were the exception that proved the rule: most wives had considerable latitude to participate in the economic sphere through their husband's accounts and with his implicit authorization.

The activities of the legislature; the advertisements placed by, for, or about women in the *Georgia Gazette*; and a number of documents among collections of family papers all are testament to the shifting and active roles occupied by working women within the newly styled export-driven economy of late colonial lowcountry Georgia.[44] White middle-class women specialized by offering services that complemented their husband's activities and cashed in on the tastes of the elite and the needs of their bondspeople. Mary Hepburn, for instance, promised gentlemen a breakfast "on the same footing as in London" and boarding on the same terms as in Charlestown, "with all the civility in her power." A tailor named Evans sought to employ several "Women who can sew neatly" in order to make clothes for ladies and gentlemen "after the newest fashion." Mary Hughes took the opportunity to "inform the Ladies" in October 1766 that she had just imported a whole range of chic accessories from London, including ribbons, French trimmings, pearl earrings and garnet necklaces, "and a great many other articles too tedious to insert." While widowhood legitimized such women's personal economic behavior, it rarely marked a substantial break from their earlier labor practices.

In contrast, for elite slaveholding women widowhood could represent an abrupt break from their earlier lifestyles. The royal era saw the emergence of a minority of households in which matriarchs and their daughters could afford to perform practically no physical labor, operating purely in a supervisory capacity and emulating the lifestyles of older elites in Britain, Virginia, the West Indies, and South Carolina. Elite wives were much less likely than their poorer counterparts to participate in the mundane and complicated administration of their husband's finances. As a result, upon widowhood many preferred to delegate responsibility to kinsmen, other executors, or even appoint outsiders to deal with their husband's estate. Ingeborg Dornan concluded from her study of lowcountry slaveholding widows that "on the whole, [they] may not have been eager to enter the planting business," and that many discharged their affairs to others.[45] After all, wills tended to provide for them amply, and they could often quite easily sell off property and live off the interest on the proceeds. However, especially while a wealthy female slaveholder was married, some extradomestic commercial responsibilities fell within her domain, although money rarely changed hands in such transactions. Sarah Gibbons, wife of William Sr., bought a number of items from various stores that tied in with her perceived feminine duties as mother and guardian of the family. She bought presents and clothing for her children and dealt with the health care of the white members of the Gibbons household.[46] It was probably also her decision to send her daughters Sally and Polly to board with Judith Swinton in 1766 and later with Betty Wright.[47] When she was widowed in February 1771, Sarah Gibbons was named an executor, but she appears to have played little part in the business of tidying up his debts, tasks that were left to John Martin (his kinsman) and Reverend Zubly. Indeed, her accounts were mixed up with those of her oldest son, William Jr., partly because her husband's estate was not settled until Sarah's death in 1790. Sarah's little direct involvement amounted to a few payments that she made in 1772–73. She paid bills for veal and beef, mending a chair, a black horse of 14.2 hands, a two-wheeled carriage, and painting her house.[48] This comprises relatively little evidence of economic activity for an owner of 2,950 acres and 83 slaves in Christ Church Parish in 1773.[49]

Nonetheless, as numerous colonial wills, deeds, and conveyances show, a minority of wealthy widows did undertake personally to administer their inherited estate, either for their own benefit or for their children's. As Kirsten Wood has recently argued of southern slaveholding widows in the early national era, such women occupied an unorthodox and sometimes uncomfortable position within the shifting matrix of race, class, and gender.[50] Though fleeting, their custodianship of legal and economic power created potential challenges to society's gender norms, awkward situations not so much in dealings with bondspeople as with white males of lesser standing: overseers and contractors. The limited timescale of a widow's control of resources was something of a saving grace for those who sought to retain a patriarchal southern slave society. These rare women, anomalies in a culture of male-to-male inheritance, were indulged and embraced as part of the system. As with royal families of old, Georgia's new plantation blue bloods bemoaned the failure of a male line but accepted the need to respect regent queens, who symbolized the system even as they belied it; a minority were allowed, in essence, to become temporary males and hold "mastery." Lowcountry widows thus acted as custodians not only of familial wealth but also of social superiority, strengthening systems of subjection according to race (white woman over blacks), class (elite woman over lesser whites), and gender (woman as temporary male). Although displaying distinctly feminine characteristics in their inheritance, use, and redistribution of bondspeople, elite slaveholding widows almost inadvertently perpetuated the institution of southern paternalism. They ensured the smooth transition of lands, slaves, and ideals to future generations.

The contraction in occupational breadth among lowcountry white women relied heavily upon the labor of slaves. Betty Wood has thoroughly explored the economic behavior of bondswomen held in the Georgia lowcountry during the late colonial era, but a brief summary here will suffice to emphasize the stark differences in livelihoods.[51] While all bondspeople suffered tremendous physical and practical constraints upon their agency and were equal in status before the law, their labor patterns show huge differences, most notably between those living on plantations and those living in urban environments, principally, Savannah, Darien, and Sunbury. These differences applied both to the labor that slaves performed for their masters and mistresses and to slaves' independent economic activity.

The tasks allocated to enslaved field hands working on plantations appear to have differed little, regardless of gender. Frustratingly, virtually no sources have survived that give us any inkling of how the earliest generations of Georgia bondswomen coped with, or felt about, their daunting array of responsibilities. James Habersham updated Isabella Wright on the progress of two young female slaves with whom she was acquainted in 1772, observing that "Peggy found the field Work at first a little hard, but she is now reconciled to it, and behaves well, as does Amey."[52] The physical labor was arduous throughout the year, typically requiring each slave to work a set amount of acreage per day—usually about a half-acre if sowing, planting, or weeding, and about a quarter-acre if hoeing or harvesting. By the final third of the eighteenth century, seasonal routines in the lowcountry were well established and involved the neat dovetailing of a variety of tasks to maximize the slaves' time and the planter's space: planting, tending, harvesting, and threshing rice; sowing, weeding, and picking corn, potatoes, and beans; clearing and preparing land (typically in winter); cultivating indigo and tobacco.[53] Pregnant bondswomen and mothers with infants received little latitude except when completely incapacitated; in 1753 an observer reported that a bondswoman at work had her child tied to her back, "and in spite of its mother's moving all the time and working hard, the child was completely still and quiet."[54] Only a handful of women on the larger plantations would find specialized employment in the planter's household that resembled the functions of their urban counterparts as cooks, maids, nurses, and seamstresses.[55]

Beyond the time claimed by planters, and particularly on the one day a week that was customarily reserved to them, slaves sought to support their own needs and desires by cultivating garden produce, engaging in small-scale manufacturing, tending livestock (principally chickens and pigs), and hunting, foraging, fishing, and trapping. They marketed their produce within and without the plantation, and, in exchange for other foodstuffs and goods, this practice allowed the plantation slave community to be self-sustaining, both physically and to a lesser degree culturally. Tobacco, for instance, was widely enjoyed by both black men and women, reflecting customs carried over from West Africa, and they either chewed the tobacco or smoked it in clay pipes. Ingenious creolized uses were frequently found for the by-products of crop production and the leftovers of garden produce, such as gourds. These might be fashioned into bed bases, utensils, canteens, toys, halters, and musical instruments such as drums and banjos—items that, as evidence from the antebellum period indicates, resounded with cultural significance.[56]

Enslaved women in urban environments manifested greater agency in the distribution of their labor and of their surplus produce. Indeed, such was the threat to white artisans and craftspeople from black street competition that by the end of the 1750s Savannah "Tradesmen" were lobbying the General Assembly to protect their interests. Though some of this petty trading and manufacturing was carried out by free blacks or slaves working on their own time, much of it was performed by slaves whose owners hired them out by the hour or the day or by owners who recouped any cash profits from their bondspeople. The flexible orbit of black peddlers, female meat and vegetable vendors, odd-jobbers, and slave craftsmen around Savannah thus placed their white owners (who wanted the profits) and their poor white urban competitors (who wanted the business) on a rare all-white collision course. The Assembly's solution—to license authorized slave vendors and introduce a badge system for marketing and a ticket system for certain manual jobs—was practically impossible to police in such a diverse and vibrant town, which on Sundays bore a stark resemblance to West African markets.[57] Bondswomen in particular carved out a dominant role in the exchange of information, pricing, and vending of a wide range of fresh foodstuffs.[58] Such women no doubt made use of the houses and hideaways in and around urban areas, some rented by blacks, that David Tubear and Adam Irick decried in February 1772 as places where "meetings of slaves are very frequent, Spirits and other liquors are sold, and Stolen goods often concealed."[59] Most female urban slaves, however, remained employed predominantly as domestic servants.

The specialization of female labor during the royal era, in the wake of the changing demographics, market expansion, and growing assertiveness of the planter elite, helped to shore up barriers between various groups of women that had been partly porous in the past. No longer would members of the aristocracy simply roll up their sleeves and hoe, as Lady Bathurst had done in 1735. No longer would the physical abuse of a black female trader be viewed as extraordinary, as in 1739. And as circles of labor association became more sharply defined, it became more difficult to break into or out of them. The elite women who gathered at Sarah Lyon's balls were wary of strangers without credentials or recommendations; the free and enslaved black women who ran Savannah's markets could be equally territorial about their wares and turfs. As density of settlement increased, personal prosperity became more and more reliant upon exploiting socioeconomic niches—whether this was washing plantation oznabrigs, importing and selling pharmaceuticals, or managing thousand-acre estates. But across the board these female niches were becoming smaller and rarer. Whether black or white, plantation or urban, whether rich, middle class, or poor, the vocational range of each subgroup of women was eroding. While contemporaries may have perceived gender predominantly as a horizontal force, seeing few (if any) common denominators among women of different races and classes, in this one sense women of all colors and statuses shared a common subjection. Within the slaves' formal and informal economies, no female occupation could equate with the preferential opportunities afforded to a minority of bondsmen who "enjoyed options that were effectively closed to bondwomen."[60] Among whites, despite their dynamic participation as retailers and consumers, and the occasional masquerading planter-widow, female vocations were also increasingly circumscribed. This provided absolutely no platform for a sense of gender affinity but rather a further reason for women to protect their differences.

CHAPTER SIX

Consolidating Gender

Each gossamer thread of a spider's web is intrinsically fine and imperfect. Only when it is artfully overlapped with countless others do the threads constitute a truly strong system, holding a form and substance that is captivating in its complexity—and capable of gripping all manner of unwary prey. Lashing the threads together is really the easy part—most spiders can do it in about an hour. Starting the web is more awkward: a floating thread is attached to a branch or a leaf, and the spider must move away—walking, jumping, and dangling until it can anchor its first drag line to the other guy lines. This process allows the web to span all kinds of encumbrances and assume an infinite variety of forms, yet it is a structure built with extremely small quantities of material; it is mainly empty space.

By the end of the colonial era a web of race and gender defined the social framework of Georgia, in emulation of other southern colonies. Three critical guy lines had proved hard to anchor in previous decades, but, once established, societal conventions swiftly intermeshed around them: the demographic normalization of the white population during the royal era, the specialization of an economy that circumscribed female roles, and the effective encoding of racial difference. Interwoven were a variety of cultural devices, although they were limited by the physical constraints upon a society that sprawled from the Appalachians to the tidewater, from the Savannah River down to Florida, and through backcountry cabins, urban dwellings, and Sea Island plantations. The growing number of concentric threads that confined late colonial Georgians to their "place" included slave codes, literature, religion, militia drilling, fashion and gentility, legislation, education, leisure patterns, courts of law, commercial networks—the list goes on. These cultural devices would create, monitor, uphold, and enforce distinctions, both consciously and subconsciously. In this chapter I will explore, insofar as the sources permit, how several of these powerful devices operated, in order to describe the process of cultural standardization that took place.

A NUMBER OF SCHOLARS have confronted the intersection of race and gender in recent years. Kathleen Brown has argued that gender and sexuality were central to the development of both slavery and the plantation elite in the society of colonial Virginia. To borrow Kenneth Lockridge's phrase, Brown dramatized how "gender was the door through which a species of racism entered colonial Virginia" in the late seventeenth century.[1] The bodily differentiation and derogatory language (such as "wench") formerly used to delineate gender and class hierarchies in early modern England were grafted onto African laborers, a process that facilitated the disempowerment of blacks alongside women in Virginia's patriarchal order. By the time slavery and gender were brought face to face in Georgia, in the middle of the eighteenth century, racial demarcation was well established across other colonies. But in post-1750 Georgia the guy lines were secured in the opposite order: here, the framework was slavery and the shifting code was that of gender. Slavery was the door through which new definitions of womanhood entered colonial Georgia.

As a host of scholars have noted, the codification of gender difference enhanced white male authority and, across the colonies, had established "a strict social hierarchy based on Anglo-American values by the time of the American Revolution."[2] In addition to protecting, isolating, and circumscribing the economic activity of women in Georgia, legislators applied considerable effort to effectively controlling the slave population. These slave codes had a perceptible and often brutal impact on the lives of the growing number of bondspeople in the province and also, in different ways, introduced measures that deeply conditioned the behavior of whites. Most fundamentally, the regulation of interracial sex—both at law and by custom—established ground rules for the most intimate kind of interaction between men and women. Two critical threads of the web met here.

In the second half of 1749 the trustees, following advice from officials in Georgia, had produced the colony's first slave code.[3] It prohibited interracial marriage and clearly articulated the consequences of transgression: "No Intermarriage between White People and Negroes shall be deemed lawful Marriages and if any White Man shall be convicted of lying with a female Negroe, or any White Woman of lying with a Male Negroe He or She shall on such conviction forfeit Ten pounds Sterling or receive such Corporal Punishment as the Court shall think proper to inflict and the Negroe shall receive Corporal Punishment."[4] This measure, while deliberately written to alter social norms involving racial intermixture in order to encourage racial separation, was actually remarkably indiscriminate in respect to gender. "White people"—whether male or female—and "Negroes"—whether male or female—were accorded an identical punishment. But plenty of discriminatory agency was left to the court's exclusively male jurors, and during the later colonial era sexism would complicate sexual behavior. While the colony abandoned or rewrote most aspects of the original slave code, a lasting legacy of the trustees was the forbidding of miscegenation, which also served as a gloomy reminder of their U-turn on slavery.

In some respects it is surprising that laws regulating interracial relations were not tightened further as slavery spread in Georgia. Punishments for sexual transgressions in Virginia and Maryland became increasingly severe as legislators sought to separate the races by barring miscegenation. Gradually, the laws appear to have had the desired effect, and voluntary interracial sexual relations occurred much less frequently after the turn of the eighteenth century.[5] In the early eighteenth century a number of colonies passed miscegenation laws (Massachusetts in 1705, North Carolina in 1715, South Carolina in 1717, Delaware in 1721, and Pennsylvania in 1725) that drew from the lessons of the Chesapeake, although Philip Morgan notes that for South Carolinians, "the yawning social chasm between most whites and most blacks bred a self-confidence about the unthinkability of interracial marriage that was absent in the Chesapeake."[6] The failure of Georgia legislators to tighten their laws reflected in part this self-same "unthinkability"; after all, many legislators had migrated from South Carolina and the West Indian islands, where only one assembly bothered to ban racial intermarriage (so far-fetched was the prospect).[7] It also reflected the huge latitude that courts were allowed in determining what constituted "proper" punishment (should a ten-pound fine not suffice).

One later law did return to the theme of interracial sex and, in doing so, projected and interlinked concerns about the perceived vulnerability of white females and the imagined predatory nature of black males. In the slave code of 1770, and for the first time in Georgia, legislators added the rape or attempted rape of a white woman by a black man to the list of capital crimes.[8] In the space of twenty years this legislation detached white womanhood from sexual agency and insisted that the only possible reason for coitus with a black man was rape. Increasing the severity of penalties for black rape of a white woman reconfirmed Georgia's southern identity; in mid-Atlantic Delaware the same crime was punishable by the severing of both ears, while in northern Rhode Island offenders could expect branding, whipping, and "transportation" (banishment, probably to the Sugar Islands).[9] Contemporary literature reinforced the legal definitions of white women as sexual victims, and newspapers provided vivid accounts of atrocities supposedly perpetrated against women by black males. On 7 April 1763 the *Georgia Gazette* informed its subscribers that a "cruel [black] wretch" in Orangeburg, South Carolina, had murdered the wife of his master, her sixteen-year-old daughter, and her suckling infant, then dressed in his master's clothes and burned the house to the ground.[10] However, while at least twenty slaves were burned alive, hung, or shot after being convicted of a crime in Georgia between 1766 and 1775, none of them was executed for white rape, and there is no evidence that such an action was ever perpetrated in the colonial era.[11] In the absence of court records from the era, little can be known for certain, but it seems clear that—as elsewhere—the sexual threat to white females was largely fictive.

Other far-reaching measures bound slavery and gendered roles between 1755 and 1759, when the Assembly instituted a series of surveillance laws that extended the responsibility for policing Georgia's slaves to more than just a handful of officers of the law. By 1757, as Betty Wood has emphasized, "all white males [between sixteen and sixty], including nonslaveholders, were being called upon to police Georgia's slaves" as members of the colonial militia or the town watch.[12] Put another way, a race-reinforcing activity was directly associated with the moment when every white boy reached adulthood—a key moment in the definition of his masculinity, civic responsibility, and independence. This would be doubly reinforced in 1770 when the law required churchgoing adult white males to pray with a gun (or a pair of pistols) and ammunition at the ready.[13] Georgia's first home-reared cohorts would grow into models of masculinity and femininity founded on racial fears.

As Georgia fell smartly into line with its northern neighbors, perhaps the only trace left of its recent interracial idiosyncrasy was an exceptional piece of legislation of 1765. This law provided that the legislature could naturalize free mulatto and mustee inhabitants, and it begrudgingly extended to them a degree of citizenship. (Ironically, the measure was partly intended to bolster militia defenses against growing fears of Indian hostilities and slave insurrections.) This law offered to free people of color "all the Rights, Priviledges, Powers and Immunities whatsoever which any Person born of British parents within this Province may, can, might, could or of Right ought to have," excepting the right to vote or to act as assemblymen.[14] Even in this odd attempt to partially enfranchise mixed-blood inhabitants, Georgians of the royal era were constructing a mythic shared white identity. Their diverse origins across the British Isles, Ireland, continental Europe, the Caribbean archipelago, and mainland North America were paling into insignificance. In any event, in 1770, with the drafting of the harshest slave code to date, Georgia dropped the clause, confirming the legal marginalization of Georgia's mixed-blood inhabitants. The matrilineal structure of Creek and Cherokee clans and the quasi-matrilineal tendencies among slave families appeared increasingly and intentionally outlandish to white Georgians, who defined themselves through paternal lines.

Legislation, in tandem with demographic change, nurtured the dissemination of ideas about nonwhites' sexual character and expansionist intentions. This was not simply a case of well-established racial preconceptions from lowcountry South Carolina taking root in lowcountry Georgia. The history of colonial America provides plentiful evidence to refute the suggestion that ambition and preconception are enough to transplant a culture. The critical facilitator of the transition to a kindred "southern" slave society was a sufficiency of white females within the young population, as achieved in the royal era. Only then could white Europeans afford to render interracial relationships illicit and effectively copy a British American (mainland) plantation society. In reality, miscegenation remained an everyday part of life in the lowcountry, as Tim Lockley has shown, but it had to be increasingly concealed behind the locked doors of individual slave owners, the curtains of whorehouses, and the impunity of overseers' depredations.[15] A Jamaican merchant visiting the lower South in 1773 made explicit the link between the frequency and visibility of sex between the races and the numbers of white women, observing that interracial liaisons "are carried on with more privacy than in our W. India Islands," where white males (such as the infamous diarist and fellow Jamaican Thomas Thistlewood) indulged in rampant sexual exploitation of their slaves.[16] Upon reflection, the merchant added, "Don't suppose Fornication is out of Fashion here, more than in other Places, No! the difference only is, that the White Girls monopolize it."[17]

In fact, white girls never had monopolized and never would corner the market on fornication with white males in Georgia. The records of the time provide a few examples, particularly among nonslaveholding whites and blacks, not only of sexual contact but also of long-standing relationships that evidently did not involve either rape or coercion, and these can only hint at the extent of illicit partnerships. Sometime before 1753 Joseph Pruniere married a typical Georgia widow, an older woman named Amie who was something of a marriage veteran. She had already outlived her first husband, the shopkeeper Peter Mallett, and her second, the planter David Jones, before she consented to wed Joseph. Like many other widows, upon remarriage she insisted upon a settlement whereby her fortune would pass not to Joseph after her death but to two children by her second marriage, son Thomas Jones and daughter Priscilla Jones. When Amie died two years later, Joseph continued to work as a merchant in Savannah, but he never remarried. At some point before or after his wife's death, he formed a relationship with his Savannah slave, who was named Maria, by whom he fathered a son, whose name was given as "Thomas, commonly called Prunieres [*sic*]." In April 1768 Joseph wrote his will, in which he officially manumitted both his partner, Maria, and his son, Thomas, who was to inherit his estate and a maintenance until he turned twenty-one. Perhaps Thomas was still no more than a boy, for his father provided alternative arrangements in the event of Thomas's not reaching this age (the estate would then go to the poor of Christ Church Parish). The decision to write the will and have it witnessed was undoubtedly intended to safeguard the interests of his immediate family and was probably prompted by sickness: Joseph Pruniere died less than a month later.[18] Another account, albeit little more than hearsay, recorded two relationships between white women and black men in 1751. Johann Martin Bolzius, noting that "such mixings or marriages are not allowed by the laws," briefly mentioned "2 white women, one French and one German, who have secretly disgraced themselves with Negroes and have borne black children," something he felt to be no less than a "terrible abomination."[19] Such relationships were rare even during the 1740s and 1750s and would fade from view in the later colonial period, a reflection of the consolidation of racial difference.

Testamentary activity leaves behind some tantalizing glimpses of relationships that resulted in the manumission of female slaves. Isaac Barksdale, a slave-owning Indian trader, manumitted only two adult slaves in his will of 1757: "Nancey," the mother of two mulatto children, and another female whom he, perhaps significantly, called "Nanney." One might speculate that he seemed to care about these children, at least more than he did about the many other slaves he bequeathed to friends and relations. But did he care about their mother and/or their nurse, whom he had already "partly freed" before his death? Charles Maran, a St. John's planter, left each member of his white family a demeaning one shilling each in 1772 and bequeathed to his associate John Couper everything else in his estate (bondspeople included), save for one female slave whom Maran manumitted. George Cuthbert, who died in the spring of 1768, left to two women annuities for the rest of their lives: the first was his wife, Mary, who was to receive three hundred pounds per annum; the second was his slave, Christina, who was to receive her freedom and twelve pounds per annum.[20] John Houstoun died childless by his wife, Hannah, but left a will that provoked widespread consternation among his relatives, for it manumitted a black woman named Doll and left six hundred dollars to each of her children.[21]

Any benign relationships, and any relationships that extended a degree of preferential treatment to selected female slaves, coexisted and overlapped with the many sexual abuses of enslaved women at the hands of white men. The opportunity to maximize on perceived racial and social superiority and pursue coerced sexual contact ranging from harassment to rape was greatest among white overseers who were managing lowcountry plantations. Although owners often went to considerable lengths to discourage relationships, many Georgia overseers took black mistresses, as they did in other plantation societies. One extreme example of this kind of exploitation was the case of Allan Bourk, an Irishman who arrived in St. John's Parish in the mid-1760s with a forged certificate of character and worked as an overseer on Kenneth Baillie's plantation. During four months there Bourk apparently infected "every negroe wench on the plantation with a foul, inveterate, and highly virulent disease," before absconding with some items, and was therefore branded as a "diabolical villain."[22] Another overseer of Christ Church Parish, Daniel Ross, specified in his will of March 1770 that his mulatto daughter Sally was to be granted her freedom and to live with and be educated by his "friend" Thomas Ross until she turned fifteen. Her mother, Phillis, however, remained a slave and was bequeathed to the same Thomas Ross, an auctioneer, along with a male slave named Sandy.[23] How long Phillis Ross remained a slave is unclear, but thanks to intervention by either familial or white benefactors, she was evidently freed sometime before 1784, when she and Sarah Baxton (another free black woman) sold a tract of two hundred acres to Philip Minis for twenty-five pounds sterling.[24]

In both the backcountry and the lowcountry, brothels provided the most obvious source of biracial sexual encounters, where the color of money was the major agent in facilitating relations. Authorities in Savannah treated interracial sex with increasing severity, and by the early national period court records suggest that those convicted of keeping a "disorderly house" or brothel could expect prison terms: a Mrs. McLean was sentenced in 1789 to forty days' imprisonment in the common jail for this misdemeanor.[25] Interracial sexual activity, then, although frequent and particularly prevalent among the poorer white and non-slaveholding classes, rarely led to the creation of functioning family units. The children of enslaved women were deemed to be slaves, and, despite occasional evidence of the acknowledgment and freeing of mulatto children by fathers, the legal infeasibility of marriage and the growing cultural stigma made biracial families a practical impossibility, especially in the lowcountry.

The combination of demographic balance, legal sanctions, and racial preconceptions swiftly eroded overt interracial interaction between whites and nonwhites—and a shift in Indian relations coincided with the tightening of the public laws of slavery. Native Americans in the Southeast increasingly declined to share cognate ties with the new waves of Georgia's backcountry immigrants who sought land without offering goods or protection—and, crucially, who were no longer impelled to compromise by a shortage of wives. Unlike the troupe of Indian traders who had become familiar with and even became acclimated to Creek ways—an open-mindedness admittedly born of self-interest—the Appalachian arrivals of the late 1750s and particularly the 1760s had no interest in (literally) wooing their new neighbors.

Like their lowcountry counterparts, the waves of pioneer settlers who descended the mountain valleys into the Georgia backcountry after 1763 brought with them large numbers of white women and rigid racial prejudices, this time forged not on the plantations of South Carolina and the Caribbean but in the frontier wilderness of Pennsylvania, Virginia, and North Carolina. As Ed Cashin has noted, these settlers often had in common only that "they did not know, or want to know, Indians."²⁶ Tensions escalated and, as elsewhere across the colonial backcountry, frequently came to a head following isolated incidents of misbehavior by either white or red renegades and newcomers. The Creek confederacy included enough river-based horticultural chiefdoms and acted with enough semblance of unity to represent a potent threat to the whole colony, and Georgia's governors went to great pains to avoid alienating it. In a letter dated 5 May 1757 Governor Ellis warned that "until [an extension of British territory] is effected it is much to be feared that our Back Settlers will always be harassed by them [Creek Indians]."²⁷ This harassment escalated into more serious violence in the summer of 1758 when a raiding party of Indians "robbed and murdered a whole family." The violence, like several occurrences that had preceded it or were to follow, was complicated by the arrival of new elements on both sides of the cultural frontier. Just as the colonial government struggled to control the movements, actions, and reactions of white "trespassers" in the backcountry, so the Creeks had trouble controlling the behavior of volatile individuals, bands, or migrant Cherokees—who were probably responsible on this occasion, for Henry Ellis described the perpetrators as "straggling Indians from the Northward (who are now settled in the Creek Country)."²⁸

After the Cherokee War erupted in South Carolina in late 1759—encouraged and supported by the French—Georgia's backcountry settlers were forced to flock to the stockade and fortified church in Augusta. The Cherokees launched an offensive across the Savannah River in late January 1760. They raided Thomas Williams's house and trading post—and murdered and scalped his wife and child. This attack, seventy miles northwest of Augusta, was followed by the killing of John Burns and his wife about twenty miles to the southeast. Only the friendship of Georgia traders with the Creeks, and the latter's enmity toward the Cherokees, prevented the frontier from being overrun.²⁹ By early March, and thanks in part to the diplomatic (and expensive) assistance of Mary Musgrove Matthews Bosomworth, the menace died down, and Governor Ellis could assert that "the Cherokees will not drive us into the sea as they threatened."³⁰ However, the continuing violence in South Carolina and the wavering attitude of several Creek leaders made a number of upcountry settlers extremely uneasy.³¹ In March 1762 William Greenwood was concerned enough about relations with the Native Americans in his vicinity to request that his land grant for his wife and two children be relocated to Buck Head.³²

A critical factor in the stability of Georgia's Anglo-Indian frontier was the treatment of Creek women by whites. During the Cherokee War, Governor Ellis informed the Board of Trade that the colony must take responsibility for "subsisting their Wives and Children in their absence when they go to War."³³ By the mid-1760s the breakdown of relations across the Anglo-Indian gender border was an early indicator of a more general collapse. White men were not only no longer marrying Creek women but were mistreating them. In the words of the Oakchoys king at a meeting in 1764 to resolve a number of murders and incidents near Augusta: "Many of these disturbances is owing to white men, who are very guilty with Women that have husbands. If a woman brings any thing to the House of a white man, let him pay her, and let her go again, or if a free single woman chooses to live with a white man, we have nothing to say against it, but many white men who are very Impudent and occasions uneasiness." He added, truthfully if tactfully, "I do not mean all white people."[34] Governor Wright similarly found a shift in cross-cultural gender relations to be central to the deterioration in Creek relations, but his perspective on accountability was somewhat different. Wright felt that the difficulties with the Creeks stemmed from the marriages of several Creek leaders to Cherokee women, unions that made the husbands "avowedly and professedly in the French and Cherokee Interest" rather than under British influence.[35]

White and red relations in the backcountry frontier were steadily deteriorating throughout the late 1760s and 1770s.[36] Trouble was rife enough during 1771 to prompt the colonial government to request regular soldiers to help support the new families that were arriving, for without armed assistance, "Men would be afraid to bring in their families and to trust their Wives and Children there."[37] Increasingly, the newest Georgians on the frontier, in contrast to the Indian traders, had no intention of interacting in a peaceable way with their Native American neighbors, and the new arrivals were impatient with the argument that the lands they were hungrily eying had been reserved for Indian hunting. The arrival of a number of settlers unfamiliar with and intolerant of Creek and Cherokee culture precipitated confusion, distrust, and frequent acts of violence and murder.

These were not simply Indian raids prompted by discontent with white occupation of lands beyond the ceded territory; rather, they were often incidents perpetrated by whites. When two unarmed young Cherokees on a boundary-marking expedition called at the cabin of Hezekiah Collins on the Broad River for some refreshment, Collins's wife offered them something to eat inside, whereupon Collins returned and killed both youths, the second with an axe. It is impossible to gauge exactly what motivated this violence beyond some combination of fear and hatred. Perhaps it was prompted by jealousy of his wife's attention; perhaps he rescued her from danger; perhaps she was in cahoots with him and delayed them intentionally. Either way, the governor and the superintendent of Indian Affairs posted rewards for Collins's arrest and put out another proclamation, ordering all trespassers to leave the Ceded Lands.[38]

In a separate incident four months later, a group of Creek Indians vented their anger by attacking the Shirrel family, which had settled near Augusta; the battle lasted six hours. Five settlers were killed, out of a household of five white men, three black men, and twelve women and children. When the Creek party arrived at about nine in the morning, the *Georgia Gazette* reported, the Shirrels "ran for shelter into the houses, and by the encouragement and good example of a Negroe fellow, who shot one of the Head Indians through the eye, those that were able fought them." When a scouting party of militia and rangers was assembled to retaliate, the soldiers lost three men to the Indians.[39] Far from the comparative normality of the lowcountry, and especially in the northwest and in the south, unusual permutations of cultural, racial, and gender interaction continued to characterize the Georgia frontier. In the Shirrel battle a man of African origin (possibly a slave) killed a Native American chief and in so doing encouraged both male and female whites of European origin to defend their home and each other.[40] On the southern frontier near St. Marys River in October 1767 more than a dozen Indians raided white settlements in revenge for a whipping they had received for alleged horse stealing. A witness testified that the Indians were "painted black," a color feared by whites in the borderlands not just because southeastern Indians used it as a sign of war but also because of the bands of runaway slaves that roamed the region.[41]

Even on the eve of the American Revolution, the proximity of peoples of Indian, African, and Euro-American heritage remained "one of the most prominent features of the region," Alan Gallay observes.[42] The historians Adele Logan Alexander and Kathryn Braund have demonstrated that the shifting grounds of cultural interaction generated shadowy aftershocks in encounters involving free blacks, runaways, slaves, and Indians in southeastern Georgia. Runaway slaves often joined nearby Indian villages, sometimes adopting the dress of the Creeks, serving as interpreters, and enjoying greater freedoms and privileges than they did among the whites. On other occasions Indian raiding parties absconded with slaves and allowed no change in their chattel status, employing them on their own lands, and producing cultural and gender encounters on very different terms.[43]

WHILE THE WEB of gender and race was weakest at its edges, it was most powerful at its center, where the lives of the white Georgia elite became inextricably bound up by cultural standards that reinforced its hierarchies. Since the heritage of the elite was diverse—an odd medley of trusteeship success stories, transplants from South Carolina (of various generations), and capital investors from the Caribbean and Britain—its members could not rely upon titles or inherited blood but sought to be aristocratic in the original sense of the word: the best. In their circles of association, material possessions, and their behavior, members of the Georgia elite aimed to be at once ostentatious and inaccessible, desperately emulating European fashions and corresponding with their designated peers in other colonies. The youngest child of the Atlantic world screamed, politely, for attention as an outpost of respectability.

What allowed this aristocracy to flower resplendently was intermarriage. Intermarriage by members of the first families at once provided opportunities to highlight their special celebrity status and, more crucially, to establish a way for them to bar entrance by outsiders—which was especially important because the late colonial Georgia slaveholding elite lacked an integrated community in either geographic or religious senses. Through their policy of intermarriage members of the elite created dense layers of interlocking kin networks that cemented familial loyalties, reciprocal obligations, and political allegiances. This was, of course, a long-tested colonial policy and to some extent another import from South Carolina, where, as Edward Pearson has noted, joining the leading families through matrimony became a critical instrument of class formation.[44] Naturally, shared economic and political interests could and did generate circles of association that excluded familial interaction, but intermarriage was recognized as another method of perpetuating social distinctions. The Gibbonses, Butlers, McIntoshes, Bryans, Houstouns, Grahams, Crookes, and so on formed a population that was almost entirely distinct from the rest of the colony, which could only aspire to become associated with so hallowed a fellowship.[45] Like fashion and education, marriage became a device for isolating and perpetuating the community of the elite in Georgia. These weddings were recorded in the local newspapers and solemnized by ceremonies performed in proper churches in Christ Church (Savannah) or Charlestown by recognized and respected ministers. Although these marriages explicitly celebrated the uniting of two people, and two prominent families, they implicitly heralded the successful exclusion of many more. At the other end of the marital spectrum—as I discussed in chapter 5—the extension of unusual power and protection to wealthy widows made it less likely that they would need or desire to remarry and therefore less likely that the pool of blue blood would be diluted.

Courtship among the elite was a formal process that revolved around the high society of Savannah and Charlestown. Within the social whirl of dinners, visits, clubs, and balls, young men and women participated in a carefully choreographed series of encounters that were dependent upon factors such as wealth, geography, socioreligious and particularly parental influences, and, of course, physical attraction. Where these occurred depended very much on the season, as John Bartram observed when traveling through the lower South in September 1765. He noted that many of "the best inhabitants" lived only at "thair seats in winter" and that those who remained during the sultry summer months tended to venture out for a ride only every fortnight or so, sometimes with "thair Ladies with them & and children in A chair." They preferred to remain within the confines of their commodious "piazzas," screened from the sunshine, where "much conversation both sitting & walking is held."[46] Young members of the elite formed their marital choices during these public and private encounters, but the overwhelming majority required the consent of both sets of parents. No evidence remains of marriages arranged by the parents, and only circumstantial evidence is extant of those arranged by grooms and the bride's parents—namely, those involving an older groom and a very young bride. Parental influence during courtship and formal consent to marriage were thus two separate stages at which fathers and mothers could look to refine their children's marital decisions. In other classes and circumstances such consent was unnecessary, as it was at law, but for the young elite of late eighteenth-century Georgia, marrying without parental consent was an unthinkable evil that could be extremely dangerous to both their social and financial prospects.

George Jones left parental consultation until the last minute in his engagement to marry Polly Gibbons. He wrote to his father, Noble Wimberley Jones, in November 1784, seeking permission to ask for her hand and conscious that he had already acted somewhat ahead of himself.

> My Honoured Sir,
> The subject I now purpose addressing you on, having made its way into somewhat general conversation, and fearing it might reach you by some other channel and perhaps in false colours, have therefore thought it my duty to the best of Parents, to acquaint you with the whole of the Transactions.

This was not a good start. The young suitor's request was not really voluntary but compelled because his engagement was already a subject of gossip in Savannah. He would have to work for his permission and labored over the next twenty-six lines to convince his "ever honoured Parent," for whose advice George had "invariably the great respect," that this was a good match, that Polly was the One. He concluded,

> I flatter myself my dear Parent that my duty and affection will be confessed and accepted by you, in thus humbly submitting the sentiments of my heart to your consideration, and hope for another mark of your goodness and condescention in making me happy by your and my dear Mother's approbation and consent and I shall then be your truly happy and most assuredly most obedient and dutiful son, George Jones.[47]

The key factors, as presented by George Jones in this letter, revolve around his attempt to persuade his father that his choice is adroit. It is patently clear that

George is talking not just man to man but more specifically in the submissive language of son to father. George actually mentions little about the personality or circumstances of Polly but maintains a businesslike attitude toward the subject, except for expressing his own feelings. He stresses that he is not rushing into an unwise relationship, having been enamored for a lengthy period, and remarks that the presence and advances of various other "objects" have not distracted him from his course. George is thus attempting to close to his father all possible avenues of objection: George has been patient; he has not been tempted by other women; his paramour is perfectly suited to him. George's manifest efforts are testimony to the necessity of obtaining parental consent, that it was more than just a formality to advancing to the final stage of courtship. Two months later George sent another letter to his father, having evidently been in frequent correspondence: his father had written twice in the previous week, but sadly neither "very affectionate" letter has survived.

It becomes evident from this second letter that George's father had assured his son of his parents' support without actually giving full assent. Rather, it appears that his parents urged caution and deliberation, advice that understandably frustrated George, who was fighting not just to secure consent but also to prevent social embarrassment. "Agreeable to your hint, I have seriously, maturely and deliberately canvassed the whole matter both as to *time* and *choice* and every thing else I can think of; and must once more declare to you my dear Father, that my attachment for the Object in question is irrevocably fixed." This rather emotionless description of Polly served not only to lend a weighty and rational feel to the language but also—as revealed later in the letter—to ensure some security against dissemination of its contents. George rescinds his previous objections to mentioning the matter to other members of the family—in particular his sister—but he "would wish it to stop there." George then makes a play to accelerate his intended marriage to Polly, informing his father that, "Unless you absolutely forbid it, and some cogent reasons shall militate against it, I have proposed the *time* for the completion of my happiness to be on or about the beginning of the next Month."[48] Noble Wimberley Jones evidently agreed to offer his son the consent that he implored, for a couple of weeks later the *Gazette of the State of Georgia* announced that George was married on a Tuesday evening to Miss Mary Gibbons, "a young lady endowed with every accomplishment that can make the married state truly happy."[49]

Parental consent to marital choices was a reinforcing thread that ensured continuity between generations as well as across them. For what was important to fathers and mothers (as evidenced by George's mention of his own mother) instantly became important to children contemplating marriage. Parental attitudes were at least easy to identify and even, on occasion, possible to change. Other aspects of courtship may have been more frustrating for both parties involved. Elite courtship occurred beneath a veneer of social etiquette and gender-based conversational protocol. The successful suitor of either gender had not only to obey publicly the rules of propriety but also to understand the nuances of body language and fashion, pick up and relay pertinent gossip, and fulfill obligations with regard to the timing and exposition of the marriage proposal. The process of elite courtship was fundamentally paradoxical. Formal and stilted protocol accompanied the pursuit of base instincts. Businesslike attitudes in correspondence and among parents accompanied the rise of the romantic movement in literature and music. Confidence in dress and conversation disguised insecurities and belied an overwhelming fear of failure. The Jewish merchant Levi Sheftall recorded in his short autobiography that, when he was about twenty-three, he "had an inclination to settle my self with a Companion for life which I well knew would be very pleasing to my good parents."[50] Although he provides few details, the first young lady upon whom he had fixed his thoughts rejected Sheftall, a setback that was evidently devastating. He commented, "I will confess that my sufferings on her account nearly cost me my life." In 1765, when he was twenty-five, Levi picked himself up and actually became engaged to a lady in Charlestown, but he decided to break off the engagement due to the "imprudence of her (tyrant) Aunt"—again suggesting that near relations played important roles. Levi Sheftall at last became a successful suitor when he was twenty-eight, comparatively late. By then his business acumen and capital were marking him as a respectable potential husband, and, sure enough, during a business trip to the West Indies, he married Sarah Delamotta on 25 May 1768. Her parents were probably heavily involved in the matchmaking; she was just fourteen years, four months, and ten days old. Sarah's young age at marriage was the major factor in the Sheftall family's eventual size; she bore twelve children between 1769 and 1796.[51]

For young women especially, courtship was a period in which—as Eleanor Boatwright has put it—they enjoyed "power, prestige, and glory."[52] Any enjoyment of the process, however, was tempered not only by the prospect of a resultant and constraining marriage but by the far more ominous shadow of an absence of marriage. The years of courtship were short and vital to the elite, which suffered more than any other group from the caricaturing of the unconventional. Contemporaries' ridicule of aging unmarried women was well documented, and many subscribed to the opinion of Dr. Brickett: "She that continues unmarried until twenty is reckoned a stale-maid which is a very indifferent character."[53] Some commentators observed that these pressures seemed to anaesthetize the behavior of elite white females of marriageable age. When traveling in the lower South (albeit in the first decade of the nineteenth century), the prominent Philadelphia ornithologist Alexander Wilson noted that

> nothing has surprised me more than the cold, melancholy reserve of the females, of the best families, in South Carolina and Georgia. Old and young, single and married, all have that dull frigid insipidity, and reserve, which is attributed to solitary old maids. Even in their own houses they scarce utter anything to a stranger but yes or no, and one is perpetually puzzled to know whether it proceeds from awkwardness or dislike. Those who have been at some of their Balls [in Charleston] say that the ladies hardly even speak or smile, but dance with as much gravity, as if they were performing some ceremony of devotion. On the contrary, the Negro wenches are all sprightliness and gayety.[54]

But although the lowcountry lady, when she approached her prospective legitimate sexual partners, may have looked "as if she were picking up a live coal in one hand and a dead rat in the other," as Winthrop Jordan put it, and some contemporary males perceived it, she certainly did not feel that way.[55]

Precious few words remain that were written from the girls' perspective, but the recollections of Elizabeth Lichtenstein Johnson of her own adolescent experiences in colonial and Revolutionary Savannah suggest that for all the external torpor, there was internal torment. This was a nerve-wracking time, for sure, especially for a girl with no mother to guide her, but it was also exciting and animated. "Betsey" vividly remembered the attentions of various suitors and in particular the first time she set eyes upon her future husband, a young beau who "had resisted all the beauty and fashion he had left [in New York], and found something in a simple child of nature to make him not many weeks after change his sentiments. Such was the romance of the olden times!"[56] True, this last statement reminds us that she was gazing back through rose-tinted Loyalist spectacles and probably no small number of cataracts too, as she was writing in 1836, when she was seventy-two. But she remembered that "I could get over my bashful timidity.... I was glad to get into the drawing-room before they [Loyalist officers] arrived; and to take wine at dinner with one of these gay soldiers called a deep blush into my cheeks."[57]

In fact, when her father became concerned that she was enjoying herself too much and sent her back to her aunt's, she remarked that "this was rather a damper to my youthful heart."[58] Caught between the forces of her father's wishes and her own desires, between her painfully learned subscription to patriarchal authority and the romance that she had dreamed and increasingly read about, Elizabeth fled upstairs where she "wept most abundantly," in large measure out of guilt. The persistent captain William Johnston was not put off.

Elizabeth Lichtenstein Johnston "in later life." Johnson harbored mixed memories of her childhood and adolescence in colonial and Revolutionary Georgia. A fervent loyalist, she looked back fondly on her courtship and marriage, at fifteen years old, to William Martin Johnson, a captain in the New York Volunteers. Her subsequent experiences as a Loyalist refugee and oftentimes single parent were more melancholy. She would bear ten children in a host of locations across the British Atlantic world, including Savannah, Charleston, St. Augustine, Edinburgh, Jamaica, and finally Nova Scotia. Courtesy of the Hargrett Rare Book and Manuscript Library, University of Georgia Libraries.

When he persuaded a mutual friend, probably Mrs. Eliza Houstoun, to follow Elizabeth to her aunt's rural plantation and request her company, her aunt obstinately refused because of her "stiff notions of female decorum."[59] Fathers, aunts, mothers, and extended kin were thus constantly on the defense against the wily pubescent and romantic machinations of the young. Their voices, frequently absent during the trusteeship, now seemed to echo up the stairways of every plantation household. They were sentinels of the principles of gendered behavior and, by extension, of the exclusivity of the elite.

Elizabeth Lichtenstein Johnston teases her readers by adding, "whether she [her aging aunt] convinced me then I will not say, but this I now know, she was right and had proper ideas of female reserve."[60] This tells us both that the gendered decorum of the late eighteenth century was to persist and in part *how* it persisted: any acts of defiance were to be stripped from the historical record ("I will not say").

During the period of courtship and the publishing of banns, a number of wealthy Georgia couples and/or their relatives decided to formulate a settlement, or marriage contract, before the ceremony took place. The settlement constituted a woman's greatest protection against the loss of her property or inheritance to avaricious husbands or children. A wife could retain control of her separate estate in several ways: by conveyance to a trustee before her marriage;

by prenuptial agreement between the parties; by postnuptial settlement (under which a husband conveyed his wife's property to a third party to hold for her); and by gift or legacy specifically establishing the woman's sole ownership and legally disavowing her husband's claim.

A substantial proportion of such contracts were drawn up by widows, who understandably preferred not to see their fortunes (and thus any existing children's fortunes) dispersed when they remarried. Marriage settlements were not the exclusive prerogative of remarrying widows, however. Newly engaged women who had never married before or, more commonly, their relations could similarly insist on receiving a substantial portion of property or possessions in case of the prospective groom's demise—such a settlement was made before the marriage of Mordecai Sheftall and Frances Hart was "solemnized according to the Jewish Custom Rites" in 1761.[61] Prenuptial agreements, especially those involving women in possession of or expected to inherit substantial fortunes, were an important preoccupation in the weeks leading up to the wedding. Although one might expect that among the elite the composition of these documents was a result of discourse between the two patriarchs—the father and future husband—this was not always the case. Mary Jones requested the advice of her lawyer and friend John Farley in April 1780 specifically regarding her forthcoming marriage to James Bullock. Farley confirmed to Mary Jones that the draft of a prenuptial agreement shown to him by Bullock would "probably operate in a Court of chancery," mentioning that the closeness of the wedding day prohibited its revision. Farley stated that he had been assured that Bullock would "fulfil his Engagement to your satisfaction." Mary was evidently happy enough with this consultation to go ahead with the prenuptial agreement, which read: "Mary is possessed of a Considerable estate, in her own right . . . which she is desirous to [illegible] and keep in her own power and right to dispose of by will or otherways she may think fit after and notwithstanding such intended marriage the aforesaid James does hereby give up his claim and renounce for himself his heirs . . . any right and claim."[62]

Such agreements acted as more than simple legal protection of the bride's property from the clutches of her husband. The willingness of a male suitor to sign one was also a manifestation of his attachment and commitment to the marriage. Leaving the female's property out of the marital equation confirmed that the groom was undertaking the union for more than financial reasons. After all, should the union be successful, the wife could always leave her protected property to her husband and/or their children. Twice-widowed Elizabeth Mercer, for instance, formed a contract with her third husband, Charles Pryce, in 1757 and two years later wrote a will making over her entire real and personal estate to him—although she lived until 1768.[63] Wills of husbands demonstrate that it was a common practice to formally return to their wife, in accordance with their marriage contract, property or possessions that the wife had brought to the marriage. Cash, cattle, land, furniture, and slaves were all returned by testators to the widows who had brought them to the marriage and had a prenuptial agreement.[64] Other marriage-related documents were drawn up to protect the rights and property of the husband from legal action by his wife's relatives or guardians. A prenuptial settlement signed by John and Sarah Cuthbert in 1755 records that they waived any claims upon the person and property of their daughter Sarah Threadcraft on the eve of her marriage to Lachlan McIntosh, whether for clothing, lodging, washing, schooling, or anything else whatsoever. Lachlan was obviously concerned about becoming accountable for these costs, which her stepfather might otherwise have attempted to recover.[65]

The opinions of fathers and mothers (and tyrannical aunts) were not the only cultural vehicles for expressing and encouraging stiff notions of female decorum. Newspapers and printing presses, which had simply not existed in Georgia during the trusteeship, offered manifold pieces of social commentary extracted from across the British Atlantic world and, occasionally, written by local subscribers. The local weeklies published notices of marriage that venerated specific virtues. They also, of course, published obituaries, final and lasting tributes to the deceased that provide strong indicators of contemporary perceptions of the ideal roles within marriage and the family (as well as nuggets of demographic information). By publicly distinguishing the superlative from the everyday, obituaries effectively raised the dead to a fictive perfection and set a bar at which the living could aim.

Philip Minis, supposedly the first white male child born in Georgia, died at the age of fifty-five on 6 March 1789. His obituary in the *Gazette* of the next week recorded that his "disconsolate" widow, Judith, and his "venerable" mother, Abigail, deplored the loss of a man who had in life been "an affectionate husband, dutiful son, tender father and kind brother."[66] The same adjectives were often applied elsewhere, in particular with reference to affectionate spouses and tender parents. Some obituaries were more detailed than the concise newspaper death notices. Levi Sheftall's son wrote of him that he was "actively alive to the welfare of his affectionate wife and dutiful children," highlighting Levi's familial virtues.[67]

Indeed, remarkably little variation is to be found in the extant obituaries of late colonial Georgia. Deceased husbands and wives were both frequently described as affectionate, apparently regardless of gender or age. This homogeneity of descriptive language served to unify and reinforce elite ideals of marital behavior. The adjective *affectionate* straddled both genders and placed them in a familial environment, removed from overt sexual passion but suggestive of warmth and devotion. Obituaries celebrated faithfulness and tenderness less frequently, and deceased parents might be congratulated on their vigilance and indulgence, among other things. The terminology was intended to link the deceased as closely in death to the ideal of gentility as the subject had aspired to be in life. [68]

The death of young elite women attracted particular attention from the local news section of Savannah's *Georgia Gazette*, which published short obituaries or poems. Miss Dorinda Ashe was hailed as "at once your sex's envy and their pride."[69] Miss Agnes Bryan achieved even higher regard, combining "a female softness, with a manly mind."[70] Only by setting up and sharing enough examples of what it meant to have a "manly mind" or to be a "sex's envy" could opinions converge on a gendered decorum that was neither rational nor innate but socially constructed. What having a "manly mind" actually meant to a Frenchman or a Puritan or an African or an Englishwoman or a Creek Indian was different. But these obituaries made sure that Georgia had a gender consensus for all to see and to impart. What did it mean to have a "manly mind" in late colonial Georgia? It meant to be like Agnes Bryan.

Older women were exalted as paragons of society, as was Mrs. Mary Elliott, who was hailed not only as a tender mother and affectionate wife (the usual spiel) but also as a "sincere friend and affable companion"; Mrs. Mary Ann Yonge's conduct in life was described as exemplary, as a "faithful Wife, an indulgent Mother, and a good Christian."[71] Among the obituaries of the elite of late colonial Georgia, as elsewhere in the British Atlantic world, the conception of idealized wifely behavior was rooted, ultimately, in docility. However, the paternalistic origins of this conception must be fully acknowledged: women's docility was celebrated only with regard to white male figures, and particularly familial figures—husbands and sons—who most frequently penned the obituaries. Obedience to husbands found public postmortem expression in the form of affection and faithfulness, whereas tenderness and indulgence characterized devotion to children. In contrast to these relatively passive traits, elite women's relationships with other groups were recorded as active and vibrant: as friends they were supportive, sincere, and affable; as Christians they were eager and pious; as neighbors, kind and charitable; as mistresses, just and humane.

In the process of sharing gendered ideals, as in sharing tea parties, recipes, or fashion tips, members of the elite marked out their territory. In practice the attitudes displayed (or published) in a public environment were rarely a genuine reflection of interpersonal dynamics. Behind the doors of the household, and especially behind the bedroom doors, the complexities of personalities and relationships refracted ideals into realities. In fact, to read different sections of the same newspapers is to get a very different sense of how contemporaries viewed gender characteristics, of how gender was perceived in courtship or in marriage. The literature of social commentary—letters, proverbs, poems, and comments—frequently addressed the subject and was often more nuanced and earthy than formulaic tombstone pleasantries. Some pieces were no doubt included by the editor, James Johnston, who, occasionally short on material, might seek to fill his pages with entertaining allegories and anecdotes. Other pieces were composed by subscribers or sent in and published at their request.

Much of the satire that obsessed readers of the *Georgia Gazette* during the last third of the eighteenth century drew directly from wider English patterns in the poetic expression of marriage, which shifted toward the glorification of domesticity and celebration of affective bonding in marriage.[72] Other pieces were also heavily influenced by British publications. One writer, "Philaretus" (fond of virtue), urged Georgia women in early 1768 to emulate Samuel Richardson's fictional heroine Clarissa (see the appendix)—and many Georgian ladies may have likened their own situations to islands of purity surrounded by high seas of vice and battering waves of immorality. Ironically, Philaretus was encouraging them to read a piece that convincingly portrayed the abuse of patriarchal power and the dire consequences of resisting it. In fact, as "Philafiddlesticks" pointed out in the subsequent issue of the *Gazette*, Philaretus himself was the most obvious mimic. Attesting to the interconnectedness of the late eighteenth-century literary Atlantic are his plagiarism of his arguments from an English magazine, the *Spectator* (perhaps he hoped to get away with it in light of the provincial Georgian readership), and his having been caught.[73]

In all, Georgians received a cacophony of advice from different quarters—from seventeenth-century romantic poems to caustic contemporary slanders. They were told to follow the tenets of classical philosophy, to emulate the Quakers, to use caution and discretion in their courtship, and not to be deceived by gaudy dress or influenced by lust. They were also told that marital violence works, that the most foolish people in society are wives who part with their inheritance, husbands who leave their wife as sole executor (with full power to apportion to their children), and men who have no estate but marry a woman without a fortune.

Girls were urged to marry, although this would render them "the passive slaves of custom's tyrant reign," because fertility is a gift from God and aging unmarried women die "neglected by the young and fair."[74] Wives were begged not to become obsessive and thereby allow their behavioral traits—such as being superstitious, cleaning obsessively, or speaking only in sentences—to dominate their marriage. Youths were warned that bachelorhood should be only a transitional phase and that without a legitimate partnership they were inferior and incomplete, leaving to posterity only "Doubts, Fears, Bashfulness, Irresolution, Uncertainty, Fickleness, [and] Obstinacy."[75] Marriage, apparently an institution "fashionable" to deride, was defended as "the cement of society, the foundation of all social bliss, worthy of God to institute, and honourable for man to observe."[76] Marriage was also attacked as a means of chaining men to the yoke of scolding wives, whose tyrannical abuse encouraged bachelors to remain single—despite their sexual urges and their need to accumulate wealth.

Despite this range of advice proffered in the pieces published by and for Georgians during the final third of the eighteenth century, some general observations about contemporary perceptions of marriage are possible. First, it is immediately obvious that almost all the social commentary printed in the papers was written by and for elite men. Although the *Gazette* had both male and female subscribers, and both genders advertised and placed notices, the letters and poems demonstrate a dominant male perspective in their content. This holds true whether the contributors write to inform, amuse, or advise and whether they support or attack aspects of marriage.

The contributions to the *Georgia Gazette* suggest that these men had two broad approaches toward marriage. The first, as represented by such works as "The Rose," "A Pastoral," and "A Batchelor's Will," and by contributors writing under the pseudonyms of "Smart," "Philaretus," "A Husband," and "Philanthropos" (see the appendix for examples by Philaretus and Philanthropos), is essentially positive about the merits of the institution.[77] The content of these pieces, although occasionally and gently comic, is largely didactic in nature: paternally instructive, and old-fashioned in style and intention. Marriage is an institution worthy of celebration in its platonic state but also one that the actions of its participants may pervert. Caution is required in courtship, appreciation of female strengths and weaknesses is vital both before and during marriage, and constant analysis and refinement of the marital state must not only be undertaken but also conveyed to wives and the younger generation.

In contrast, works such as "The Spirit of Contradiction" and the writings of "Philotomy" and "Anti-Vixen" represent a negative and derogatory view of women and marriage (see the appendix for an offering from Anti-Vixen).[78] These pieces uphold bachelorhood and promiscuity in the face of a skeptical critique of womanhood that implicitly identifies marriage as a backward step for the female character. The tone of these pieces is caustically and aggressively comic—suggesting in turn remedies for malfunctioning marriages that range from domestic violence through financial sanctions and ultimately (if surreally) to amputation. The authors make no effort to suggest moral alternatives. If anything, they demonstrate a preference for the immoral and unorthodox: the bachelor with no estate who marries a single woman with no fortune is, in this dissenting analysis, a fool. Indeed, the very concept of a malfunctioning marriage—according to these contributors—is somewhat tautological.

Where the two approaches to the concept of marriage do overlap is in the mutual awareness of the destructive force of arguments and disputes within marriage. Although both offer explanations for the occurrence of marital disagreements, only the paternalistic contributors offer a plausible rationalization and any kind of solution. The dissenting view presents conflict within marriage as almost inevitable, as predominantly the fault of the wife—because of either her defective character or her disobedient behavior, which can be remedied only in the short term. The paternalistic view holds that problematic marriages are a reflection of problematic personalities, of *either* male or female. Thus the male is cautioned to be prudent and temperate in his actions and choices (including those before marriage), whereas the female is urged to be responsive and self-aware: to live up to the ideals presented in literature (e.g., Clarissa) and those virtues venerated in Georgia obituaries.

The letter of Philanthropos makes clear that the paternalist contributors were well aware of the existence of a more squalid, dissenting, and even fashionable view of marriage among a minority of their contemporaries. The perceived attractions of remaining a promiscuous bachelor, or—for that matter—a chaste virgin, were recognized and rejected (e.g., in "Batchelor's Will" and "A Pastoral," as well as by Philanthropos) on the grounds that to do so offered nothing to the future and meant failing to fulfill one's obligations to society. Marriage was tied through metaphors of construction ("the cement of society"), fertility (vines and growth), and transition (death of bachelorhood) to personal development—the attaining of a higher individual state in both man and woman. In the absence of a dominant denomination or a thorough creed within the colony, this was as close as many elite Georgians publicly came to answering the universal conundrum: Why are we here? The appeal of using such writings to explain the moral ordering of society was its apparent timelessness, yet as Felicity Nussbaum and Laura Brown have noted, eighteenth-century literature was nonetheless "an historically produced category."[79] In the newspapers the paternalistic defense of an "orthodoxy" of marriage against various seditious opinions and practices revealed both its limits and its extent, like glistening dew on a web.

THE ELITE'S CONTROL of legislative and judicial authority—as signified, for instance, by the slave-patrolling militia—facilitated the diffusion of consensuses about gender and race throughout the colony. It was aided by the desire of many nonelites, whether white or black, to emulate their economic betters in dress and behavior. Louis LeClerc de Milfort recounted that one backcountry wife had gone to great (and comedic) lengths to impress him with her fashionable manners, by attempting to use tea leaves.[80] In October 1775, even as colonists further north turned to homespun clothing to register their solidarity against British impositions, the Georgia grand jurors (who essentially ran local government in the colonial era, responding to complaints and issuing regulations to do with road building, bridge maintenance, the operation of jails, and such) expressed concerns about the "excessive and costly apparel" worn by people of color in Savannah, in imitation of their "betters."[81] Finally, local authorities such as church bodies tried to hold their communities together culturally across different classes. Every church that has left records, including the Lutheran Salzburgers, the Congregational church at Midway, and the Quaker Meetinghouse at Wrightsborough, took steps to castigate members who, if they didn't break the letter of the law, broke gender codes loaded with moral significance—for instance, husbands who were excessively violent toward their wives. In 1770 St. John's Parish suspended three men of substance for mistreating their wives—an example to all and sundry that socioeconomic status should not theoretically affect gendered behavior.[82]

Across the colony the indiscriminate dynamics of each relationship were underscored by a specific conception of the places of husband and wife in the social and domestic order. Little evidence exists to shed light on the standardization of protocol among the nonelite, especially in the backcountry. We may expect that practices belied theory far more openly—that the virtues of affection, devotion, and tenderness were less celebrated than functional skills and that the letter of the law or the dogma of the church was less constraining. The snooty records of churches in Ebenezer and Wrightsborough certainly seem to intimate that many settlers outside their cherished communities continued to indulge in what Richard Godbeer has termed "pragmatic" and "popular" folk traditions of marriage—informal, impromptu, and inexpensive.[83] Nonetheless, stabilizing the demography of the region lent ballast to marital practices. For instance, as separation became less common, it accrued a growing cultural stigma. One separation in 1767 resulted in tragedy when, a year after refusing to pay the debts of his wife, Margaret, the barber John Frentz found her at the house of her friend, a widow named Catherine Williams. There, he "asked her to make up their differences and go home with him, but on her refusing to comply, he immediately went to the door, and presenting a gun to her, which he brought with him as he said to kill a rabbit, fired it, and killed her on the spot." John Frentz was apprehended, and hanged in January 1769.[84]

The records of a Quaker community that settled in the Georgia backcountry offer further circumstantial evidence that the colony had consolidated a racially demarcated gender system that was increasingly normative and universal. About forty Quaker families from Orange County, North Carolina, had settled Wrightsborough Township in 1767, led by Joseph Maddock and Jonathan Sell.[85] Although the Georgia land-granting committee had specifically laid out and reserved land for this group of two hundred men, women, and children, the Quakers constituted only a minority of the inhabitants of the region. The unusually close coexistence of Quakers with non-Quakers in Wrightsborough was largely ascribable to the community's proximity to Creek settlements. Maddock was surely aware that the presence of non-Quakers nearby, while undesirable under normal circumstances, offered the Society of Friends some military protection against Indian attack (which their pacifistic religion forbade them to provide for themselves).[86] With their lands and persons thus secured, they hoped to go about their everyday lives in peace, upholding the peculiarities and practices of their faith.

Quaker marriages theoretically conformed to the banns system, announcing marital intention twice in successive months before the monthly meetings. Quaker couples therefore expected a period of formal engagement longer than most others in colonial and Revolutionary Georgia—a minimum delay of eight weeks before they could marry. The structure of Quaker marriage in Georgia was that both prospective spouses appeared before the meetinghouse assembly and declared their marital intention, whereupon the Men's Meeting appointed a committee (usually of two people) to investigate the prospective groom's "life and conversation and clearness in relation to marriage with others," and the Women's Meeting reciprocated. In the case of remarriage the congregation took further action to ensure that any children from the first marriage were adequately provided for. If these inquiries found nothing to obstruct the marriage, the couple—after again reaffirming their intention to marry—were left at "liberty to consummate their marriage according to good order," and the same committee of investigation became responsible for producing a marriage certificate and ensuring that the wedding was accomplished in good order. M. A. Candler has suggested that Quakers broke a taboo if they married at home instead of in meeting, but although this may have been true of other Quaker communities, the evidence from Men's Monthly Meeting minutes for the Georgia settlers suggests otherwise. Marriages actually took place at the liberty of the betrothed couple—that is, at the local meetinghouse of the bride or perhaps in the home—but under the supervision of a number of people appointed by both Men's and Women's Meetings.[87]

Joseph Maddock's decision to settle near other groups of colonists, although prudent in terms of providing physical defense for the Quakers, left the community open to a far more insidious form of decomposition: intermarriage with outsiders. Meetinghouse minutes show that marriages to outsiders actually outnumbered exclusively Quaker unions, twenty-six to twenty. Furthermore, in more than half the cases such "outgoings in marriage" resulted in immediate expulsion from the religious community.[88] Rather than subscribing to the gendered expectations of their elders and forerunners, young Georgia Quakers found mainstream customs and practices too attractive to resist. Frequenting "places of diversion," and manifesting a "Loose Disorderly Disposition" through their dress and language, they danced their way out of narrow orthodoxy and into another, wider one.[89] Only if guilty parties produced an immediate condemnation of their own actions were they allowed to continue to attend meetings, as in the case of James Vernon in May 1775.[90]

Whether a Quaker received permission to continue to attend meetings after marriage to an outsider also varied significantly according to the gender of the offender. According to the minutes, equal numbers of women and men married outside the Society of Friends (twenty-six in all), yet women made up 79 percent of those expelled and just 17 percent of those who remained. This is largely ascribable to the reticence of many female Quakers to hand in a paper of self-condemnation but may also be a reflection of more stringent expectations within the Women's Monthly Meeting than the men's. Catherine Sidwell, upon her marriage to an outsider named Mendenhall, was excoriated for having "tolerated and encouraged Fidling [sic] and Dancing" in October 1783. Catherine was at first adamant that she would appeal her expulsion but was persuaded not to by a committee appointed by the Quakers in February 1784. Two years later she was still fighting to be readmitted to the Society, producing testimony in October 1786 in which she condemned her disorderly marriage and conduct. The Quakers postponed their decision on the matter, stating that their major concern—the "chiefest obstruction from receiving her offering"—was the distance she lived from other Friends.[91]

Few other women who married outsiders shared Catherine Sidwell Mendenhall's desperation to remain within the fold despite her marriage. Most women, newly married to non-Quakers, appeared "in no inclinable disposition" or "desirous of condemning" their actions to their old meetinghouse. Through their act of marriage they had already moved away from the Society—often literally as well as figuratively. Their loss was keenly felt by the community of Quakers, whose elders eventually issued an announcement—or series of "advices"—in 1786, to be read in both Men's and Women's Meetings, stating "that early care be taken to advise and deal with such as appear inclinable to marry contrary to discipline and if parents give their consent to or connive at their children therein that they and those who may attend such marriages be dealt with accordingly."[92] This statement suggests that the factors leading to mixed marriages were more than the mere proximity of Quakers to non-Quakers. Although an era of revolution and the turbulence of the backcountry afforded young adult Quakers the opportunity to rebel against the influences of parents and elders, this announcement acknowledges that parents and friends were often coconspirators in the dilution of the Quaker community. When a daughter was torn between suitors who were wealthy, landholding outsiders and poorer and perhaps younger male Quakers, and when she asked advice or permission from her parents (as nearly all Quakers did), they in turn faced a similar dilemma: to ensure a secure future for their child or to back the fading tenets of their Society of Friends. As the numbers of Quakers declined, the alternative prospect was that of a community forced to sanction intermarriage between blood relatives. Critics often mockingly associated incest and sexual deviance with Quakers during the seventeenth and eighteenth centuries.[93] In this case, however, the elders of Wrightsborough themselves cautioned "that care be taken to advise those who may appear inclinable, against marrying with too near kindred."[94] The flaming light of truth was running out of torchbearers, their numbers drained by the increasingly homogeneous counterculture beyond their control.

Quaker authorities made other attempts to sustain levels of membership and devotion to the faith. They amended Quaker policy in Wrightsborough in May 1782 in an effort to maintain the membership of children whose parent(s) had been disowned by the meeting. The new policy stated that such children "shall be looked upon to have full Right in Membership until they forfeit it by their own Misconduct."[95] In contrast to those who chose or were forced to leave the Quaker community, few settlers in the region chose or were allowed to convert to the Society of Friends. The meetings accepted six requests by non-Quakers between 1773 and 1792, and all were made by women. The process of acceptance depended upon the applicant's recent behavior under the scrutiny of the Women's Meeting, but the lack of those minutes means we know about only successful applicants, as recorded in passing by the Men's Meeting. Three of the accepted women, Ruth Sidwell, Sarah Sanders, and Rebecca Farmer, were already wives of Quaker men. Having lived in the community for a period, they were able to give a good account of themselves over time—in Sarah's case, "some Considerable time past." They also stood to gain some credibility from the influential positions of their husbands. The other three women who joined the Society of Friends were single, two of them mothers, and all received united support from the Women's Meeting.[96]

GEORGIA'S SLAVE POPULATION was denied the right to form marriages recognized by law.[97] Since there was no theory or orthodoxy, the character of slave marriages and relationships varied widely and was dependent upon a host of variables. Two themes seem to pervade the few historical records relating to slave unions and families of the colonial era: their intrinsic precariousness and their intrinsic fortitude. Starkly apparent to inhabitants of late colonial Georgia was that external powers could dissolve slave relationships at any second, and the slaves involved had no formal recourse to appeal. This power of severance occasioned more fear among bondspeople than the whip, chain, or any kind of corporal punishment. It was not only a demeaning reminder of their status but a critical mechanism by which the regime of slavery would be extended throughout the colony (and, later, the state). This was the part of the web that caught the most prey. Slaveholders were involved, indirectly and directly, in ordering bondspeople's sexual relations and, by extension, relations between the genders.

The sex ratio and age structure of the enslaved population of Georgia undoubtedly affected opportunities for sexual congress and family formation. Indirectly, the artificial whims of a host of white planters, merchants, and African slave traders had already predetermined a black population that was demographically skewed to begin with (see chapter 4). The limited age structure of slave imports and the constraints placed on the mobility of the population fundamentally affected birth, death, and marriage rates. The physical abuses and psychological damage associated with their status increased slave mortality and reduced slave fertility in many different ways. Everyday influences included limited diet, accommodation and clothing, corporal punishments, labor intensity, and epidemiological exposure.

But the interaction of demographic and socioeconomic variables was more complex than this. The coherence of slave communities and families was influenced not only by the makeup of the black population and by the direct constraints of their imposed condition as slaves. It was also affected by the demographic attributes of the white slaveholding population. Since, as in other plantation colonies, owners were free to separate black couples and families as they wished, the familial cycles of slaveholders were often key determinants of the timing of separation. White male life expectancy, in other words, was not just a statistic of concern for lowcountry patriarchs; it also marked a potential rupture point in the familial lives of their slaves. The same holds true for the age at which white females married, a transition often accompanied by the provision of a dowry, which often included slaves. Other white demographic waypoints that might affect slave family structures included rates of remarriage, fecundity, and, where wet-nursing was concerned, even slaveholders' infant mortality rate.

For example, as a direct result of bequests in 153 colonial wills, more than fifteen hundred slaves were transferred to other owners in Georgia—and although this sample may include a number of bondspeople who were bequeathed by multiple testators, it is certainly an underestimate (and probably by significant margin) of the total number of slaves who were transferred at the death of their owner in colonial Georgia. Nearly 11 percent were transferred alone, a significant proportion given that only 1.47 percent of slaves were the only slaves held by an owner, according to the land grant data. Perhaps even more ominous for slave familial prospects were the gender preferences of testators. Female slaves were considerably more likely to be bequeathed to female relatives and friends, as occurred in 88 percent of identifiable cases (96). Conversely, male slaves were left to male legatees in 74 percent of identifiable instances (57). These levels of bias in testamentary activity, if representative, would cast doubt on any assertions of widespread white respect for the permanence of bondspeople's relationships.

In contrast, between 1755 and 1775 fewer than twenty slaveholders specified in their will that certain slaves were to remain together, and only a handful of testators (including three who had fathered mulatto children) manumitted their slaves. In his will dated April 1766, Bryan Kelly did both, freeing an entire family of slaves consisting of a father named Dick, his wife, Juno, and their three children, Paris, Venus, and Tulip.[98] The experience of slave marriage and parenthood was enormously dependent upon the predisposition and character of the slaveholders, whose deaths and marriages typically marked juncture points for the family lives of their bondspeople—though debt repayment, a poor harvest, or a lost wager could equally prompt estate revision and thus black separation. In particular, Betty Wood has identified the "moral and religious inclinations and economic interest of the owner[s]" as crucial variables.[99] When Button Gwinnett's creditors called in his debts in the early 1770s, the upshot was a major life change for the bondswoman Doll and her young children, Judith and Flora, who were forced to move away from St. Catherines Island when they were sold to James Read in Savannah.[100] One of the most prominent slaveholders of the province, Jonathan Bryan, had—according to his historical biographer, Alan Gallay—a concept of bondspeople as family, which led him to respect the actual families formed by his slaves.[101] The majority of owners prioritized necessity or convenience over consideration of black familial attachments. Many owners underestimated the strength of the bonds across and between generations of slaves, fugitives, and free blacks, which offered structures of association and familiarity in a world that was otherwise often devoid of comfort.

The manifest control exerted by white importers and white owners rendered slave cohabitation (whether as partners or as family) intrinsically precarious and often fleeting. In particular, whites' control affected and structured the creation of relationships. But between the dictates of owners, in the spaces between the concentric threads, male and female slaves found ways to cultivate, continue, and fortify relationships in defiance of every imperative outside that of the human heart. Separation, whether real or anticipated, prompted a significant number of bondspeople to run away, a dramatic and dangerous course of action. Among all runaways for whom information survives (provided, it should be noted, by the slaveholders themselves), 8 percent were believed to be attempting to rejoin friends and relations from whom they had been separated, while another 9 percent were thought to be harbored by other blacks, not people who were family or friends.[102] These percentages become considerably more significant if one does not count the large number of newly arrived slaves who dominated the ranks of fugitives—Africans who had not had the time or inclination to forge new familial relationships (except relatives or acquaintances transported on the same ships).[103] Although Georgia's pattern was similar to South Carolinian fugitive patterns in many respects, Peter Wood's observation that white owners in the older province "were only occasionally aware" of black family connections does not hold up so well in Georgia, where those who took out advertisements for fugitives often outlined significant amounts of information pertaining to their slaves' kinship networks.[104]

Just sixteen notices placed about runaways between 1766 and 1780 gave details of the escape of an adult male with an adult female or a reference to marriage.[105] Although not all these pairings may have involved marriage, we may expect that the majority of these fugitives were motivated (even if only as a secondary consideration) by the opportunity to reach freedom in the company of a sexual partner. Nine of the notices make actual reference to a marriage. Of the remaining seven, two concern an "elderly fellow" and a woman aged forty; one concerns a pair of "young negroes"; one involves a man of twenty-two and woman of eighteen; and three give no details of age or relative age. About half of the unmarried fugitive bondswomen were described in stigmatized sexual language—as "naturally lusty," "a lusty wench," and "a very likely wench." Their running away in the company of a black man seemed to reinforce slaveholders' understandings of black female sexuality as loose and immoral and to reassert the pointlessness of slave marriages. In contrast, only one of the nine married bondswomen was described as "likely" (attractive). This suggests that the slaveholders who permitted their slaves to marry perhaps understood their marital condition to render them somehow morally superior, although other factors (such as the age of the runaways or the cost of the advertisements) may have influenced the descriptions.

In the overall patterns of escape—as revealed in the newspapers—it was nevertheless unusual for individual men to team up with women except when they had a preexisting bond. Having a bond served to nullify or at least justify the added risks encumbered when traveling in a pair. These partner-fugitives thus ran against the trend of the majority of advertised escapes, which consisted solely of males. Betty Wood estimates that only about 13 percent of runaways consisted of women, which is similar to patterns in South Carolina and Virginia. It is likely that, as in South Carolina, female absences were "less likely to prompt public advertising" because of their mobility and visiting patterns. One Georgia notice suggests that women's presence posed problems for groups of men attempting to secure permanent freedom. On or around 18 November 1774 four newly imported male slaves in their early twenties escaped with a female in a small canoe on the Ogeechee River. They later abandoned the woman ashore, where she was found and, upon interrogation, revealed that the others "intended to go to look for their country, and that the boat was not big enough to carry her with them." However, this incident should not be allowed to disguise the considerable numbers of mixed male and female slaves who did escape in groups larger than two, which accounted for more than eleven advertisements.[106]

The marriages and relationships noted in the advertisements of runaways encompassed an eclectic range of ages, origins, skills, and circumstances. In July 1766 a couple made up of an "elderly fellow" named Pero and a woman called Chloe, who had an injured right hand, absconded from the estate of William Smith, and his widow, Elizabeth, reported them as fugitives in the *Gazette*.[107] The two relatively old slaves were obviously recaptured, because two years later the pair—this time their names were spelled as "Peroe and Cloe," and they were now owned by Thomas Young of Vernonburgh—ran away again. Young complained that they "have often run away before, and it is supposed that they enticed the others away, and it is thought they are gone towards some of the Sea Islands."[108] The onset of age and disability was evidently insufficient to deter this couple from repeated attempts to reach freedom together. Most other runaway couples were more representative of the youthful age structure of the slave population as a whole.

As was customary when placing a notice announcing the disappearance of any slave, the owners carefully described the married fugitives and those we may assume to have been partners in the hope that they would be identified and apprehended. The slaves took with them a variety of skills and possessions. "Bridge," described as a forty-year-old prime sawyer, held the dubious honor of having been enslaved by three different European powers, a wife seventeen years his junior, and the ability to speak Portuguese and Spanish. Other married slaves spoke French and English and had occupations ranging from cooper to washerwoman to herder to grass cutter. Some were expected to commit "several outrages," whereas others would apparently be forgiven if they returned within a week or two.[109] They carried away clothes and licenses to work, canoes, and other belongings. Owners anticipated that some would flee "Northward," others "to Augusta and the Indian nation," some to relatives as far away as Mobile, and still others might "endeavour to pass as free." Overall, they appear to have represented a fair cross section of both urban and plantation slave communities. Not one of the fugitive couples took children with them.

Of course, leaving children behind should not be interpreted as suggestive of a contemporary devaluing of enslaved familial relations. If anything, the opposite is true. Put another way: no notices in the extant copies of the *Georgia Gazette* between 1766 and 1780 record the flight of nuclear families of more than one generation. The sources about runaways, sporadic though they are, reinforce the assertion made by Henry Melchior Mühlenberg in 1775 that slaves "love their families dearly, and none runs away from the other."[110] For slave parents the added responsibility of a child and the solace of a shared emotional investment appear to have been conducive to remaining on their owners' estate. For some this may well have been a burden, another chain tying bondspeople to their immediate environment but this time wrought of mental and emotional links. Others may have disregarded such connections or indeed been unaware of them. For many, though, parenthood may not have been an entirely negative experience. In Georgia, as elsewhere, through reproduction and through family formation, slaves were able to create, re-create, and reinforce their acculturated identities.

Parenthood was a double-edged sword for the enslaved population of late colonial Georgia. It offered at once the opportunity to create, enjoy, and be stripped of the solace offered by a family. Families rarely ran away en masse, perhaps recognizing that theirs was a life of comparative hope. To be separated from or bereft of such emotional support engendered the opposite reaction with surprising frequency. Several notices give details of mothers who ran away with children—whose ages ranged from infancy to eight years—but make no mention of a father. The majority of single female runaways, however, were without children. Of these ten women, most were younger than eighteen and were unlikely to have had children, although nothing conclusive can be assumed from such a small sample and in the absence of corroborating information.

The development and defense of slave families against the forces of external separation generated important outcomes for both blacks and whites. As Betty Wood has noted, "The West and West-Central African women brought against their will to the Georgia Lowcountry after 1750 were no more homogeneous than American women of European ancestry."[111] But by the end of the eighteenth century, a certain degree of cultural standardization had taken place. Much of it owed to the dramatic rise of evangelical Protestant ideologies and rituals in the slave quarters, where Methodism and Baptism in particular proliferated in the 1770s and beyond. Much of it owed to the circles of association delineated by bondspeople's labor patterns—both on plantations and in

> RUN AWAY from Augusta, A MUSTEE FELLOW, named HARRY. He is middle aged, and has a halt in his walk from a rheumatick complaint he is subject to. He has carried off with him his wife, named CASSANDRA, a tall slim young black wench. The fellow is very artful and plausible, and both he and his wife are well known about Savannah, though it is supposed they may endeavour to get to the Indian nation, or to Mobille, where the wench's parents and other relations live. Whoever will apprehend them, and deliver them to me at Augusta, or to the Warden of the Work-house at Savannah, shall receive 20s sterling reward for each, besides all reasonable charges; and if any persons harbour them they may expect to be prosecuted.
>   ANDREW JOHNSTON.

Runaway slave notice in the *Georgia Gazette*, 1 November 1769. This advertisement, commissioned by a slave owner, offered a reward to anyone who helped to return a married slave couple who had run away from his estate. Like scores of other advertisements, it provided information about the fugitives and their appearance. It also leaves evidence of known kinship connections among bondspeople: the husband was apparently "mustee" (part-Indian), while the wife was known to have relations in Mobile. Courtesy of the Georgia Historical Society, 1 November 1769, *Georgia Gazette*.

urban areas. But the salient sphere in which Georgia's people of African origin converged, both literally and metaphorically, was the family. Insofar as we can identify slaves as having held ideals and objectives in common, they prioritized family members over the interests of same-sex associates, frequently above and beyond their own welfare.[112] The virtues of affection, tenderness, and loyalty were precious commodities in light of the many constraints on slaves' time and space, and whites rarely remarked upon these virtues. In part, this reflected that most slaves chose to hide them; in part, it reflected that most slaveholders chose to overlook them. Either way, both owners and slaves were swift to apprehend that slave children often acted as an adhesive that bound sexual partners together and, in a larger sense, generations of bondspeople. Both hostages and aspirations, the children tied the interests of slaves to the interests of their owners.

In November 1796 George Jones, whose ardent professions of love a dozen years earlier had forced his parents to relent on the matter of his first marriage, received a letter from his second wife, Sarah Campbell Jones.[113] She enclosed a list of slaves' names at his request, since he planned to redistribute their laborers for the winter months. Though acting on his instructions, Sarah herself made recommendations and added several X's to the number he had specified. She explained: "They are the children of those that I suppose you will send down, as they would not wish to leave any of their children. They won't make but half hands; . . . I suppose Lancaster, when he finds all his children is coming down, will be coming to you about it, therefore I mention it to you, if he should do it &

you choose to indulge him with me, he could not be so unreasonable as to want the whole of them. Howsoever, you can settle that matter better than I can."[114]

This offhand remark, a casual line about mundane plantation business, offers insight into the operation of the patriarchal web that had formed across Georgia by the end of the century. The threads that Sarah Campbell Jones's words reveal are many. Most obvious are the lines of formal authority. She makes perfectly clear that her husband holds ultimate control over her own actions and those of their slaves. Of secondary significance are her own lines of influence—for she has chosen to "indulge" a number of slaves according to her own knowledge and judgment, and she is evidently literate in the language of plantation management. Finally, a tertiary degree of informal agency is revealed in the hands of the bondspeople in question, whom, we are told, are likely not only to mobilize in defense of their familial interests but to hold certain expectations about their privileges. Thus, while it would be "unreasonable" of Lancaster to expect to remain with all his children, his owners expected him to negotiate some allowance. This fragment of bargaining power, like prison visiting rights, offered just enough incentive in the critical realm of family access to prevent uproar. It was at once a victory for individual slaves and an informal forfeit consciously surrendered by slaveholders to help consolidate a stable form of plantation slavery.

WHAT, THEN, OF the spider? Who was responsible for this artful interweaving? The term *arachnid* originates from a Greek myth that recounted a tapestry-weaving contest between two females. Vying for superiority, a Lydian named Arachne had the temerity not only to outweave her immortal opponent, Athena, but in doing so to slight the goddess by graphically representing a stunning range of past sexual abuses performed by male gods against female mortals.[115] Athena's fury turned to pity when Arachne tried to hang herself, and Athena transformed her rival into a spider to hang and weave for eternity. This tale, dripping with gendered meanings, has not been of great use to historians of late colonial slave societies, who have preferred to unilaterally equate the weavers of webs with those who stood most to gain—elite white males. But to acknowledge, as the legend does, the significance of same-gender competition, specialized skills, sexual jealousy, and female power is to extend arachnid agency beyond a narrow set of consciously conspiratorial white men.

Acknowledging that the spider was multilateral is not a defense of slavery, patriarchy, or the contemptible actions of their principal beneficiaries. There is no doubt that wealthy white men instituted most of the formal measures that regulated Georgia society in the late colonial era. In their capacity as legislators, jurors, and slaveholders, they mobilized in defense of their own oft-converging interests—commercially, militarily, and socially. But it is inaccurate to view their actions retrospectively as a malicious design to progressively oppress and victimize all others or, as the Declaration of Independence put it, "a history of repeated injuries and usurpations, all having in direct object the establishment of an absolute Tyranny." To do so is to lose sight of both the involvement of others in the construction of the web and the full extent of the ruling clique's own self-deception. Anthony Stokes, chief justice of colonial Georgia, was ludicrously able to maintain that "Georgia continued under the King's Government to be one of the most free and happy countries in the world; justice was regularly and impartially administered, oppression was unknown, the taxes levied on the subject were trifling, and every man that had industry became opulent."[116] This was not a sanitized assertion consciously intended to promote future prospects or to perpetuate a mythology that advantaged those in power, for it was written by a Loyalist long after the British had lost the Revolutionary War.

The spider that artfully interweaved cultural devices to consolidate a racially and sexually prescriptive patriarchal society in late colonial Georgia relied upon the self-interest of the colony's inhabitants, male and female, young and old, white and black, often acting outside formal or public life. As each subgroup sought to advance its own immediate interests, working on discrete threads, it was oblivious to the larger significance of its actions—and that the web would hold tighter for future generations. Even at the start of the twenty-first century, despite hundreds of years of struggle, discernible cobwebs remain.

Elite white women willingly participated in ensuring their own social prominence above women and men of other classes and races—accepting and perpetuating customs of gentility and slave ownership. They were not simply parroting their husbands and fathers but advising them and sustaining beliefs that operated in the interests of their immediate family. If the 1770 law making black attempted rape of white females a capital crime was a symbolic assertion of white males' sexual supremacy (and perhaps anxiety), it was empowering in a far more practical sense for white mistresses in their relations with slaves. Among the nonelite, and particularly in a colony where upward mobility was still possible, the natural desire to emulate the high and mighty proved critical in perpetuating racially and socially engendered understandings of morality and virtue. Even as wealthy families sought to plug the holes through intermarriage, the porous nature of the young Georgia aristocracy, unlike the more closed societies of elite Virginia, Massachusetts, or Britain, gave hope to would-be arrivals. Material prosperity and especially landownership increasingly made cultural bedfellows out of the disparate communities of settlers, who reached broad—though never universal—consensuses about their own "British" identity and the "others" all around them. Finally, even slaves and free blacks labored on threads that would inadvertently anchor their descendants to a system of subjugation, often choosing as individuals (and often regardless of owners' intent) to embrace the ransomable family unit as a primary mechanism of social organization and affiliation.

By the end of the colonial era the surviving children of Georgia's early European-born settlers were behaving in ways that their mothers and fathers could never have anticipated. The attitudes toward race and gender of three historical actors with very different loyalties highlight the fundamental presumptions that they nonetheless shared in common. All three were avid patriots— one for the British, one for the Creeks, and one for the nascent Americans. Fervent Loyalist Elizabeth Lichtenstein Johnston, who described the American Revolution as "the scum rising to the top," was the only daughter of a Russian pilot (Johann Lichtenstein) and a French Huguenot (Catherine Delegal), born in 1764. Her relatives were by no means significant slaveholders, owning just three slaves according to a land grant application in 1766, but she remembered that her Tory father had been saved from arrest in 1776 by "a sensible, plausible black man, who had been brought up as a pet . . . and who was greatly attached to the family."[117] Alexander McGillivray, born in 1750 the only son of a Scottish trader (Lachlan McGillivray) and a Wind Clan Creek mother (Sehoy Marchand), was "too Scottish to be Creek and too Creek to be British," according to Ed Cashin.[118] As Kathryn Braund has noted, Alexander McGillivray became "the best-known Indian slaveholder during the revolutionary period," owning at least fifty slaves by 1790, whom he put to work partly in imitation of American plantations and partly according to more benign Creek traditions of slavery.[119]

Perhaps the clearest indication that Georgia evolved a distinctive and recognizable system of patriarchy and gendered power in the final third of the eighteenth century was the behavior of elite Georgians that was unacceptable outside their indigenous environment. Joseph Habersham, born in Georgia in 1751, one year after Alexander McGillivray, was eighteen when he was sent by his English father, James Habersham, to an academy in Woolwich, England, to round off his polite education. Initially, Joseph struggled to discard his colonial sensibilities.[120] He was expelled in August 1769 for upbraiding an English maid, becoming violent with her in the same manner "as the Negroes get in Georgia when they do amiss." This instinctive beating, while absolutely in line with his inherited principles of class, race, and gender protocol, was unacceptable to Joseph's new wardens. This was England, not Georgia, where beatings would be administered at different times and on different terms. It didn't help that the mistress of the house was the mother-in-law of the master of Woolwich Academy.[121] Joseph's guardian in England, William Knox, was understandably distressed and embarrassed by these proceedings. He determined to keep a closer eye on Joseph's development and by April 1770 was apparently making excellent progress, declaring that "Joe is indeed a very good Lad and has left off to be an American much easier and earlier than any youth of the Country that ever I knew came here."[122] But time proved Knox's statement to be woefully inaccurate. The distinctive regionalism of Habersham's loyalties was not to be so easily washed off. Within a few years of returning to Georgia, Joseph Habersham had become an officer in the Continental Army and would be responsible for arresting his father's close friend, Governor James Wright, in 1776.

The three disparate examples of Elizabeth Lichtenstein, Alexander McGillivray, and Joseph Habersham convey a flavor of the diverse origins of Georgia's eighteenth-century inhabitants—from England, Scotland, Russia, France, the Creek nation, and Carolina. If anything, these three were unusually cosmopolitan. Lichtenstein wrote to her grandparents in St. Petersburg, Russia, when she was seven; McGillivray was apprenticed to two urban merchant firms; Habersham was schooled at a Presbyterian college in New Jersey and later at Woolwich Academy. But despite their differing understandings of patriotism and loyalty, despite the fact that each would fight for a very different political brand of Georgia, their conditioned understandings of the sexual and racial ordering of society were extremely similar.[123] This shared psychological investment in social ordering ensured that the bloody revolution and the civil war that eclipsed the province between 1776 and 1783 in the contest for independence, for all the material damage it did, would not permanently disfigure the web.

EPILOGUE

Revolution?

"This is a frontier Province, bordering upon the Indian, and too near the Spanish Settlements, both of which 'ere long, may be our declared Enemies," predicted the members of Georgia's Council of Safety (the body that contested royal rule and sought to mobilize Revolutionaries in the province) in a letter to Gov. James Wright on 8 August 1775. "It is extensive without Populous habitation, and a dreadful Enemy within its Bosom; and an Assault from either of them might be excitement to the others, and would reduce the Inhabitants to the Miserable alternative, either of being Sacrificed, or of Evacuating the Province."[1] They were not far wrong. The impact of the American Revolution upon the society and economy of Georgia, and more specifically the war that accompanied it in the South between 1779 and 1782, was devastating. As the youngest colony/state at the time of Revolution, Georgia contained more than its fair share of Tories, those loyal to the Crown, a situation that eventually prompted the British to concentrate on the lowcountry as a military foothold. Wright and his councilmen, who had been gently overthrown by moderate Patriots in 1776, returned to the province after British troops successfully invaded Savannah in December 1778. Though the self-proclaimed objective of the British army was the "pacification" of the South, its arrival in fact signaled the breakdown of justice, escalation of violence, and complete stagnation of the economies of Georgia and, later, South Carolina.[2] Raids from eastern Florida, the Creek Nation, and the sea (by both pirates and enemy naval detachments) accounted for substantial disruption of the plantation routine and the forcible impressment of slaves. Partisan warfare in the backcountry was fierce and retaliatory: plunderers carried off anything movable and frequently damaged or destroyed buildings and growing crops. Abandonment and neglect ravaged and ruined many lowcountry plantations, especially the irrigation systems so necessary to rice planting. Roads and bridges were damaged, trading paths severed, and in parts of the province steady immigration changed to headlong emigration.

The physical redistribution of Georgia's human population and material goods had the potential to radically change the social as well as the political character of the province. One does not have to amble too far down a counterfactual path to see imagined alternative outcomes in the aftermath of revolution. Even if we take for granted, in time, a successful regime overthrow and the institution of republican government (which was by no means a certain eventuality), the late colonial elite had been irrevocably split by its ideological differences, with many of its members fighting for, and leaving with, the British Crown. From the top down, new directions in government, and new directions from government, could have aided the construction of a new cultural web, just as they had in the 1750s and 1760s. From the bottom up, the sands of society had also shifted dramatically. The Revolutionary War saw the backcountry assume a greater significance in the province's fortunes, while in the tidewater thousands of slaves seized the opportunity to run away. Yet for all this constitutional and physical upheaval, in 1790, when a national census was first conducted, Georgia bore a damning, bloated resemblance to the Georgia of 1770. According to the census returns, the province now contained 82,548 people, including 29,264 slaves (35 percent) and 25,739 white females (now virtually equal in proportion to white males). Demography, society, and economy would recover with astonishing speed from the whirlwind of revolution—nursed by familiar remedies like slave trading and land granting. Crucially, for all the short-term upheaval, the web would hold fast.

During the American Revolution, as during the trusteeship, the practical significance of women's roles was impossible to conceal beneath a veneer of gendered suppression—though it left little impression upon the extant sources. Although many members of the elite were able to move wives and families to comparatively safe havens to the north (or across the Atlantic), most women were forced to deal with the circumstances in Georgia, and their assumption of greater economic responsibility, as well as sole familial predominance in the absence of husbands and fathers, belied the perception of feminine fragility that had been constructed during the decades before the Revolution.[3]

Civil and military authorities, particularly those at the top, tried desperately to ignore women as passive victims of the war but were repeatedly forced to recognize their myriad agency. On 4 January 1781 the *Royal Georgia Gazette* (which had been published under this name since 1779) gave notice of an exodus of slaves from Mary Thomas's plantation that was led by Old Ross, a fifty-six-year-old Ibo woman, and included, among others, two of her daughters (one married), a son, and a granddaughter.[4] In this case—as in hundreds of others—the familial relations between slaves, and particularly the central role played by the matriarch, formed a core around which group action was coordinated in defiance of slaveholders.[5] In the meantime, even white women were breaching guidelines of conduct by exercising conspiratorial political agency in their domestic and extradomestic activity. In August 1778 the Patriots' Council of Safety became so frustrated about the active support that Georgia Tory women were giving to enemy raiders from Florida that it ordered the women cast out of their homesteads on the Ogeechee River, "from which they have so easy a communication with their husbands and afford them so great assistance and help in their plundering schemes." The council complained ominously that in this instance "humanity itself must yield to Necessity and the public good."[6] Yet just ten months earlier, in October 1777, the civil authorities had abandoned a plan to sell confiscated Tory estates because of the "numberless Acts of Injustice" that might be committed by selling land owned or occupied by "Widows, Orphans, Minors, [and] Friends."[7]

As localized conflict spread into the backcountry after the British occupied Savannah and Charlestown in December 1778 and May 1780, respectively, Patriot women provided similar resistance to Tory control. By July 1780 the only parts of Georgia under Patriot control were Wilkes County and the upper part of Richmond County. Like the Patriot assembly before him, Col. Thomas Brown, the local Tory leader, decided that he would have to evacuate the women in the region in order to ensure security. Giving their correspondence with Patriots as a reason, he ordered families out of Georgia to North Carolina, a journey of approximately two hundred miles.[8] Later in the war Brown's movements continued to be reported by vital female observers, such as the anonymous girl from Savannah who informed Lt. Col. James Jackson of the Georgia Militia that she had seen Brown in town but none of Brown's men, and she noted that "there are but few in Town." She also provided Jackson with the location of their two remaining outposts.[9]

The fighting in Georgia temporarily altered the position of white women—whether elite or nonelite, Tory or Patriot—with respect to their familial and societal environs. In many cases the boundaries of gendered labor patterns shifted, demanding a greater occupational diversity for both women and children, as had been the case during the turbulent trusteeship years. Once-shared marital economic responsibilities now often fell upon abandoned wives and widows, whose ability to continue to operate bore witness to their undocumented contributions within marriage. If anything, conditions during the Revolution made even day-to-day transactions more difficult to complete.[10] Given the circumstances, few wives can have relished the opportunity to wield more direct familial jurisdiction or economic responsibility. They were liable to be without the physical support of both their adult sons and the choice firearms owned by the household, which obviously made it more difficult to protect property from assailants or effectively resist personal attack.[11]

Cynthia Kierner notes that in the southern backcountry, perhaps more than anywhere else in Revolutionary America, "women were among the perpetrators . . . of wartime violence." However, much of this activity was either in self-defense or rather indirect—for instance, in the ostentatious use of stolen goods, the probable actions of female camp followers, or the vocal expression of partisan sentiment.[12] In Georgia the legend of Nancy Hart offers the best-known and the least substantiated example of female resilience during the ravages of 1779–81. According to the legend, she was forced to prepare food and plentiful drink for five of the murderers of Col. John Dooly, a Patriot hero. Hart supposedly sent her daughter to the spring for water and to warn the Patriots in the neighborhood that Tories were in her cabin. When the Tories discovered her removing the murderers' muskets through a crack in the log wall and confronted her, Hart shot one of them dead and soon repeated the deed. The other three accepted Hart's demand that they "surrender their ugly Tory carcasses to a Whig woman" and were strung up in a nearby tree. The murderers had faced the particular embarrassment of capture—indeed, execution—by a female whose supposed vulnerability they had planned to exploit.[13] No doubt such incidents did occur from time to time, but the very mythologizing of Hart's actions reminds us that white women were rarely able, in practice, to defend their homesteads—far more frequently choosing to evacuate with choice possessions, sometimes including slaves.[14] A Quaker report emphasized that in the backcountry "passive innocence on their part was no avail; the torrent of rage leveled all distinction, age nor sex afforded no security against violence."[15]

The perception that white women were passively innocent, though occasionally contradicted (as by the actions of the Council of Safety and Col. Thomas Brown), was more than just a comfortable fiction. It played a crucial part in maintaining a degree of social continuity between the halcyon days of the past and the insecurity of the Revolutionary present. Gendered modeling, however inaccurate, offered a moral lifeline to both Tories and Patriots at a time of profound uncertainty; it seemed to provide an assurance that certain facets of Georgia life were uncontested and deeply rooted. Neither Patriots nor Tories required women to take an oath of abjuration, declaring their loyalty to the state, as both factions deemed women to be apolitical.[16] Though the British and the Americans (as they would become) differed in their policies concerning the treatment of slaves, Indians, and white men, they marched in tandem insofar as white women were concerned.

The determination to uphold understandings of gendered place, masculinity, and femininity was frequently advantageous to women. Elite women in particular consciously overacted their parts, maximized their ambiguous political status, and fired off barrages of submissive petitions and pleas as the mortars landed around them. Elizabeth Lichtenstein—at the tender age of twelve—had been forced by her Loyalist grandfather to sign a petition begging that her father's confiscated property be deeded to her, a request to which the Patriot Board of Commissioners, which was responsible for the redistribution of land, evidently acceded.[17] Her property was therefore not sold—as was that of many other Loyalists'—and she commented that one or two cases besides hers showed that "they did not give the property to wives and children whose husbands and fathers had been forced away as mine had been."[18] If the young Loyalist Elizabeth Lichtenstein was given the benefit of the doubt because of her gender, so too was the aging Patriot Abigail Minis. Minis, a wealthy Jewish widow and tavern keeper well known in Savannah, had actually supplied provisions and "sundry articles" to the allied French and American army outside Savannah in 1779.[19] Despite these blatantly rebellious actions, the octogenarian widow later successfully petitioned the occupying British to allow her to leave for Charlestown. Minis applied to the reinstalled Governor Wright, mentioning her five daughters (whose political inclination was unimportant) but not her only son, Philip, who had already been branded a vile Patriot (and had acted as paymaster and commissary general of the Continental troops in 1776). The British allowed her to leave Savannah in a boat laden with her helpless daughters and all their personal property under a flag of truce. She retained legal possession of all her goods, slaves, and property—the latter administered in her absence by a trustee.[20] Similarly, John Habersham, a prisoner of the British forces in September 1780, urged a female friend to reapply to Gen. Charles Cornwallis for his parole. Habersham sensed that a submissive female applicant might be the best way to gain his early release, in order to accompany his sister-in-law to Virginia.[21]

Consciously complying with ideals of masculinity and femininity was an intricate part of the Revolutionary experience of the Gwinnett family. Button Gwinnett, an Englishman who had migrated to the colony in 1765, was a signer of the Declaration of Independence in 1776 and was instrumental in framing Georgia's first constitution in 1777. When Continental general Lachlan McIntosh called him a scoundrel at a public meeting not long after, Gwinnett demanded a duel to defend his honor, which took place at sunrise on Friday, 16 May. Such duels, an exclusively white male phenomenon, yoked a code of elite southern masculinity to older European practices. The likes of Benjamin Franklin and George Washington may have decried duels, but they were too important for elite Georgians—even those fighting for the same cause—to abandon.[22] According to the biographer Charles Francis Jenkins, the macho brag and bluster did not end there. McIntosh requested a distance of eight feet and that the duelists be allowed to face one another. His second, the same Joseph Habersham who had once beaten an English maid like a Georgia slave, and was now expressing his adult male identity in another capacity, felt it his duty to insist upon an extra step. After the first exchange Gwinnett, even with his thighbone shot through in what would, with the onset of gangrene, become a mortal wound, had the temerity to offer another shot if his second would help him up.

Letter from Abigail Minis to (probably) Mordecai Sheftall, 14 January 1780. In this letter, the wealthy Jewish widow sought to recoup funds she had spent on provisioning the Continental army that besieged British-occupied Savannah in October 1779, providing her correspondent with receipts and asking him to make inquiries. In peacetime Minis had been a notable figure in Savannah, having assumed management of a mercantile firm and tavern after the death of her husband, Abraham, in 1757. Ever astute, during the war she opportunistically relocated to South Carolina. Courtesy of the Georgia Historical Society, Minis Papers #568.

His wife, widowed a few days later, eventually decided to write to Congress and request the removal of her husband's killer from his military command.[23] Her first petition was rejected, so Ann Gwinnett penned two more detailed letters in which she outlined the background of the dispute between the two men. She concluded that "the blood of the slain cries for vengeance, the widow and orphan in unutterable and inexpressible grief seek to you in the midst of it for relief."[24]

Ann Gwinnett's letters reveal an explicit awareness that she is acting outside her gendered station. In providing Congress with her opinions about the state of the Revolution in Georgia—how the "St. John's men was your first friends," the "Western people are likewise very true," and that "Savannah is Mostly filld [with] Tories," she knew that she was contravening gender boundaries that constrained her as a passive innocent. But she felt that the truth of her impressions was powerful enough to sanction her actions, as evidenced by one sentence in particular: "These things (tho from a Woman, & it is not our sphere, yet I cannot help it) are all true." Her desperation to reveal her personal impressions of the Revolution in Georgia was strong enough to compel her consciously to act beyond accepted gender boundaries.

If women frequently made use of gendered expectations—even as they contravened them—to advance their personal interests, men also on occasion sought advantage. During the siege of Savannah by an allied French and American amphibian force in October 1779, both British and Patriot forces exploited the presence of large numbers of women and children in the town. Neither side allowed the civilians to leave, in an effort to maneuver the other side into giving up. General McIntosh first requested that Maj. Gen. Augustine Prevost of the British army allow women and children (including McIntosh's own family) to leave before the bombardment began. Prevost refused, evidently hoping that the presence of women and children would preclude the Patriots' use of heavy artillery. After several days of shelling Prevost changed his mind and wrote to his French opponent, Count Charles Henri d'Estaing, suggesting that the helpless civilians should be sent downriver under the protection of a French warship. The count refused and gave no reason. The French later apologized to Prevost, blaming the refusal on the Americans, in particular "that scoundrel" Gen. Benjamin Lincoln, who may have been concerned about provisioning the civilians.[25] The special consideration afforded white women according to the dictates of paternalism and gentility was not always beneficial to them.

As suggested explicitly in the petitions of Ann Gwinnett, and implicitly in the recollections of Elizabeth Lichtenstein Johnston and the mythologizing of Nancy Hart, the Revolution fell in theory outside the woman's sphere. Yet as revealed by the actions of these same three people, and the plethora of strategies that other women adopted, in practice the Revolution in Georgia affected women—and was affected by women—in myriad ways. Women were responsible for relaying counterintelligence, sustaining households or families in adversity and flight, and responding directly to the political and military exigencies of the respective combatants. Often in competition with other women, they exploited or flouted racial laws and gender conventions to suit their immediate needs. For elite white women in particular, this tended to mean upholding a facade of neutrality and innocence. Like Oscar Wilde's Dorian Gray, they would retain a perfect, timeless form in one incarnation, while they flagrantly belied it in another. How aware these women were of their charade is hard to fathom and certainly varied according to age and background. But their willingness—either out of expedience or conditioning—to conform to paternalistic models of gendered behavior during the conflict laid a foundation for replicating the web in the early national era. Colonial Georgia had, as Jack Greene put it, "seemed forever to be destined to be going against history," a place of rapid changes in the face of external continuities.[26] In contrast, the continued theoretical subscription to racial and sexual ties ensured that Georgia's Revolutionary experience was one of stubborn cultural continuity in the face of momentous short-term upheaval.

CONCLUSION

Colonial Georgia had made a long journey in the space of half a century. At its inception it was a well-intended but poorly planned utopian scheme expected by elite Britons to transform an "empty" land into an imperial Eden. Their project gradually unraveled, leaving only an odd mishmash of rather disheartened settlers and a sense of metropolitan dismay, until finally, at midcentury they reluctantly withdrew their involvement. To the delight of another set of British administrators, during the royal era the colony metamorphosed, swiftly fattening its population and developing features more typical of other southern provinces. To the horror of the British, during the American Revolution their promising colony, which Harold Davis has neatly labeled a "fledgling province," turned out to be of the republican variety.

What underwrote the transformation of Georgia was the social, and especially racial, reconstruction of relations between the sexes. Eighteenth-century authorities were always acutely aware of the potency of this element, of the importance of women's presence and of their economic and social behavior. Initially, the trustees had banned slavery and prohibited female inheritance, in a desperate effort to preempt the sorts of racial and sexual complications that might combine to deform their project. In so doing, they did more than attempt to shape the economy of early Georgia: they acknowledged that, together, gender and race relations lay at the heart of political power, cultural authority, and, ultimately, colonial identity. Equally cognizant of the potency of gender and race, royal officials had reversed these policies, protecting female inheritance and encouraging slavery, consciously importing models and supplies from elsewhere to boost the colony's development. By the end of the colonial era racial and gendered behavioral codes in Georgia were intermeshed in a system so resilient that even a political revolution and an accompanying war could not displace it.

The promotional literature circulated to publicize the Georgia project in the 1730s showed that the trustees viewed females as pivotal to the success of their frontier colony. They believed that the presence of women would act as security against its abandonment by men. The trustees acknowledged that women would preserve the health of male colonists—by providing foodstuffs, cleaning, mending, and nursing. The trustees agreed that females alone had the skills to ensure regular routines, welfare support, and social stability. The trustees also asserted that women could play a unique role in Georgia, strengthening the integrity of Britain's commercial empire through the cultivation of silk. The women that the trustees wanted were to be harbingers of cultural authority: industrious within their domestic realms and sericulture, subservient to their husbands, and providing the foundation of moral and religious order. They were also to be white women, for these roles, with their reliance upon what might loosely be termed orthodox European understandings of household structure and Christianity, precluded serious consideration of familial intermixing with Indian (or African) females. The trustees theoretically banned female landholding to protect gender relations from the challenges that might arise from clusters of propertied widows or young heiresses. Publicists neatly attached these hopes to wider objectives in eighteenth-century British philanthropy: the advancement of imperial demography and commerce, and the extension of the Anglican Church to convert supposedly inferior races—particularly the indigenous peoples of the lower South, whose souls had been coveted for decades by the Society for the Propagation of the Gospel. Attesting to the success of the trustees' formula were the substantial contributions to the Georgia trust by elite Englishwomen, who welcomed the opportunity to attach themselves to a venture with such a reputable gendered and religious framework.

If female roles were conceptually important to the founding philosophy and sponsorship of the Georgia trustees, they were pragmatically even more critical to the settlers themselves. Colonists and their leaders swiftly realized that orderly households were not just indicators of civilization or microcosms of societal stability. In the early years of settlement orderly households were a matter of life and death for individuals, communities, and potentially colonial projects too. Thanks in part to the trustees' planning, women arrived from England, Scotland, and Germanic Europe in the kinds of kinship groupings that provided the sex ratios that had figured so prominently in New England's dramatic population growth a century earlier. But, as with so many colonies in the less-hospitable southern summer environment, the mortality of seasoning would play a more prominent role than fertility, tearing holes in the family structures and expectations of settlers. The imbalanced age structure of the early population further compromised growth, as did the decision of so many to abandon the province in light of its manifest disabilities. Unable to fend for themselves domestically as individuals or demographically as a colony, those settlers who remained were dependent on trustee officials, who were desperately seeking more young white females, just as their Virginia counterparts had in the early seventeenth century.

In fact, the situation in Georgia was far more complex than its antecedents. First, though exotic and little understood, the region was far from a "New World" waiting to be mapped out, even from a European perspective. More than two hundred years had elapsed since the first Europeans had arrived at the mouth of the Savannah River with Spaniard Pedro de Quejos on 3 May 1525. The Spanish did not remain long—abandoned seventeenth-century Spanish Franciscan missions dotted the coast—but since the 1680s South Carolinian traders and occasional missionaries had become familiar with the peoples whose lands would be granted by royal charter to the trustees in 1732. In other words, the canvas upon which the trustees sought to sketch a copy of a mythic ancient English social order was not blank when they began, even if one overlooks (as contemporaries so often did) the presence of the Amerindian population. Second, and more distinctively, the communities that arrived in trusteeship Georgia, either through sponsorship or by their own means, were of far more diverse origins than virtually any other British American colony at inception. The Georgia settlers were not purely English, purely British, or even purely European. The common cultural ground occupied by these migrants from London, the Rhineland, the Scottish Highlands, Austria, the Italian piedmont, Ireland, South Carolina, the Iberian peninsula, provincial England, and so on consisted of little more than a shared faith in the Old Testament (the initially unwelcome presence of Sephardic Jews loosened the monopoly of Christianity among migrants) and a loose subscription to patrilineal familial organization and the institution of marriage.

Demographic conditions forced those who survived seasoning and remained in Georgia to draw from this common gendered ground. While it proved unthinkable for single males to learn even an expedient proficiency in feminized domestic skills, it proved eminently possible to break down ethnic prejudices and even, to a lesser extent, racial ones, by intermarrying. Settlers reappraised their preconceptions as they adjusted their cohabiting, courtship, marital, and familial practices to cope with the unbalanced demographic and economic environment in which they found themselves. Systems and life cycles that had appeared fixed by tradition and custom proved to be malleable, as colonists frantically sought to anchor themselves and their children against the howling winds and fast-running tides of the frontier. People married surprisingly young, remarried surprisingly quickly, and selected partners from other settlements, other denominations, other nations, and even other races.

This demographic upheaval had repercussions for all inhabitants—male and female, young and old, native and newcomer. In conjunction with commercial expediency, the social imbalances underwrote the proliferation of relationships between Georgia traders and Amerindian females. At best the uneven demographics tested, and at worst they eroded, the strength of communal identity, organized religion, and familial authority. The economic and social experiences of women in Georgia, like those of their colonial antecedents and unlike those of their counterparts elsewhere in more established societies, were extreme at both ends of the spectrum. One end signified a descent toward powerlessness, victimization, and exploitation, the experience of countless widowed mothers and indentured servant girls. The other end signified an increase in social power and economic agency, seized in Georgia by the likes of Mary Musgrove Matthews Bosomworth, Marie Camuse, and Elizabeth Penrose. Their vocal presence in the trusteeship records reminds us that female power mongers were by no means a seventeenth-century oddity, limited in time, and largely confined to white Englishwomen of respectable birth. The likes of Margaret Brent (who clamored for a vote in Maryland in 1647), Anne Hutchinson (who clamored for theological parity in early Massachusetts), and Lady Frances Berkeley (who was a significant force in late seventeenth-century Virginia) have led several historians, such as Cynthia Kierner, to suggest that "unabashedly powerful public women such as Brent and Berkeley would have no eighteenth-century counterparts."[1] The unusual conditions in trusteeship Georgia challenged gendered legal, economic, cultural, and familial practices and allowed remarkable latitude, particularly to women with control of information, connections, and a certain flexibility of character. But male and female settlers alike understood that they were on the frontier and that this was a function of the frontier—never accepting in their language that commonplace patterns were anything more than commonplace expressions of societal dysfunctionality. The unorthodox gendered interaction of early colonists, decried by the likes of George Whitefield, was in itself both a cause and a symptom of the trusteeship's failure.

The transition to direct royal control in the mid-eighteenth century brought about a number of quite remarkable transformations in Georgia. The increase in institutional authority and formal legislation, the waves of migration and population explosion, and the regulation of racial slavery brought formalized practices that inhibited the elasticity in women's experiences. Increasingly like their counterparts in other colonies, and particularly southern colonies, Georgia women of all classes and races would operate inside rather than despite an established patriarchal society.

Between the 1750s and 1770s royal administrators distributed vast acreage, wrenched from Native Americans, to thousands of new migrants who had converged upon Georgia from across the Atlantic world (and especially from other British American colonies). The administrators shared with the trustees before them an ardent desire for an orderly gender organization to underpin a newly orderly society. But unlike the trustees, the royal administrators presided over an influx of forces potentially subversive to this order: plantation slavery and backcountry disorder. They sought to encourage the settlement of families and communities, to deter the arrival of young single males whose actions—as overseers for absentee planters in the lowcountry or renegades and pilferers in the backcountry—would undermine the structural integrity and nascent identity of the colony. In so doing, the administrators acknowledged the reciprocal influences of gender and settlement and began to describe and define ideals of masculinity and femininity. By the time the Revolution interrupted the royal era, the demography of whites in the province had swelled and stabilized, bolstered by an almost even sex ratio and growing numbers of children. The black population was comprised overwhelmingly of slaves, imported initially from other colonies and later from Africa. Although, as elsewhere, slave fertility at first faltered as a result of the plantation regime, the Middle Passage, and seasoning, black family formation was in the interests of both planters and slaves, and in all likelihood natural population growth began to complement the slave trade by the 1770s.

The transformation of Georgia into a prosperous slave society significantly altered women's economic roles within the colony, encouraging diversification and specialization. Incorporating both black and white women, the changes could be viewed again as a kind of polarization—for now women could occupy positions of remarkable affluence as white elite propertied widows and positions of overwhelming poverty as black slaves who were denied ownership even of their own labor and their own bodies in perpetuity. Although females shared an important common subjection on the basis of their gender within their different economic worlds, slavery categorically divided them so effectively as to render any commonality all but invisible. Most female slaves labored alongside male slaves in the fast-expanding rice and indigo plantations of the lowcountry, though some occupied more specialized roles in the households of larger plantations. Those bondswomen held in an urban environment tended to act in various capacities as domestic servants, but some manifested greater agency in the distribution of their labor and of their surplus produce, particularly those who were market traders. The domestic and agricultural labor of slaves allowed for a contraction in occupational breadth for many lowcountry white women, while the rise in credit and consumerism that accompanied the development of a planter elite paved the way for specialization of services, manufacturing, and retail in proto-urban environments. As a result fewer white women in the royal era would need to engage in multiple vocations than their counterparts during the trusteeship, although those settling the southern and western frontiers continued to adopt the flexible labor strategies that were necessary to survival.

Women's economic activity was increasingly regularized at law, as legislators dispensed with the vagaries of trusteeship policies and sought to place the colony on a surer footing. This brought Georgia more firmly into line with other southern colonies, particularly South Carolina. The provincial assembly's resolutions about feme sole trading and married women's conveyance rights, along with notices placed in newspapers by husbands who were denying credit to their wives, were suggestive of two paradoxical features of women's participation in the late colonial economy. First, the laws and advertisements indicated that, in practice, women were regular and active commercial agents in the marketplace despite the constraints of marriages that formally disenfranchised them. Second, the laws and advertisements indicated that when this female agency was contested, the letter of the law was unmistakably clear: it abrogated their activities.

The stabilization of the population and economy during the royal era made possible the standardization of far more than just rules about conveying land. During these years myriad cultural devices were introduced and normalized and together acted like a web to lend cohesion and shape to the identity of the province. Slave codes, literature, fashion, education, intermarriage, and other influences created, monitored, and enforced distinctions. Among the more important features of this web was its protection at the center of a white planter elite whose customs and behavior consciously emulated other elites in metropolitan Europe and cosmopolitan Charlestown (and that would, itself, be emulated by would-be gentry among the lower and middling orders in Georgia). Another critical step was the creation of a mythic shared white identity and the abasement of nonwhite populations through slave codes and the regulation of interracial sex. As the population grew, mobility and circles of association narrowed. Mainstream practices challenged the attempted exceptionalism of communities such as the Quakers, partly subsuming ethnic or religious diversity and breaking down friendly ties across racial boundaries, for instance, eroding the middle ground formerly occupied by Indian traders, their clients, and their children. Of course, the web was weaker at its fringes and still consisted largely of empty space—a space in which Georgians belied their prescribed places by engaging in interracial sex, rebelling against parental wishes, running away or resisting slavery, expressing seditious opinions about the value of marriage or religion, and bullying their husbands. But as the experience of the American Revolution demonstrated, Georgia had evolved a powerful and surprisingly resilient system of behavioral codes predicated upon the gendered and racial ordering of society. Woven from the economic, social, and familial self-interest of every constituent part, it would not easily be torn apart.

APPENDIX

Included in this appendix are three excerpts from the *Georgia Gazette* that reflect the diverse influences and contrasting opinions about female behavior that circulated locally during the late colonial era. The *Gazette*'s inclusion of such literature, selectively plagiarized from British sources, revealed not only the continuing significance of Atlantic-world connections, and common interests in the institution of marriage, but also a growing awareness that the operation of gender defined a society's identity and integrity.

In the first letter, from "Philaretus," the author outlines a set of virtues that he feels all women should aim to attain. Philaretus draws consciously upon a literary model, Samuel Richardson's fictional Clarissa, to paint a "picture of a good and accomplished woman." The letter from "Philanthropos" presents a more original and thorough articulation of idealized gender relations and specifically their operation within the institution of marriage. Taking a stand against what he perceives as a "torrent of corruption" and the willingness of young men to deride the value of marriage, Philanthropos leaps to its defense, stressing the sanctity of the institution and its role in sculpting a proper Christian society. The final excerpt, the letter from "Anti-Vixen," offers an example of precisely the kind of burlesquing that offended the sensibilities of Philanthropos, proposing as it does a comic tax upon wives who scold their husbands, in an era when Anglo-American taxation was something of a sore point.

Letter from "Philaretus" (6 January 1768)

Philaretus writes to the printer and attempts "the picture of a good and accomplished woman," which he equates with Samuel Richardson's fictional Clarissa.

> CLARISSA is not in the very bloom of youth, but an exact symmetry and a beautiful inexpressible comliness and agreeableness run through and compose the whole of her external form and amiable person, which, together with that easy and graceful carriage and deportment strike with irresistible force, and command respect: while the more beautiful and exalted perfection of her mind add fresh lustre and force to the external beauties of her person, which, embellished as it is by nature, make it a fit lodging for so pure a mind, where dwell all the graces and virtues requisite to adorn the woman and the christian. Who can see Clarissa without feeling in his breast at once the glow of love and the tenderness of friendship? But though those attractives create desire, yet you stand corrected by the decency and easiness, not the severity of her virtue. That virtue, sweetness and good humour, which is so visibly expressed in her face, naturally diffuse themselves into her every word and action.
>
> [Despite being] followed by a crowd of lovers . . . she, being a kind and affectionate mother, prefers, for the sake of her family, the single to the married state, and is proof against all the solicitations of love.

Philaretus concludes: "So rare a pattern of female excellence ought not to be concealed, but should be set forth to the view and imitation of the world."

Letter from "Philanthropos" (14 September 1768)

> To the PRINTER of the GEORGIA GAZETTE.
> *Strange product must that union make,*
> *Where* SHE*'s a fool, and* HE*'s a Rake.*

MARRIAGE was instituted as early as our first parents; its end was the propagation of the human race, and to render it effectual to that purpose, the all-wise Creator formed both sexes susceptible of the most tender passions and affections, with a desire for this sacred union. Man, variable man, soon departed from that innocence and simplicity in which he was at first created. His passions made for obedience unhappily usurped the fountain of reason, and thereby destroyed that subordination and harmony in which consisted the true freedom and serenity of his soul. From this depravation of our intellectual powers, there immediately arose a vicious propensity to the irregular enjoyment of animal pleasure, in opposition to the law and institution which the great BEING had designed for our happiness. LOVE, that delicate refinement known but to few, could now no longer effectually exert her power, so as to secure to herself the sole possession of any heart: Men became slaves to divers lusts, and eagerly trod the flow'ry paths of vice, unmindful of the woeful consequences of such a conduct, and what, in its original appointment, was intended for a perpetual fountain of domestick sweets, became the source of numberless evils, of jealousies, and of death. The Heathen Poet elegantly describes this state of fallen love;

> *In amore haec omnia insunt vitia: injuriae,*
> *Suspiciones, inimicitiae, induciae,*
> *Bellum, pax rursum.*

But we must not imagine this tableau hath any resemblance to those pure, worthy, and chaste bosoms, which are under the guidance of virtue, and as yet free from the corruptions, the detestable corruptions that are in the world through lust. No, love is not a vice but in vicious hearts; when it is nourished in such, it can there produce nothing but shameful and irregular desires; it can form no designs but criminal ones, and be followed by nothing but troubles, cares, and misery. However fashionable it is at present for the libertine to burlesque and condemn matrimony, yet let him not dare to deny its comforts, such as he's a stranger to, and perhaps unhappily incapable of enjoying: He must confess it in his sober moments to be the cement of society, the foundation of all social bliss, worthy of God to institute, and honourable for man to observe. The luxury of the present times, together with an affectation in too many of appearing more vicious than they really are, contribute not a little to the many witticisms daily bestowed on this happy state; but let those wits, those very pretty fellows, remember, that if they have bad principles, which render them incapable of rational and social happiness, they should lay blame no where but on themselves; they should crack their jokes at home, and examine whether the singularity of their manners does not make them considered by the thinking and sober part of both sexes as enemies to society, as bad men, and most inconsistent triflers. It must be acknowledged that all the votaries of Hymen, all in wedlock are not happy; indeed it is evident too many are wretchedly miserable, groaning under bondage; but this will afford no argument to quarrel with the institution; the question is, are the parties that take upon themselves this solemn obligation fit for and worthy of it? Is SHE, in the language of my mott, a FOOL? Is HE a RAKE? Blunt interrogatories, but very important. Miseries are frequently the children of imprudence; and how can corrupt hearts find happiness in themselves? How can persons of vicious characters, who mean nothing but deception in all their actions, blame a state of life, because inadequate to their absurd expectations, and which state can only improve the condition of the virtuous, and for whose refined pleasures, through the darkness of their understandings, and the vitiated bent of their minds, they are absolutely unfit, unworthy, and incapable. Much hath been said on this subject by many writers; too much cannot be said: It is high time to make a stand against this prevailing torrent of corruption, to vindicate the honour of the most amiable sex, and to demonstrate, that a man is not *weak*, though he takes one *weaker* than himself; that he is not irrational, when he obeys laws human and divine; that he is not inconsistent, when he extends the sphere of his relative duties, and gives himself opportunities to become a tender parent, and affectionate husband, a good citizen, and an honest man, and by so doing lays up for himself a good foundation against the time to come. But on what foundation doth the libertine build, and what end doth he propose to himself? See him in his old age miserably enervated and shattered by debauchery, and held in contempt by his fellow-creatures; forgetful of the obligations of society, he hath only lived for the indulgence of his sensual appetites, and now, what is the fruit of all his labour? Does he feel the infirmities of a tottering patched up body, and are the arrows of the Almighty levelled against him, wounding his guilty conscience, which at length is alarmed with innumerable fears? And has he no one whom he can call his own, no child, no friend, to bind up his wounds, and pour in oil and wine to comfort him?—Wretched Being!—Thou hast rejected the gifts of Heaven, and dost thou not deserve this? If the profest Bucks of our times cannot see the impropriety of their pursuits, I could wish, in order to beget in them a reverence for virtuous love, the following words of Milton were engraven on their hearts as with the pen of a diamond: Slight impressions will not reclaim from a false taste, but surely these delicate sentiments, with many others of this great man, may demand attention, and be of some weight:

> *Love not the lowest end of human life,*
> —— *Love refines*
> *The thoughts and heart enlarges: hath her seat*
> *In reason and is judicious: is the scale*
> *By which to heav'nly love thou mayest ascend:*

> *Not back in carnal pleasure: for which cause,*
> *Among the beasts no mate for thee was found.*
> PHILANTHROPOS

Letter from "Anti-Vixen" (20 April 1774)

A NEW TAX PROPOSED

A PROFESSED scold is at once the most disagreeable and obnoxious being in the world. She not only renders herself completely disagreeable, but casts a general stigma upon the whole sex; and I will venture to say there are many old batchelors, who would long since have entered into the state of wedlock, had they not been deterred from it by some female relation or acquaintance, whose *great talents* in this way made them fear they might meet with a wife whose genius was of the same turn. The maidens and widows of this island have a just plea to petition parliament for the transportation of every professed vixen in the kingdom; or, if this should be thought too severe, they should at least be taxed, to silence them; though probably they might scold the more for it. I know a very ingenious old gentleman, who has never had the courage to engage in matrimony, who gives it as his opinion, that the innumerable batchelors every where to be found, remain so more through the fear of being scolded to death, than from any mercenary cause, or far less from any real disposition for celibacy. He has, indeed, furnished me with hints of taxing the race of shrews, having put into my hand the following proportion, which he thinks very reasonable.

Scolding every morning	20£. per annum.
Twice a day	30.
Three times	40.
Every other day	10.
Once a week, if not on Sundays	5.
On Sundays	10.
Scolding a husband into a consumption, the jaundice, or any lingering disorder	100.
Scolding a husband to death	500.
Scolding herself into hystericks	000.

This calculation is made for a woman who brings 5000£. to her fortune, which, indeed, my friend says is the least portion a vixen should have; so that the penalties must be proportionably augmented to the increase of this fortune.

A tax upon batchelors has long since been talked of, and by many judged reasonable; but I do not think this would be striking at the root of the evil, as it plainly appears that the real source of the complaint, *celibacy*, is to be traced to this female vice, which cannot be too speedily, or too completely eradicated. I am, &c.

ANTI-VIXEN

NOTES

Introduction

1. Spalding and Wilson, *Women on the Colonial Frontier*, iv.
2. For a succinct explanation and deconstruction of the myth of the golden age, see Norton, "Evolution of White Women's Experience," 593–619. See also Ulrich, *Good Wives*, 35–50; Salmon, *Women and the Law of Property*, 185–93.
3. *Col.Rec.*, 20:208.

Prologue. The Georgia Plan

1. For a useful broad discussion of the interplay between gender and colonization in the British Atlantic world, see Pearsall, "Gender," 113–32. For an examination of the major English theorists whose ideas were played out in early colonial societies (especially Robert Filmer and John Locke), see Norton, *Founding Mothers and Fathers*. For a detailed analysis of the construction of gender among the Cherokees, see Perdue, *Cherokee Women*, 13–40.
2. Specific understandings about sexuality and femininity were evolving, but Robert Shoemaker's survey of English society between 1650 and 1850 (*Gender in English Society*) suggests that little changed over time in the extent to which men's and women's lives were segregated according to their gender, refuting the notion of a separation of spheres.
3. Campbell, "'When Men Women Turn,'" 83.
4. Laurence, *Women in England*, 84.
5. Oglethorpe, *Some Account*, 9, 22, 29. Oglethorpe celebrated in his preface that in successful empires, husbands could always find wives, stating of ancient Rome that "no Woman who was not deformed (the Vestal Virgins only excepted) ever lived to the age of 25 years unmarried." He felt that more recently Louis XIV had missed a trick by overlooking women when he built a magnificent hospital that consigned his invalid soldiers to celibacy in the 1670s; instead, the Sun King should have paired them off with wives and sent them off to New France to populate and stabilize the French colonies. Oglethorpe is aware that inappropriate gendered behavior is liable to compromise colonization—suggesting that white "Violencys committed upon their [Indian] Wives" explained in part the eruption of the Yamassee War in 1715, when several Native American tribes unusually combined their assault and threatened to eradicate white settlement in South Carolina. Equally, he warns that the presence of "effeminate fellow[s]" could cause problems (Oglethorpe, *Some Account*, 6).
6. Ver Steeg, *Origins of a Southern Mosaic*, xii. For more detailed histories of the background to the colonization of Georgia, see H. Davis, *Fledgling Province*, 1–32; Coleman, *Colonial Georgia*; Coleman, *History of Georgia*, 9–71; B. Wood, *Slavery in Colonial Georgia*, 1–24; Reese, *Colonial Georgia*; Taylor, *Georgia Plan*.

7. See Tailfer, *True and Historical Narrative*; B. Wood, *Slavery in Colonial Georgia*, esp. chaps. 2, 3, and 5.

8. Quoted in Boorstin, *Americans*, 71.

9. For the trustees' most important promotional literature, see *Most Delightful Country*, and Spalding, "Some Sermons." For a discussion of disputes about authorship of these early promotional tracts, see Baine, "James Oglethorpe."

10. Oglethorpe, *Some Account*, xiv, 44.

11. Ver Steeg, *Origins of a Southern Mosaic*, 102.

12. Oglethorpe, *Some Account*, xx.

13. The pamphlet added: "And in Sicknes the having their Wives to nurse them may recover many who would inevitably perish were they to have no succour but from careless or unskilful Comrades" (Oglethorpe, *Some Account*, 26).

14. Oglethorpe, *Some Account*, 29.

15. Ibid., 32.

16. Ibid., 4. See also *Most Delightful Country*, 133, 159. For a discussion of imagery relating to bees and colonization in the seventeenth century, see Kupperman, "Beehive," 272–92.

17. His account is reprinted in *Most Delightful Country*.

18. *Most Delightful Country*, 142. Oglethorpe went on to argue that "most of the Poor in Great Britain, who are maintain'd by Charity, are capable of this, tho' not of harder labour" (144).

19. *Most Delightful Country*, 159. For Martyn's estimate see p. 165; for Oglethorpe's quote about family earnings, see p. 137.

20. Indeed, Benjamin Martyn boldly began his *Reasons for Establishing the Colony of Georgia* by asserting that "it is undoubtedly a self-evident Maxim, that the Wealth of a Nation consists in the Number of her People."

21. Oglethorpe, *Some Account*, 40–41.

22. Ibid., 43.

23. Andrew, *Philanthropy and Police*; the listed charities are the Foundling Hospital, Marine Society, Lambeth Asylum, Lying-in Charity, Magdalen Hospital, and British Lying-in Hospital. Those that constituted "major donors" (listed in her appendix) contributed to at least three of the charities named.

24. Andrew, *Philanthropy and Police*, 67.

25. For the subscription numbers for London charities, see Andrew, *Philanthropy and Police*, 72. Figures for Georgia donors are derived from analysis of the trustees' benefaction lists in *Col.Rec.*, vol. 4. For the support extended to poor London women in the mid-eighteenth century by such institutions, see Hitchcock, " 'Unlawfully Begotten on Her Body,' " 75–78. Studies of the gendering of benevolence in southern colonies in the late eighteenth century have identified similar preoccupations with providing sisterly or maternal aid to less privileged women and children. See Bellows, *Benevolence among Slaveholders*; Lockley, "Encounters," 41–43.

26. *Col.Rec.*, 1:85.

27. The other two categories used in the trustees' records of benefactions were "for

the Uses of the Colony" and "for the Advancement of Botany." These figures are derived from the benefaction lists in *Col.Rec.*, vol. 4.

28. *Col.Rec.*, 2:152; 1:273, 305, 350.

29. Ibid., 1:271.

30. Ibid., 1:275, 278. For the benefactions see 1:221, 232, 237, 246, 270; 2:152.

31. Guerrini, "The Hungry Soul." For Betty Hastings's recommendation, see *Col.Rec.*, 1:217.

32. The Countess of Huntingdon requested a tract of more than twenty thousand acres, preferably on good farming land near a river, on which to settle a number of handpicked families to be settled "at her own Expence," though the trustees prevaricated (*Col.Rec.*, 2:496). For an account of her involvement with the Georgia colony, see Schlenther, "To Convert the Poor People."

33. Measures theoretically banning women from landownership were taken to ensure that sufficient able-bodied men were present to act as a militia against possible Spanish incursions. See Caldwell, "Women Landholders," 184–85.

One. *Population*

1. McCusker and Menard, *Economy of British America*, 229. Maris Vinovskis reiterated this point in his introductory essay for *Studies in American Historical Demography*, 2–11.

2. Ready, *Castle Builders*, 55.

3. Gemery, "Emigration," 179–231. The estimate of the South Carolina population is from P. Wood, *Black Majority*, 152.

4. Ready, *Castle Builders*, 24–25; *Col.Rec.*, 5:41, 452; Fries, *Moravians in Georgia*; H. Davis, *Fledgling Province*, 17–18.

5. Coleman, *History of Georgia*, 62.

6. *List*; Ready, *Castle Builders*, 41–47; the quote is from Ver Steeg, *Origins of a Southern Mosaic*, 102.

7. Carr and Walsh, "Planter's Wife," 138.

8. Galenson, "Settlement and Growth of the Colonies," 179.

9. For a discussion of gender imbalance in the French colonies, see Moogk, *Nouvelle France*, 105–20.

10. *Collections*, 3:104, 113.

11. Ibid., 3:144. Oglethorpe also remarked in the same letter: "We have found also that the married Soldiers live easiest many of them having turned out very industrious Planters."

12. *Col.Rec.*, 21:457.

13. Ibid., 2:388.

14. Ibid., 21:295. For more on the activities of Scottish recruiters, see Parker, *Scottish Highlanders*, 61–67.

15. E. Morgan, *American Slavery, American Freedom*, 95; *Col.Rec.*, 20:167–68; W. Stephens, *Journal of William Stephens*, 18 February 1745.

16. Ready, *Castle Builders*, 55; Cates, " 'The Seasoning,' " 146–58.

17. *Col.Rec.*, 20:5.

18. Ibid., 20:407.

19. Wrigley, Davies, Oeppen, and Schofield, *English Population History*, 364–65. Other factors significant in influencing the birth interval in a given community were the frequency of intercourse, the length of breast-feeding, and the levels of stillbirths. See Wrigley et al., *English Population History*, chap. 7.

20. *Col.Rec.*, 20:361.

21. Ready, *Castle Builders*, 28; *Det.Rep.*, 1:44. The quotes are from *Det.Rep.*, 2:75.

22. For these deaths see *Det.Rep.*, 2:48, 51, 56; for the quote see 2:63. The new midwife promised to be "satisfied with whatever people want to give her after she has give the lying-in-women every possible attention and care" (*Det.Rep.*, 2:70).

23. For the quotes see *Det.Rep.*, 5:23, 8:397.

24. W. Stephens, *Journal of William Stephens*, 26 June 1745.

25. *Col.Rec.*, 2:142–43.

26. *Det.Rep.*, 2:78; *Col.Rec.*, 20:19.

27. *Col.Rec.*, 20:167–68.

28. Ibid., 21:137.

29. Wesley, *Journal of the Rev. John Wesley*, 152.

30. H. Davis, *Fledgling Province*, 89.

31. *Col.Rec.*, 2:275–78, 448; 6:43. For the quote see 2:275.

32. For an analysis of the role of the family in describing the South as a sociogeographical entity, see Blake Smith, "In Search of the Family," 21–36.

33. The most comprehensive volume on patterns of remarriage and their implications is Dupâquier et al., *Marriage and Remarriage*, 3–4.

34. Wells, "Quaker Marriage Patterns."

35. *Det.Rep.*, 1:13, 16.

36. W. Stephens, *Journal of William Stephens*, 4 April 1745. See also the marriage of schoolgirl Mary Bolton to her teacher, the wealthy James Habersham, at Bethesda in December 1740, in *Col.Rec.*, 4a:59.

37. *Col.Rec.*, 6:121.

38. Ibid., 20:234.

39. Temple and Coleman, *Georgia Journeys*, 195.

40. Menard, "Economic and Social Development," and Galenson, "Settlement and Growth of the Colonies"; the quote from Franklin may be found in *Papers of Benjamin Franklin*, 228. Galenson observes that "the tendency for higher southern fertility due to the earlier ages at marriage might have been offset by higher southern mortality rates, which meant that fewer marriages completed their normal fertility in the South than the North" (185), whereas Menard identifies a "distinct marriage pattern" as "women in the South—white or black, rich or poor, tidewater or backcountry—married earlier and in higher proportions than in England or the northern colonies" (255–57). For contemporaries' demographic analysis see Malthus, *Essay on the Principle of Population*, esp. 105–6, and Franklin's "Observations Concerning the Increase of Mankind," in his *Papers*, 225–34.

41. Wells, "Quaker Marriage Patterns," 424; Wrigley et al., *English Population History*, 172.

42. Georgia cases compiled from references in *Col.Rec.*; *Det.Rep.*; *List*; Temple and Coleman, *Georgia Journeys*.

43. *Col.Rec.*, 20:170.

44. *Det.Rep.*, 1:103; *Col.Rec.*, 4a:74, 131.

45. *Col.Rec.*, 4a:101.

46. William Stephens added that Slack also bought Harris presents to testify to his love: a gold ring and new engraved pewter. Stephens also shrewdly observed that it could not "be doubted, but our Lover would take equal Care to see the Widow's Cattle bear his Mark with a Hot Iron very soon; for they were now looked upon as Man and wife betroth'd, and nothing wanting but the Office of Matrimony, by a proper Minister" (*Col.Rec.*, 4a:100–101; for her husband's debts see 2:410).

47. *Col.Rec.*, 20:207–9.

48. Ibid., 20:415–16.

49. McCain, *Georgia as a Proprietary Province*, 243; Lipscomb, "Land Granting," 40–51.

50. *Col.Rec.*, 20:338–40; *Egmont*, 2:380. For more information on the minister, Daniel McLachlan, see Parker, *Scottish Highlanders in Colonial Georgia*, 62–63.

Two. *Economy*

1. *Col.Rec.*, 20:275, 6:262; W. Stephens, *Journal of William Stephens*, 22 March 1744.

2. *Col.Rec.*, 20:394.

3. Ibid., 4:394–95.

4. Dayton, *Women before the Bar*.

5. Lady Bathurst's eulogy was recorded in the *South Carolina Gazette*, 8 May 1736. Anne Bradstreet's 1643 epitaph is quoted in Ulrich, *Good Wives*, vii. Wesley's note appears on p. 375 of his *Journal*.

6. *Col.Rec.*, 20:15; Moore, *Voyage to Georgia*, 10 (quote), 14, 31. Women traveling on the *London Merchant* and *Simond* also washed linen while they were ashore (*Col.Rec.*, 21:137–38).

7. The Minis household boasted a pair of bellows, a hanging shelf, four flatirons, a gridiron, an iron dripping pan, a spit, tongs, a frying pan, two iron skillets and pot hooks, three iron pots and two pans, five kettles, a warming pan, and five pewter candle makers (Estate of Abraham Minis, 30 June 1757, Inventory Book F, 49–51, Georgia Estate Records, Georgia Department of Archives and History, Atlanta). The dig is detailed in Honerkamp, *Colonial Life on the Georgia Coast*.

8. Ewing, "Rights of Women," 1; Rogers, "Shadowy Presence," 14–21; *Col.Rec.*, 4:627. For a concise account of the kinds of chores this "&c." encompassed, see Woloch, *Women and the American Experience*, 25.

9. For the quotes see *Col.Rec.*, 22:250–51, 348; *Det.Rep.*, 4:113. The example of dutiful sons is in *Det.Rep.*, 18:132. Ruprecht Steiner paid two-thirds of his crops and butter to a family of servants who offered to care for his house and three undisciplined children

(*Det.Rep.*, 14:200). The trustees' recommendations for the employment of newly arrived servants in 1738 underlines the importance of surrogate housekeepers in the absence of wives or mothers: one woman servant was placed in the service of the trustees' secretary, William Stephens, and one with John Brown, both men living alone (*Col.Rec.*, 22:250–51).

10. *Col.Rec.*, 4:454; W. Stephens, *Journal of William Stephens*, 15 October 1743; *Col.Rec.*, 20:150 (Hill quote). Also see Fant, "Labor Policy of the Trustees," 1–16. More recent commentaries on labor in the colony include B. Wood, *Slavery in Colonial Georgia*, chaps. 1–5.

11. *Det.Rep.*, 17:268, 14:93 (quote). Tim Lockley engages with the replacement of white servants by slaves in the late colonial era (see Lockley, "Encounters," chap. 4).

12. *Col.Rec.*, 1:445.

13. Ready, *Castle Builders*, 6 (quote), 104. On preadaptation see E. Jones, "European Background."

14. *Col.Rec.*, 21:80; *Det.Rep.*, 1:176, 3:63.

15. *Col.Rec.*, 4:543, 680; 6:74; 20:359–60. Both men and women did the work to keep up a property and its garden, as demonstrated by the petition of Mary Fage, who was "praying some consideration," when the trustees sold her lot in Highgate, for improvements that both she and her late husband, Peter, made (*Col.Rec.*, 2:348).

16. Ready, *Castle Builders*, 104; *Col.Rec.*, 4:100 (Harris comment); 20:357–58.

17. *Det.Rep.*, 1:91; *Col.Rec.*, 25:252–60.

18. *Col.Rec.*, 20:23, 141. The Salzburger community in particular, again bringing genuine experience from their homeland, was quick to capitalize on the livestock provided by the trustees: "Some of the people now have milk-giving cows, for which they cannot thank God enough. And some of them have begun to make fresh butter, which is very rare in this colony and especially amongst us" (*Det.Rep.*, 2:92–93).

19. *Col.Rec.*, 2:251, 277; 6:62.

20. *Det.Rep.*, 1:32; *Col.Rec.*, 2:374. Harold Davis lists the men who served as schoolmaster from 1736 on (*Fledgling Province*, 234–36).

21. *Collections*, 4:17.

22. Whitefield, *Account of Money Received*, 1–2; *Col.Rec.*, 2:109.

23. *Col.Rec.*, 20:27–31.

24. Ibid., 2:100, 375–76; *Col.Wills*, William Harvey; *Col.Rec.*, 4:259.

25. Ewing, "Rights of Women," 2.

26. *Col.Rec.*, 6:51.

27. The colonies she studied were Maryland, Virginia, and South Carolina, as well as Massachusetts, Connecticut, New York, and Pennsylvania. See Salmon, *Women and the Law of Property*.

28. For a recent survey of the changing nature of women's livelihoods in early modern England, see Laurence, *Women in England*, 108–43, 273.

29. Norton, "Evolution of White Women's Experience," 296; *Col.Rec.*, 2:100, 6:31; *Col.Wills*, John Martin Bolzius.

30. *Col.Rec.*, 4:310, 386.

31. Mary Hodges Townsend complained that Thomas Jones "supplies Shops with

Goods by wholesale, Whilst he undersells them by retale; And that he has a Pettiaugua or large boat, and no other Boat can expect Employment when his wants any" (*Col.Rec.*, 1:371). For Emery quotes, see *Col.Rec.*, 2:287–88, 4a:114.

32. *Col.Rec.*, 4:344.

33. *Det.Rep.*, 4:8, 6:122, 8:17 (Ortmann quote). Mrs. Pichler caused outrage by selling goods to the English "at a price far in excess of that demanded by the rules of common decency" (*Det.Rep.*, 4:88), while an Englishwoman from Old Ebenezer similarly journeyed to the Salzburgers several times to sell barrels of rendered beef fat (*Det.Rep.*, 6:122, 8:37).

34. *Det.Rep.*, 10:58; also see 9:27, 38, 317; 15:7. Such part-time employment supplemented the income that Mrs. Ortmann derived from teaching.

35. W. Stephens, *Journal of William Stephens*, 8 February 1744.

36. The commentator is Bolzius, quoted in Loewald, Staricka, and Taylor, "Johann Martin Bolzius," 235. Other examples include vintners, weavers, and flax spinners (*Col. Rec.*, 2:391; 20:353; 25:163–64, 363; 29:190, 327).

37. Spalding and Wilson, *Women on the Colonial Frontier*, 25.

38. *Col.Rec.*, 6:149–50.

39. Ibid., 1:505, 6:166. By working as a mantua maker in Frederica, Anne Harris similarly provided for her son, William, and her mother after Anne's husband died in 1737 (Spalding and Wilson, *Women on the Colonial Frontier*, 25).

40. Bartlett, "Eighteenth Century Georgia Women," 76; Temple and Coleman, *Georgia Journeys*, 144; *Egmont*, 3:202.

41. W. Stephens, *Journal of William Stephens*, 25 August 1743. At least one woman was actually commissioned to trade in alcohol: Mary Morels supplied wine to the Indians in Savannah, for which she was reimbursed by the trustees, who spent considerable sums on presents to pacify and impress the Creeks and Chickasaws. Her claim for three pounds was examined and reduced to £2 8s. (*Col.Rec.*, 7:214).

42. *Col.Rec.*, 4:90, 29:67; *List*, 47; Temple and Coleman, *Georgia Journeys*, 144.

43. For references to Penrose, see *Col.Rec.*, 2:363, 410; 4:211–12, 222, 327, 361–62, 365; 4a:153, 158–59, 163, 174; 5:395; 20:285, 334; *Col.Wills*, John Penrose; Temple and Coleman, *Georgia Journeys*, 165. For the Hetherington quote see *Col.Rec.*, 20:275.

44. *List*, 40.

45. *Col.Rec.*, 20:334.

46. Ibid., 20:285.

47. H. Davis, *Fledgling Province*, 118; W. Stephens, *Journal of William Stephens*, 4 May 1744. Similarly, the Freemasons were an influential enough body in 1735 for comment to be made about a preponderance of its members on juries: Paul Amatis hinted that the reason some people did not have to pay fines for selling rum was because they were Masons (*Col.Rec.*, 20:373, 383, 369).

48. *Col.Rec.*, 2:452, 4:624, 20:287–89, 23:287; *List*, 24.

49. Ibid., 22:pt. 1, 229; W. Stephens, *Journal of William Stephens*, 78; Temple and Coleman, *Georgia Journeys*, 210–11; Spalding and Wilson, *Women on the Colonial Frontier*, 25.

50. Account of the conversation proudly recorded in *Egmont*, 2:387. In fact, the topic had been raised because the queen had heard rumors that the silk was Italian, not Georgian. Egmont explained that the trustees had "debauched [persuaded] two Italians" (the Amatis brothers).

51. *Collections*, 107–11.

52. *Col.Rec.*, 4:310–11. For an analysis of the motivation of poor women, see Lockley, "Encounters," 88–91.

53. *Det.Rep.*, 11:46, 14:74, 17:137, 18:217; *Col.Rec.*, 25:378, 500.

54. Davis, *Fledgling Province*, 161.

55. Stewart, "*What Nature Suffers to Groe*," 2.

56. Cited in H. Davis, *Fledgling Province*, 122.

57. For an excellent discussion of lowcountry planters' experimentation and apprehensively modernist approach, see Chaplin, *Anxious Pursuit*. Those with a more cosmopolitan outlook included, for example, the Earl of Halifax, Henry Ellis, Charles Townshend, James Wright, and Benjamin Franklin. Overall, it is clear that British administrators of Georgia during the royal era took the prospect of silk extremely seriously indeed. In the transition from a proprietorship to a Crown colony, the items that attracted the most lavish parliamentary grants were the governor's salary on the one hand and the "encouragement to the Growth and Culture of Silk" on the other (both one thousand pounds) (Col.Rec., 37:pt. 1, 207). Familiar names in Anglo-American commerce such as George Montagu Dunk (Earl of Halifax) and Charles Townshend interested themselves in Georgia's silk prospects (Col.Rec., 39:187).

58. B. Wood, *Slavery in Colonial Georgia*, 137–38. South Carolinian rice had been the product of earlier experimentation and peaked in 1740 with the production of about forty-three million pounds valued at about £100,000. As a consequence "lowcountry planters concentrated on rice, their most profitable staple, and had little time for anything else"(Menard, "Economic and Social Development of the South," 275–76). By 1770 Georgia's rice and indigo crops were worth more than £40,000 (283–85).

59. Martyn, *Reasons for Establishing the Colony of Georgia* (London, 1733), in *Collections*, 1:204. Poem from J. Stephens, *Georgia, and Two Other Occasional Poems*, 9–10.

60. Boreman, *Compendious Account*.

61. *Col.Rec.*, 1:100, 20:3 (quote).

62. W. Stephens, *Journal of William Stephens*, 22 March 1744; *Egmont*, 3:155; *Col.Rec.*, 25:62, 181.

63. *Col.Rec.*, 1:406; 4a:134; 6:6–7, 85–86.

64. Camuse retired to Purysburg, where at least her French mother tongue could be properly understood, and died sometime before June 1749. A complete list of references to Camuse in the records is as follows: *Col.Rec.*, 1:100, 362, 392, 406, 527–29; 2:276, 416–21, 428; 4a:134, 136, 141, 146, 231–32; 6:6–7, 85–86, 95, 190–91, 251; 25:62, 140–41, 169, 179–81; 26:92; 28:pt. 1, 103; also *Det.Rep.*, 18:4–5, 201; W. Stephens, *Journal of William Stephens*, 4 February 1744, 20 March 1744, 27 March 1745; Moore, *Voyage to Georgia*, 30; *Egmont*, 3:155. For references to Anderson see *Col.Rec.*, 1:547; 6:166, 190–91, 206, 218, 251, 323; 25:140–41; 26:145, 426–31.

65. Ibid., 1:527–28, 4a:134, 1:539.

66. *Col.Rec.*, 1:545, 552, 568–69; 4a:134; 25:369–73, 500; 26:92, 218; for the quote see 25:373.

67. *Det.Rep.*, 15:4. The slave was apparently brought down while pregnant and the next year bore a little girl.

68. *Col.Rec.*, 1:544, 2:498–500.

69. Ibid., 26:332, 289, 231; 28:pt. 2, 154.

70. For statistics and information on silk production in Georgia, see *Col.Rec.*, 1:392, 529, 532; 4a:134; 25:140–41; 28:pt. 1, 125–27, 213, 341, 377, 445; 28:pt. 2, 49; Cashin, *Governor Henry Ellis*, 118–21; W. Smith, *Georgia Gentlemen*, 111, 118, 121–22; G. Jones, "John Adam Treutlen's Origin and Rise," 221–22; Bonner, *History of Georgia Agriculture*, 16–17; P. Stephens, "Silk Industry in Georgia"; McKinstry, "Silk Culture in the Colony of Georgia"; W. Smith, "Utopia's Last Chance?"

71. Habersham to Hillsborough, 24 April 1772, *Collections*, 6:173–74.

72. *Col.Rec.*, 28:pt. 1, 162. In 1758 the Savannah filature was consumed by a raging fire in which half the cocoons were lost (two to three thousand pounds), along with all the utensils, forty pounds in cash, and other valuables; Ed Cashin reckoned that "a record amount of silk would have been produced." On the bright side, the heroic efforts of some sailors prevented the flames from spreading to the building next door, which contained the provincial arms and ammunition (Cashin, *Governor Henry Ellis*, 120). Two years later, in 1760, an unusually cold February devastated the budding mulberry leaves; Ebenezer pastors reported that four widows' silk efforts had failed, probably because of poor weather (*Det.Rep.*, 17:168). In July 1761 only 325 pounds of raw silk had been wound off at the Savannah filature on account of "excessive, hard and unseasonable Frosts" (*Col.Rec.*, 28:pt. 1, 341).

73. Temple and Coleman, *Georgia Journeys*, 53–56. Lucy Mouse was granted Mr. Dobell's vacated "small Hut . . . convenient for a single person" but denied further compensation for her cattle on Skidaway on 18 August 1748 (*Col.Rec.*, 25:319).

74. For secondary sources that discuss the life of Mary Musgrove Matthews Bosomworth, see Gillespie, "Sexual Politics of Race and Gender"; Coulter, "Mary Musgrove"; Baine, "Myths of Mary Musgrove." For primary references see *Col.Rec.*, 1:277, 286, 487, 537–38; 2:263; 4:49–50, 217–20, 327–28, 518; 4a:86, 103, 160, 219; 6:72, 111, 176, 252, 256, 264, 268, 272, 274, 277, 305–6, 355; 20:64–65, 122–23, 141, 173, 237–38, 246, 452; 26:405; 27:1, 7, 24–25, 66–280; 28:pt. 1, 75, 228, 315; *Det.Rep.*, 4:34.; *Col.Wills*, John Musgrove, Jacob Matthews; W. Stephens, *Journal of William Stephens*, 88, 90; *Egmont*, 2:313, 375, 486.

75. Coulter, "Mary Musgrove," 5.

76. *Col.Rec.*, 26:405.

77. Gillespie, "Sexual Politics of Race and Gender," 189.

78. *Col.Rec.*, 7:277.

79. Ibid., 6:264, 271; 28:pt. 1, 75; 20:173; land grant detailed in 28:pt. 1, 315.

80. *Col.Rec.*, 20:173; Coulter, "Mary Musgrove," 30.

81. Mary Musgrove Matthews Bosomworth was not the only Native American female translator used by the colonists and who made the most of the benefits of racial inter-

marriage in the sphere of communication. Edward Jenkins was asked to inquire about Indian discontent "with a Lingester [linguist] which was Bartlets wife" (*Col.Rec.*, 20:185).

82. *Det.Rep.*, 5:96, 6:21 (quote), 9:203.

83. W. Stephens, *Journal of William Stephens*, 19 July 1744; *Col.Wills*, John Teasdale; *Det.Rep.*, 7:147, 108. For elaboration see *Col.Rec.*, 5:659. *Det.Rep.*, 7:108, 147, 214; 18:56; 21:106; 13:95.

Three. *Family and Community*

1. *Col.Rec.*, 2:466–67, 6:118–23; W. Stephens, *Journal of William Stephens*, 31 October 1744, 23 November 1744, 27 November 1744, 1 December 1744.

2. Unfortunately, no one recorded the exact ages of many settlers to whom the colonial records refer. It is sometimes possible to find individuals in multiple sources (such as lists of transatlantic passengers, town inhabitants, or information from wills) and figure out their ages by cross-referencing. But where this is impractical, I am compelled to adopt the vaguer terms of reference used by contemporary commentators. In general, references to "girls" seem to have applied to females as old as eighteen, although those between their midteens and early twenties were often referred to as "young" (e.g. "young woman," "young servant," or "young wife"). In the case of the Spencer family (which I discuss later in this chapter), we might infer from various references that at the time of his second marriage William was about forty, his second wife about sixteen, and his two daughters by his first marriage somewhere between six and thirteen—but these estimates are necessarily speculative.

3. *Col.Rec.*, 26:6 (quote about daughters); *List*, 49; *Col.Rec.*, 30:240; W. Stephens, *Journal of William Stephens*, 2 January 1745, 6 January 1745.

4. *Col.Rec.*, 25:105.

5. Ibid., 2:7.

6. Ibid., 25:105; W. Stephens, *Journal of William Stephens*, 9 and 16 January 1745.

7. *Col.Rec.*, 25:105–6; *Col.Wills*, Spencer; for quotes see *Col.Rec.*, 26:7, 276.

8. Ready, *Castle Builders*, 24–25, 59.

9. Mühlenberg, *Notebook of a Colonial Clergyman*, 2.

10. *Col.Rec.*, 4a:271; *Det.Rep.*, 10:17.

11. *Det.Rep.*, 17:19. In 1759 they asked the Ebenezer pastors to be married and to move into the Lutheran district—but the pastors were unable to promise this, having first to "inquire what the law of the land" was in this matter. Sadly, no record is left of the result of the pastors' inquiry into the Virginian's petition.

12. *Egmont*, 3:196.

13. Braund, "Guardians of Tradition," 240. For a detailed examination of several marriages between white traders and Creek women, see pp. 249–50.

14. Sweet, *Negotiating for Georgia*.

15. Cashin, *Lachlin McGillivray*, 315; Temple and Coleman, *Georgia Journeys*, 143; for the quote see *Col.Rec.*, 20:426–27. George Galphin noted in November 1750 that "all the traders can justify that we have been often in danger of our Lives" (*Col.Rec.*, 6:355).

16. Cashin, *Lachlin McGillivray*, 72, 74–75; *Col.Rec.*, 22:pt. 1, 229; Braund, "Guardians of Tradition," 250–51. Alexander apprenticed under the merchant Samuel Elbert and later Inglis and Company.

17. For an excellent appraisal of Mary Musgrove Matthews Bosomworth's cultural brokering, and its limitations, see Gillespie, "Sexual Politics of Gender."

18. *Col.Rec.*, 4:518–19; *Col.Wills*, Jacob Matthews—written 14 January 1740, in which Jacob leaves the entire estate in America to Mary. Otherwise, Mary would have received only a dower (a third) of Matthews's possessions.

19. For excellent, detailed studies of some of these communities, see Parker, *Scottish Highlanders*, and G. Jones, *Georgia Dutch*.

20. *Col.Rec.*, 20:284.

21. Whitefield, *George Whitefield's Journals*, 500; R. Bolton, *Genealogical and Biographical Account*, 86; W. B. Stephens, "Sketch of the Life of James Habersham," 158; Lambert, *James Habersham*, 41–42.

22. *Col.Rec.*, 4a:59.

23. *Det.Rep.*, 14:158, 160.

24. Ibid., 8:167, 178; for the quotes see 8:183, 192, 197.

25. Ibid., 8:167, 178, 183, 192, 197, 315, 402; 9:47; 18:22. The couple had their first reported tiff in mid-July 1741 and another in September when Holy Communion was withheld.

26. *Det.Rep.*, 3:277, 13:63, 14:97, 17:166. Bolzius remarked that forced marriage was "accustomed to bring forth such fruit." The wife in question confessed her lack of love for her husband to another woman, who advised her "to pray devoutly and eagerly to God to grant her the love she was lacking"; in response, the wife prayed sincerely while shedding "many thousands of tears" (*Det.Rep.*, 8:306).

27. *Col.Rec.*, 4:495, 499; 20:301; W. Stephens, *Journal of William Stephens*, 21 March 1744; for the quotes see *Col.Rec.*, 4:430, 449, 588. Per the records contained in *Col.Wills*, 22 percent of the 236 wills that left bequests to wives specified that at least a portion of her bequest was dependent upon her remaining a widow.

28. For an excellent discussion of religion in early Georgia, see H. Davis, *Fledgling Province*, 193–232.

29. Clarke, *History of the S.P.C.K.*, 137.

30. *Det.Rep.*, 5:135, 10:117.

31. Ibid., 1:103.

32. Ibid., 2:21.

33. Ibid., 3:240; 4:15, 34, 82, 188; 7:115; 8:421.

34. *List*, 74; *Det.Rep.*, 9:238.

35. *Det.Rep.*, 10:17.

36. *Col.Rec.*, 25:19–24, 33–35, 57, 121; *Det.Rep.*, 8:130.

37. *Col.Rec.*, 20:285, 301–3.

38. Ibid., 21:288.

39. *Det.Rep.*, 9:148. For Oglethorpe's campaign against the Spanish, see Spalding, "Oglethorpe, Georgia, and the Spanish Threat," and Jackson, "Behind the Lines."

40. *Det.Rep.*, 5:239, 6:172. One German husband could not persuade his English wife

to sell everything and move to the Ebenezer settlements as he wished (16:38). Patrick Graham, who had become president of the colony in 1752, encouraged Bolzius to marry a number of English candidates in 1753 (16:8).

41. Temple and Coleman, *Georgia Journeys*, 143; *Col. Wills*, Derizous.

42. *Col.Rec.*, 1:573, 7:9–10, 20:144–46; for the quotes see 20:146, 2:520. In this respect some of the conditions in Georgia reflected similarities to the London environment. See Hitchcock, " 'Unlawfully Begotten on Her Body,' " 70–87.

43. *Col.Rec.*, 20:456.

44. Temple and Coleman, *Georgia Journeys*, 77–79; *Col.Rec.*, 4:259; 20:229; 21:57–58; *List*, 81. For incidences of wife selling in England between 1760 and 1800 (of which he found forty-two cases), see Thompson, *Customs in Common*, 404–67.

45. *Det.Rep.*, 8:130; Snyder, "Tree with Two Different Fruits"; *List*, 68–69; Ready, *Castle Builders*, 24–25. See "Sheftall Diary," ms. 921, Levi Sheftall Family Papers, University of Georgia Libraries, Athens. Families that intermarried were the Sheftalls, Harts, Delamottas, Minises, Pollocks, Depasses, Canteses, and Nolochs. Jewish brides' listed ages at marriage suggest a younger female age than was prevalent in other communities in the royal and Revolutionary periods.

46. Snyder, "Tree with Two Different Fruits," 863, 865, 877–78.

47. Gillespie, "Sexual Politics of Gender," 188.

48. Cashin, *Lachlan McGillivray*, 70. For details of Creek and Cherokee processes, see Braund, "Guardians of Tradition," 240–41; Perdue, *Cherokee Women*, 42–46; Morris, *Bringing of Wonder*; Cashin, *Lachlan McGillivray*, 70–80. Other sources are Corkran, *Creek Frontier*, and Hawkins, *Combination of a Sketch*. Bolzius observed that the Indians' basic marriage contract explained why "the men do no work but go hunting and see to the meat and skins, while the women plant corn, beans, and gourds," adding in parentheses that "they do not need any laundry" (*Det.Rep.*, 6:257).

49. *Det.Rep.*, 1:143.

50. Paine, *Complete Writings*, 2:119–20.

51. For discussions of adultery and its resolution among the Creeks, see Braund, "Guardians of Tradition," 247; among the Cherokees, see Perdue, *Cherokee Women*, 56–59.

52. Von Reck's report appears in *Det.Rep.*, 1:145.

53. Similarly, women conveyed their wealth or prestige by adornment of their hair, through the use of ribbons, thimbles worn as tinkling cones, beads, and so on, that made manifest that they were related to a good hunter and well provided for. The most important information revealed by the appearance of any Indian (often proudly displayed in male tattoos) was their tribal affiliation.

54. On Cherokee marital practices see Perdue, *Cherokee Women*, 17–60; Hudson, *Southeastern Indians*, 321; Alexander, *Ambiguous Lives*, 29; *Det.Rep.*, 1:67; 6:257.

55. As Kathryn Braund has argued in "Guardians of Tradition," "Hunting temporarily disrupted the pattern of matrilocal residence, accentuated the influence of a woman's husband on her family, and tended to loosen the authority of the matrilineal clan system" (245). For a comprehensive discussion of the shifting nature of Creek Indian trade, see Braund, *Deerskins and Duffels*.

56. For a comprehensive account of the frequency and experiences of mixed-blood descendants, see Perdue, "Mixed Blood" Indians.

57. For the quote see Det.Rep., 2:91. On polygamy see Braund, "Guardians of Tradition," 241; Perdue, Cherokee Women, 44. In fact, polygamy was not unknown in Creek and Cherokee society, but few husbands could support more than one familial unit.

58. Det.Rep., 4:166; 6:65, 192; 8:19; 16:71; for the quote see 11:4. For a full analysis of relations between Georgia's Germanic immigrants, see Jones, Georgia Dutch.

59. Col.Rec., 2:93–94.

60. Det.Rep., 1:100, 104; 2:12, 15, 45; 3:54; for quotes see 1:109, 2:134.

61. Col.Rec., 20:184 (Jenkins quote); Det.Rep., 2:203; 3:243, 250; 4:71; 6:259, 267.

62. Det.Rep., 8:275.

63. Ibid., 8:244, 250, 305, 318, 362; 13:124; 18:75; for quotes see 5:73, 6:187.

64. See, for instance, Carr and Walsh, "Planter's Wife"; Norton, "Evolution of White Women's Experience"; Biemer, Women and Property; M. Dunn, "Saints and Sisters."

65. Laurence, Women in England, 274.

66. Ebel, "Women and the Wesleys," 227–42; Col.Rec., 4a:177–78; Coulter, "Mary Musgrove," 1–30. For more detailed commentaries on the undeveloped state of communication and transportation, see Ready, Castle Builders, 322–30, and H. Davis, Fledgling Province, 44–58.

67. Det.Rep., 16:31.

Four. *Immigration and Settlement*

1. The plantations used black labor even before the legalization of slavery in 1750 (B. Wood, Slavery in Colonial Georgia, 76; Lockley, "Encounters," 68–69).

2. Russell Menard estimated the population in 1775 at 27,600, although contemporary estimates were higher. Menard posits 14,000 whites, 13,000 blacks, and 600 Indians (Menard, "Economic and Social Development," 253).

3. The Governor's Council handled land grants at its first meeting of every month. Because it is useful to distinguish its land-granting activities from its other duties, I refer to it as the "land-granting committee," or the "committee" when it is concerned solely with land grants and as the "Governor's Council," or "council," when other matters are at stake.

4. Col.Rec., 28:pt. 1, 455.

5. Ibid., 9:415.

6. At the nominal cost of one shilling per ten acres (Lipscomb, "Land Granting in Colonial Georgia," 68).

7. Lipscomb, "Land Granting in Colonial Georgia," 63–64. Petitioners were asked to clear 5 percent of their total acreage per annum, a regulation designed to prevent wide absenteeism and vast areas of uncultivated land. This requirement was changed in 1758 to clearing three of every fifty acres within three years.

8. Lipscomb, "Land Granting in Colonial Georgia," 62.

9. Of course, the land grant data have existed for some time in published form within the broader collection known as *Colonial Records of the State of Georgia* and first printed

in 1904, and several historians have found them useful in exploring the process of land occupation in early Georgia. Robert Lipscomb, in his master's thesis, "Land Granting in Colonial Georgia," tabulated grants made between 1732 and 1772 and charted periods of high and low land-granting activity in the royal period. David Chesnutt explored South Carolina's expansion into colonial Georgia between 1720 and 1765 in his doctoral dissertation of 1973. Chesnutt observed that because of identification problems, his "portrait of Carolina's greatest period of expansion into colonial Georgia is of a qualitative rather than a quantitative nature." He chose to use the land grant data sparingly, having decided that their frequent failure to give the origin of petitioners rendered "a numerical analysis of the period from 1755–1765 valueless" (Chesnutt, "South Carolinian Expansion," 51, 53). In this chapter I hope to demonstrate that a reappraisal of this data is far from valueless but can tell us a great deal about the patterns of immigration during the boom era of colonial population growth in Georgia. More recent work by Alan Gallay, Lee Ann Caldwell, and Kenneth Coleman has used elements of the data set to investigate the expansion of plantation systems, female property holders, and Indian land cession, among other issues. Their contributions have revolved more around the nature and location of the actual grants than around the composition of the petitioners. They have determined that most of the 390,645 acres granted in the first decade of royal government (1752–63) were coastal—mainland or island—and that the largest landholders were South Carolinians who brought with them large numbers of slaves. These historians have explored the importance of tidewater lands to the plantation cultivation of rice and indigo, and they have identified an "agricultural revolution" during the era of royal government, when the colony became characterized by coastal plantations in the lowcountry and familial subsistence farms on the western and northern frontiers. Gallay in particular, in his study of the life of Jonathan Bryan, has put the land grant information to good use, highlighting at once how planters could accrue land and use the same system to distribute patronage and display prestige. See Gallay, *Formation of a Planter Elite*; Caldwell, "Women Landholders of Colonial Georgia"; Coleman, *Colonial Georgia*.

10. Coleman, *Colonial Georgia*, 224.

11. Chesnutt, "South Carolinian Expansion," 51.

12. Ibid., 70, 125–27. The data from land grant applications challenge Alan Gallay's estimates of Carolinian migrants during the 1750s and 1760s. See Gallay, *Formation of a Planter Elite*, 213n41. Gallay uses Chesnutt's compilation of identified migrants to calculate that before 1765, 330 Carolinians applied for land in Georgia (Chesnutt, "South Carolinian Expansion," appendix, 216–30). Gallay removes 10 percent of these as his estimate of claims made in children's names (therefore discountable) before multiplying by an "average family size" factor of five. He therefore emerges with an estimate of 1,485 white South Carolinians arriving in Georgia by 1765. These data indicate that ninety-three land grant petitioners identified themselves as South Carolinians by 1765. If these ninety-three are representative of the Chesnutt-identified 330 South Carolinians—and there is no reason to assume that they are not—then Gallay's assumptions are probably leading to an overestimation of the numbers of white South Carolinian immigrants in the 1750s and early 1760s. The data show that *married* South Carolinian migrants during

this period had an average family size of 4.8 people—that is, 4 percent less than Gallay's factor. More important, Gallay fails to take into account that 28 percent of the white arrivals had no family at all—they were single male applicants. If the land grant data are assumed to be representative and multiplied by a coefficient to encompass Chesnutt's 330 identified Carolinians, we reach an overall estimate of 1,228 white migrants, 17 percent fewer than Gallay's estimate. These petitions consisted of 93 men, 67 wives, and 186 children. Refinements made to Gallay's estimate from analysis of the land grant applications again support the assumption that the settlement of Georgia was actualized by a high proportion of young settlers and smaller families. Gallay himself evidently believed that his method of determining numbers of migrants had overestimated the arrivals: he found that his figure was at "the high end," constituting 2–3 percent of the total white South Carolinian population in a given year between 1751–60, and stating that "it is much more likely that less than 1 percent of the white Carolinians moved to Georgia in the 1750s." Seen in this light, the land grant data support Gallay's broader conception that "the migration southward was significant, but by no means was it an avalanche"—if not his quantitative manipulation.

13. Chesnutt, "South Carolinian Expansion," 125–26.

14. Gallay, *Formation of a Planter Elite*, 63.

15. See Chesnutt, "South Carolinian Expansion," 124; B. Wood, *Slavery in Colonial Georgia*, 90.

16. *Col.Rec.*, 11:330 31.

17. Ibid., 27:63.

18. Cashin, *Governor Henry Ellis*, 56–57. See, for example, Henry Ellis's memorandum to the Board of Trade dated 5 October 1756.

19. Coulter, "Acadians in Georgia"; Cashin, *Governor Henry Ellis*, 96–99. Governor Reynolds initially allowed only the first transport ship of French Acadians, "120 People mostly women and children," to land at Savannah, refusing the second boatload, which "had 280 mostly men" onboard (*Col.Rec.*, 28:pt. 1, 142).

20. Chesnutt, "South Carolinian Expansion," 161, 168.

21. The northwestern acreage was secured in the Treaty of Augusta, while the southern extension of Georgia's territory was confirmed by royal proclamation of 7 October 1763.

22. Gallay notes that "in the late 1760s, planters became willing to move far south of the main settlements about Savannah." Georgia eventually won control but was forced to accommodate South Carolinian claims for grants that had been issued by South Carolina governor Thomas Boone. The competition for this area is indicative of its perceived desirability for the expansion of plantation slavery (Gallay, *Formation of a Planter Elite*, 101–4; the quote appears on p. 96).

23. Coleman, *Colonial Georgia*, 227.

24. The system I have used to categorize applications as "low" or "up" country is based on an analysis of the location sought by the grantee according to a topographical atlas of the area. Petitions for land in areas substantially comprised of "wetland" or "forested wetland" have been identified as lowcountry locations. Although far from perfect, the topographical system of categorizing the grants offers further insight into the pattern of

settlement. Of the 1,833 distinct petitions, 65 are impossible to categorize because of a lack of information from the applicant. Furthermore, my decision to use only the latest petition of each identifiable applicant means that a significant proportion of these 1,833 petitions were made by people already possessing land in Georgia. However, few landholders applied for a radically different location in their subsequent petitions. As backcountry settlers had little need of wetland territory, most repeat claimants requested land next door to their own or close by. Those who did reapply for land in a different part of the province were generally wealthier lowcountry settlers who sprouted new projects to take best advantage of their labor supply. Only rarely might these projects be in the upcountry—when a lumber mill might be a commercial enterprise or practical necessity.

25. *Col.Rec.*, 10:502.

26. Chesnutt, "South Carolinian Expansion," 76; Lipscomb, "Land Granting in Colonial Georgia," 57.

27. Ellis first suggested a ceiling on family grants in early 1757 (*Col.Rec.*, 28:15). The Board of Trade disagreed with his position—which went against the interests of most of the leading councilmen (Ellis to Board of Trade, 24 April 1759; *Col.Rec.*, 28:pt. 1, 300–301.

28. *Col.Rec.*, 17:205.

29. Ibid., 9:604, August 1766.

30. Coleman, *Colonial Georgia*, 225.

31. Cashin, "From Creeks to Crackers," 69–75.

32. Governor Wright's address to the Assembly, October 1765 (*Col.Rec.*, 17:206).

33. R. Davis, *Wilkes County Papers*, 37.

34. It was rare for petitioners to have their applications rejected, but this occurred from time to time—occasionally with a justification's being recorded. In some cases this justification might be spurious—for instance, the committee rejected several petitions because the governor or committee members wanted the same plot of land. Alan Gallay's treatment of this aspect of the data gives a number of examples indicating how patronage and prestige could be used to advance one's claim for land, and he rightly observes that the committee members, all of whom were councilman) regulated Georgia's land system through legislation and "careful control of the distribution of land" (Gallay, *Formation of a Planter Elite*, 90–91). Gallay plotted the gradually dropping percentage of rejections per annum for the whole data series in his appendix 2 (170). A chi-squared test produces the most obvious indication that the committee was acting to streamline the population makeup of the growing colony. This test of association between acceptance and marriage in 2,030 distinct records (one degree of independence) suggests that the two factors are significantly related (i.e., the probability that they are not is less than 0.1 percent). The committee accepted 1,949 applications in all, comprising 651 from single men and 1,298 from married men. It rejected 81 applications, 42 of which were made by single men and 39 by married men.

35. *Col.Rec.*, 10:318–19, 11:152, 153. Eventually, in March 1772, the land-granting committee resolved "that for the future no Applications shall be received at the Board for lands in this province from or on behalf of any Person or persons not residing within the same" (*Col.Rec.*, 11:253).

36. *Col.Rec.*, 20:319, October 1767. In November 1769, for example, Edmund Bugg's claim to land was rejected because it appeared "that Bugg was now living in Virginia and his Family was never in the Province nor had he ever had any Settlement therein" (10:944).

37. Children in John Demos's study of Rhode Island averaged 3.27 per family (Demos, "Families in Colonial Bristol, Rhode Island"). See also Greven, "Family Structure in Seventeenth-Century Andover," 78–80.

38. Data generated from *Col. Wills*.

39. Galenson, "Settlement and Growth," 185; Wrigley, Davies, Oeppen, and Schofield, *English Population History*, 135. Unfortunately, several American historians appear to continue to rely on the questionable figures generated by Lawrence Stone.

40. Chestnutt, "South Carolinian Expansion," 118; B. Wood, *Slavery in Colonial Georgia*, 92.

41. The reservation of land at Wrightsborough operated on a slightly different headright system than in other areas. It appears that single men who arrived were given one hundred acres (as usual) but also could reserve an adjoining hundred acres in anticipation of their future families. An Irish reservation was also in operation in St. George's Parish (near Lambert's Big Creek) during 1769. For overviews of the Quaker settlements, see Candler, *Quakers of Wrightsborough*, and R. Davis, *Quaker Records in Georgia*, 1–17.

42. Gallay, *Formation of the Planter Elite*, 100.

43. McCurry, *Masters of Small Worlds*, esp. 72–85.

44. Gray and Wood, "Transition from Indentured to Involuntary Servitude," 363.

45. Elite families benefited from their ability to move at short notice from urbanized areas to country homes and vice versa. For instance, in June 1764, when a vessel from Curaçao brought smallpox into the province, the threat was far more serious for poorer families, which depended on their daily labor to support themselves and lacked the options of hiring nurses or moving to the countryside to be inoculated in a controlled environment (*GG.*, 7 June 1764, 12 July 1764).

46. Chesnutt, "South Carolinian Expansion," 111–12.

47. 1765–68 file, William Gibbons Jr. Papers, University of Georgia Libraries, Athens.

48. *GG.*, 10 May 1769, 23 May 1770; B. Wood, *Slavery in Colonial Georgia*, 171–73. The *Georgia Gazette* was the colony's first newspaper, and it was published weekly from its inception in the spring of 1763 by the specialist printer James Johnston in Savannah. Johnston's publishing of the *Gazette* reflected the political travails of the colony/state: publication was suspended for six months during the Stamp Act crisis in 1765 and temporarily abandoned with the onset of the American Revolution in 1776; the newspaper was reincarnated as the *Royal Georgia Gazette* during the brief era of British occupation between 1779 and 1782, and again as the *Gazette of the State of Georgia* between 1783 and 1788, before reverting to its original title in 1788 (still under the direction of James Johnston, from 1790 in conjunction with Nicholas Johnston).

49. *Col.Rec.*, 11:227, 12:212–13, 253–54; R. Davis, *Quaker Records in Georgia*, 204–5, 255–59.

50. For Moody see *Col.Rec.*, 9:413–14, 10:17; for Venning see 9:503.

51. Twenty-six percent of all widows who applied for land applied with more than ten slaves, whereas just 13 percent of the overall applicants applied with more than ten slaves. For examples of widows claiming their headrights, see *Col.Rec.*, 9:162 (Mary Bach/Liemburger), 183 (Mary Johnson/Douglass), 186 (Elizabeth Cross/Marcer/Pryce), 685 (Elizabeth Butler), Mary Gilbert, Sarah Bevill, Hannah Vincent, Christina Perkins, Mary Larescy.

52. *Col.Rec.*, 7:889, 287; 9:639–40.

53. Ibid., 8:65–66, 7:582, 10:73–74; 9:730.

54. See land grant, November 1769, in *Col.Rec.*, vol. 10. Other examples of the latitude extended to women include Mary Douglass, who received surplus land (*Col.Rec.*, 11:3). Mary Tannatt petitioned to change her granted lands as "not being convenient for her purpose" (11:102). Widow Sarah Spencer obtained an extension of her lands (on a branch of the Little Mortar) (11:192). Abigail Minis found that the thirty-seven acres of surplus land from her last grant was in fact comprised of seventy-four acres and asked for and obtained the surplus thirty-seven (12:156). Elizabeth Butler petitioned for twenty-three acres in addition to her previous request for one hundred acres, "which if granted would be very Convenient" (granted) (12:201).

55. *Col.Rec.*, 8:150–51. Consideration of her petition was postponed.

56. Ibid., 8:258.

57. See land grant petitions of Sarah Bevill in November 1766 and February 1767 in *Col.Rec.*, vols. 9 and 10. The partners were Sarah Bevill, Nathaniel Miller, William Coulson, and Abraham Lundy.

58. *Col.Rec.*, 8:697. Peter Rietter similarly capitalized on his marriage to Ann Sunier (since she already had a daughter, Paula) in March 1766—when he was probably in his mid- to late twenties, for six years earlier he claimed he had "arrived at manhood" (9:490).Other examples of remarried spouses' taking advantage of the land grant system include James Grierson and Katherine Pettygrew; Nicholas Cavenah and the widow of William Pugh.

59. *Col.Rec.*, 10:158–59, 392–93, 605–6.

60. Ibid., 9:406. See also the grant to John Winn of land located "East of land granted Lydia Saunders," who had married him.

61. Thomas Tripp, a carpenter, left behind no fewer than six daughters who all received a share in his Savannah town lot. See vol. 10 of *Col.Rec.* for land grant requested by Thomas Lee in December 1769. Legatees were Elizabeth Snook (dead), Rebecca Lee, Mary Dews, Grace Lyon, and Sarah and Ann Tripp (spinsters).

62. Deposition of Henry Yonge to the governor dated 17 May 1774 (*Col.Rec.*, 12:401–2).

63. See Lipscomb, "Land Granting in Colonial Georgia," table 11.

64. Col.Rec., 38:pt. 1A, 151–52.

65. Independent of Wright's account, William De Brahm put the Georgia population at 16,000 whites (2,000 fewer than Wright) and 13,000 blacks (2,000 fewer) (Col.Rec., 39:464). Wright was not in the best position to accurately estimate the Georgia population in the early 1770s because he had been in England for about eighteen months. He had taken a leave of absence, sailing on 10 July 1771 to visit London, where he was able to press

in person for the acquisition of more land from the Creeks and Cherokees, overcoming the initial reticence of Lord Hillsborough and apparently the king himself (Cashin, *Lachlan McGillivray*, 272–79). When the Board of Trade secured the king's blessing for the proposal on 9 November 1772, Wright—the sponsor of the plan—was awarded a baronetcy. He returned to Georgia in early 1773 and was given a congratulatory address by the colonial assembly on 15 February (*Col.Rec.*, 27:687–89). James Wright's 1773 estimate to the Board of Trade of the Georgia population was made in the conscious awareness that the province needed to continue to display high growth rates in order to validate his press for the purchase of extra territory. There is thus good reason to suspect that Wright's figures, rounded for the first time to the nearest thousand, and influenced by his diplomatic efforts of the preceding two years, were probably considerably higher than the actual population present in 1773.

66. Yasuba, *Birth Rates of the White Population in the United States*, 61.

67. *Col.Rec.*, 12:347–48.

68. For a full account of the New Purchase, see Cashin, *Lachlin McGillivray*, chap. 15.

69. Wright reported that he had sold 55,650 acres of the Ceded Lands, which were purchased by 1,413 white settlers and 300 blacks.

70. Wright to Hillsborough, December 1771, in *Documents of the American Revolution*, 3:269–75.

71. *Documents of the American Revolution*, 5:113–18; *Col.Rec.*, 38:pt. 1A, 4–8, 9–10. Of course, as the historian Edward Cashin has observed, Habersham could not enforce the edict—short of calling out the militia—so it failed to resolve the problem (*Lachlan McGillivray*, 273).

72. R. S. Davis states that "at least 300 families moved to the Ceded Lands from other American colonies," mainly from the Carolinas (*Wilkes County Papers*, 25). On 15 July 1773 Wright reserved the following portions of the Ceded Lands: 75,000 acres for one hundred families from Long Cane in South Carolina; 50,000 acres for Presbyterians from North Carolina and Pennsylvania; 40,000 acres for South Carolinians from the north side of the Savannah River (*Col.Rec.*, 12:371–76; R. Davis, *Quaker Records in Georgia*, 204–5, 255–59). Note that an adult was a person aged eighteen or older; average family size was based on married units.

73. The lower South had the highest average annual regional growth rates on the mainland for most of the colonial era, but Georgia's contribution was noticeable only between about 1755 and 1775. David Galenson calculates that average annual regional growth rates on the mainland during 1650–1770 ranged from a low of 2.7 percent for New England, through 3.3 percent for the upper South and 4.2 percent for the Middle Colonies, to a high of 5.5 percent for the lower South ("Settlement and Growth of the Colonies," 169–70, 178).

74. *Col.Rec.*, 11:320, 323, 332, 333–34.

75. Ibid., 12:386–87.

76. Lachlan McIntosh to Jack McIntosh, 1 October 1774, ms. 2868, McIntosh Family Papers, University of Georgia Libraries, Athens.

77. Berlin, *Many Thousands Gone*.

78. Noble W. Jones to his wife, Sarah, 22 August 1785, ms. 1127, Noble Jones Family Papers, University of Georgia Libraries, Athens.

79. For detailed considerations of slavery in the late colonial lowcountry, see Berlin, *Many Thousands Gone*, 142–73; B. Wood, *Slavery in Colonial Georgia*, 110–30; P. Wood, *Black Majority*, 195–326.

80. The distribution of enslaved men and women varied according to the size of the holding: on estates with fewer than ten slaves, the ratio was as low as 119:100 and on holdings with more than forty slaves as high as 152:100. See B. Wood, *Slavery in Colonial Georgia*, 105.

81. See Littlefield, *Rice and Slaves*, 56–72. For an account of the punishing nature of sugar plantations, see Follett, "Heat, Sex, and Sugar," 510–39.

82. J. Morgan, "This Is 'Mines.' "

83. Peter Wood identified 663 people by gender for inventories filed in the eighteen months after 1 January 1730. He calculated that on these estates with more than ten slaves, 64.2 percent were men and 35.8 percent women (*Black Majority*, 155). In South Carolina more than 40 percent of slaves came from the rice-growing regions of Upper Guinea and Senegambia. Another 40 percent came from Angola (Tanner, *Settling of North America*, 51–52).

84. *Trans-Atlantic Slave Trade*. Betty Wood analyzes the origins of twenty-five hundred slaves shipped from West Africa in *Slavery in Colonial Georgia*, 103.

85. *Det.Rep.*, 16:20.

86. Loewald, Staricka, and Taylor, "Johann Martin Bolzius," 236.

87. B. Wood, *Slavery in Colonial Georgia*, 101.

88. Ibid., 105.

89. Habersham to Knox, 24 July 1772, *Collections*, 6:193–94. Herbert Klein has concluded that across all of North America a "positive growth rate was masked by the inability of African-born women to reproduce their arriving cohorts, and their positive rates would only become manifest and influence total slave population growth when the volume and ratio of African immigrants declined significantly" (*Atlantic Slave Trade*, 167).

90. Just as in South Carolina, where the large black population had scarcely sustained itself during the several decades after 1720, so Georgia slaves experienced the same phenomenon in the 1750s through 1770s (P. Wood, *Black Majority*, 163–64).

91. B. Wood, *Slavery in Colonial Georgia*, 106–7.

92. Klein, *Atlantic Slave Trade*, 126, 166–67.

93. *Col.Rec.*, 26:22. According to James Habersham, there were 280 whites and 536 blacks settled at Midway on 9 January 1752 (26:374).

94. *Det.Rep.*, 16:20.

95. *GG.*, 13 April 1768, 1 November 1769.

96. Ibid., 27 April 1774.

97. No information about the ages of those auctioned was apparent from the records (*Det.Rep.*, 16:217).

98. B. Wood, *Slavery in Colonial Georgia*, 98, 100.

Five. Expansion and Contraction

1. *Col. Wills*, various. For examples of declining inheritance elsewhere, see Berkin, *First Generations*, 17–18; Brown, *Good Wives*, 290; Norton, *Founding Mothers*, 147; Kierner, *Beyond the Household*, 12; Salmon, *Women and the Law of Property*, 147–60.
2. *Col. Rec.*, 16:423, 426, 428, 430, 455, 466, 469–70, 474, 487.
3. American Antiquarian Society, *Early American Imprints*, Series 1, No. 41370.
4. Salmon, *Women and the Law of Property*, 39.
5. "Release in Fee-simple: Mrs. Anne Bard to John Smith, baker," "Legal Papers," folder 78, Wallace-Owens Family Papers, Colonial Dames of America Historical Collections, Georgia Historical Society, Savannah.
6. *Col. Rec.*, 16:726.
7. American Antiquarian Society, *Early American Imprints*, Series 1, No. 41382.
8. Colonial Conveyances, book C-1 (cutoff date 24 April 1760), Georgia Department of Archives and History, Atlanta.
9. Ibid., books S, U, and V. Book S contains 79 shared conveyances out of 190 recorded between January 1759 and January 1769. Book U contains 47 shared conveyances out of 163 recorded between October 1755 and December 1769. Book V contains 89 shared conveyances out of 229 recorded between July 1753 and June 1771.
10. For references to the bill and its tortuous passage, see *Col. Rec.*, 16:28–29, 31, 36, 42, 45.
11. Salmon, *Women and the Law of Property*, 46.
12. Cashin, *Governor Henry Ellis*, 63–65.
13. Greene, "Travails of an Infant Colony," 296–98.
14. Ingeborg Dornan provides a more complete analysis of slaveholding widows' economic activities in Savannah and Charlestown in "Women Slaveholders," 143–91.
15. The total price for these items came to £17.3s.9d, and the bill was paid off in December. See William Gibbons Jr. Papers, 1728–1803, University of Georgia Libraries, Athens, p. 10.
16. Gibbons Papers, pp. 37 (1757–58), 59 (1759), 191 (1760–63).
17. Ibid., 252. The widows Amelia Alther and Elizabeth Tannatt dealt more directly with the Gibbonses; see pp. 69, 197.
18. For a cross section of examples see the following dates in the *Georgia Gazette*: 2 February 1764, Abigail Minis, Mary Smith, Catherine Zettler all take out licenses to keep taverns or retail goods; 20 August 1766, Jean Campbell advertises her millinery and mantua-making business; 7 January 1767, Mary O'Neal takes out a license for tavern keeping; 25 February 1767, Mary Somers offers to board children; 3 June 1767, Mary Stedman gives up teaching and recommends Judith Swinton; 23 March 1768, Mary Blake holds a ball; 28 September 1768, Mrs. Colgreve teaches sewing and reading; 12 January 1774, Mary Martin advertises her services as milliner and mantua maker from Paris; 18 July 1775, Mary Garrety teaches; 22 November 1775, Jane Stutz opens a boarding house.
19. *GG.*, 5 January 1764.
20. Ibid., 30 August 1775.

21. Ibid., 25 October 1775.

22. *Col.Wills*, Vincent.

23. Letterbook, 16 February 1771, 15 February 1774, undated (prob. 1775–76), 11 March 1776, ms. 1127, Noble Jones Family Papers, University of Georgia Libraries, Athens. Hannah Vincent was asked to procure, among other things, cotton bed lining, mirrors, thimbles, and needles, Dr. James's fever powders, six boxes of Keysers Pills, curtains, window tacks, marking ink and nibs, a black cloak, and a mahogany tea chest.

24. Mary Jenkins, p. 10; Hannah Vincent, pp. 112, 138–40, 249; Jane Mauve, pp. 275, 289; Ann Greene, p. 286; Penelope Humphryss [sic] p. 367; Ann Milledge, p. 454; Alis. Forbes, p. 555; Eliza Wright, 643, all in Gibbons Papers.

25. *GG.*, 6 October and 15 December 1763, 7 November 1765.

26. Colonial Conveyances, book O, 255; *GG.*, 2 February 1764, 15 November 1764, 10 January 1765, 7 January 1767, 11 March 1767, 21 December 1768, 11 January 1769; *Col.Wills*, Pages.

27. Excluding the school established at Bethesda, which was expanded to an "academy" by George Whitefield during the royal period. For a comprehensive account of the institution's history, see Cashin, *Beloved Bethesda*.

28. See, for example, the advertisement by James Cosgreve and wife, *GG.*, 21 June 1769.

29. See, for instance, the Savannah schools listed in E. D. Johnston, *Houstouns of Georgia*, 343.

30. E. L. Johnston and Eaton, *Recollections*, 43–44.

31. *GG.*, 24 May 1775, 31 May 1775, 22 November 1775.

32. *Gaz.S.G.*, 15 June 1786; *GG.*, 19 September 1793.

33. *GG.*, 29 September 1796.

34. Ibid., 2 August 1769. Elizabeth Bedon offered reading, writing, arithmetic, and all kinds of needlework. She charged £5 a year for day scholars, £12 for "day boarders," and £25 for night boarders.

35. Quote taken from B. Wood, *Slavery in Colonial Georgia*, 163; for a general discussion of the religious teaching of slaves, see pp. 159–65.

36. *Det.Rep.*, 11:32, 17:194, 197.

37. Ibid., 15:275.

38. Ibid., 15:4, 44, 272.

39. *GG.*, 21 February 1765.

40. For the quotes see *GG.*, 17 and 24 September 1766, 3 August 1768.

41. For the quotes see *GG.*, 12 July 1769, 20 April 1774, 4 October 1764, 7 November 1765, 3 December 1766, 6 September 1775.

42. *GG.*, 4 April 1765.

43. Ibid., 11 June 1766.

44. The Gibbons Papers, which consist of the records of rice plantations near Savannah and other family accounts (1728–1803), show women—including feme coverts—not as major players but frequently as supporting actors on the urban economic stage. The collection shows that the family's finances consisted essentially of several large accounts with sizable companies that catered to whole plantations and a number of small receipts

for specialist goods purchased and services paid for. It shows that women of all statuses—from elite widows to wives and spinsters of the lower classes—played an active role in the growing economy of the 1750s. Consistency in billing patterns suggests that the Gibbons family used the following major companies for larger accounts: Robert Bolton (saddler), David Tubear (gunsmith), Morel & Cooper and later Clay & Habersham (general merchants), John Wilson (tailor), Sheftall & Unseld (food retail), John Farley (building materials), James Johnston (books), Eppinger & Williams (builders and plasterers).

45. Dornan, "Women Slaveholders," 222.

46. Penknives and stockings for boys, p. 98; goods from the physician John Ludwig Mayer in 1761 and 1763, pp. 127, 206; ointments from Henry Lewis Bourquin, p. 295; women's clothing from Penelope Humphryss, p. 367, all in Gibbons Papers.

47. Judith Swinton charged £3.15s per child per quarter, p. 254,; Betty Wright in 1771 was charging £6 per quarter, p. 464, both in Gibbons Papers.

48. Gibbons Papers, pp. 499, 504, 512, 522, 523, 542.

49. Introduction to microfilm of Gibbons Papers, p. 42.

50. K. Wood, *Masterful Women*.

51. For a comprehensive discussion of the public and private economic activity of slaves in the Georgia lowcountry, see B. Wood, *Women's Work, Men's Work*.

52. Quoted in F. Lambert, *James Habersham*, 140.

53. B. Wood, *Slavery in Colonial Georgia*, 137–38.

54. *Det.Rep.*, 16.138.

55. B. Wood, *Women's Work, Men's Work*, 106.

56. *Drums and Shadows*; B. Wood, *Women's Work, Men's Work*, 38–42.

57. Solutions found in 1758, 1763, and 1774 universally served the interests of the planter elite, which sought to retain the utmost flexibility for its disposition of slaves and curb the prices and wages charged by white competitors.

58. B. Wood, *Women's Work, Men's Work*, 82–87.

59. *Col.Rec.*, 12:214.

60. B. Wood, *Women's Work, Men's Work*, 106.

Six. Consolidating Gender

1. See Kenneth Lockridge's book review of K. Brown, *Good Wives*, in *Journal of Social History* 31, no. 3 (March 1998): 731.

2. Clinton and Gillespie, *Devil's Lane*, xv.

3. For a comprehensive treatment of this code, see B. Wood, *Slavery in Colonial Georgia*, 80–87.

4. *Col.Rec.*, 25:434.

5. Paul Finkelman has posited that Virginia's lawmakers in the seventeenth century quite deliberately set out to alter social norms involving sex in order to encourage racial separation (see "Crimes of Love," 126).

6. P. Morgan, *Slave Counterpoint*, 17. For discussions of these miscegenation laws, see Morgan's first chapter and Jordan, *White over Black*, 138–44.

7. Jordan, *White over Black*, 140n8. It was the Montserrat assembly that banned intermarriage.

8. B. Wood, *Slavery in Colonial Georgia*, 129; *Col.Rec.*, 19:pt. 1, 220.

9. Jordan, *White over Black*, 157.

10. *GG.*, 7 April 1763.

11. B. Wood, *Slavery in Colonial Georgia*, 193.

12. Ibid., 123–24.

13. "An act for the better security of the inhabitants by obliging the male white persons to carry fire arms to places of public worship, February 1770" (*Col.Rec.*, 19:137–40).

14. Ibid., 18:659.

15. Lockley, *Lines in the Sand*, 51–56.

16. G. Moulton to unknown recipient, 23 January 1773, no. 75 in Additional Manuscripts Index no. 22677 (Correspondence of Jamaican Planters and Merchants), British Museum. For a compelling insight into Anglo-Jamaican sexual relations, see Burnard, *Mastery, Tyranny, and Desire*.

17. G. Moulton to unknown recipient.

18. *Col.Wills*, Joseph Prenieres [*sic*]; Amie Pruniere. Maria may have been one of four slaves purchased by Joseph Pruniere from Samuel Piles in July 1761 for £152. The kinship networks united by Amie's previous marriages clearly continued to correspond, since her first father-in-law, Gideon Mallet, loaned Amie's daughter from her second marriage, Priscilla Jones, the sum of £28 on 11 February 1757. See Abstracts of Georgia Bonds, Deeds of Gift, Sales, Colonial Book J, 1755–62, 217, 73, Georgia Department of Archives and History, Atlanta.

19. Loewald, Staricka, and Taylor, "Johann Martin Bolzius," pt. 1, 235. He added in respect to white-Indian sexual relations, "Up among the Indian nations the merchants and their white servants treat the heathenish women and their daughters in the same way. The children are half-Indian in colour and remain, unfortunately, heathens" (235).

20. *Col.Wills*, Barksdale, Maran, Cuthbert.

21. E. D. Johnston, *Houstouns of Georgia*, 285.

22. *GG.*, 19 September 1765. For other examples of overseers' sexual predations, see B. Wood, *Slavery in Colonial Georgia*, 141.

23. *Col.Wills*, Ross.

24. "Miscellaneous Deeds," No. 1505, box 1, folder 2, Minis Family Papers, Georgia Historical Society, Savannah.

25. For a summation of the evidence of and attitudes toward prostitution in the early national period, see Lockley, *Lines in the Sand*, 56.

26. Cashin, "From Creeks to Crackers," 71. Governor Wright was increasingly concerned about the presence of those variously called vagabonds, strollers, stragglers, banditti, and crackers. Interestingly, the Indians referred to this type as "Virginians" and complained primarily that they spoiled the hunting grounds by killing buffalo, bear, and deer (Cashin, *Lachlan McGillivray*, 235–36, 288).

27. *Col.Rec.*, 28:pt. 1, 17.

28. Ibid., 166.

29. See Cashin, *Lachlan McGillivray*, chap. 10.

30. Ibid., 197. See also *Col.Rec.*, 28:pt. 1, 216, 228.

31. In June 1760 Ellis remarked that hundreds of families had left their homes and were moving to other provinces. This probably was an exaggeration, but his observation that "we may expect many more will follow, if a War with the Creeks should prove unavoidable" undoubtedly hit the mark (*Col.Rec.*, 28:pt. 1, 252).

32. *Col.Rec.*, 8:650.

33. Ibid., 28:pt. 1, 246.

34. Ibid., pt. 2, 42, emphasis added.

35. Ibid., pt. 1, 293.

36. See Braund, "Creek Indians, Blacks, and Slavery," 610–14.

37. *Col.Rec.*, 28:pt. 2, 357.

38. Cashin, *Lachlan McGillivray*, 280–81.

39. *GG.*, 2 February 1774, 16 February 1774; Col.Rec., 38:15–17.

40. No land grant was made to a "Shirrel," but headright was claimed by a William Shirley for himself, his wife, and five children in April 1767 at MacBean's Swamp, near Augusta. He possessed no slaves, according to this petition in *Col.Rec.*, vol. 10.

41. The Indians avenged themselves by shooting three men and ransacking and torching a number of properties. When other colonists returned to the scene they "found (in a Branch) Mrs. Wilder taking care of her husband who was wounded in the leg, and afterwards found Baker & Cummins by their grones [sic] in the thicket who were both still sensible." Baker and Cummins died on the way to the ferry, and it may be assumed that they (along with Jeremiah Wilder) were the men who had administered the whipping in the weeks before. The postman for the region was understandably worried by these events, because he had to travel alone all the way to St. Augustine, Florida. He went so far as to leave all his money with a colonist, along with a letter for his wife, should he never return. Three Indians who were at the house were identified by witnesses by the names of "Billy Jonston, Nathicks & Chessey," suggesting that the cycle of retribution would continue (Col.Rec., 37:pt. 1, 260, William Clark's deposition; 262, James Lemon's deposition).

42. Gallay, *Formation of a Planter Elite*, 127. David Hackett Fischer goes so far as to observe that the militant attitude of the frontier people—at least, those who were Scots Irish, with roots in the border countries of northern Britain—had a cultural basis grounded in their Old World customs and experiences (Fischer, *Albion's Seed*, 758).

43. Alexander, *Ambiguous Lives*, 23; Braund, "Creeks, Blacks, and Slavery," 614–16.

44. Pearson, "Planters Full of Money," 303–4.

45. For a good example of the elite intermarriage of one family, see E. D. Johnston, *Houstouns of Georgia*, 293–94.

46. J. Bartram, "Diary of a Journey" (25–26 September 1765), 30.

47. George Jones to Noble Wimberley Jones, 23 November 1784, ms. 1127, Noble Jones Family Papers, University of Georgia Libraries, Athens. Polly was obviously a nickname—her real name was Mary Gibbons. George concluded his case as follows: "One thing Dear Sir I would wish further to observe: I have for Eighteen months or

two years past placed my affections on this young Lady, and notwithstanding a variety of other objects may have presented I have still found my partiality for her continue & must confess to you it would be attended with painful reluctance that I could immediately relinquish it."

48. George Jones to Noble Wimberley Jones, 18 January 1785, ms. 1127, Jones Family Papers.

49. *Gaz.S.Ga.*, 3 February 1785.

50. Ms. 921, 23:25, Levi Sheftall Family Papers, University of Georgia Libraries, Athens.

51. As recorded by Levi Sheftall in what is described as "Benjamin Sheftall's Diary, 1733–1800," 23:3, Sheftall Family Papers.

52. Boatwright, *Status of Women*, 31.

53. Dr. Brickett, who practiced at Edenton, North Carolina, around 1731, is quoted in Calhoun, *Social History*, 1:245.

54. Wilson to William Bartram, 8 March 1809, in Wilson, *Poems and Literary Prose*, 1:167–68.

55. Jordan, *White over Black*, 149.

56. E. L. Johnston and Eaton, *Recollections*, 52.

57. Ibid., 53.

58. Ibid., 54.

59. Ibid., 55.

60. Ibid.

61. "Excerpt from Marriage Settlement of Mordecai Sheftall and Frances Hart, 1761," No. 1505, box 1, folder 2, Minis Family Papers, Georgia Historical Society, Savannah.

62. Consultation document and marriage agreement, ms. 1127, Jones Family Papers. The agreement, dated 20 April 1780, was witnessed by James Deveaux and Sarah Jones.

63. *Col.Wills*, Pryce.

64. Ibid., Altherr, Barnard, Cunningham, Cuthbert (George), Cuthbert (James), Heyd, Martin, Schweiger.

65. Ms. 921, folder 9, McIntosh Family Papers, University of Georgia Libraries, Athens.

66. Death notice in *Georgia Gazette*, 12 March 1789, no. 1505, box 1, folder 4, Minis Family Papers.

67. Undated obituary in ms. 921, 24:3, Sheftall Family Papers.

68. On gentility and obituaries see F. Lambert, *James Habersham*, 141–43; B. Wood, *Gender, Race, and Rank*, 38.

69. *GG.*, 21 February 1770. See also obituary of Miss Sally Read, *GG.*, 30 August 1774.

70. *GG.*, 29 November 1774.

71. Ibid., 19 January 1774, 30 March 1774; Mary Law was described as "a tender mother, and a loving and affectionate wife," in the paper of 2 March 1774. Katherine Stith revered in *Gaz.S.Ga.*, 6 July 1786; Mrs. Houstoun, 21 April 1791.

72. Whether this is reflective of a weakening of patriarchal control of mating arrangements during the long eighteenth century (the progressive viewpoint) or an indication that such control adjusted in subtle ways to continue to operate (the revisionist viewpoint) has been widely debated. For a broader analysis of English marriage poetry during this period, see Horne, *Making a Heaven of Hell*.

73. *GG.*, 6 January 1768. Philafiddlesticks comments that "the amiable picture of Clarissa in your last paper is so very much alike to that of Emilia I now send you from the Spectator No. 302" (*GG.*, 13 January 1768).

74. *GG.*, 10 June 1767.

75. Ibid., 13 July 1768.

76. Ibid., 14 September 1768.

77. See the *Gazettes* of 4 March 1767 ("The Rose"), 10 June 1767 ("A Pastoral"), and 13 July 1768 ("A Batchelor's Will"). For examples of contributions from "Smart" and "A Husband," see the issues of 12 April 1764 and 11 November 1767, respectively.

78. For "The Spirit of Contradiction," by "R. Lloyd, M.A.," see the *Gazette* of 7 February 1765; Philotomy's offering appeared in the *Gazette* on 20 May 1767.

79. Nussbaum and Brown, *New Eighteenth Century*, 13.

80. Milfort, *Memoirs*, 87. For a succinct account of her rather confused tea making, see Cashin, "From Creeks to Crackers," 72.

81. *GG.*, 18 October 1775.

82. Lockley, *Lines in the Sand*, 153–54.

83. Godbeer, *Sexual Revolution in Early America*.

84. *GG.*, 20 July 1768. See also advertisement by Frentz denying his wife access to his credit on 12 August 1767 and notice of his execution on 11 January 1769.

85. For more details about the migration, see Candler, *Quakers of Wrightsborough*; Davis, *Quaker Records in Georgia*.

86. Monthly meetings, and therefore records, were established on 4 November 1773, but the register of marriages and the minutes of the Women's Monthly Meeting have not survived. All that remains, as compiled by Robert Scott Davis, are twentieth-century handwritten transcripts of the minutes of the Men's Monthly Meeting (1773–92) and of the birth and death records. See Davis, *Quaker Records in Georgia*, 17.

87. The formal betrothal took the form of an oath: "Friends, you are my witnesses that, in the presence of you, I take this my Friend, ———, to be my wife, promising to be a loving and true husband to her and to live in the good order of truth, so long as it shall please the Lord that we live together or until death" (Candler, *Quakers of Wrightsborough*, 22).

88. For listed expulsions see Davis, *Quaker Records in Georgia*, June 1780, June 1781, September 1782, August 1784, September 1784, January 1785 (2), May 1785, September 1786, August 1789, October 1790, February 1791, September 1791 (2).

89. Three sisters, Rachel, Olive, and Abigail Barns, were cast out in February 1782 for these activities. William Cooper was expelled simply for going to a "disorderly wedding" in April 1773 (Davis, *Quaker Records in Georgia*).

90. Apologetic condemnations were offered for such activities. See Davis, *Quaker Records in Georgia*, May and October 1775, July 1776, June and July 1785, February and August 1789, January and February 1790, May, June, and September 1791, April 1792.

91. In 1792, nine years after her marriage, Catherine made the long journey to Wrightsborough and appeared before the meeting to offer her paper of condemnation in person. At last she was readmitted into membership and promptly requested a certificate to travel to Deepriver Monthly Meeting in North Carolina. Catherine Sidwell Mendenhall's situa-

tion was considered in the following minutes: Davis, *Quaker Records in Georgia*, October 1783, October and November 1786, November and December 1792.

92. Davis, *Quaker Records in Georgia*, December 1786.

93. Contemporary perceptions of Quaker sexuality are briefly discussed in Levy, *Quakers and the American Family*, 82–84.

94. Davis, *Quaker Records in Georgia*, December 1786.

95. Ibid., May 1782. The extent to which this measure, which effectively jumped a generation, offset the dwindling numbers of full Quakers is difficult to ascertain. It was largely dependent upon the circumstances and attitudes of the parents toward the Society that had barred them, as well as the ages of the children in question. All that can be firmly asserted is that such measures provide further indications of contemporary concern about the dilution of Quaker society in the Georgia backcountry.

96. Davis, *Quaker Records in Georgia*, May 1778, October 1782, October 1785, August 1789, May 1791, May 1792.

97. B. Wood, *Slavery in Colonial Georgia*, 155.

98. *Col. Wills*, Mary Bryan, Heriot Crooke, Hariot Crooke Jr., George Cuthbert, John Flerl, John Forbes, Gasper Garbut, Benjamin Goldwire, Priscilla Houstoun, William Jones, Bryan Kelly, Theobald Kieffer, John Luptan, Charles Maran, Clement Martin, William Moore, Thomas Peacock, John Pettycrow, Joseph Pruniere, Daniel Ross, John Roviere. Theobald Kieffer, a small planter from Ebenezer, specified in his bequests (fulfilled on 5 March 1767) to his two sons and four daughters that his slaves were to be paired off as couples and families.

99. B. Wood, *Slavery in Colonial Georgia*, 155.

100. Jenkins, *Button Gwinnett*, 49.

101. Gallay, *Formation of a Planter Elite*, 164. Bryan's paternalistic ideology was apparently transmitted to his kin, several of whom took the extremely rare step in eighteenth-century Georgia of freeing bondspeople. Two of Bryan's sons freed favored slaves, as did his son-in-law John Houstoun (98).

102. B. Wood, *Slavery in Colonial Georgia*, 182.

103. Of those fugitives whose origins are specified in the records, Betty Wood calculates that 45 percent were newly enslaved, 30 percent were born in Africa, and 25 percent were born in the Americas (*Slavery in Colonial Georgia*, 176).

104. P. Wood, *Black Majority*, 248.

105. *GG.*, 2 July 1766, Bridgle and Celia (married); 23 July 1766, Pero and Chloe; 23 July 1766, Boson and Betty; 30 July 1766, Billy (married); 21 January 1767, London and Nanny (married); 19 August 1767, Cuffy and Bersheba; 13 April 1768, John (married); 13 July 1768, Cato and Judy (married); 26 July 1769, Peroe and Cloe; 1 November 1769, Harry and Cassandra (married); 23 May 1770, Tom and Bella (married); 27 July 1774, Polydore (married); 2 November 1774, Sampson and Felico; 14 December 1774, London and Juno (married); 25 October 1775, Boson and Daphney; June 22 1780, Anonymous and Cloe.

106. *GG.*, 25 January 1775. More than 160 different owners placed advertisements for 453 fugitives between 1763 and 1775. See B. Wood, *Slavery in Colonial Georgia*, 170–72; P. Wood, *Black Majority*, 241.

107. *GG.*, 23 July 1766.
108. Ibid., 26 July 1768.
109. How this information was to communicate itself from a subscriber-only newspaper to illiterate underground slaves is an interesting question.
110. Mühlenberg, *Notebook of a Colonial Clergyman*, 2:675.
111. B. Wood, *Gender, Race and Rank*, 5–7.
112. See, for instance, B. Wood, *Gender, Race, and Rank*, 25–27.
113. Mary Gibbons Jones died on 25 July 1792 (*GG.*, 26 July 1792). Macartan Campbell died in Richmond County in 1793 (*GG.*, 28 November 1793). Dr. George Jones married again, to the widow Jane Campbell, in 1795 (*GG.*, 19 March 1795).
114. Sarah Jones to George Jones, 18 November 1796, ms. 1127, Jones Family Papers.
115. Ovid, *The Metamorphoses*, trans. David Raeburn (New York: Penguin, 2004), bk. 6, ll. 1–145.
116. A. Stokes, *A View of the Constitution of the British Colonies in North America and the West Indies* . . . (London, 1783), 139, quoted in Reese, *Colonial Georgia*, 6–7.
117. E. L. Johnston and Eaton, *Recollections*, 45; land grant application of John Lightenstone dated September 1766. The land grant of two hundred acres in St. Andrew's Parish was awarded in March 1767.
118. For a comprehensive overview of Alexander's origins, see Cashin, *Lachlan McGillivray*. The quote appears on p. 80.
119. Braund, "Creeks, Blacks, and Slavery," 619, 625–26.
120. The educational opportunities afforded a minority of late colonial children such as Joseph Habersham were a function of the prosperous commercial and demographic conditions—and stood in sharp contrast to the more physically demanding and illiterate childhoods of trusteeship orphans, black slaves, and a majority of poor whites. What remains clear even from a brief reading of the sources is that children's roles in the families of colonial Georgia varied according to broader trends in population density and marriage patterns, as well as local and personal circumstances. Before the stabilizing of mortality rates and sex ratios in the white population, family formation was a process of merging disparate components and accommodating high numbers of orphans and stepchildren. Before the widespread use of bondspeople (particularly in the lowcountry), children's capacity to perform even minor duties was vital to the prosperity of families and even communities. Before the specialization of the education sector, children received a limited amount and quality of teaching, reflecting both a low supply of keen itinerant tutors and low levels of demand from parents who required their children's services at home and would instruct them there when necessary. The *Georgia Gazette* gives evidence of an increasingly large choice in both private and public teachers, specialized tutors, boarding schools, academies, and wet nurses. Access to educational institutions for poorer white children was further supported by charities, parish relief, and the sponsorship of clubs and societies. Even a small proportion of slave children received a limited degree of attention in the Christianized teaching of men such as Joseph Ottolenghe and Bartholomew Zouberbuhler. Not all parents chose to have their children educated in Georgia. In fact, those with sufficient funds at their disposal more often than not sent

their sons and daughters elsewhere to receive their education, most commonly to the northernmost American colonies and to England. This was usually deemed a worthwhile investment only for older children, aged fourteen to eighteen, because exposure to other environments as well as professional training would reinforce their understanding of polite society. Submission and civility were demanded of colonial youths of both genders, who were required to drop habits picked up in America and cultivate European traits. Patrick and George Houstoun, fifteen and twelve, respectively, were sent to school near New York in 1791 (E. D. Johnston, *Houstouns of Georgia*). Similarly, the two older Habersham boys, James and Joseph, were sent to Princeton College in the early 1760s (Smith, "Georgia Gentlemen," 121–22, 176).

121. William Knox to James Habersham, 26 August 1769, collection 337, item 17, James Habersham Papers, Georgia Historical Society.

122. William Knox to James Habersham, 5 April 1770, collection 337, item 20, Habersham Papers.

123. McGillivray, who was invited to treaty negotiations at New York, was described by Abigail Adams as one who "dresses in our own fashion, speaks English like a native . . . is not very dark, [and is] much of a gentleman" (Abigail Adams to Mary Cranch, 8 August 1790, quoted in Wright, *Creeks and Seminoles*, 61). For a discussion of Elizabeth Lichtenstein Johnston and female decorum, see *Recollections* by Johnston and Eaton.

Epilogue. *Revolution?*

1. *Col.Rec.*, 12:421–23.

2. For more complete accounts of the effects of Revolution in Georgia, see Coleman, *American Revolution in Georgia*; Frey, *Water from the Rock*; Hall, *Land and Allegiance*. Before the fighting began, Georgia had exported twenty to twenty-five thousand barrels of rice a year and had consumed a significant amount internally. In 1780 Governor Wright stated that no more than two thousand barrels would be put on the market—and that none of this would be available for export (*Collections*, 10:79; Coleman, *American Revolution in Georgia*, 170).

3. For a more detailed discussion see Marsh, "Women and the American Revolution in Georgia."

4. *Roy.GG.*, 4 January 1781.

5. Just as kinship ties structured the practicalities of escape, so they frequently defined the objectives and/or destination of fugitives. The Philipsburg Proclamation, and the ebb and flow of the opposing armies, naturally drew thousands of bondspeople into the British military camp, but this was far from a universal target for fugitives, and many were thought to be searching for relatives, like the twenty-four-year-old Patt, whose mother, Lady, lived on a plantation in Carolina (*Roy.GG.*, 22 June 1780). Equally, kinship ties of marriage and particularly motherhood could act as powerful disincentives to running away: infants and young children are conspicuous in their absence among the fugitive advertisements, just as they had been in pre-Revolutionary years. Given the "depth of commitment to the dream of freedom" expressed in the actions of slaves during

the war, the liability that children posed to any bid for escape is not in itself sufficient to explain their absence. Rather, it is likely that many black mothers, blessed and burdened with the physical and emotional responsibility for an infant's welfare, made the rational choice to remain in the comparative safety of their owners. It was the lesser of a variety of evils (the quote is from Frey, *Water from the Rock*, 118–19). There are no exact figures for how many Loyalists left Savannah in July 1782. Just before the evacuation, one source stated that six thousand people, black and white, were encamped at Savannah, awaiting transportation away from the province. Gen. Guy Carleton said that ten families with 1,508 slaves went from Savannah to Jamaica (Coleman, *American Revolution in Georgia*, 145; Hall, *Land and Allegiance*, 160–63).

6. Before the arrival of a British occupation force in 1778–79, the biggest military threat to Patriot Georgia came from raids from the south by Florida scouts and rangers and their Native American allies between 1776 and 1778. For a more complete account of the effects of the Revolutionary War on the society of the Deep South, see Frey, *Water from the Rock*, 206–42. These raids, unlike the vicious fighting in northwest Georgia during 1779–82, were purposeful and effective. The perpetrators were refugees to Florida from across colonial America who were seeking to provide livestock and foodstuffs for their dependents in St. Augustine as well as to disrupt the economic productivity of the southern lowcountry and its rich herds of cattle. According to the historian Leslie Hall, nearly seven thousand refugees made their way to eastern Florida as a result of newly invoked expulsion laws passed by the Patriot Council of Safety, and many traveled through the backcountry of Georgia and South Carolina (*Land and Allegiance*, 66). For a discussion of the Florida rangers' activities, see Coleman, *American Revolution in Georgia*, 97–108. Connections between and within nonelite Georgia Tory families facilitated the efficacy of these attacks on the property of the local gentry. Coleman remarked that the Tory families evicted from the Ogeechee "carried Georgia plans to Florida" (*American Revolution in Georgia*, 108). Hall, *Land and Allegiance*, 67, also refers to the incident.

7. Joseph Clay to Henry Laurens, 16 October 1777, *Collections*, 8:201.

8. The refugees, including the wives of Patriot generals Elijah and John Twiggs and Col. Andrew Williamson, apparently arrived in North Carolina "almost famished with hunger and some never recovered" (Hawes, "Miscellaneous Papers of James Jackson," 73). These were probably the four hundred women and children found by General Clarke in late September as they were trying to escape the Tory ravaging of the upcountry (Williams, "Colonial Elijah Clarke," 151–58).

9. Jackson to unknown recipient, 30 October 1781, Hawes, "Miscellaneous Papers of James Jackson," 55.

10. When Peter Tondee, the tavern keeper and early Revolutionary leader, died in 1775, his widow, Lucy, continued to operate their popular tavern under American, British, and returned American governments. On 5 August 1782 the Patriot Provincial Assembly apparently awarded "Mrs. Tondee" the first fifteen pounds that next came into the public treasury to pay for the "use of her room" (*Rev.Rec.*, 3:187). Leah Minis wrote two notes to Mordecai Sheftall that testify to the upheaval in and around Savannah. She apologized that it was "not in our Power to send anything else at this time" other than a little coffee

and sugar, and she stated that she and her family had heard nothing from their friends in Carolina for two months, "which makes us very unhappy" (Minis to Sheftall, 15 March and 16 July 1777, no. 1505, box 1, folder 3, "Leah Minis Sub-series," Minis Family Papers, Georgia Historical Society, Savannah).

11. For example, two privates were court-martialed on 1 July 1782 for raiding the property of civilians. John May was acquitted of breaking open a Mrs. Rain's smokehouse and stealing meat, while William Cowan was turned over for trial by civil powers for his alleged theft of two horses from a Miss Fox (Hawes, "Miscellaneous Papers of James Jackson," 56–57). Many references to plundering and pillage were reported in the *Royal Georgia Gazette*, such as the murder and scalping of a Mrs. Hearn, her year-old child, and her brother, Sylvanus Bird. The attackers carried off three horseloads of valuable effects after torching the house and barn. Another time, a Mrs. Pendarvis was forced to watch as her husband was killed with another man ninety yards from his house (Hall, *Land and Allegiance*, 138, 154).

12. Kierner, *Southern Women in Revolution*, 18.

13. Coulter, "Nancy Hart," 118–51; Coleman, *American Revolution in Georgia*, 132–33.

14. An unrelated court case brought in Wilkes County against Hannah Caudle in 1790 highlights not only the violence and lawlessness of the backcountry but also the time required to untangle the complexities produced during the conflict. One witness testified that sometime after the siege of Augusta in the spring of 1781, a Patriot detachment arrived at the house of Richard Caudle (Hannah's husband), which the militiamen "would have burned down if they had not gotten the door open." They next allegedly tortured Gregory Caudle, then aged fourteen or fifteen, to learn the whereabouts of the family's slaves, who were presumably hidden with Hannah but later discovered (R. Davis, *Wilkes County Papers*, 141).

15. Report sent from Savannah to London Quakers, 9 January 1782, R. Davis, *Quaker Records in Georgia*, 160. Mark Candler's assertion that the "Georgia Quakers, as a sect, were non-combatants in the war" receives little support from the Meeting House minutes—in which examples abound between 1778 and 1780 of young male Quakers' being castigated for joining militia, bearing arms, and plundering (M. Candler, *Quakers of Wrightsborough*, 20; R. Davis, *Quaker Records in Georgia*, 157–58).

16. The Patriot government issued a resolve on 1 March 1778 requiring all *white male* inhabitants aged sixteen or older to take an oath of abjuration, declaring their loyalty to the state. A British proclamation of 3 January 1779 demanded allegiance of a similar constituency, with no mention of women.

17. E. L. Johnston and Eaton, *Recollections*, 46.

18. Ibid., 47.

19. Abigail Minis experienced considerable difficulties in reclaiming payment for these supplies because of the complex state of Continental finances. She (apparently personally) gave her invoices to Gen. Benjamin Lincoln, who promised to have them settled, but after communications with Philadelphia broke down, she applied to Col. Alexander Wylly and later asked a friend to seek out the money on her behalf. She recorded the details of her dilemma in a letter, probably to Mordecai Sheftall, from Charleston dated

16 January 1780, no. 568, items 1, Minis Colonial Papers, 1768–93, Georgia Historical Society. See also article entitled "Abigail Minis, Matriarch," by Rabbi Saul Rubin, no. 1505, box 1, folder 2, Minis Family Papers.

20. An inventory of Abigail Minis's estate taken on 3 March 1795 valued it at £689.9s.8d (Minis Family Papers). See also the petitions of Hannah Noble (seeking restitution for cattle plundering in August 1778) and a Mrs. Crughton (seeking leave to take her slaves to St. Augustine in a boat under a flag of truce) in *Rev.Rec.*, 2:85, 90.

21. John Habersham's letter opened by condoling his sister-in-law Isabella Habersham on the loss of her only child but ended with the pointed question: "Might yet your united application be the means of procuring leave for me to conduct you to the Northward?" (item 2, collection 338, John Habersham Papers, Habersham Family Papers, Georgia Historical Society).

22. Another leader of the radical Whig faction in Georgia, George Wells, would also be killed in a duel, in his case by Maj. James Jackson in 1780 (Hall, *Land and Allegiance*, 95).

23. Smith, "Georgia Gentlemen," 282; Jenkins, *Button Gwinnett*, 152, 233–40.

24. Jenkins, *Button Gwinnett*, 162–64; the quote is from p. 164. For transcriptions of the letters see 233–40.

25. See Hall, *Land and Allegiance*, 91–92.

26. J. P. Greene, "Travails of an Infant Colony," 303.

Conclusion

1. Kierner, *Beyond the Household*, 10. Mary Beth Norton emphasizes the preponderance of powerful women, and symbolic Filmerian mothers in the seventeenth-century Northeast, noting that "most such incidents occurred in New England and within two decades of the colonies' founding" (*Founding Mothers*, 403). For more details on these prominent Englishwomen in colonial settings, see Lebsock, "A Share of Honour," 26–27; E. T. James, James, and Boyer, *Notable American Women*, 1:236–37; Norton, *Founding Mothers*, 281–87, 359–99.

BIBLIOGRAPHY

Primary Sources

MANUSCRIPT COLLECTIONS
Georgia Department of Archives and History, Atlanta
   Bonds, Deeds of Gift, Sales
   Colonial Conveyances
   Georgia Estate Records
   Land Grant Records
Georgia Historical Society, Savannah
   Colonial Dames of America Historical Collections
   Habersham Family Papers
   Minis Colonial Papers, 1768–93
   Minis Family Papers
National Archives, London
   Colonial Office
University Library, Cambridge
   Gazette of the State of Georgia (microfilm), 1783–88
   Georgia Gazette (microfilm), 1763–76, 1788–1800
   Royal Georgia Gazette (microfilm), 1779–82
   South Carolina Gazette (microfilm), 1732–75
University of Georgia Libraries, Athens
   Keith Read Collection
      Levi Sheftall Family Papers
      McIntosh Family Papers
      Noble Jones Family Papers, 1754–1838
   William Gibbons Jr. Papers, 1728–1803 (microfilm)
University of Warwick Library, Coventry
   Pierce Butler Plantation Papers, 1744–1822 (microfilm)
   Unpublished Colonial Records, vols. 33–39 (microfilm)

PUBLISHED COLLECTIONS AND CONTEMPORARY SOURCES
Abstracts of Colonial Wills of the State of Georgia, 1733–1777. Atlanta: Reprint Co., 1962.
American Antiquarian Society, ed. *Early American Imprints, 1639–1800*. Series 1, Evans [microform]. New York: Readex, 1981–82.
Bartram, John. "Diary of a Journey through the Carolinas, Georgia, and Florida from July 1, 1765 to April 10, 1766." Edited by Francis Harper. *Transactions of the American Philosophical Society* 33, no. 1 (December 1942):i–120.
Bartram, William. "Travels in Georgia, and Florida, 1773–74. A Report to Dr. John

Fothergill." Edited by Francis Harper. *Transactions of the American Philosophical Society* 33, no. 2 (November 1943): 121–242.

Beckemeyer, Frances Howell, comp. *Abstracts of Georgia Colonial Conveyance Book, C-1, 1750–1761.* Atlanta: R. J. Taylor Jr. Foundation, 1975.

Benham, Daniel. *Memoirs of James Hutton Comprising the Annals of His Life, and Connection with the United Brethren.* London: Hamilton, Adams, 1856.

Boreman, Thomas. *A Compendious Account of the Whole Art of Breeding, Nursing, and the Right Ordering of the Silk-Worm.* London, 1733.

Collections of the Georgia Historical Society. 22 vols. Savannah: Georgia Historical Society, 1840–1996.

The Colonial Records of the State of Georgia. 32 vols. to date. Atlanta and Athens: various printers, 1904–16, 1976–.

Coulter, E. Merton, and Albert Berry Saye, eds. *A List of the Early Settlers of Georgia.* Athens: University of Georgia Press, 1949.

Davis, Robert Scott, comp. *Quaker Records in Georgia: Wrightsborough, 1772–1793: Friendsborough, 1776–1777.* Augusta, Ga.: Augusta Genealogical Society, 1986.

———, comp. *The Wilkes County Papers, 1773–1833: A Compilation of the Genealogical Information Found in Collections of Loose Court, Estate, Land, School, Military, Marriage, and Other Records of the Ceded Lands and Wilkes County, Georgia, from 1773 to 1833, with a Few Additional Papers from Earlier and Later Periods.* Easley, S.C.: Southern Historical Press, 1979.

Documents of the American Revolution, 1770–1783 (Colonial Office Series). Edited by K. G. Davies. Shannon: Irish University Press, 1972–81.

Drums and Shadows: Survival Studies among the Georgia Coastal Negroes. Introduction by Charles Joyner. Photographs by Muriel and Malcolm Bell Jr. Athens: University of Georgia Press, 1986.

Franklin, Benjamin. *The Papers of Benjamin Franklin.* 4 vols. Edited by Leonard W. Labaree. New Haven, Conn.: Yale University Press, 1961.

Greene, Evarts Boutell, and Virginia D. Harrington. *American Population before the Federal Census of 1790.* New York: Columbia University Press, 1932.

Hawes, Lilla M., ed. "Miscellaneous Papers of James Jackson, 1781–1798." Serialized in *Georgia Historical Quarterly* 37 (March, June, September, and December 1953).

Hawkins, Benjamin. *A Combination of a Sketch of the Creek Country, in the Years 1798 and 1799; and, Letters of Benjamin Hawkins, 1796–1806.* Spartanburg, S.C.: Reprint Co., 1974.

Johnston, Elizabeth Lichtenstein, and Arthur Wentworth Hamilton Eaton. *Recollections of a Georgia Loyalist.* New York: M. F. Mansfield, 1901.

Jones, George Fenwick, ed. *Detailed Reports on the Salzburger Emigrants Who Settled in America, Edited by Samuel Urlsperger.* 17 vols. Athens: University of Georgia Press, 1968.

Loewald, Klaus G., Beverly Staricka, and Paul S. Taylor, eds. "Johann Martin Bolzius Answers a Questionnaire on Carolina and Georgia." *William and Mary Quarterly* 14 (1957): 218–61; 15 (1958): 228–52.

Malthus, Thomas Robert. *An Essay on the Principle of Population.* London: 1798.
Milfort, Louis. *Memoirs or, A Quick Glance at My Various Travels and My Sojourn in the Creek Nation.* Translated and edited by Ben C. McCary. Savannah, Ga.: Beehive Press, 1972.
Moore, Francis. *A Voyage to Georgia, Begun in the Year 1735, Containing an Account of the Settling of the Town of Frederica, in the Southern Part of the Province; and a Description of the Soil, Air, Birds, Beasts, Trees, Rivers, Islands, &c.* London: Jacob Robinson, 1744.
The Most Delightful Country of the Universe Promotional Literature of the Colony of Georgia, 1717–1734. Introduction by Trevor R. Reese. Savannah, Ga.: Beehive Press, 1972.
Mühlenberg, Henry Melchior. *The Notebook of a Colonial Clergyman: Condensed from the Journals of Henry Melchior Mühlenberg.* 3 vols. Translated and edited by Theodore G. Tappert and John W. Doberstein. Philadelphia: Muhlenberg Press, 1958.
Oglethorpe, James Edward. *Some Account of the Design of the Trustees for Establishing Colonys in America.* Edited by Rodney M. Baine and Phinizy Spalding. Athens: University of Georgia Press, 1990.
Paine, Thomas. *The Complete Writings of Thomas Paine.* Collected and edited by Philip Sheldon Foner. New York: Citadel, 1945.
Percival, John. *Diary of Viscount Percival, afterwards First Earl of Egmont.* 3 vols. Edited by R. A. Roberts and United Kingdom Historical Manuscripts Commission. London: H. M. Stationery Office, 1920–23.
The Revolutionary Records of the State of Georgia. 3 vols. Atlanta: Franklin-Turner, 1908.
Shipton, Clifford Kenyon, James E. Mooney, and Roger P. Bristol, eds. *National Index of American Imprints through 1800; the Short-Title Evans.* Worcester, Mass.: American Antiquarian Society, 1969.
Stephens, John C., ed. *Georgia, and Two Other Occasional Poems on the Founding of the Colony, 1736.* Atlanta: Emory University Publications, 1950.
Stephens, W. B. "A Sketch of the Life of James Habersham." *Georgia Historical Quarterly* 3 (December 1919): 158.
Stephens, William. *The Journal of William Stephens, 1741–45.* Edited by E. Merton Coulter. Athens: University of Georgia Press, 1959.
Tailfer, Patrick. *A True and Historical Narrative of the Colony of Georgia by P. Tailfer and Others.* Edited by Clarence L. Ver Steeg. Athens: University of Georgia Press, 1960.
The Trans-Atlantic Slave Trade: A Database on CD-ROM. Cambridge, Cambridge University Press, 1999.
Two Pamphlets on the Province of Georgia: A Sermon by William Berriman (1739) and An Impartial Enquiry, etc. by Benjamin Martyn (1741). WPA mimeograph, California State Library, San Francisco, 1940.
Walker, George Fuller, comp. *Abstracts of Georgia Colonial Book J, 1755–1762.* Atlanta: R. J. Taylor Jr. Foundation, 1978.

Wesley, John. *The Journal of the Rev. John Wesley Enlarged from Original Mss., with Notes from Unpublished Diaries, Annotations, Maps, and Illustrations*. Edited by Nehemiah Curnock et al. London: R. Culley, 1909.
Whitefield, George. *An Account of Money Received and Disbursed for the Orphan-house in Georgia*. London: Printed by W. Strahan for T. Cooper at the Globe in Pater-noster-row, and sold by R. Hett at the Bible and Crown in the Poultry, 1741.
————. *Journals*. London: Banner of Truth Trust, 1960.
Wilson, Alexander. *The Poems and Literary Prose of Alexander Wilson, the American Ornithologist*. Paisley, Scotland: A. Gardner, 1876.

Secondary Works
Alexander, Adele Logan. *Ambiguous Lives: Free Women of Color in Rural Georgia, 1789–1879*. Fayetteville: University of Arkansas Press, 1991.
Anderson, Karen. *Chain Her by One Foot: The Subjugation of Women in Seventeenth-century New France*. London: Routledge, 1991.
Andrew, Donna T. *Philanthropy and Police: London Charity in the Eighteenth Century*. Princeton, N.J.: Princeton University Press, 1989.
Archer, Richard. "New England Mosaic: A Demographic Analysis for the Seventeenth Century." *William and Mary Quarterly* 47, no. 4 (1990): 477–502.
Armitage, David, and M. J. Braddick, eds. *The British Atlantic World, 1500–1800*. New York: Palgrave Macmillan, 2002.
Baine, Rodney M. "James Oglethorpe and the Early Promotional Literature for Georgia." *William and Mary Quarterly* 45, no. 1 (January 1988): 100–106.
————. "Myths of Mary Musgrove." *Georgia Historical Quarterly* 76 (summer 1992): 428–35.
Bartlett, Helen R. "Eighteenth-century Georgia Women." Ph.D. diss., University of Maryland, 1939.
Bellows, Barbara L. *Benevolence among Slaveholders: Assisting the Poor in Charleston, 1670–1860*. Baton Rouge: Louisiana State University Press, 1993.
Berkin, Carol. *First Generations: Women in Colonial America*. New York: Hill and Wang, 1996.
Berlin, Ira. *Many Thousands Gone: The First Two Centuries of Slavery in North America*. Cambridge, Mass.: Harvard University Press, 1998.
Biemer, Linda. *Women and Property in Colonial New York: The Transition from Dutch to English Law, 1643–1727*. Ann Arbor: University of Michigan Press, 1983.
Blake Smith, Daniel. "In Search of the Family in the Colonial South." In Jordan and Skemp, *Race and Family in the Colonial South*, 21–36.
Boatwright, Eleanor Miot. *Status of Women in Georgia, 1783–1860*. Scholarship in Women's History, vol. 2. New York: Carlson, 1994.
Bolton, Robert. *Genealogical and Biographical Account of the Family of Bolton in England and America*. New York: J. A. Gray, 1862.
Bonner, James C. *A History of Georgia Agriculture, 1732–1860*. Athens: University of Georgia Press, 1964.

Boorstin, Daniel J. *The Americans, the Colonial Experience.* New York: Random House, 1958.
Braund, Kathryn E. Holland. "The Creek Indians, Blacks, and Slavery." *Journal of Southern History* 57, no. 4 (November 1991): 601–36.
———. *Deerskins and Duffels: Creek Indian Trade with Anglo-America, 1685–1815.* Lincoln: University of Nebraska Press, 1993.
———. "Guardians of Tradition and Handmaidens to Change: Women's Roles in Creek Economic and Social Life during the Eighteenth Century." *American Indian Quarterly* 14, no. 3 (1990): 239–58.
Brown, Kathleen M. "Brave New Worlds: Women's and Gender History." *William and Mary Quarterly* 50, no. 2 (April 1993): 311–28.
———. *Good Wives, Nasty Wenches, and Anxious Patriarchs: Gender, Race, and Power in Colonial Virginia.* Chapel Hill: Published for the Institute of Early American History and Culture, Williamsburg, Virginia, by the University of North Carolina Press, 1996.
Buel, Joy Day, and Richard Buel. *The Way of Duty: A Woman and Her Family in Revolutionary America.* New York: W. W. Norton, 1984.
Burnard, Trevor. "Inheritance and Independence: Women's Status in Early Colonial Jamaica." *William and Mary Quarterly* 48, no. 1 (January 1991): 93–114.
———. *Mastery, Tyranny, and Desire: Thomas Thistlewood and His Slaves in the Anglo-Jamaican World.* Chapel Hill: University of North Carolina Press, 2004.
Caldwell, Lee Ann. "Women Landholders of Colonial Georgia." In Jackson and Spalding, *Forty Years of Diversity,* 183–97.
Calhoun, Arthur W. *A Social History of the American Family from Colonial Times to the Present.* Cleveland, Ohio: Arthur H. Clark, 1917.
Campbell, Jill. "'When Men Women Turn': Gender Reversals in Fielding's Plays." In Nussbaum and Brown, *New Eighteenth Century,* 62–84.
Candler, Mark A. *The Quakers of Wrightsborough, Georgia.* New York, 1911.
Carr, Lois G., and Lorena S. Walsh. "The Planter's Wife: The Experience of White Women in Seventeenth Century Maryland." *William and Mary Quarterly* 34 (1977): 542–71.
Cashin, Edward J. *Beloved Bethesda: A History of George Whitefield's Home for Boys, 1740–2000.* Macon, Ga.: Mercer University Press, 2001.
———. "From Creeks to Crackers." In Crass et al., *Southern Colonial Backcountry,* 69–75.
———. *Governor Henry Ellis and the Transformation of British North America.* Athens: University of Georgia Press, 1994.
———. *Lachlan McGillivray, Indian Trader: The Shaping of the Southern Colonial Frontier.* Athens: University of Georgia Press, 1992.
Cates, Gerald L. "'The Seasoning': Disease and Death among the First Colonists of Georgia." *Georgia Historical Quarterly* 64 (1979): 146–58.
Chaplin, Joyce E. *An Anxious Pursuit: Agricultural Innovation and Modernity in the Lower South, 1730–1815.* Chapel Hill: University of North Carolina Press, 1993.

———. "Tidal Rice Cultivation and the Problem of Slavery in South Carolina and Georgia." *Georgia Historical Quarterly* 49, no. 1 (January 1992): 29–61.
Chesnutt, David R. "South Carolinian Expansion into Colonial Georgia." Ph.D. diss., University of Georgia, 1973.
Clarke, William Kemp Lowther. *A History of the S.P.C.K.* London: S.P.C.K., 1959.
Clinton, Catherine, and Michele Gillespie, eds. *The Devil's Lane: Sex and Race in the Early South*. New York: Oxford University Press, 1997.
Coleman, Kenneth. *The American Revolution in Georgia, 1763–1789*. Athens: University of Georgia Press, 1958.
———. *Colonial Georgia: A History*. New York: Scribner, 1976.
———, ed. *A History of Georgia*. Athens: University of Georgia Press, 1977.
Corkran, David H. *The Creek Frontier, 1540–1783*. Norman: University of Oklahoma Press, 1967.
Coulter, E. M. "The Acadians in Georgia." *Georgia Historical Quarterly* 47 (1963): 68–75.
———. "Mary Musgrove, 'Queen of the Creeks': A Chapter of Early Georgia Troubles." *Georgia Historical Quarterly* 11 (1927): 1–30.
———. "Nancy Hart, Georgia Heroine of the Revolution: The Story of the Growth of a Tradition." *Georgia Historical Quarterly* 39 (1955): 118–51.
Crane, Verner Winslow. *The Southern Frontier, 1670–1732*. New York: W. W. Norton, 1981.
Crass, David Colin, Steven D. Smith, Martha A. Zierden, and Richard D. Brooks, eds. *The Southern Colonial Backcountry: Interdisciplinary Perspectives on Frontier Communities*. Knoxville: University of Tennessee Press, 1998.
Davis, Harold E. *The Fledgling Province: Social and Cultural Life in Colonial Georgia, 1733–1776*. Chapel Hill: Published for the Institute of Early American History and Culture, Williamsburg, Virginia, by the University of North Carolina Press, 1976.
Dayton, Cornelia Hughes. *Women before the Bar: Gender, Law, and Society in Connecticut, 1639–1789*. Chapel Hill: University of North Carolina Press, 1995.
Demos, John. "Families in Colonial Bristol, Rhode Island: An Exercise in Historical Demography." In Vinovskis, *Studies in American Historical Demography*, 99–110.
Dornan, Ingeborg. "Women Slaveholders in the Georgia and South Carolina Low Country, 1750–1775." Ph.D. diss., University of Cambridge, 2001.
Dunn, Mary M. "Saints and Sisters: Congregational and Quaker Women in the Early Colonial Period." In J. W. James, *Women in American Religion*, 27–46.
Dunn, Richard S. "The Trustees of Georgia and the House of Commons, 1732–1752." *William and Mary Quarterly* 11, no. 4 (October 1954): 551–65.
Dupâquier, Jacques, ed. *Marriage and Remarriage in Populations of the Past*. New York: Academic Press, 1981.
Ebel, Carol. "Women and the Wesleys at Frederica, 1736–1737." In P. Spalding and Wilson, *Women on the Colonial Frontier*, 27–41.
Engerman, Stanley L., and Robert E. Gallman, eds. *The Cambridge Economic History of the United States*. New York: Cambridge University Press, 1996–2000.

Ewing, Anne. "The Rights of Women in Colonial Georgia: An Overview." In P. Spalding and Wilson, *Women on the Colonial Frontier*, 1–6.

Fant, H. B. "The Labor Policy of the Trustees." *Georgia Historical Quarterly* 16 (1932): 1–16.

Finkelman, Paul. "Crimes of Love, Misdemeanors of Passion: The Regulation of Race and Sex in the Colonial South." In Clinton and Gillespie, *Devil's Lane*, 124–39.

Fischer, David Hackett. *Albion's Seed: Four British Folkways in America*. New York: Oxford University Press, 1989.

Follett, R. "Heat, Sex, and Sugar: Pregnancy and Childbearing in the Slave Quarters." *Journal of Family History* 28, no. 4 (October 2003): 510–39.

Fraser, Walter J., R. Frank Saunders, and Jon L. Wakelyn, eds. *The Web of Southern Social Relations: Women, Family, and Education*. Athens: University of Georgia Press, 1985.

Frey, Sylvia R. *Water from the Rock: Black Resistance in a Revolutionary Age*. Princeton, N.J.: Princeton University Press, 1991.

Fries, Adelaide L. *The Moravians in Georgia, 1735–1740*. Raleigh, N.C.: Printed for the author by Edwards and Broughton, 1905.

Galenson, David W. "The Settlement and Growth of the Colonies: Population, Labor, and Economic Development." In Engerman and Gallman, *Cambridge Economic History of the United States*, 135–207.

Gallay, Alan. *The Formation of a Planter Elite: Jonathan Bryan and the Southern Colonial Frontier*. Athens: University of Georgia Press, 1989.

———. "Jonathan Bryan's Plantation Empire: Land, Politics, and the Formation of a Ruling Class in Colonial Georgia." *William and Mary Quarterly* 45, no. 2 (April 1988): 253–79.

Gemery, H. A. "Emigration from the British Isles to the New World, 1630–1700: Inferences from Colonial Populations." *Research in Economic History* 5 (1980): 179–231.

Gillespie, Michelle. "The Sexual Politics of Race and Gender: Mary Musgrove and the Georgia Trustees." In Clinton and Gillespie, *Devil's Lane*, 187–205.

Godbeer, Richard. *Sexual Revolution in Early America*. Baltimore: Johns Hopkins University Press, 2002.

Gray, Ralph, and Betty Wood. "The Transition from Indentured to Involuntary Servitude in Colonial Georgia." *Explorations in Economic History* 13, no. 4 (1976): 353–70.

Green, E. R. R. "Queensborough Township: Scotch-Irish Emigration and the Expansion of Georgia, 1763–1776." *William and Mary Quarterly* 17, no. 2 (April 1960): 183–99.

Greene, Jack P. "Travails of an Infant Colony: The Search for Viability, Coherence, and Identity in Colonial Georgia." In Jackson and Spalding, *Forty Years of Diversity*, 278–309.

Greene, Jack P., Rosemary Brana-Shute, and Randy J. Sparks, eds. *Money, Trade, and Power: The Evolution of Colonial South Carolina's Plantation Society*. Columbia: University of South Carolina Press, 2001.

Greven, Philip J. "Family Structure in Seventeenth-century Andover, Massachusetts." *William and Mary Quarterly* 23, no. 2 (April 1966): 235–56.

Guerrini, Anita. "The Hungry Soul: George Cheyne and the Construction of Femininity." *Eighteenth-Century Studies* 32, no. 3 (spring 1999): 279–91.

Hall, Leslie. *Land and Allegiance in Revolutionary Georgia.* Athens: University of Georgia Press, 2001.

Hitchcock, Tim. "'Unlawfully Begotten on Her Body': Illegitimacy and the Parish Poor in St. Luke's, Chelsea." In Hitchcock, King, and Sharpe, *Chronicling Poverty,* 70–87.

Hitchcock, Tim, Peter King, and Pamela Sharpe, eds. *Chronicling Poverty: The Voices and Strategies of the English Poor, 1640–1840.* New York: St. Martin's Press, 1997.

Hoffer, Peter Charles, ed. *Colonial Women and Domesticity: Selected Articles on Gender in Early America.* New York: Garland, 1988.

Honerkamp, Nick. *Colonial Life on the Georgia Coast.* St. Simons Island, Ga.: Fort Frederica Association, 1977.

Horne, William C. *Making a Heaven of Hell: The Problem of the Companionate Ideal in English Marriage Poetry, 1650–1800.* Athens: University of Georgia Press, 1993.

Hudson, Charles M. *The Southeastern Indians.* Knoxville: University of Tennessee Press, 1976.

Hufton, Olwen H. *The Prospect before Her: A History of Women in Western Europe.* New York: Alfred A. Knopf, 1996–.

Inscoe, John C., ed. *James Edward Oglethorpe: New Perspectives on His Life and Legacy.* Athens: University of Georgia Press, 1997.

Jackson, Harvey H. "Behind the Lines: Oglethorpe, Savannah, and the War of Jenkins' Ear." In Inscoe, *James Edward Oglethorpe,* 61–91.

———. *Lachlan McIntosh and the Politics of Revolutionary Georgia.* Athens: University of Georgia Press, 1979.

Jackson, Harvey H., and Phinizy Spalding, eds. *Forty Years of Diversity: Essays on Colonial Georgia.* Athens: University of Georgia Press, 1984.

James, E. T., J. W. James, and P. Boyer, eds. *Notable American Women, 1607–1950: A Biographical Dictionary.* 3 vols. Cambridge, Mass.: Harvard University Press, 1971.

James, Janet W., ed. *Women in American Religion.* Philadelphia: University of Pennsylvania Press, 1989.

Jenkins, Charles Francis. *Button Gwinnett, Signer of the Declaration of Independence.* New York: Doubleday, Page, 1926.

Johnston, Edith Duncan. *The Houstouns of Georgia.* Athens: University of Georgia Press, 1950.

Jones, E. L. "The European Background." In Engerman and Gallman, *Cambridge Economic History,* 95–134.

Jones, George Fenwick. *The Georgia Dutch: From the Rhine and Danube to the Savannah, 1733–1783.* Athens: University of Georgia Press, 1992.

———. *The Germans of Colonial Georgia, 1733–1783.* Baltimore: Clearfield, 1986.

———. "John Adam Treutlen's Origin and Rise to Prominence." In Jackson and Spalding, *Forty Years of Diversity,* 217–28.

Jordan, Winthrop D. *White over Black: American Attitudes toward the Negro, 1550–1812.* Chapel Hill: Published for the Institute of Early American History and Culture at Williamsburg, Virginia, by the University of North Carolina Press, 1968.
Kierner, Cynthia A. *Beyond the Household: Women's Place in the Early South, 1700–1835.* Ithaca, N.Y.: Cornell University Press, 1998.
———. *Southern Women in Revolution, 1776–1800: Personal and Political Narratives.* Columbia: University of South Carolina Press, 1998.
Klein, Herbert S. *The Atlantic Slave Trade.* New York: Cambridge University Press, 1999.
Kupperman, Karen Ordahl. "The Beehive as a Model for Colonial Design." In Karen O. Kupperman, ed., *America in European Consciousness, 1493–1750,* 272–92. Chapel Hill: Published for the Institute of Early American History and Culture, Williamsburg, Virginia, by the University of North Carolina Press, 1995.
Lambert, Frank. *James Habersham: Loyalty, Politics, and Commerce in Colonial Georgia.* Athens: University of Georgia Press, 2005.
Lambert, Robert S. "The Confiscation of Loyalist Property in Georgia, 1782–1786." *William and Mary Quarterly* 20, no. 1 (January 1963): 80–94.
Laurence, Anne. *Women in England, 1500–1760: A Social History.* New York: St. Martin's Press, 1994.
Lebsock, Suzanne. *"A Share of Honour": Virginia Women, 1600–1945.* Richmond: Virginia Women's Cultural History Project, 1984.
———. *The Free Women of Petersburg: Status and Culture in a Southern Town, 1784–1860.* New York: W. W. Norton, 1984.
Levy, Barry. *Quakers and the American Family: British Settlement in the Delaware Valley.* New York: Oxford University Press, 1988.
Lipscomb, R. G. "Land Granting in Colonial Georgia." MA thesis, University of Maryland, 1970.
Littlefield, Daniel C. "Plantations, Paternalism, and Profitability: Factors Affecting African Demography in the Old British Empire." *Journal of Southern History* 47, no. 2 (May 1981): 167–82.
———. *Rice and Slaves: Ethnicity and the Slave Trade in Colonial South Carolina.* Urbana: University of Illinois Press, 1991.
Lockley, Timothy James. "Encounters between Non-slaveholding Whites and Afro-Americans in Lowcountry Georgia, c. 1750–c. 1830." Ph.D. diss., University of Cambridge, 1996.
———. *Lines in the Sand: Race and Class in Lowcountry Georgia, 1750–1860.* Athens: University of Georgia Press, 2001.
Lockridge, Kenneth A. *On the Sources of Patriarchal Rage: The Commonplace Books of William Byrd and Thomas Jefferson and the Gendering of Power in the Eighteenth Century.* New York: New York University Press, 1992.
McCain, James Ross. *Georgia as a Proprietary Province.* Boston: R. G. Badger, 1917.
McCurry, Stephanie. *Masters of Small Worlds: Yeoman Households, Gender Relations, and the Political Culture of the Antebellum South Carolina Low Country.* New York: Oxford University Press, 1995.

McCusker, John J., and Russell R. Menard. *The Economy of British America, 1607–1789.* Chapel Hill: Published for the Institute of Early American History and Culture, Williamsburg, Virginia, by the University of North Carolina Press, 1985.

McKinstry, Mary Thomas. "Silk Culture in the Colony of Georgia." *Georgia Historical Quarterly* 14 (1930): 225–35.

Marsh, Ben J. "Women and the American Revolution in Georgia." *Georgia Historical Quarterly* 88 (2004): 157–78.

Menard, Russell R. "Economic and Social Development of the South." In Engerman and Gallman, *Cambridge Economic History,* 249–96.

Moogk, Peter. *La Nouvelle France: The Making of French Canada—A Cultural History.* East Lansing: Michigan State University Press, 2000.

Morgan, Edmund Sears. *American Slavery, American Freedom: The Ordeal of Colonial Virginia.* New York: W. W. Norton, 1975.

Morgan, Jennifer L. "'Some Could Suckle over Their Shoulders': Male Travelers, Female Bodies, and the Gendering of Racial Ideology, 1500–1700." *William and Mary Quarterly* 54, no. 1 (January 1997): 167–92.

———. "This Is 'Mines': Slavery and Reproduction in Colonial Barbados and South Carolina." In Greene et al., *Money, Trade, and Power.*

Morgan, Philip D. *Slave Counterpoint: Black Culture in the Eighteenth-century Chesapeake and Lowcountry.* Chapel Hill: Published for the Omohundro Institute of Early American History and Culture, Williamsburg, Virginia, by the University of North Carolina Press, 1998.

———. "Work and Culture: The Task System and the World of Lowcountry Blacks, 1700–1880." *William and Mary Quarterly* 39, no. 4 (October 1982): 563–99.

Morris, Michael P. *The Bringing of Wonder: Trade and the Indians of the Southeast, 1700–1783.* Westport, Conn.: Greenwood, 1999.

Norton, Mary Beth. "The Evolution of White Women's Experience in Early America." *American Historical Review* 89, no. 3 (June 1984): 593–619.

———. *Founding Mothers and Fathers: Gendered Power and the Forming of American Society.* New York: Alfred A. Knopf, 1996.

Nussbaum, Felicity, and Laura Brown, eds. *The New Eighteenth Century: Theory, Politics, English Literature.* New York: Methuen, 1987.

Nwokeji, G. Ugo. "African Conceptions of Gender and the Slave Traffic." *William and Mary Quarterly* 58, no. 1 (January 2001): 47–68.

Parker, Anthony W. *Scottish Highlanders in Colonial Georgia: The Recruitment, Emigration, and Settlement at Darien, 1735–1748.* Athens: University of Georgia Press, 1997.

Pearsall, Sarah M. S. "Gender." In Armitage and Braddick, *British Atlantic World,* 113–32.

Pearson, Ed. "Planters Full of Money: The Self-Fashioning of the Eighteenth-century South Carolina Elite." In Greene et al., *Money, Trade, and Power.*

Perdue, Theda. *Cherokee Women: Gender and Culture Change, 1700–1835.* Lincoln: University of Nebraska Press, 1998.

———. "Mixed Blood" Indians: Racial Construction in the Early South. Athens: University of Georgia Press, 2003.
Piker, Joshua Aaron. *Okfuskee: A Creek Indian Town in Colonial America*. Cambridge, Mass.: Harvard University Press, 2004.
Ready, Milton. *The Castle Builders: Georgia's Economy under the Trustees, 1732–1754*. New York: Arno, 1978.
Reese, Trevor Richard. *Colonial Georgia: A Study in British Imperial Policy in the Eighteenth Century*. Athens: University of Georgia Press, 1963.
Rogers, Anne Frazer. "A Shadowy Presence: Women at Frederica." In Spalding and Wilson, *Women on the Colonial Frontier*, 14–21.
Salmon, Marylynn. *Women and the Law of Property in Early America*. Chapel Hill: University of North Carolina Press, 1986.
Schlenther, Boyd S. "To Convert the Poor People in America: The Bethesda Orphanage and the Thwarted Zeal of the Countess of Huntingdon." *Georgia Historical Quarterly* 77 (1994): 225–56.
Scott, J. Thomas. "Success and Yet Failure: Women in Early Frederica." In Spalding and Wilson, *Women on the Colonial Frontier*, 22–26.
Sharpe, Pamela. *Women's Work: The English Experience, 1650–1914*. New York: Arnold, 1998.
Shoemaker, Robert B. *Gender in English Society, 1650–1850: The Emergence of Separate Spheres*. New York: Longman, 1998.
Smith, W. Calvin. "Georgia Gentlemen: The Habershams of Eighteenth-century Savannah." Ph.D. diss., University of North Carolina, 1971.
———. "Utopia's Last Chance? The Georgia Silk Boomlet of 1751." *Georgia Historical Quarterly* 59 (1975): 25–37.
Snyder, Holly. "A Tree with Two Different Fruits: The Jewish Encounter with German Pietists in the Eighteenth-Century Atlantic World." *William and Mary Quarterly* 58, no. 4 (October 2001): 855–82.
———. "Queens of the Household: The Jewish Women of British America, 1700–1800." In Jonathan D. Sarna and Pamela S. Nadell, eds., *Women and American Judaism: Historical Perspectives*, 15–45. Waltham, Mass.: Brandeis University Press, 2001.
Spalding, Phinizy. "Oglethorpe, Georgia, and the Spanish Threat." In Inscoe, *James Edward Oglethorpe*, 61–91.
———. "Some Sermons Preached before the Trustees of Colonial Georgia." *Georgia Historical Quarterly* 57 (1973): 332–46.
Spalding, Phinizy, and Pamela B. Wilson, eds. *Women on the Colonial Frontier: A Study of Frederica and Early Georgia*. St. Simons Island, Ga.: Fort Frederica Association in cooperation with Fort Frederica National Monument, National Park Service, U.S. Department of the Interior, 1995.
Stephens, Pauline Tyson. "The Silk Industry in Georgia." *Georgia Review* 7 (spring 1953): 39–49.
Stewart, Mart A. "'Policies of Nature and Vegetables': Hugh Anderson, the Georgia

Experiment, and the Political Use of Natural Philosophy." *Georgia Historical Quarterly* 77 (1993): 473–96.

———. "What Nature Suffers to Groe": Life, Labor, and Landscape on the Georgia Coast, 1680–1920.* Athens: University of Georgia Press, 1996.

Sturtz, Linda L. *Within Her Power: Propertied Women in Colonial Virginia.* New York: Routledge, 2002.

Sweet, Julie Anne. *Negotiating for Georgia: British-Creek Relations in the Trustee Era, 1733–1752.* Athens: University of Georgia Press, 2005.

Tate, Thad W. *Race and Family in the Colonial South: Essays.* Edited by Winthrop D. Jordan and Sheila L. Skemp. Jackson: University Press of Mississippi, 1987.

Taylor, Paul Schuster. *Georgia Plan: 1732–1752.* Berkeley: Institute of Business and Economic Research, University of California, 1971.

Temple, Sarah Blackwell Gober, and Kenneth Coleman. *Georgia Journeys, Being an Account of the Lives of Georgia's Original Settlers and Many Other Early Settlers.* Athens: University of Georgia Press, 1961.

Thompson, E. P. *Customs in Common.* New York: New Press, distributed by W. W. Norton, 1991.

Ulrich, Laurel. *Good Wives: Image and Reality in the Lives of Women in Northern New England, 1650–1750.* New York: Alfred A. Knopf, 1982.

Valenze, Deborah M. *The First Industrial Woman.* New York: Oxford University Press, 1995.

Ver Steeg, Clarence Lester. *Origins of a Southern Mosaic: Studies of Early Carolina and Georgia.* Athens: University of Georgia Press, 1975.

Vinovskis, Maris. *Studies in American Historical Demography.* New York: Academic Press, 1979.

Walsh, Lorena S. "The Experience and Status of Women in the Chesapeake." In Fraser, Saunders, and Wakelyn, *Web of Southern Social Relations,* 1–18.

Wells, Robert V. "Quaker Marriage Patterns in a Colonial Perspective." *William and Mary Quarterly* 29, no. 3 (July 1972): 415–42.

Williams, S. C. "Colonel Elijah Clarke in the Tennessee Country." *Georgia Historical Quarterly* 25 (1941): 151–58.

Woloch, Nancy. *Women and the American Experience.* New York: Alfred A. Knopf, 1984.

Wood, Betty. *Gender, Race, and Rank in a Revolutionary Age: The Georgia Lowcountry, 1750–1820.* Athens: University of Georgia Press, 2000.

———. *Slavery in Colonial Georgia, 1730–1775.* Athens: University of Georgia Press, 1984.

———. "White Women, Black Slaves and the Law in Early National Georgia: The Sunbury Petition of 1791." *Historical Journal* 35, no. 3 (September 1992): 611–22.

———. *Women's Work, Men's Work: The Informal Slave Economies of Lowcountry Georgia.* Athens: University of Georgia Press, 1995.

Wood, Kirsten E. *Masterful Women: Slaveholding Widows from the American Revolution through the Civil War.* Chapel Hill: University of North Carolina Press, 2004.

Wood, Peter H. *Black Majority Negroes in Colonial South Carolina from 1670 through the Stono Rebellion.* New York: Alfred A. Knopf, 1974.

Wright, J. Leitch. *Creeks and Seminoles: The Destruction and Regeneration of the Muscogulge People.* Lincoln: University of Nebraska Press, 1986.

Wrigley, E. A., R. S. Davies, J. E. Oeppen, and R. S. Schofield, eds. *English Population History from Family Reconstitution, 1580–1837.* New York: Cambridge University Press, 1997.

Yasuba, Yasukichi. *Birth Rates of the White Population in the United States.* Baltimore: Johns Hopkins University Press, 1962.

INDEX

Abercorn, 50, 75, 87
academies. *See* teaching
Acadians, 101
Africa: customs from, 139–40, 172; slave trade from, 38, 117–21 passim, 170, 191; mentioned, 1, 99, 109, 111, 160. *See also* slavery; slaves
agriculture: animal husbandry, 43–45, 96, 109, 113, 135, 139, 171; gardening during trusteeship, 29, 43–44; slave gardens, 139–40. *See also* plantations
Alcock, Thomas, 13
alcohol: consumption of, 26, 51, 80, 135; prohibition of, 9; sale of, 62, 130, 131, 140, 203n47; trade in, 203n41. *See also* tavern keeping
Altamaha River, 62, 78, 100, 102, 111
Amatis, Nicholas, 57, 76, 204n50
Amey (bondswoman), 139
Anderson, Elizabeth, 50, 59, 112
Anglican ministers, sermons for the trustees by, 10, 16
Angola. *See* Africa
Arthur, Francis, 114
Ashe, Dorinda, 160
Associates of Dr. Bray, 8, 10
Augusta, 71; and backcountry unrest, 149, 150, 151, 228n14; marital disputes in, 136; mentioned, 73, 74, 102, 104, 105, 171
Austria, 28, 189. *See also* Salzburgers
Avery, Margaret, 67, 68–69

backcountry: banditry in, 104, 105, 149–51; customs in, 163–64; race relations in, 148–51; during Revolution, 179, 181–82; settlement of, 101–5, 109–10, 116–17, 190–91
Bahamas, 130

Baillie, Kenneth, 147–48
balls, 132, 152, 156
baptism, 78
Baptists, 172
Barbados, 37, 98, 118. *See also* West Indies
Bard, Anne, 126
Barksdale, Isaac, 107, 147
Barnard, Edward, 105, 116
Barnard, Jane, 113–14
Bartram, John, 152–53
Bateman, Mary, 130
Bathurst, Francis, 31, 44
Bathurst, Lady, 39, 140
Beaufain, Hector Beringer de, 56
Bedon, Elizabeth, 133
bees, 11, 44
Belfast, 111
Bennet, Ann, 53
Berkeley, Frances, 190
Bermuda, 98, 108
Bethany, 88
Bethesda orphanage, 18, 41, 46
Bevill, Mary, 113
bigamy, 81
Bland, Elizabeth, 36
Bliss, Ann, 46
Board of Presidents and Assistants, 67, 122
Board of Trade, 95, 96, 98, 149, 212n27, 215n65
Bolzius, Johann Martin, 28, 73; on domestic arrangements, 41, 65, 66, 74, 88, 89; on interracial relations, 147; on labor, 43; on marriage, 77–78; on sericulture, 58, 59, 60; on slaves, 120; will of, 48
Boreman, Thomas, 57
Bosomworth, Mary Musgrove Matthews, 62–63, 65, 72–73, 85, 91, 113; mentioned, 149, 190

245

Bosomworth, Thomas, 62
Bourk, Allan, 147–48
Bourquin, Henrietta, 131
Bourquin, Henry Lewis, 111, 131, 219n46
Brahm, William De, 214n65
Breed, Sarah, 113
Brent, Margaret, 190
Bridgle (bondsman), 171
Broad River, 150
Brown, Thomas, 111, 181, 182
Bryan, Agnes, 160
Bryan, Jonathan, 100, 134, 169
Butler, Elizabeth Elliott, 112, 113–14

Camuse, Marie, 55, 58–59, 65, 190
capital punishment, 117, 118, 144–45, 164
Caroline of Ansbach, Queen, 53
Cassandra (bondswoman), 122
Causton, Martha, 48, 55–56
Causton, Thomas, 32, 39–40, 52, 56, 79
census, 180
charity. *See* philanthropy
Charlestown: goods and services in, 40, 110, 137; and Malcontents, 9; marriages in, 82, 152, 155; migration to, 67, 183; and Revolution, 181, 183; and slavery, 70, 123; mentioned, 29, 192
Cherokees, 83–86, 116; and war, 149–51; mentioned, 7, 145
Chesapeake: demographic comparisons with, 21, 24–25, 26, 95, 188; gender in, 37, 89, 143, 144, 190, 219n5; migration from, 98–99, 109, 117, 148, 220n26; and Revolution, 183; and slave trade, 120; mentioned, 1, 2, 3
Cheyne, George, 17
Chickasaws, 71, 83, 91
Chloe (bondswoman), 171
Christ Church Parish, 69, 102, 138, 146, 148
Christie, Thomas, 71, 76
Christina (bondswoman), 147
cohabitation, 73, 76, 80, 169
Collins, Hezekiah, 150

Commons House of Assembly, 100, 125–26, 129
Compass, Isaac, 82
Congregationalists, 99, 109, 164
Connecticut, 37. *See also* New England
conveyances, 125–27
Coram, Thomas, 15
Council of Safety, 179, 180, 182
crackers, 116–17, 149–51, 220n26
Creeks: and blacks, 151, 176; communal organization of, 83–86; land cessions of, 101–2, 116; and marriage, 71–73, 78, 84–86, 148–51; unrest by, 62–63, 104, 117, 149–51; mentioned, 5, 7, 36, 81, 145, 160
Crooke, Heriot, 112, 224n98
Cunningham, Ann, 131
Curaçao, 213n45
Cuthbert, George, 147, 224n98

Darien, 73, 113, 124
Darque (bondswoman), 111
Defoe, Daniel, 13
Delaware, 89, 144. *See also* Chesapeake
Derby, 53
Derizous, Daniel, 80
disease: and nursing, 46, 110; and seasoning, 23, 26, 27, 116, 188; smallpox, 213n45; yellow fever, 113
Doll (Gwinnett's bondswoman), 169
Doll (Houstoun's bondswoman), 147
Dunbar, George, 23, 43
Dutch, 31, 47, 70, 82, 89, 118
Dye (bondswoman), 118

Ebenezer: and economic practices, 44, 49; religion in, 77, 164; school in, 45, 46; sericulture in, 60, 61; sex ratio in, 25, 27–28, 79; mentioned, 73, 74, 87, 88. *See also* Salzburgers
education. *See* teaching
Egmont, Earl of, 8, 10, 22, 35, 50, 52; mentioned, 53, 58

Elliott, Grey, 126, 127
Elliott, Mary, 160
Ellis, Henry, 63, 104, 125, 127, 149
Emery, Ann, 48
England: differences from, 5, 27, 31, 32, 40, 44, 107; gender in, 7–8, 47, 48, 90, 176; migration from, 8, 22, 67, 98–99; poor relief in, 12; mentioned, 34, 36, 40, 57, 59, 65, 81, 160
Eveleigh, Samuel, 29, 44

Farley, John, 158
fashion, 130, 134, 137, 152–53
feme sole trading: during royal era, 127–29; during trusteeship, 47
Fielding, Henry, 7
Fitch, Ann, 113
Fitz, Margaret, 46–47
Fitzwalter, Joseph, 72, 80
Fitzwalter, Penelope, 47
Florida: opening of, 102; and Revolution, 179, 180, 227n6; Spanish influence in, 4, 8, 9, 22, 62, 101; mentioned, 117, 142, 221n41
France: and Acadians, 101; colonial sex ratios of, 25, 197n5; diplomacy with, 4, 8, 22, 72, 85, 115; settlers from, 28, 79, 133, 147, 176; and Seven Years' War, 86, 100–101; mentioned, 160
Franklin, Benjamin, 32, 183
Frederica: and archaeology, 40, 41; economy in, 43, 50, 53; and marriage, 25; and midwifery, 30; sexual relations in, 78, 82; mentioned, 79, 91, 95
free blacks, 122, 140, 148, 164, 175–76, 206n11; and manumission, 132, 146–47, 169. *See also* mixed race, people of
Freemasons, 132, 203n47
French and Indian War. *See* Seven Years' War
Frentz, John, 164
Friendsborough, 112
Fryer, Sarah, 113

Galphin, George, 72, 206n15
Gay, John, 13
gender, 187–92; and colonization, 7–8, 10–13, 89–92; and consolidation with race, 142–51, 176–77; and economic roles, 63, 65–66, 83–86, 135–37, 181; and inheritance, 125, 138, 169; and labor, 41–42, 124–25, 130, 138–41; and legislation, 125–29, 143–44; and literature, 159–63; and patriarchy, 156–57, 160, 174–77; and philanthropy, 15–18; and Revolution, 180, 182–86; and settlement during royal era, 104–6, 110, 112–14, 115, 116, 123; and slavery, 140–41
General Assembly, 104, 118, 125, 127, 140, 145
George II, King, 8, 36, 53, 62
Germany, settlers from: and appearance, 71, 84; and customs, 48, 75; and language, 46, 77, 79–80; and marriage, 71, 75, 77, 80, 86–87, 147; Moravians, 22–23; and relations with Jews, 82; and servants, 45, 71, 78–79; mentioned, 28, 43, 55, 70, 114, 188. *See also* Salzburgers
Gibbons, Joseph, 110–11
Gibbons, Mary, 153–54
Gibbons, William, 111, 130, 132, 137
Gilbert, Elizabeth, 76
Gold Coast. *See* Africa
Governor's Council, 99, 126, 129, 131
Graham, Jean, 112
Grimmiger, Abraham, 79
Gronau, Israel Christian, 28, 74
Gruber, Maria, 49, 88
Gwinnett, Ann, 183–85
Gwinnett, Button, 169, 183

Habersham, James: on land granting, 99, 116; and legislation, 128; marriage of, 73; on silk cultivation, 56, 60, 61; and slaves, 121, 134, 139; sons of, 176–77, 183
Habersham, John, 183
Habersham, Joseph, 176, 183

Halifax, Earl of, 96, 204n57
Hamilton, Robert, 136
Hannah (bondswoman), 122
Harris, Ann, 32, 44
Harris, James, 60
Harrison, Elizabeth, 30
Hart, Frances, 158
Hart, Nancy, 182, 185
Hastings, Betty, 17
Hastings, Selina (Countess of Huntingdon), 17–18
Hawkins, Thomas, 46
Heinrich, Ann Magdalena, 71, 78
Helvingstine, Anne Dorothy, 50
Hepburn, Mary, 137
Heron, Alexander, 43, 62
Hillsborough, Lord, 116, 205n71
Hogarth, William, 13
Honduras, 98. *See also* West Indies
housekeeping: preconceptions about, 11, 31, 188; during trusteeship, 38–43, 188. *See also* marriage
housing, 9, 40, 152–53
Houstoun, John, 147
Huber, Margaretha, 87–88
Huber, Maria Magdalena, 87
Hughes, Mary, 137
Huntingdon, Countess of (Selina Hastings), 17–18
Hutchinson, Anne, 1, 190
Hutchinsons Island, 45

immigration: and family size, 107–8, 112, 115–16; during royal era, 95–106, 108–9, 111–12, 115–17, 123; during trusteeship, 22–27, 90
indentured servants: abuse of, 34, 36, 71, 78, 79, 88; employment of, 41–42, 45, 46, 55, 78; marriage of, 77; during royal era, 111–12; mentioned, 31, 33
Indian trade, 62, 63, 72, 84, 86, 116
indigo, 96, 99–100, 129–30, 135, 139, 191

Ireland: migration from, 98, 111, 213n41; settlers from, 72, 80, 147; mentioned, 7, 86, 189

Jackson, James, 181
Jamaica, 37, 82, 98, 117, 119. *See also* West Indies
Jenkins, Edward, 76, 79, 88, 206n81
Jews, 22–23, 70, 82, 155, 158, 189
Johnson, William, 85
Johnston, Elizabeth Lichtenstein, 132–33, 156–57, 176–77, 182–83, 185
Johnston, James, 161, 213n48, 219n44
Johnston, William, 156–57
Jones, George, 153–54, 173–74
Jones, Mary, 158
Jones, Noble, 33, 128, 131–32
Jones, Noble W., 118, 153–54
Jones, Sarah Campbell, 173–74
Jones, Thomas, 55–56

Kalcher, Margaretha, 49
Kellaway, Elizabeth Hughes West, 76
Kellet, Alexander, 128, 129
Kieffer, Maria, 134
Knox, William, 176–77

Lancaster (bondsman), 173–74
land grants: during Revolution, 182–83; during royal era, 97–99, 101–6, 107–8, 115, 164–65; and slaves, 110–12; during trusteeship, 31, 34; and women, 109–15
Leeward Islands, 37, 98–99, 112, 119, 122, 220n7
Lincoln, Benjamin, 185, 228n19
Lines, Martha, 130
Lombe, Thomas, 53
London: agents in, 131–32; charities in, 15; decadence in, 13, 51, 80; fashions in, 137; travel from, 26; travel to, 116, 129; mentioned, 8, 9, 39, 43, 48, 69, 189

lowcountry: economy of, 99–100, 137–41; race relations in, 142–48; settlement of, 101–5, 190–91; mentioned, 21, 123, 129
Loyalists, 156, 175, 179, 180–81, 183
Lyon, Sarah, 132, 140

MacBean, Archibald, 25
Mackintosh, Winiwood, 113
Maddock, Joseph, 109, 164–65
Mahoney, Florence, 131
Malcontents, 9, 23, 52, 99
Malpas, Elizabeth, 80
Malthus, Thomas, 32
Manson, William, 111–12
manufacturing, 38–39, 49–50, 53, 66, 130–31, 140. *See also* sewing; silk
manumission, 132, 146–47, 169. *See also* free blacks
Maran, Charles, 147
Maria (bondwoman), 146
marriage: ages at, 30–31, 32, 73, 107, 155–57, 168; celebrations of, 86–87, 164, 166; economic cooperation within, 65–66, 130–33; among the elite, 152–59; ideal of, 34, 161–63; interethnic, 69–70, 79–80, 82, 165–67; interracial, 70, 71–73, 83–86, 143–47; and land granting, 105–6, 112–14; legal definitions of and legislation about, 39, 47, 125–29; and overseers, 134–35; parental involvement in, 33, 74–76, 106–7, 152–57, 166–67; and prenuptial contracts, 157–59; and religion, 80, 165; and separation, 80, 84–85, 135–37. *See also* cohabitation; remarriage; slavery: and marriage
Martyn, Benjamin, 10, 12, 57
Maryland: gender in, 144, 190; migration from, 109, 117; sex ratio, 24; mentioned, 98. *See also* Chesapeake
masculinity: and attitudes toward marriage, 162–63; and dueling, 183; and landownership, 106; and race, 144–45; and separation, 135–36

Massachusetts, 39, 109, 117, 144, 175, 190. *See also* New England
Matthews, Jacob, 72–73
McCarty, Lydia, 136
McDonald, Norman, 98
McGillivray, Alexander, 72, 85, 176–77
McGillivray, Lachlan, 72, 176
McIntosh, Lachlan, 117, 159, 183, 185
Mellichamp, Hannah Willoughby Watkins, 81
Mendenhall, Catherine Sidwell, 166
Mercer, Elizabeth, 158
Methodists, 172; and charismatic revivalism, 17–18. *See also* Wesley, John; Whitefield, George
Midway, 99, 109, 164
midwifery, 26, 28–30
Milfort, Louis LeClerc de, 163
millinery. *See* sewing
Minis, Abigail, 113–14, 130, 159, 183, 214n54, 217n18
Minis, Philip, 148, 159, 183
mixed race, people of: among Amerindians, 85, 148; mulattos, 132, 144–45, 146–47, 148, 169
Mobile, 119, 122, 171–72
Montserrat. *See* Leeward Islands
Moodie, Ann, 112
Moore, Francis, 40
Moravians, 22–23
Mouse, Lucy, 50, 61–62, 114
Mühlenberg, Henry Melchior, 71, 172
mulattos. *See* mixed race, people of

New England: demographic comparisons with, 21–22, 24–25, 26, 82, 95, 107; gender in, 37, 39, 89, 190; migration from, 109; miscegenation laws in, 144; and slave trade, 120; mentioned, 1, 2, 3, 82, 188
New France. *See* France
New Hampshire, 37. *See also* New England
New Jersey, 98, 177

New York: gender in, 89; migration from, 22, 98; mentioned, 51, 82, 86, 117, 156
Newcastle upon Tyne, 111–12
Newfoundland, 98
Newport River, 111
newspapers: ads by men in, barring wives from credit, 135–37; ads by women in, for goods or services, 130–33; ads in, for overseers, 134–35; atrocities described in, 144, 150–51; obituaries in, 159–61; social commentary in, 160–63, 193–96. *See also* slaves: and fugitiveness
North Carolina: migration from, 97, 99, 109, 117, 148, 164; miscegenation laws in, 144; and Revolution, 181
nursing, 46–47, 198n13. *See also* disease

Oates, Elizabeth, 135
obituaries. *See* newspapers
Ockstead, plantation at, 55–56
Oconee River, 116
Ogeechee River: and escaped slaves, 171; and Revolution, 181; settlement on, 97, 100, 101, 109, 113, 116
Oglethorpe, James Edward: correspondence of, 25, 26, 29, 44, 57, 80; and Mary Bosomworth, 62; military leadership of, 9, 25, 79; and promotional pamphleteering, 8–12. *See also* trustees
Ohio Valley, 37, 117
Old Ross (bondswoman), 180
Orkney Islands, 111
orphans, 15, 26, 74, 87–89, 91. *See also* Bethesda orphanage
Ortmann, Juliana, 46, 48, 49, 78
Ottolenghe, Joseph, 225n120
overseers, 104, 134–35, 147–48
oznabrig, 134, 141

Pages, Margaret, 132
Parker, Robert, Jr., 3, 33, 44, 73
Peggy (bondswoman), 139

Pennsylvania: gender in, 89; migration from, 22, 98, 109, 112, 148; miscegenation laws in, 144; mentioned, 82, 117
Penrose, Elizabeth, 51–52, 65, 190
Pensyre, Samuel, 80
Percival, Catherine Parker, 53
Percival, John Viscount. *See* Egmont, Earl of
Perkins, Catherine, 50
Pero (bondsman), 171
petitions, 112–13, 114–15, 182–85
pharmaceuticals, 111, 130, 131, 141
philanthropy: in England, 12–13, 15; and gender, 15–18, 188
plantations: abuse on, 147–48; conditions of labor on, 121, 138–39; establishing of, 99–100, 102, 110–11; management of, 134–35, 137–38; residence on, 152–53; during Revolution, 179; slave numbers on, 118–19, 120; mentioned, 112, 117
poetry, 57, 160–63
polygamy, 86, 120
Portsmouth, 29
Presbyterians, 177, 215n72
Prevost, Augustine, 185
prostitution, 51, 78–79, 81, 146, 148
Pruniere, Amie Mallett Jones, 146
Purysburg, 28, 68, 76, 79, 204n64

Quakers: in Georgia, 109, 161, 164–67, 182, 192; in Middle Colonies, 31, 32, 82, 89; mentioned, 51
Queensborough, 111, 117
Quejos, Pedro de, 189
Quincy, Samuel, 26

rape, 71, 78–79, 144–48 passim, 175
Rauner, Maria Magdalena, 49, 66
remarriage: during royal era, 113–14, 165; during trusteeship, 30–31, 32–33, 69
Remington, Jonathan, 136

retail, women's involvement in, 48, 128–32, 134
Revolutionary War, 115, 179–86
Reynolds, John, 10, 97, 100–101, 104, 128, 129
Rhode Island, 82, 106, 117, 144. *See also* New England
rice, 56–57, 99–100, 129–30; and labor, 139; during Revolution, 179, 226n2; mentioned, 96, 135, 191
Richardson, Samuel, 161
Riedelsperger, Anna, 65
Robinson, Pickering, 60
Ross, Daniel, 148
Ross, Phillis, 148
Royal African Company, 17, 38
Russia, 176, 177

Sale, Elizabeth, 33
Salzburgers: customs of, 87; and demography, 25, 27–28; and economy, 43–44, 53, 202n18; household arrangements of, 42, 48, 65–66, 164; and marriage, 31, 70, 74–75, 77–78, 80; and midwifery, 28; migration of, 71; and sericulture, 59–60; support of refugees by, 79; and teaching, 45–46
Satilla River, 100, 112
Savage, Loveless, 104
Savannah: British occupation of, 179, 181; Continental army siege of, 183, 185; early population of, 22, 26, 29–30, 73, 79; filatures in, 59–60; Indian fears in, 62, 91; interracial relations in, 146–47, 148; jail of, 81, 148; market of, 124, 126, 130, 140; orphans in, 87, 88; renting in, 136, 140; schooling in, 45, 46, 132–33; and sexual debauchery, 79, 80–81, 82, 148; and slaves, 111, 140, 169; taverns in, 51–52, 130, 132; and weddings, 67–68, 78, 152, 156; wharf of, 47
Savannah River, 99–100, 109; mentioned, 72, 101, 102, 142, 149, 189

schools. *See* teaching
Scotland: and interethnic unions, 70, 71, 79–80, 84, 86; migration from, 25, 98–99, 189; settlers from, 23, 73, 98, 111; mentioned, 35, 80, 188
Senegambia. *See* Africa
sericulture. *See* silk
Seven Years' War, 86, 100–101
sewing: during royal era, 131, 132, 137; during trusteeship, 49, 61, 69. *See also* manufacturing
Sheftall, Benjamin, 82
Sheftall, Levi, 155, 159
Sheftall, Mordecai, 158, 227n10, 228n19
Shortner, Mary, 113
Sierra Leone. *See* Africa
silk: cultivation of, in Georgia, 53–61, 96; in promotional literature, 8, 11–12
Simeon, Mary, 79
Skidoway Island, 61
Slack, John, 32
slavery, 38, 117–19, 190–91; and marriage, 120, 143, 167–74; prohibition of, 9, 38; references to, during trusteeship, 44, 48–49, 70–71; and sericulture, 60–61; slave codes, 100, 104, 118, 140, 143–45. *See also* Africa; slaves
slaves: dress of, 134, 164; education of, 134; employment of, 138–41, 171; and families, 139, 145, 148, 167–74, 176, 180; and fugitiveness, 70–71, 111, 122, 151, 169–73, 180; on Gibbons plantation, 110–11; inherited by minors, 114–15; manumission of, 132, 146–47, 169; population of, 98, 102, 110, 111, 118–23, 168–69; provisioning of, 134, 171; and Revolution, 226n5; and surveillance, 145. *See also* Africa; slavery
Society for the Promotion of Christian Knowledge, 17, 77
Society for the Propagation of the Gospel, 188

South Carolina: economy of, 37–38, 47, 189, 204n58; legislation in, 100, 126, 128, 191; migration from, 22, 99–100, 102–13 passim, 117, 152, 210n12; population of, 22; and Revolution, 179; and slavery, 118, 119–20, 122, 144, 170–71. *See also* Charlestown
Spencer, William, 67–69, 73, 74, 81
spinsters, 155–56, 161
St. Andrew Parish, 102
St. Catherines Island, 169
St. David Parish, 102
St. George Parish, 104, 112, 117, 213n41
St. John Parish, 63, 102, 107, 147, 164, 185
St. Kitts. *See* Leeward Islands
St. Mary Parish, 102
St. Marys River, 100, 102, 108, 151
St. Patrick Parish, 102
St. Paul Parish, 104
St. Petersburg, 177
St. Phillip Parish, 112
St. Thomas Parish, 102
Stanley, Elizabeth, 26, 29–30, 79
stepchildren, 67–69, 76, 87–89, 114, 225n120
Stephens, William: on Bethesda, 41; on early demography, 26, 31; on marriage, 32–33, 74; on sericulture, 55, 59; on taverns, 51, 52
Stokes, Anthony, 175
Sulamith (bondswoman), 134
Sunbury, 117, 124
Swinton, Judith, 138, 217n18
Swiss, 45, 70

tavern keeping: during royal era, 130, 132; during trusteeship, 50–53, 61, 66; mentioned, 72
teaching: during royal era, 132–34, 138, 225n120; during trusteeship, 45–46; mentioned, 89
Teasdale, John, 66
Terry, John, 78

tobacco, 109, 139
Tomochichi, 72
Townsend, Mary Hodges, 48, 51–52
Triboudet, Lucretia, 134
trustees, 8; encouragement of sericulture by, 53–61; expectations of, 34; and philanthropy, 12–13, 15, 18, 188; promotional propaganda of, 8–12, 18, 24, 57, 105, 187–88; regulations of, on land granting, 9, 31, 34, 47, 68, 128; regulations of, on liquor, 9, 50–51; regulations of, on slave ownership, 9, 60, 95, 99, 143–44, 187; selection of settlers by, 24; and surrender of charter, 95–96. *See also* Egmont, Earl of; Oglethorpe, James Edward
Turner, Sarah, 76
Tybee Island, 48, 113

Union Society, 132
Urlsperger, Samuel, 25, 31

Vat, John, 23, 27, 43
Venning, Mary, 112
Venture, Fort, 62, 78
Vernonburgh, 171
Vincent, Hannah, 113, 131–32
Virginia: gender in, 126, 137, 143, 144, 190, 219n5; migration from, 109, 117, 148, 220n26; and Revolution, 183; sex ratio in, 24, 26, 188; and slavery, 37, 118, 119, 170–71; mentioned, 11, 51, 71, 83, 175, 213n36. *See also* Chesapeake
Von Reck, Philip, 84

War of Jenkins' Ear, 9, 66, 79
Washington, George, 85, 183
Wesley, John, 16, 29–30, 39, 76
West, Elizabeth Little, 87
West Indies: economy of, 37–38; Jewish marriages in, 82, 155; migration from, 22, 99, 111, 112, 122–23; slavery in, 119, 144, 146; views on, 117

Whitefield, George, 16–17, 32, 46, 76, 77, 190
widows: during royal era, 112–14, 130, 158; and slaveholding, 137–38; during trusteeship, 27, 32–35 passim, 43, 52–53, 76. *See also* remarriage; wills
Wilkins, Ann, 112
wills: and familial life cycle, 106–7; and marriage contracts, 132, 158–59; and nomination of executors, 125; and royal era widows, 137–38; and slaves, 146–47, 168–69; and trusteeship widows, 76
Wilson, Alexander, 156
Wilson, Mary Riedelsperger, 114
Windward Coast. *See* Africa
Woolwich, 176, 177

Wright, James: arrest of, 177; on Indian problems, 150; and legislation, 127; and migration, 96, 101–2, 104, 105, 115–17; and Revolution, 179, 183; on silk cultivation, 61
Wright, Penelope, 52
Wrightsborough, 109, 164–65, 167

Yamassee War, 197n5
Yonge, Henry, 115
Yonge, Mary Ann, 160
Young, Thomas, 171

Zettler, Elisabetha Catharina Kieffer, 74–75, 134, 217n18
Zettler, Matthias, 74–75
Zouberbuhler, Bartholomew, 225n120
Zubly, John J., 138

www.ingramcontent.com/pod-product-compliance
Lightning Source LLC
Chambersburg PA
CBHW032146230426
43672CB00011B/2461